Sixteen essays in the social and economic history of the ancient world by a leading historian of classical antiquity are here brought conveniently together. Three overlapping sections deal with the urban economy and society, peasants and the rural economy, and food-supply and food-crisis. While focusing on eleven centuries of antiquity from archaic Greece to late imperial Rome, the essays include theoretical and comparative analyses of food-crisis and pastoralism, and an interdisciplinary study of the health status of the people of Rome using physical anthropology and nutritional science. A variety of subjects are treated, from the misconduct of a builders' association in late antique Sardis, to a survey of the cultural associations and physiological effects of the broad bean. The essays, of which two appear in English for the first time, are presented together with bibliographical addenda by Walter Scheidel, which summarize and assess research stimulated by the original and often provocative theses and approaches of the author.

CITIES, PEASANTS AND FOOD
IN CLASSICAL ANTIQUITY

CITIES, PEASANTS AND FOOD IN CLASSICAL ANTIQUITY

ESSAYS IN SOCIAL AND ECONOMIC HISTORY

PETER GARNSEY
*Professor of the History of Classical Antiquity,
University of Cambridge*

Edited with addenda by
WALTER SCHEIDEL
*Moses and Mary Finley Research Fellow in Ancient History,
Darwin College, University of Cambridge*

PUBLISHED BY THE PRESS SYNDICATE OF THE UNIVERSITY OF CAMBRIDGE
The Pitt Building, Trumpington Street, Cambridge, United Kingdom

CAMBRIDGE UNIVERSITY PRESS
The Edinburgh Building, Cambridge CB2 2RU, UK
40 West 20th Street, New York NY 10011–4211, USA
477 Williamstown Road, Port Melbourne, VIC 3207, Australia
Ruiz de Alarcón 13, 28014 Madrid, Spain
Dock House, The Waterfront, Cape Town 8001, South Africa

http://www.cambridge.org

© Cambridge University Press 1998

This book is in copyright. Subject to statutory exception
and to the provisions of relevant collective licensing agreements,
no reproduction of any part may take place without
the written permission of Cambridge University Press.

First published 1998
First paperback edition 2004

Typeset in 9.75/12.5 pt Times Ten

A catalogue record for this book is available from the British Library

Library of Congress cataloguing in publication data

Garnsey, Peter.
Cities, peasants, and food in classical antiquity: essays in
social and economic history / Peter Garnsey; edited with addenda by
Walter Scheidel.
p. cm.
Includes bibliographical references and index.
ISBN 0 521 59147 3 hardback
1. Cities and towns, Ancient – Rome. 2. Peasantry – Rome – History.
3. Food supply – Rome – History. 4. Food supply – Greece – History.
I. Scheidel, Walter, 1966– . II. Title.
HT114.G37 1998
307.76'0938–dc21   97–25203 CIP

ISBN 0 521 59147 3 hardback
ISBN 0 521 89290 2 paperback

Transferred to digital printing 2004

TO MY TEACHERS, YOUNG AND OLD

CONTENTS

Preface xi
Editor's preface xiii
Acknowledgements xv
List of abbreviations xvii

PART I CITIES

1 Aspects of the decline of the urban aristocracy in the empire *3*
2 Independent freedmen and the economy of Roman Italy under the Principate *28*
3 Economy and society of Mediolanum under the Principate *45*
4 Urban property investment in Roman society *63*
5 An association of builders in late antique Sardis *77*

PART II PEASANTS

6 Peasants in ancient Roman society *91*
7 Where did Italian peasants live? *107*
8 Non-slave labour in the Roman world *134*
9 Prolegomenon to a study of the land in the later Roman empire *151*
10 Mountain economies in southern Europe *166*

PART III FOOD

11 Grain for Athens *183*
12 The yield of the land in ancient Greece *201*
13 The bean: substance and symbol *214*
14 Mass diet and nutrition in the city of Rome *226*
15 Child rearing in ancient Italy *253*
16 Famine in history *272*

Bibliography 293
Index 330

PREFACE

A scholar is formed by his or her teachers. I am an eternal student. When my capacity to learn from colleagues and students (especially from students) has gone, retirement will be overdue.

J. J. Nicholls, a modest man and an admirable teacher, introduced me to ancient history. He was learned in the history of the Roman constitution, and an *appassionato* of Cicero's *De republica*. My Oxford history tutors were G. E. M. de Ste. Croix, of New College (which I entered in 1961) and C. E. 'Tom Brown' Stevens of Magdalen, the former a passionate polemicist, the latter an outrageously eccentric genius. I was Fergus Millar's first graduate pupil (from 1963). He set a high standard and a fast pace. The fruit of a month's hard labour would come back to me the next day together with pages of hand-written addenda and corrigenda. The atmosphere was friendly and supportive. I watched Ronald Syme work magic on inscriptions copied from stone, turning them into living Romans. He passed on to me one of his honorary doctorates and much more. Peter Parsons was a witty guide to the society of Oxyrhynchus for a term. P. A. Brunt, Martin Frederiksen and Tony Honoré were willing and formidable critics of my early work. George Cawkwell, a benevolent and charismatic giant, was my host when I took up a Junior Research Fellowship at University College, and encouraged and watched over my first efforts at teaching undergraduates. John Matthews was my contemporary and friend. I must have caught from him the late imperial bug, carrying it unawares for a time.

In 1967 I joined the staff of the Classics Department at Berkeley, when W. K. Pritchett was chairman. He was pugnacious in combat, but a loyal backer of youth and talent. Paul Alexander's classes on Late Antiquity, which I 'audited' as a junior colleague, made a deep impression. It was the time of 'the troubles'. A refugee from Nazi Germany, he would shake his head in sorrow while rioting guardsmen met flower power with tear gas beneath his windows. I talked philosophy with Michael Frede in the Café Mediterraneum.

The Sather Lecturers at Berkeley were then mostly Cantabrigians. The last of them was Moses Finley, like Charlie Chaplin returning to the USA for the first time since the McCarthy era. When in due course I moved to Cambridge (in 1973), I joined him at Jesus College, the seat not long before of Denys Page, A. H. M. Jones, H. Lloyd-Jones, and

D. R. Shackleton Bailey. Finley did not expect others to share his taste for controversy, nor did he require pious allegiance to his 'line'. My intellectual horizons expanded under his influence, often as a direct result of the challenges he set me: to take his place in a lecture series on political theory or in a London seminar on peasants. Famine appealed to me because it demanded a broad, comparative and interdisciplinary approach, and was a new subject (in ancient history). Famine was my idea not his, but I cannot imagine myself having undertaken it in another place or at another time. For this and other work done in my Cambridge period, I have drawn heavily and gratefully on the intellectual resources of this community and beyond, that is to say, on my teachers, young and old, who are too numerous to name.

I began research as a Roman social historian with an interest in the relationship between law and society and the bases of social stratification. *Social status and legal privilege in the Roman empire* was a treatment of the theme of legal discrimination, encompassing criminal law, private law and legal procedure. My abiding interest in Roman law, and in intellectual history, as shown in *Ideas of slavery from Aristotle to Augustine*, and elsewhere, are not represented in the present volume.

The Roman empire: economy, society and culture was written with Richard Saller, who contributed, in particular, highly original work on family and patronage. The ground for this work was prepared with a series of articles on urban and rural society and economy, local government institutions and imperialism. The social and economic history dimension of this research is drawn on here, alongside papers written in preparation for, or following up, *Famine and food supply in the Graeco-Roman world*, and another for a forthcoming book on *Food and society in classical antiquity*.

I am deeply indebted to my colleague and friend Walter Scheidel for editing these papers. They would not have appeared in this or any other form without his intervention, given that I was disinclined either to revise them or reproduce them uncorrected. As it is, a reader interested in any of the matters covered can find here a corrected version of the original paper (in addition, two papers are here published in English for the first time), accompanied by a pithy summary of the 'state of the question' with up-to-date bibliography and independent assessment.

I owe thanks also, not for the first time, to Pauline Hire of Cambridge University Press for her tolerance and patience.

PETER GARNSEY

EDITOR'S PREFACE

The text of all but two of the sixteen papers assembled in this volume has been reprinted unchanged except for the correction of a minor inaccuracy, the revision or removal of obsolete references to forthcoming research, and the exclusion of illustrations from the final chapter. Two pieces (chapters 5 and 13) are published here in English for the first time and differ in points of detail from the original French versions. A number of inconsistencies have been removed from the references to modern scholarship, all of which have been consolidated into a bibliography at the end of the volume. New material has been confined to the addenda that conclude most of the chapters. These supplements offer concise overviews of pertinent research undertaken subsequent to the publication of a particular essay. Although I have reviewed a wide range of recent scholarship, and in some cases also referred to forthcoming publications, the addenda are not intended to be exhaustive. Special attention has been devoted to contributions which respond to and elaborate on the original articles. As a consequence, individual addenda vary greatly in length, therein reflecting trends in recent scholarship as well as the limits of editorial competence. For the same reasons, four chapters did not seem to require any addenda.

The completion of the addendum to chapter 11 has been greatly facilitated by the generosity of Graham Oliver, Ronald Stroud and Michael Whitby who made their work accessible in advance of publication. John Patterson most helpfully provided us with a bibliography of work in field archaeology pertinent to chapter 7. We are also grateful to Robin Osborne, Peter Rhodes and Reinhard Selinger for their advice and logistical support in obtaining material and information. On a more personal note, I would like to thank Peter Garnsey for inviting me to participate in this project.

WALTER SCHEIDEL

ACKNOWLEDGEMENTS

Chapters 1-16 were published in their original form in the following publications, and we are grateful for permission to reprint them.

1. Aspects of the decline of the urban aristocracy in the empire: from *Aufstieg und Niedergang der römischen Welt*, II, 1, ed. H. Temporini (Berlin and New York: De Gruyter, 1974), 229-52
2. Independent freedmen and the economy of Roman Italy under the Principate: from *Klio* 63 (1981), 359-71
3. Economy and society of Mediolanum under the Principate: from *Papers of the British School at Rome* 44 (1975), 13-27
4. Urban property investment: from *Studies in Roman property*, ed. M. I. Finley (Cambridge: Cambridge University Press, 1976), 123-36, 190-3
5. Les travailleurs du bâtiment de Sardes et l'économie urbaine du bas-empire: from *L'origine des richesses dépensées dans la ville antique*, ed. P. Leveau (Aix-en-Provence: Université de Provence, 1985), 147-60
6. Peasants in ancient Roman society: from *Journal of Peasant Studies* 3 (1976), 221-35
7. Where did Italian peasants live?: from *Proceedings of the Cambridge Philological Society* 25 (1979), 1-25
8. Non-slave labour in the Roman world: from *Non-slave labour in the Greco-Roman world*, ed. P. Garnsey (Cambridge: Cambridge Philological Society, 1980), 34-47
9. Prolegomenon to a study of the land in the later Roman empire: from *Energeia: studies on ancient history and epigraphy presented to H. W. Pleket*, eds. J. H. M. Strubbe, R. A. Tybout and H. S. Versnel (Amsterdam: J. C. Gieben, 1996), 135-53
10. Mountain economies in southern Europe: from *Pastoral economies in classical antiquity*, ed. C. R. Whittaker (Cambridge: Cambridge Philological Society, 1988), 196-209
11. Grain for Athens: from *Crux: essays presented to G. E. M. de Ste. Croix on his 75th birthday*, eds. P. A. Cartledge and F. D. Harvey (London: Duckworth, 1985), 62-75
12. Yield of the land: from *Agriculture in Greece*, ed. B. Wells (Stockholm: Swedish Institute in Athens, 1992), 147-53

13. La fève: substance et symbole: from *La sociabilité à table: commensalité et convivialité à travers les âges*, eds. M. Aurell, O. Dumoulin and F. Thélamon (Rouen: Publications de l'Université de Rouen, 1992), 317–23

14. Mass diet and nutrition in the city of Rome: from *Nourrir la plèbe: actes du colloque tenu à Genèvre les 28 et 29. IX. 1989 en hommage à Denis van Berchem*, ed. A. Giovannini (Basel and Kassel: F. Reinhardt, 1991), 67–101

15. Child rearing in ancient Italy: from *The family in Italy from antiquity to the present*, eds. D. Kertzer and R. Saller (New Haven and London: Yale University Press, 1991), 48–65

16. Famine in history: from *Understanding Catastrophe*, ed. J. Bourriau (Cambridge: Cambridge University Press, 1992), 65–99

Note: The original pagination of articles is indicated at the top of each page, and the original page divisions are marked in the text by a pair of vertical lines, ||.

ABBREVIATIONS

A E   *L'année épigraphique*
C A H   *Cambridge ancient history*
C I L   *Corpus inscriptionum latinarum*
F I R A   *Fontes iuris romani anteiustiniani*
I G   *Inscriptiones graecae*
I G R R   *Inscriptiones graecae ad res romanas pertinentes*
I L S   *Inscriptiones latinae selectae*
Inscr.It. *Inscriptiones Italiae*
N S   *Notizie degli scavi dell'antichità*
P G   *Patrologia graeca*
P.Oxy   *The Oxyrhynchus papyri*
P I R   *Prosopographia imperii romani*
R E   *Real-Encyclopädie der classischen Altertumswissenschaft*
S E G   *Supplementum epigraphicum graecum*
S I G[3]   *Sylloge inscriptionum graecarum* (3rd edn)

Other abbreviations are as found in the *Oxford Classical Dictionary*, 3rd edn. Periodicals in the bibliography are abbreviated in accordance with *L'Année Philologique*.

PART I
CITIES

I

ASPECTS OF THE DECLINE OF THE URBAN ARISTOCRACY IN THE EMPIRE

1. INTRODUCTION

The theme of decline and fall remains irresistible to historians of the Roman Empire. No one who has tangled with the issue can be unaware that the decline of the aristocracy of the cities was closely bound up with the decline of the Empire at large.

The main outlines are well known and uncontroversial. The members of the local councils of cities, that is, the decurions or *curiales*, bore the brunt of the financial burdens of the imperial administration. At one time, local office carried sufficient prestige and privilege to compensate for the expenditures it entailed. By the fourth if not late-third century, however, because of the mounting costs of government, external interference in city administration, and a decline in local prosperity, it had lost its appeal. In the early Empire service in the local council of a city was both voluntary and sought-after; by the fourth century, it was compulsory, to be evaded if at all possible. Faced with the flight of decurions from their cities, the central administration sought to block the escape-routes, both by restricting the entry of decurions into other professions or occupations, including the clergy, the army and the imperial administration itself, and by forcing sons to follow fathers into local government. This policy pointed to the eventual transformation of the local aristocracy into a hereditary order. If this was the aim of the central administration, it was never achieved. Clear evidence for this is the succession of imperial decrees which are || collected in the 'Theodosian Code' ordering that errant decurions be returned to their *patriae* to perform liturgies. A decree that has gained its end does not have to be continually reenacted. It has even been argued, largely on the basis of the legal evidence, that social mobility was greater in the later Roman Empire than under the Principate. This is very doubtful. But at least it can be acknowledged that a considerable degree of mobility characterized the society of the late Empire.[1]

---

[1] The thesis is that of Jones (1970) 79–96. It is in practice impossible to evaluate the argument on the basis of the evidence presented in the article. I am indebted to M. I. Finley

The broad outlines of the process of decline, then, are familiar, and accounts of the general phenomenon abound. But we lack a comprehensive analysis of the stages by which:

(1) the cost of curial liturgies increased,
(2) office-holding and liturgy-performing in the cities lost their voluntary nature, and
(3) the *ordo* of decurions became progressively ingrown and self-perpetuating.

These three overlapping subjects are all highly complex. An adequate treatment of each would require consideration of a very large body of evidence from all parts of the empire. This article is purely preparatory. My aim with respect to the first two topics (which I propose to treat together) is to initiate what I believe to be a fruitful line of inquiry. As regards the third topic, I will attempt, by proposing a novel thesis, to make more intelligible the process by which the curial class became largely hereditary.

II. COMPULSION AND THE COST OF OFFICE

There are some well-known legal texts relevant to the Severan period which point to the existence of compulsion in municipal politics. For example, Septimius Severus in one ruling relating to the repetition of office distinguished between 'unwilling' and 'willing' office-holders.[2] Moreover, frequent references are made to sons of decurions who have been nominated to the council, to magistracies or liturgies against the will of their fathers.[3] These passages might have set scholars searching for others of earlier date with similar implications, or stimulated a more general inquiry into the conditions of municipal government in the preceding period. In fact, the Antonine period has virtually been passed over and discussion of the question of compulsion has revolved around a few texts from the Flavio-Trajanic age. One is a clause in the Flavian charter for Malaga, which sets up a procedure to be followed in cases where too few candidates have offered themselves for magistracies.[4] Another is a letter of Trajan to Pliny, then governor of Bithynia-Pontus, which may refer to men who became decurions against their will (*inviti ... decuriones*).[5]

---

and R. P. Duncan-Jones for criticisms of an earlier draft of this paper. Responsibility for the conclusions is mine.

[2] *Dig.* 50.1.18: 'Divus Severus rescripsit intervalla temporum in continuandis oneribus invitis, non etiam volentibus concessa, dum ne quis continuet honorem'.

[3] E.g. *Dig.* 50.1.21 pr.; 50.2.6.4; 50.2.7.3; cf. 50.1.2 pr.: 'consensisse autem pater decurionatui filii videtur, si praesens nominationi non contradixit.'

[4] *FIRA* 2nd edn, I, no. 24, p. 209, ch. LI.   [5] Pliny, *Ep.* 10.113.

DECLINE OF THE URBAN ARISTOCRACY

The clause in the law of Malaga is not good evidence of 'the growing unpopularity of office'.[6] We cannot assume that it was inserted in a charter for the first time on this occasion. It is more likely to have been tralatician than newly invented, either for Malaga or for the newly chartered Spanish towns in general.[7] As for its purpose, it is best regarded as a safety clause designed to cope with emergencies. It might be invoked, for example, when famine or plague threatened to leave a state leaderless. Acraephia in Boeotia suffered some kind of natural disaster ('the destruction of the land') early in Claudius' reign, and special measures had to be taken to have polemarchs appointed. It is unclear whether death or financial loss was responsible for the temporary dearth of officials there.[8] Athens was beset with chronic 'anarchy' under Domitian, probably as a result of economic difficulties. Between AD 82 and 92 it seems that no Athenian served as archon. But in time conditions improved and wealthy Athenians were again prepared to take on their expensive highest magistracy.[9] There is no evidence that antipathy to office-holding was a permanent feature of the municipal scene in Greece or anywhere else in the late first century AD.[10] ||

The closing sentence of Trajan's letter to Pliny is undoubtedly corrupt, and emendation is in order. *Invitati* for *inviti* has not won support. The arguments on both sides, however, are inconclusive.[11] Moreover, the

---

[6] Last (1934) 466. [7] For the last suggestion, see Sherwin-White (1966) 724.
[8] *SEG* xv (1958), 330, ll. 47ff.
[9] This was not, however, the last taste Athens had of Anarchia. See Graindor (1922) 11–12 (causes); 291–8 nos. 64, 68, 127, 130, 143, 161 (examples); Day (1942) 240–1.
[10] Last (1934) 466, cites, with Trajan's letter and the law for Malaga, *Dig.* 50.4.12: 'Cui muneris publici vacatio datur, non remittitur ei, ne magistratus fiat, quia id ad honorem magis quam ad munera pertinet. cetera omnia, quae ad tempus extra ordinem exiguntur, veluti munitio viarum, ab huiusmodi persona exigenda non sunt.' The context of this comment of the Trajanic lawyer Iavolenus Priscus is difficult to establish. Last seems to assume that it was prompted by attempts of some to avoid magistracies by pleading *vacatio*. Even if he is right about the background to the ruling, it must be emphasized that this is an isolated text and should not be made to bear too much weight. At the most, the passage would suggest that there was no universal scramble for magistracies. But the text can equally be interpreted as a legal clarification of an ambiguous situation, issued possibly but not necessarily in response to an inquiry, rather than as a judgement which was meant to apply in specific disputes. In this connection it should be noticed that the opinion covers extraordinary liturgies as well as magistracies.
[11] See Sherwin-White (1966) 722–3; *contra* Jones (1968) 137–8. Goold (1964) 327–8 (cf. Bowersock (1965) 148 n. 3), argues that the grant of legal privileges to decurions (which he dates from Hadrianic times) was made to compensate them for the high costs of office. Cf. Garnsey (1970) 170, n. 1 and 5 passim. Sherwin-White appears to have the better of the historical argument. On the surface the period from Vespasian to Trajan was an age of expansion. More communities acquired municipal rights and therefore local councils (as in Spain), and existing councils grew in size (as in Bithynia, see Pliny, *Ep.* 10.112; Dio 40.14). Pliny, *Ep.* 10.79 is evidence of competition for office. It might,

whole controversy may be misdirected. Trajan may have referred in his letter to decurions who were reluctant not to serve as decurions, but to pay an entry fee.[12] One could therefore retain *inviti* without committing oneself to the judgement that the letter alludes to compulsory recruitment of decurions in Bithynian cities.

There are thus no firm indications of a malaise in municipal government in the last quarter of the first century. The sources of the post-Trajanic period present a different picture. Here we turn to the legal evidence, which has been largely neglected.

A passage of Marcianus runs as follows:

> 'Everyone is compelled to perform the liturgy of envoy in his turn. However, no one is to be forced to perform the liturgy unless those introduced before him into the council have done so. But if a mission demands men from the highest rank, and those who are summoned in their turn are from the lower grades, then the order should be disregarded.' This was Hadrian's reply to the people of Clazomenai.[13]

Presumably the last sentence contains Hadrian's rescript, or Marcianus' summary of the rescript. It is this sentence which reveals that there was an acknowledged division between *primores viri* and *inferiores* in the council of Clazomenai, perhaps an average second-class Asian city. It is not stated in what respect the *inferiores* were deficient. They may have included relatively new arrivals in the council and therefore men who lacked experience; but there is no hint in the text that they were just this group. More probably the two groups were unequal in terms of prestige and wealth.

A second rescript of Hadrian, which may or may not be the rescript to Clazomenai in another form, is cited by Callistratus. The jurist purports to give Hadrian's own words. The relevant sentence reads:

> The Divine Hadrian sent a rescript on the subject of the repetition of liturgies which ran as follows: I am resolved that if there are no others suitable for the performance of this liturgy, men should be appointed from among those who have performed it already.[14]

Idonei (suitable) is a term of approbation applied to men of position, prestige and substance. It is the last quality mentioned, however, which appears to be given emphasis in legal texts.[15] It is likely that for the proper

---

of course, be true that the sources, such as they are, give us a superficial and slanted impression of conditions in the cities. The sources for the period that follows, however, are better balanced.

[12] Cf. Pliny, *Ep.* 10.39.5. For another explanation, see Pleket (1971) 236.
[13] *Dig.* 50.7.5.5; cf. 50.2.7 pr. (a later text, referring to *honores* as well as *munera*).
[14] *Dig.* 50.4.14.6. [15] E.g. *Dig.* 50.4.6 pr. – 1; 50.4.11.1.

performance of the unnamed liturgy to which Hadrian refers possession of wealth rather than experience or influence was the prime necessity.

The language of the rescripts becomes plainer. 'It should be understood,' wrote Marcianus, 'that a debtor to the state cannot perform an embassy. This was a reply of the Divine Pius to Claudius Saturninus and Faustinus.'[16] Pius' successors, Marcus and Verus, faced the question of whether debtors to the state could undertake office. It is not clear whether the differentiation of two kinds of debtors is that of the jurist who cites their decision, Ulpian, or is based on this or another imperial ruling. In any case, the statement that men might fall into debt as a result of the performance of some administrative office is something of a revelation. The whole passage runs as follows:

> It is certain that state-debtors cannot be invited to take up magistracies, unless they have first made reparation for the debt they owed to the state. But as state-debtors we should regard only those left in debt as a result of an administrative office. Those who are not debtors as a result of office but have borrowed money from the state are not so placed that they should be prevented from holding magistracies. Clearly it is an adequate solution that a man should give surety either in the form of security or suitable guarantors: that was the reply of the Divine brothers to Aufidius Herennianus.[17]

Now the provision of surety was required not only of debtors. Another rescript of Marcus and Verus rules that 'those who perform a magistracy under compulsion no less that those who have assumed office of their own free will should give security'.[18] In the late Republic sureties and securities were demanded of those magistrates who handled public money, as a guarantee against embezzlement.[19] We may suspect that the exaction of security from all magistrates in the Antonine period had the double motivation of protecting the cities against both embezzlement and the possible insolvency of their officials.[20]

In general, the several rescripts cited establish that the disabilities of at least some *inferiores* within the curial order were pecuniary. Confirmation, if it is needed, is provided by another rescript of Marcus and Verus quoted by Ulpian immediately before his discussion of state-debtors:

> The following pronouncement is made in a rescript of the Divine brothers to Rutilius Lupus: 'The constitution in which it is laid down that the holding

---

[16] *Dig.* 50.7.5. pr.   [17] *Dig.* 50.4.6.1.   [18] *Dig.* 50.1.38.6.
[19] E.g. *FIRA* 2nd edn, I, no. 18, p. 167, ll. 1–25 (Lex mun. Tar.).
[20] In Egypt in the third century there was a real danger that a magistrate might abscond because of bankruptcy or fear of bankruptcy. See *P. Oxy.* 12. 1415.11; cf. *CPHerm.* 97.13.

of magistracies should be dependent upon the time of election as a decurion should be retained as long as all the men concerned are capable and sufficient. However, if certain individuals are so weak and impoverished that they are not only unequal to public office but in addition scarcely able to maintain their standard of living from their own resources, then it is less suitable, and in fact not at all proper, that they should be entrusted with a magistracy, especially when there are some whose appointment would be consistent with their wealth and the honour of the city. Let the rich therefore be informed that they should not use the law as a pretext, and that it is right to inquire into the time of admission into the council only in the case of those who achieve the dignity of office by virtue of their possessions.'[21]

The rescript is remarkable for its length and lucidity of detail. It demonstrates the existence of a sharp cleavage between rich and poor in the council. The rich, by clinging to the rota system and insisting that what was written in the law should be implemented, were aggravating the already unhappy situation of the poor, if they had not actually brought about or contributed to their impoverishment. The verdict of the emperors is that wealth rather than seniority is the essential qualification for office.

Finally, a rescript of Marcus had the same import:

Though it be laid down by municipal law that men whose rank is sure should be preferred in office, it should nevertheless be understood that this law is to be complied with if the men concerned are suitable. This ruling is contained in a rescript of the divine Marcus.[22]

Thus affluence was not universal among the upper-classes in the cities even in the Antonine age, which is generally thought to have been a period of high prosperity. Some councillors were, relatively speaking, indigent. Their further decline could be arrested, and their curial status preserved, only if they were excused magistracies and liturgies, at least for the immediate future. We cannot of course estimate on the basis of these rescripts whether this was the lot of a sizeable number or only of a few; nor do the rescripts reveal how representative of the more prosperous group of decurions were those who showed a reluctance to take on more than their share of administrative responsibilities. It is nevertheless possible to make certain deductions of a general nature concerning conditions of office-holding in the cities. The first is that the central authorities had recourse to compulsion in order to ensure the regular performance of magistracies and liturgies. In doing so they overrode local rules. The rescripts show that the cities (or some cities) had their own regulations which had the function of maintaining a steady flow of administrators and liturgizers.

[21] *Dig.* 50.14.6 pr.   [22] *Dig.* 50.4.11.1.

The rescript of Hadrian to Clazomenai mentions a rota system for the performance of embassies. A passage of Ulpian, citing the Augustan jurist Labeo, suggests that the system, or something like it, was known at the beginning of the Empire:

> Labeo writes that if, when one man is due for an embassy, the *duumvir* imposes the burden on another, no action can be instituted for injury on account of the labour enjoined.[23]

We do not know if the rota system applied in the case of other liturgies. It did exist for magistracies: Marcus and Verus mention it, referring back to a constitution of an unknown emperor.[24] There is no way of ascertaining when it was first introduced into municipal law, or how widely it was used. At any rate, by the early second century the system was in danger of breaking down, and the emperors were called upon to resolve the difficulty. The second point that emerges from the rescripts is a closely related one. It was above all the financial responsibilities of councillors which brought about the intervention of the emperors. There were members of the council who simply could not afford to hold a magistracy or perform a liturgy when their turn came to do so. Again, it was presumably the cost of office rather than lack of patriotism in itself which made men who were more comfortably off unwilling to offer themselves for iteration of office or to accept nomination for extra duties without demur.

These two facts of local politics, the high cost of membership of the council and the presence of compulsion, are perhaps by now sufficiently established. What does need further investigation is the question of whether there was a deterioration in the climate of local government in the first half of the second century. It is interesting in this connection that the rescripts thus far discussed fall within the period from Hadrian to Marcus. There is, however, additional pertinent material to be found in the juristic writings. It will be seen that it is concentrated in the same period. It concerns eligibility for liturgies.

Public liturgies were performed in the main by decurions. Others indeed were eligible.[25] But their numbers were reduced by imperial grants of immunity. Decurions as such never benefited from such grants. In principle they were exempted from liturgies only by illness.[26] It was illegal to pay one's way out of a liturgy.[27] An appeal against a nomination might be

---

[23] *Dig.* 47.10.13.5.   [24] *Dig.* 50.4.6. pr.
[25] Public liturgies included embassies, duty as judge of law suits or advocate for the city, preservation of public order, tax-collection, supervision of public post and of aqueducts, repair of buildings, construction of or repair of roads, heating of baths, provision of animals for transport, the sheltering and equipping of troops.
[26] *Dig.* 50.4.18.11.   [27] Ibid. 16 pr. – 1.

lodged.[28] Alternatively, the nominee might attempt to pass on the liturgy to the nominator by ceding him perhaps two-thirds of his property (given the approval of the provincial governor).[29] This, however, was a drastic step which jeopardized the status of the ceder. It was thus in the interests of city councils that the circle of those who held the privilege of immunity from liturgies should be restricted, or at least not widened. It could also be argued that an imposition of restrictions on immunity is at least prima-facie evidence that councillors were feeling the pressure of liturgies and were increasingly reluctant to bear them. The earliest rescripts known to us which cut back the number of exemptions belong to the first half of the second century.

Antoninus Pius issued the quite general order to Ennius Proculus, the governor of Africa, that he should inspect the law of each city to see whether those who were immune from liturgies had been granted immunity for only a limited period of time.[30] A time-limit was enforced in the case of traders, as a comment of Scaevola, Marcus Aurelius' jurist, shows.[31] But the most important condition of exemption for traders was that they should be engaged in the transportation of supplies to Rome. This regulation is ascribed to Hadrian.[32] The same emperor excluded from immunity rich traders who did not invest a sizeable proportion of their funds in trade and did not use profits to increase the scale of their trading activities.[33] Pius advised that whenever an inquiry was made about a trader it should be ascertained whether he was merely pretending to be a trader in order to escape liturgies.[34] Evidently traders were watched fairly closely. In the case of philosophers, rhetors, grammarians and doctors, it was Pius who first imposed strict limitations on their immunity. Hadrian had allowed them immunity;[35] but the privilege must have been taken up on a greater scale than had been anticipated, or else the administration, under pressure, no doubt, from local councils, had second thoughts. By Pius' regulation,[36] cities of small size were permitted to grant immunity to five doctors, three sophists and three grammarians. Medium-sized cities were allowed seven doctors, four sophists and four grammarians with immunity, and the largest could excuse from liturgies ten doctors, five sophists and five grammarians. Another ruling, attributed to Pius, gave grounds for hope to those

---

[28] *Dig.* 50.5.1 pr. An appeal might succeed, for example, where the appellant could show that he was entitled to a short *vacatio* before repeating a liturgy or magistracy. See *Cod.Iust.* 10.41.2–3.
[29] See Jones (1940) 185.   [30] *Dig.* 50.6.6.1.   [31] *Dig.* 50.4.5.
[32] *Dig.* 50.6.6.3; 5.   [33] Ibid. 6.8.   [34] Ibid. 6.9.
[35] *Dig.* 27.1.6.8. Hadrian's contribution may have been no more than the addition of philosophers to the group of professionals who already had immunity. See Bowersock (1969) 32ff.
[36] Ibid. 6.2.

excluded from the lists. The 'exceedingly learned' (ἄγαν ἐπιστήμονες) could claim immunity.[37] In his long battle against public burdens Aelius Aristides seems to have appealed to this enactment, in so far as he employed legal arguments (that is, as opposed to the argument from his ill-health).[38] However, it appears that it was often less the legal situation than the applicant's standing with the authorities which counted. Philiskos the Thessalian, as professor of rhetoric at Athens, might have expected immunity. He had the privilege, until it was taken away by Caracalla. Philostratus, who tells the story, goes on to relate that Caracalla subsequently decreed exemption for Philostratus of Lemnos, aged twenty-four, as a reward for declamation.[39]

In reducing exemptions the emperors were assisting the cause of the decurions, who bore the brunt of public liturgies. The space devoted by lawyers to problems connected with origin and domicile is further evidence that central and local authorities were on the hunt for potential performers of liturgies.[40] Inquiries on such matters were chiefly designed to find out whether some individual or group was liable to undertake liturgies. The Trajanic jurist Neratius discussed the question of the *origo* of a bastard.[41] Hadrian concerned himself with the status of *incolae*, or foreign residents: Diocletian knew of a Hadrianic edict which dealt with the difference between *cives* and *incolae*.[42] Furthermore, we know of one dispute concerning an *incola* which came before Hadrian. A city claimed liturgy-service from a man who, it alleged, was an *incola*. He disputed the allegation, presumably on the grounds that he had not established *domicilium* in the city. Hadrian ruled that the defendant should plead his case before the governor of the province to which the claimant city belonged.[43] This decision broke the principle *actio sequitur forum rei* and made the defeat of the defendant more likely. It should be noticed that all parties assumed that if the defendant lost he would have to submit to liturgies in two cities. The principle of the double liability of *incolae* was known to Gaius.[44] Perhaps the rule had not long been in existence.

To sum up: the legal developments outlined above had a bearing on the position of decurions, for they were largely responsible for the performance of liturgies. The search for extra-curial liturgizers was led by councils

---

[37] Ibid. 6.10. See Nutton (1971).
[38] Ael. Arist., *Or.* 50.72ff. (ed. Keil). See Bowersock (1969) 36ff.
[39] Philostr. *VS* p. 622ff., ed. W. C. Wright (Loeb). On veterans, see Sander (1958), 203ff. Either Pius or Marcus allowed veterans only five years exemption; see Mitteis and Wilcken (1912) no. 396 (AD 172). By Severan times they were subject (apparently without restriction) to patrimonial liturgies, see *Dig.* 50.5.7.
[40] Some of them were perhaps required for *munera sordida*, but liturgizers of that kind were less difficult to find. On *origo* see Nörr (1965).
[41] *Dig.* 50.1.9.   [42] *Cod.Iust.* 10.40.7 pr.; cf. ibid. 2 pr.
[43] *Dig.* 50.1.37 pr.   [44] Ibid. 29.

anxious to lighten their load. They sought and gained the cooperation of the Roman authorities. The hunt for liturgizers and the close investigation of immunity claims were not confined to the Severan and post-Severan ages. The crucial discussion on the subject of *muneris publici vacatio* took place in the early decades of the second century. Official attitudes on matters relevant to residence and origin were fully shaped by the accession of Pius. Subsequently only refinements were added.[45]

The bulk of the public expenditures of the local aristocracy was associated directly or indirectly with the performance of magistracies and liturgies. The preceding section has, I believe, demonstrated that the pressure of liturgies had mounted by the first half of the second century AD. It remains to see whether council membership was becoming more burdensome in the same period because of other duties, especially those connected with magistracies.

The jurist Callistratus stated that magistracies might or might not involve their holders in expenditure (whereas public liturgies inevitably carried expenditure).[46] This statement cannot apply in the Eastern provinces of the empire, where the traditional functions of magistrates, sometimes mainly decorative, sometimes real and significant, either disappeared entirely in Roman times or declined substantially in importance, having been supplanted or overshadowed by the requirement of the giving of bounty to the city. In the West the principle was established early that magistrates should meet some of the costs incurred by the state during their year of office. Thus duovirs and aediles were required at least as early as the mid-first century BC to help pay for the religious games and festivals which they themselves organized. This was probably the origin of the *summa honoraria* or statutory fee, which, it is generally assumed, was virtually universal in the *municipia* and *coloniae* in the first century AD.[47] ||

There is no indication that statutory fees were higher in the second century than in the first. Nor, as far as is known, did any office-bearers pay fees who had not paid them in an earlier period.

There were, however, two developments in Trajan's reign which require brief discussion. The first concerns voluntary payments by magistrates, the second a statutory fee for members of the council.

Pomponius reports a Trajanic constitution with these words:

> If a man promises to undertake some project in a state in his own or another's honour, he or his heir is under obligation to carry out the undertaking, according to the terms of a constitution of the Divine Trajan.[48]

---

[45] Ibid. 17.9 (Pius); 37.2 (*divi fratres*); cf. 38.3. [46] *Dig.* 50.4.14 pr.
[47] *FIRA* 2nd edn, I, no. 21, pp. 182–3, ch. 70–1 (Lex Urs.). See Duncan-Jones (1962) 65ff.; Garnsey (1971a) 323ff.
[48] *Dig.* 50.12.14. For a discussion of this text and the institution of promising in general, see Garnsey (1971b).

There is independent evidence from the same period that promised donations were not always forthcoming. Dio of Prusa threatened proconsular intervention to force the payment of money promised, while Pliny was instructed by Trajan to see to it that certain promises were not allowed to lapse.[49] Now a promise was in essence something spontaneous and self-imposed. Trajan's constitution did not alter this. It did not require promises from any who were unprepared to make them, but stated simply that such as were made were to be regarded as legally binding. On the other hand, where promise-making became customary and institutionalized – and there are indications that this may have been the case at least for a time in some parts of Africa in the second century AD – the payment could no more be avoided than the statutory impost; and this was in effect a consequence of Trajan's constitution. It is too much to claim that Trajan had this in mind, especially as we do not know how commonly promises were made in his time, even in Africa, where the evidence is largely post-Trajanic. What can be said, however, is that Trajan's attitude to promise-making was not that of the wealthy magnates who created the practice and from time to time used it as a means of demonstrating their patriotism and advancing their reputation and careers. For Trajan, promises must have appeared first and foremost as an important source of revenue, one that should not be permitted to wither away because legal sanctions to support it were lacking.

If we knew the immediate background of the constitution of Trajan we would probably find that it was requested by a governor or another imperial official. We can see gubernatorial initiative at work in a related case. Pliny as governor of Bithynia-Pontus recommended to Trajan that he should issue a general decree requiring all decurions in the province to pay a fee on entering the local council.[50] Pliny explains that such a fee had in the first instance been exacted, by whose decision it is not stated, from those || councillors appointed with Trajan's permission over and above the legal number. A previous governor, Anicius Maximus, then extended the fee to cover regular entrants into the council, but only in a few cities. Pliny obviously regarded the universalizing of the fee as a logical next step. Trajan rejected the proposal, ruling that each state should be allowed to follow its own laws. Trajan, it should be noticed, did not declare himself against an extension of the entry-fee to all the cities, but only against the imposition of the fee from above. It was presumably open to city-authorities to levy the fee, either on their own initiative or under pressure from a governor; and Trajan's decision might subsequently be reversed. There is in fact no further evidence from Bithynia relating to the entry-fee. Nevertheless it does look as if a fee became more generally demanded of

[49] Pliny, *Ep.* 10.40; Dio Chrys. *Or.* 47.19.   [50] Pliny, *Ep.* 10.112. See Garnsey (1971a).

councillors from the early second century. To be more precise, it is in this period that the Eastern evidence for an entry-fee begins. It is not substantial in volume, but nevertheless concerns cities in Asia, Macedonia, Galatia and Crete. The situation in the West is obscure, but again the first unambiguous evidence for the fee belongs to the early second century.

The appearance of the entry fee coincided with a period of expansion. In cities in the Eastern provinces in particular extensive building-programmes were undertaken with the aim both of improving the quality of amenities and of raising the stock of the community in the world at large. There was some funding from private sources, but the city treasuries probably bore the brunt of the expenditure. An entry-fee would serve the purpose of providing an additional, if modest, source of income at a time when ordinary revenues were severely taxed. The fact that the councillors were turned to for extra income was perhaps inevitable but nonetheless significant. They had always contributed to city finances as magistrates or liturgists, and also as private donors. The imposition of the entry-fee on all decurions carried the clear implication that membership of the curial order as such entailed financial obligations. The same idea is conveyed in another recommendation of Pliny, that councillors should be forced to accept on loan public funds for which willing borrowers could not be found. Trajan's rejection of the proposal was a rejection of the principle of compulsion, not of that of the collective responsibility of decurions for their city.[51]

We are faced therefore with something of a paradox. Detailed evidence has been presented which suggests that the expenses of the decurionate were increasing by the first half of the second century AD and that financial distress was not absent from the ranks of decurions. At the same time inscriptions indicate that voluntary expenditure by local benefactors reached a high point in both quantity and value in the same period. It is a fair assumption, moreover, that munificent spending increased as a result of the operation of natural factors such as the growth of wealth and the pressure of competition for office. ||

The matter requires careful investigation on a scale which cannot be attempted here. I will make two suggestions of a preliminary nature. The first is that no solution is likely to be adequate which does not take into account regional variation. It cannot be assumed that all cities enjoyed lasting prosperity in the Antonine period. Economic growth and decline did not proceed at an even pace throughout the empire, and phases of expansion or contraction of public expenditure did not necessarily coincide in different parts of the Roman world. We must also allow for the

[51] Pliny, *Ep.* 10.54–5.

occurrence of periodic fluctuations in the scale of munificence within particular cities and areas as a result of temporary changes in local conditions. Secondly, the paradox may disappear once the limitations of the sources are grasped. It is unlikely that the generous benefactors of the gift-inscriptions (or, for that matter, the poor and the selfish rich of the legal sources) were representative of the whole class of local officials and councillors. It has been plausibly argued, on the basis of the African evidence (which is comparatively full), that in that area it was rare rather than common for an official to give more to his city than the law required.[52] The message of the inscriptions from other areas, and especially from the Eastern provinces, is that voluntary spending was in the hands of comparatively few, well-established, wealthy families.

Thus the epigraphical and legal sources may not be in contradiction. One can readily believe that the Antonine age was a period of prosperity for the *primores viri* and ruin for the *inferiores* within the councils. As for the middle groups, who perhaps constituted the majority of councillors, here too the sources converge. The inscriptions suggest that the average decurion was a benefactor on a very modest level, if he gave voluntarily at all, while if the legal evidence is taken seriously, the financial pressure of magistracies and liturgies, and in general the cost of the decurionate, was becoming oppressive for more than a small minority of decurions. The position of this group was not likely to improve, given the acceptance by the imperial authorities of two principles, the principle of interference in local government and the principle of the collective responsibility of decurions for their city. If their decline, and that of the whole order, was slow, this was because economic conditions were relatively favourable and the political situation stable in the Antonine period.

III. THE HEREDITARY PRINCIPLE

The rest of this paper is devoted to an examination of the process by which membership of local councils, and therefore of the curial class, became hereditary. I believe there is a stage in this development which is missing in the scholarly accounts. My suggestion is that the task of the central administration in trying to impose the hereditary principle was considerably simplified by the fact that councils were moving spontaneously toward a closed membership, and in the process had waived a traditionally accepted constitutional principle. This was the principle that the local senates should be composed, like the senate at Rome, of men who had held

---

[52] Duncan-Jones (1963) 169.

a magistracy.[53] Sons of senators, either in Rome or in the other cities of the empire, were not *ipso facto* senators. They had to gain entry into the order, and by tradition this privilege was earned through service in a magistracy.

In fact, it is extremely unlikely that the statutory number of decurions, usually 100 in the West, could have been maintained solely by the controlled influx of ex-magistrates; deaths, elevations into higher orders, and impoverishment of individuals within the order would have created more vacancies than it was possible to fill in this way. Doubtless the local censor was frequently compelled to turn to men who lacked experience in a magistracy so as to maintain the order at full numerical strength. But if these two streams of entrants, that is, first, ex-magistrates, and second, those without magisterial experience, were to be drawn entirely from members of established families, then *novi homines* would be excluded, and the order would become self-perpetuating; and this result would be achieved without any modification of constitutional principles. However, it is possible to envisage a more efficient way of sealing-off the order, or at least of restricting the number of families who had access to it: sons of decurions and, in general, members of established families might be admitted to the council before they had held a magistracy, and tenure of magistracies might be restricted to those who were already councillors.

Several pieces of evidence suggest that this practice was introduced, in some parts of the Empire at least, perhaps in the course of the second century AD. One text shows us the development at an early stage. A letter of Pliny to Trajan written in c.AD 111[54] reveals that in the province of Bithynia over which he was governor sons of established families (whom he calls *honestorum hominum liberi*) who were under the minimum age for membership of the council (thirty) and who lacked magisterial experience, were being enrolled in the councils with men of plebeian stock (*e plebe*) who were also under age but who had held magistracies. Moreover, they were competing successfully.[55] This was against the spirit of the Pompeian law for Bithynia-Pontus, by which it was understood that ex-magistrates were the prime source of recruits for the local senate: 'lex senatorum esse voluisset qui gessisset magistratum'. Now Augustus revised some of Pompey's arrangements; but his attitude to the Pompeian principle as just stated is unclear. It is curious that Augustus lowered the minimum age for tenure of a magistracy (from thirty to twenty-two or twenty-five) without adjusting the age for entry into the senate.[56] We are justified, I think, in assuming that he did not restate the Pompeian principle and indeed that

---

[53] See Mommsen (1888) 847ff.; Marquardt (1881) 183ff.   [54] Pliny, *Ep.* 10.79.
[55] 10.79.3: 'quod alioqui factitatum adhuc et esse necessarium dicitur . . .'
[56] I follow Morris (1964) 316, who reads twenty-five, following Merrill (1903) 54. For the other view, Sherwin-White (1966) 671.

no reference was made in his edict to the means by which new members of the council were to be chosen. Whether by accident or design, Augustus left the law on this point in a state of confusion. In the century and a quarter that followed it is clear that at least some censors took advantage of this fact by enrolling sons of established families before better qualified plebeians. Trajan decided that the men who had held minor magistracies at twenty-five could enter the order before they turned thirty and that the others could not. This ruling in effect ran counter to the exclusivist mentality of the governing class; Trajan was in effect stating that age and birth were not sufficient qualifications for entry into the council.[57] There is no reason to believe, however, that his decision represented anything more than a temporary set-back for the aristocratic cause in the cities of Bithynia or in those of any other province.

The next piece of evidence is *CIL* IX 338 from Canusium in Italy, and its date is AD 223.

Canusium stood near Cannae in Apulia, on the River Aufidus, twelve miles from its mouth. The town was of Greek foundation (or received a Greek colony at an early date) and its inhabitants, as late as the Augustan period, were proverbial for their bilingualism.[58] Greek influence persisted under the Empire. Eastern traders and businessman must have been attracted to the town especially by the wool industry – the famous Apulian wool was processed in Canusium.[59] The inscription is evidence that in the Severan epoch a good proportion of the most prominent citizens of Canusium were of Greek or Eastern extraction.[60]

In AD 223 the two leading magistrates of the town, the *duoviri quinquennales* Marcus Antonius Priscus and Lucius Annius Secundus, revised the list of members of the council and had the new list inscribed in bronze and presumably displayed in the forum. It is a unique document, || the only *album decurionum* which has survived in its entirety. The other album of which we have a respectable portion comes from Thamugadi in Numidia, and belongs to the fourth century.[61]

---

[57] Despite Jones (1940) 181; (1970) 80, and Sherwin-White (1966), I see no sign that Pliny's own approach was élitist. He was simply reporting a case which had been put to him. In fact the compromise that he suggested between the Augustan edict and the Pompeian law was not in the interests of the *homines honesti* if they were attempting to block the way of the ambitious outsiders and keep the circle of official families small.

[58] Hor. *Sat.* 1.10.20: *Canusini more bilinguis*. On Canusium see Jacobone (1925).

[59] Strab. 6.3.6.9; Pliny *HN* 8.190; Columella, *Rust.* 7.2.2; *Ed. Diocl.* 19.23ff.; *Not. Dign. occ.* 11.52.

[60] Philostr. *VS* p. 551, ed. W. C. Wright (Loeb) says that Herodes Atticus 'colonized' Canusium and gave it a proper water-supply. As Dr Duncan-Jones has pointed out to me, the truth must be not that colonists (who might have included Greeks) were introduced, but that colonial status was gained for the town.

[61] *CIL* VIII 2403; 17824; Leschi (1948), 71.

Table 1.1. *The Ordo of Canusium, (AD 223) (CIL IX 338)*

quinquennalicii	aedilicii	D. Agrius Pietas
T. Ligerius Postuminus*	T. Flavius Crocalianus	Q. Iunius Silvanus
T. Annaeus Rufus	C. Ennius Marcianus	A. Kanuleius Onesimianus
L. Abuccius Proculus	Sex. Tedius Priscus	T. Pompeius Vitalis
T. Aelius Rufus*	P. Graecidius Iustus	C. Fufidius Rufus
T. Aelius Flavianus*	Ti. Claudius Candidus	T. Pompeius Alexander
M. Antonius Priscus	M. Servilius Helius	C. Lucretius Venustus iun.
L. Annius Secundus	T. Artorius Minervalis	C. Iulius Stachys
	L. Herennius Crescens	M. Athanius Felix
all. inter qq.	T. Flavius Marinus	L. Herennius Celsus
C. Galbius Soterianus*	L. Clatius Secundinus	D. Satrenius Satrenianus
L. Abuccius Iulianus	L. Abuccius Euryalus	T. Pompeius Attalus
C. Silius Antiius (sic)	P. Marcius Carpophorus	P. Esquilius Silvanus
P. Aelius Victorinus	L. Dasimius Priscus	Ti. Cl. Onesimianus iun.
	Q. Fabius Thalamus	Q. Iunius Musogenes
IIviralicii	Ti. Claudius Eutychianus	P. Rutilius Tertullinus
A. Caesellius Proculus II	M. Sempronius Sabinianus	Ti. Claudius Verus
L. Faenius Merops II	C. Ennius Priscianus	M. Ulpius Anthimus
L. Abuccius Maximianus	L. Faenius Merops iun.	P. Publicius Maximus
Q. Iunius Alexander II	M. Antonius Vindex	
M. Aemilius Marcellus		*praetextati*
C. Iulius Hospitalis	*quaestoricii*	T. Flavius Frontinus
L. Marcius Fortunatianus	L. Ceius Asclepiodotianus	C. Iulius Hospitalis iun.
C. Fulvius Satyrus	L. Abuccius Laberianus	L. Abuccius Proculus iun.
P. Libuscidius Victorinus	D. Balonius Felix	M. Aurelius Marullus
Q. Fabius Felicissimus	T. Flavius Iustus	T. Aelius Nectareus
T. Aelius Antonius	T. Flavius Quintio	L. Eggius Maximus
L. Herennius Arescusianus	M. Saufeius Constans	C. Vibius Marcellus
T. Curius Salvianus	M. Marcius Ianuarius	P. Publicius Maximus iun.
A. Kanuleius Felicissimus	P. Sergius Augurinus	L. Annius Rufus
P. Sergius Bassaeus	M. Aurilius Acrisius (sic)	L. Triccius Apollinaris iun.
P. Graecidius Firmus		M. Aurelius Iulius
M. Athanius Felicissimus	*pedani*	M. Aurelius Agrippinus
C. Vibius Octavianus	Q. Fabius Fabianus	L. Attius Ianuarius
Ti. Claudius Onesimianus	L. Vibius Iuventianus	C. Galbius Atticillianus
L. Annius Pius	P. Graecidius Vestinus	C. Vibius Faustinus
Q. Iunius Onesiphorus	P. Carinatius Agathangelus	Q. Pompeius Asclepius
C. Lucretius Venustus	C. Terentius Priscinus	L. Timinius Ponticus
A. Fabius Cassianus	C. Pomponius Cupitus	M. Aurelius Valens
L. Triccius Apollinaris	C. Peticius Dionysius	C. Galbius Amandus
M. Apronius Primus	Sex. Calpurnius Aemilianus	M. Servilius Marcellus
P. Esquilius Silvanus	N. Novius Alticus	M. Gavius Rufus
Q. Iunius Rusticus	C. Vibius Saturninus	L. Dasimius Iustus
P. Clodius Dasimianus	P. Pacilius Chrysomallus	Q. Iunius Trophimianus
L. Abuccius Felicianus	T. Pomponius Felix	T. Flavius Silvinus
	M. Aurelius Maximus	T. Flavius Fortunatus

* Equestrian patron, nos. 2, 6, 7, 5, respectively. Omitted are P. Gerellanus Modestus (1), T. Munatius Felix (3), T. Flavius Crocalianus (4), Q. Coelius Sabinianus (8). The 31 senatorial patrons are also omitted.

The inscription lists in order of importance patrons of senatorial rank (31), patrons of equestrian rank (8), *quinquennalicii*, or men who had held the duovirate in a census year (7), *allecti inter quinquennalicios*, or men who had been raised straight to the rank of *quinquennalicius*, bypassing some or all lower ranks (4), *duoviralicii*, ex-duovirs (29), *aedilicii* (19), *quaestoricii* (9), *pedani*, or decurions who had held no office (32), and *praetextati*, or young men with the *toga praetexta* who were descended from decurions or other members of official families (25).[62] The Greater Ordo, then, consisted of 160 persons (164 names are listed, but it can be assumed that four men, who occur as both *allecti* and equestrian patrons, are listed twice). Subtracting the patrons, whose membership was honorary, and the *praetextati*, who attended meetings but lacked the vote, we are left with 100, probably the standard membership of local councils in the West.

How open was the *ordo*? A superficial glance at the album reveals that membership was to a certain extent a family affair. The *gens Abuccia* is prominent. The senior member is *quinquennalicius* and the family is represented in all other categories except the *pedani*. All seven representatives bear the *praenomen* Titus. The TT. Aelii have two *quinquennalicii* who are also equestrian patrons, an ex-duovir and a *praetextatus*. As for the *quinquennales* who drew up the album, it is not fanciful to suggest that M. Antonius Priscus was related to the ex-aedile M. Antonius Vindex and L. Annius Secundus to the ex-duovir L. Annius Pius and the *praetextatus* L. Annius Rufus.[63] A connection between a senior ex-duovir L. Faenius Merops and the ex-aedile L. Faenius Merops surnamed the younger is self-evident – the two are presumably father and son. The TT. Flavii Crocaliani, equestrian patron and ex-aedile are unlikely to be one man, for the two ranks are further apart than seems appropriate. The fact that the ex-aedile is not called iunior is not telling; there were two PP. Esquilii Silvani, one an ex-duovir, the other a *pedanus*. The nature of other connections, between, for example, the five QQ. Junii, must remain hypothetical. That they are all linked in some way seems a fair assumption. It may be suggested in general that recurring *nomina* point to some kind of family connection, though the tie may be one of adoption or patronage rather than blood. ||

---

[62] Gell. *NA*. 3.18, on *pedani*. The twenty-five *praetextati* were not all sons of living decurions. Four bore gentile names that do not crop up elsewhere in the album: Eggius, Attius, Timinius, Gavius. At least one of them, L. Eggius Maximus, was from an office-holding family, see *CIL* IX 343. One wing of this family produced senators, see *PIR* 2nd edn, E, 4-10. Four other *praetextati* are Iuniores and presumably sons of the men of the same name. Of the rest (seventeen), all have a *praenomen* in common with one or more decurions who bear the same *gentilicium*.

[63] A L. Annius Rufus of the tribe Oufentina (the tribe of the town), an equestrian and patron of Canusium, is known from *CIL* IX 339 = *ILS* 5500; 340. See *PIR* 2nd edn, A 687. Cf. *CIL* IX 330; *PIR* 2nd edn, A 722 (Annia Rufina, wife of a senator).

There are, however, thirty-three members of the *ordo* who bear *nomina* that occur once only. It is clear that not all of them can be considered new men, that is to say, the first of their families to hold office or to enter the council. Four, Eggius, Attius, Timinius and Gavius, were *praetextati*, who were members of official families.[64] What of the remainder? A test of *novitas* is to hand, which, while ordinarily accepted, is yet subject to question: an imperial *nomen*, or an Eastern or 'servile' *cognomen*, or both, points to descent from slaves or from immigrants.[65] Eight of the thirty-three are 'suspect' in this way: C. Fulvius Satyrus (ex-duovir), M. Servilius Helius (ex-aedile), L. Ceius Asclepiodotianus, D. Balonius Felix (ex-quaestors), P. Carinatius Agathangelus, C. Peticius Dionysius, P. Pacilius Chrysomallus, M. Ulpius Anthimus (*pedani*).[66] We would probably be able to add to this number if we had the names of the fathers of the other twenty-five, for it was not uncommon for families of foreign or servile origin to adopt Latin *cognomina* in order to disguise their ancestry.

The test of *novitas* can be applied more widely. On a conservative estimate a further thirty-five decurions, whose *nomina* are not individual, could be added to the list of 'suspects'.[67] If these were all first-generation decurions or their sons, which is possible but in my view unlikely (see below), then the turnover within the order was rapid.

Now, eleven of the twenty-five *praetextati* can be 'shown' to be *novi* by the same criteria. This should give us pause, for *praetextati* were not the first representatives of their families to approach the *ordo*. The case of those with Greek *cognomina* is especially striking. T. Aelius Nectareus, for example, is presumably the son of one the three TT. Aelii higher in the album. They all have Latin *cognomina*: Rufus, Flavianus, Antonius. This, then, appears to be an instance of reversion from a Latin to a Greek *cognomen* in the younger generation. The album furnishes additional examples of the retention of Greek or 'servile' *cognomina*. Ti. Claudius

---

[64] See n. 62 above.

[65] See, recently, Thylander (1952) 12ff., 84 (imperial *nomen*), 123ff., esp. 125 (Greek *cognomen*). With Thylander 124, I class as 'Greek' those *cognomina* which are formed on Greek names with the aid of the suffixes *-anus* and *-inus*. On the validity of the test see below. I intend to explore this matter in detail elsewhere.

[66] We might also have doubts about N. Novius Alticus (*ped.*), as the cognomen might be a transcription of Ἁλτικος 'Leaper'. Men with names drawn from the old Roman aristocracy, such as M. Aemilius Marcellus (ex-duovir), P. Clodius Dasimianus (ex-duovir), M. Sempronius Sabinianus (ex-aedile), Sex. Calpurnius Aemilianus (*ped.*) might be descended ultimately from a freedman ancestor. There is of course no reason to suspect that these families were recently enfranchised.

[67] In the list of 'suspects' that follows, the original eight are included. *Quinq.*: nos. 4–5; *allecti*: nos. 1, 4; *duov.*: nos. 2, 6, 8, 10–12, 14, 17, 19, 21, 29; *aed.*: nos. 1, 5–6, 9, 11–12, 14–15, 18; *quaest.*: nos. 1, 3–5, 9; *ped.*: nos, 4, 6–7, 11–13, 16, 21–2, 25, 27–8, 30–1. Total: 43 (out of 100).

Onesimianus (Iunior) the *pedanus* preserves the *cognomen* of his father of the same name among the ex-duovirs; this case is paralleled by that of the two LL. Faenii Meropes, ex-duovir and ex-aedile. Again, the senior A. Kanuleius and M. Athanius, II ex-duovirs, are both Felicissimus, their putative sons Onesimianus and Felix, respectively. There was no general distaste for Greek or 'suspect' *cognomina* among members of the official class of Canusium.

It is worth dwelling on this observation for a moment. The general assumption is that in Italy Greeks and others of alien origin with social pretensions and political ambitions found it prudent or necessary to adopt Latin names and in general the life-style of the Italian city aristocracy.[68] But at Canusium there existed a group of Greeks or Easterners who had won public office and respectability and who nevertheless had an interest in preserving some vestiges at least of their former culture.[69] One is reminded of those Roman senators of the Antonine and Severan periods whose names indicate they are from the East.[70] These men had no need to disguise their background at a time when the governing class of Rome was no longer predominantly Italian and when the influence of Greek culture was at its height. Not that these magnates and the urban bourgeoisie of Canusium are comparable in standing and wealth – or lineage. For example, the C. Julii, Ti. Claudii and T. Flavii who entered the Roman aristocracy owed their citizenship to emperors of the first century; the grant was a recognition of their pre-eminence in cities and provinces. Their counterparts in Canusium probably included descendants of freedmen, whether of emperors, or of families enfranchised by emperors in East or West.[71] On the other hand, it would be a mistake to brand the Greek decurions of Canusium *novi homines* because they were Greek or because of the suspicion that their ancestors were freedmen. In the first place, as we have seen, some at least of the Greeks were in no hurry to become Latin or Italian. Secondly, families founded by freedmen could be long-lived, and

---

[68] Thylander (1952) 124, showed that not all Greeks discarded their Greek *cognomina* in favour of Latin ones. However, he did not separate high-status or status-conscious Greeks from the rest, and thus was in no position to challenge directly the assumption cited in the text. It is worth mentioning that Canusium is not included in his survey of Italian ports; nor is a more important town, where Greek names are common and in some cases persist among the governing class – Pompeii. See ibid. 56, n. 6.

[69] Cf. text to n. 58 above.   [70] Barbieri (1952) 438.

[71] Some families which received citizenship from first-century emperors may of course have survived. As for the origins of those families, a C. Iulius, Ti. Claudius, T. Aelius, and M. Aurelius (those gaining citizenship from Caracalla) might have come from either West or East; a T. Flavius or M. Ulpius was more likely to have come from the West (Rhine and Danube frontier-areas especially). A M. Aurelius deriving citizenship from Marcus was more likely to have been an imperial freedman than a free provincial.

in Italy under the Empire three generations of free birth were enough to establish a family's claim to a certain nobility.

To sum up: our attempt to estimate the degree of turnover of curial families in Canusium by an analysis of the names of the decurions was unsuccessful. The test which is commonly employed to establish *novitas* singled out immigrants or men of freedmen stock, mostly if not all from the East, but did not succeed in identifying *novi homines*. It seems that at Canusium Eastern origin had no special stigma attached to it. The basic reason must be the town's longstanding links with Greek cities of the East; it may be added that any trading centre near the Italian coast was likely to be cosmopolitan to some degree.

There is another point. Thus far we have assumed that the test of *novitas* is secure, whereas it may in fact be impugned on a number of counts. In particular, the identification of 'suspect' Latin *cognomina*, or those which may safely be regarded as slave names, is problematic. While the status of the test is in doubt it seems unwise to base our argument upon it.

Another approach is more promising, to examine the structure of the council as it is presented by the album, and in particular to try to account for the presence of the thirty-two *pedani* and twenty-five *praetextati*.

The twenty-five *praetextati* are twenty-five privileged young men from families to some degree established who were allowed to witness the council at work and to take part in its proceedings to the extent of expressing opinions. Clearly the expectation was that they would move into the council when they came of age and when vacancies appeared; and it would be strange if matters were not arranged so that a good proportion of them at least were admitted before outsiders into those vacancies. Moreover, the fact that there were twenty-five of them, exactly a quarter of the order proper, suggests that this favouritism towards established families had been institutionalized.

But how precisely did *praetextati* enter the order proper and become fully-fledged decurions? If local government in Canusium in the early third century had been run according to the principles laid down by Pompey for Bithynia, for example, the *praetextati* would presumably have been expected to compete with their plebeian rivals for a minor magistracy, probably the quaestorship, or perhaps the aedileship. If they were successful in the elections for these offices, because of merit or superior connections, in the quinquennial revision of the *ordo* their names would have been inscribed in the album of decurions after those of the old members. Furthermore, if the numbers of the *ordo* needed topping up after the admission of ex-magistrates, censors with aristocratic prejudices might have drawn the necessary supplement from *praetextati* rather than from eligible plebeians.

This was perhaps the way in which matters were ordered in traditional Canusium. But can we believe that the old system was still in operation in AD 223? The presence of thirty-two *pedani* suggests that it was not.

It is striking that the *pedani* were so many, almost a third of the *ordo*. To account for their numbers we have to imagine that there were more than a few places left vacant for second-stage entrants, that is, for those enrolled after the admission of five years' supply of minor magistrates. That is not impossible; a death-rate of twenty every five years is perhaps a liberal estimate; if the number of ex-magistrates to be admitted over the same period was ten (a conservative figure), then ten new *pedani* would have been introduced in each quinquennial year. But there is more to be said. Most of the *pedani* must have had a political future. There is nothing to show that they were any more 'plebeian' in origin than any other group in the album,[72] and a number of them certainly had fathers or relatives of high rank who would have ensured that their careers were not static. We may nonetheless ask what prospects they had of rising in the order if the lowest office or offices were dominated by men not yet admitted into the council, whether *novi homines* or *praetextati*.

A legal text from Paul's *Sentences* offers a solution to the difficulty:

> Is, qui non sit decurio, duumviratu vel aliis honoribus fungi non potest, quia decurionum honoribus plebeii fungi prohibentur.[73]

It should be noted that the restriction of magistracies to those who were already members of the council is seen by the writer as a way of blocking the ambitions of men from plebeian families, or outsiders.

The dating of the text is difficult. The work was published in the late third century, but the compilers must have taken over some material, without changing it in substance, from earlier legal treatises, including no doubt treatises of Paulus the Severan jurist.[74] Thus the text might be adduced as evidence that by the Severan age outsiders were unable to hold magistracies and therefore were unable to advance into the council on the strength of magisterial service.

The album of Canusium is securely dated to just this period. It may therefore be proposed that the situation described in Paul's *Sentences* was current at Canusium: that is to say, local office was open only to those who had already been enrolled in the council. Thus the *pedani* would have provided the minor magistrates, and first preference in filling up the gaps left by deaths and promotions would have gone to *praetextati*.

---

[72] This statement is based on the list in n. 67 above. [73] *Dig.* 50.2.7.2.
[74] For the date, see R. Marichal in Archi *et al.*, eds. (1956) 57.

The evidence considered above suggests two conclusions about conditions of municipal government in the Severan age.[75]

First, curial office had not yet lost its appeal for those outside the order; some status-seekers were still anxious for admission. The dictum of Paul's *Sentences* carries this implication: if plebeians were prevented (*prohibentur*) from holding magistracies, some of them must have wanted those magistracies. Again, it may be assumed that some, no doubt exceedingly wealthy, plebeians were gaining access to the order at Canusium, even if they cannot be positively identified.

Second, we can believe that the hereditary principle was firmly established in the institutions of local government well before the period under discussion. It was expected of sons of decurions that they would follow their fathers into local politics, unless of course they could gain access to higher careers. Similarly, sons of established families in the normal course of events would have been preferred to new men in the local magisterial elections. But if my arguments are correct, open elections where plebeians competed with *honestorum hominum liberi* may not have been a regular feature of local government under the Severans. The indications are that at Canusium – and, if the dictum of Paul's *Sentences* is taken seriously, in other towns as well – magistracies were reserved for those already admitted to the council, and ambitious outsiders had to be content with the few places left vacant after the eligible *praetextati* had been enrolled. When at a later stage the flight of curial families began and the supply of outsiders dwindled, the central administration was able to make use of institutions and practices created when faith in the hereditary principle ran high, to impose that principle by force. That time had not yet come for Severan Canusium.

Addendum

This paper comes towards the end of a series of publications on local government and the curial class beginning with *Social status and legal privilege in the Roman empire* (Garnsey (1970)) and continuing with several articles ((1971a), (1971b), (1975)). Here, G. aims to capture the dynamics and sketch the pattern of social differentiation within the municipal élite, as revealed in the way burdens and honours were distributed. He confronts the notion of a decline of this group and addresses the questions of the attractiveness of office and the mode of succession of city councillors in the face of the economic, social and legal change.

There are now a number of general studies of municipal élites in the Roman empire. On conditions in Italy, see *Les bourgeoisies* (1983); Cebeillac-Gervasoni, ed. (1996). Castrén (1975); Jongman (1988) 275–329; Los (1992b);

---

[75] I do not imply that all areas experienced similar conditions.

Mouritsen (1988), (1990) focus on Pompeii. Provincial *decuriones* are discussed by Rupprecht (1975) (with Wolff (1982)) and Mrozewicz (1989). Cf. Quaß (1993) 303–46, on the Roman East. Langhammer (1973) provides an exhaustive overview of the legal provisions regulating local government (42–188, on magistrates, 188–278, on the *ordo decurionum*). Stahl (1978) 36–63 traces symptoms of crisis in the local élites. The most comprehensive study of local government under the Principate is now Jacques (1984), esp. 321–500, on municipal careers, and 507–803, on municipal autonomy. For a competent general survey, see Weber (1993). See also Vittinghoff (1982); Abramenko (1993). Demougin (1994) discusses the structure of the municipal aristocracy of Roman Italy. Alföldy (1984) illustrates differences between the upper classes of individual cities (in Roman Spain). For a general discussion of local élites in the transition from the early to the later empire, see Brown (1978) 34–53, quoting G. (p. 14) on 33–4.

On the question of finding candidates for office (pp. 4–6), see Vittinghoff (1982) 129–37 (with reference to G.). Concerning number 51 of the *lex Malacitana* (pp. 4–5), Spitzl (1984) 32–6, esp. 36, also thinks that the provision for *nominatio* was only a formality, given that municipal office-holding must still have been attractive at that time. For discussions of *munera* borne by local magistrates and councillors (pp. 6–12), see Langhammer (1973) 237–62; Neesen (1981). On *summae honorariae* (pp. 12–13), see Langhammer (1973) 105–8; on the practice of *pollicitatio* (pp. 12–13), see Jacques (1984) 729–30; Hayashi (1989); Weber (1993) 294. The issue of wealth differentiation among *decuriones* (p. 15) is taken up by Alföldy (1985) 127–9, who emphasizes internal stratification and argues for the existence of substantial differences both within and between local élites. Jacques (1984) 507–70 devotes an entire chapter to the heterogeneity of the municipal ruling class. See also Weber (1993) 300–6. On the typical size of the *ordo decurionum* (p. 16), see Nicols (1988), who casts doubt on the notion that one hundred members were the norm (cf. Duncan-Jones (1982) 283–7), but Weber (1993) 290 defends that view. Henrik Mouritsen will return to this issue in a forthcoming article. Kleijwegt (1991) 274–6, 283–4 discusses Plin. *Ep.* 10.79–80 (pp. 16–17).

The *album* of Canusium (pp. 17–24) has continued to attract scholarly attention. Again, the most detailed discussion can be found in Jacques (1984), esp. 457–96; and see also Horstkotte (1984); Chelotti et al., eds. (1990) 45–68; Silvestrini (1990); Kleijwegt (1991) 278–83; Weber (1993) 260–3. For a study of the *album* of Thamugadi (p. 17), see Chastagnol (1978). On family ties among the councillors of Canusium (p. 19), see Jacques (1984) 514–15; Chelotti (1990). Members of certain families regularly progressed to high offices: Rupprecht (1975) 86; Weber (1993) 262–3, even though the evidence is suggestive only of a trend, not of a monopoly: Jacques (1984) 509–10, 526, 615–16; Weber (1993) 263; cf. Castrén (1975) 272–4, on Pompeii, and Jacques (1984) 513, on Thamugadi. Alföldy (1985) 170 infers from the *album* that 'the sons of decurions had no choice but to enter the *ordo* upon their inheritance of the family property' (cf. 127); this view seems unwarranted, and is rejected by Horstkotte (1984) 222 n. 72.

Garnsey (1975) 173–4 discusses the practice of interpreting Greek *cognomina* as an indication of social *novitas* (pp. 20–2). Jacques (1984) 522 accepts G's conclusion that in the case of Canusium, onomastics cannot be used to establish *novitas* but refines this position (524–5). However, Jongman (1988) 326–7, drawing on Jacques (1984) 525, demonstrates that in the *album*, the frequency of Greek *cognomina* decreases with rising status, which strongly suggests a link between onomastic characteristics and social prestige. The presence of freedmen or their descendants in city councils (p. 21) is discussed by Castrén (1981); Serrano Delgado (1988) 187–205, esp. 190–2; Abramenko (1992); Christol (1992); Los (1987), (1992b) (and cf. (1995)); Weber (1993) 267–9. Cf. also Demougin (1994); and LeGlay (1990) 629, 631; Barja de Quiroga (1995) 328 and n. 8, on the effects of the *lex Visellia*.

On the identity of the *praetextati* of Canusium (p. 22), see Horstkotte (1984) 219–22, addressing the question of whether they belonged to the *decuriones*; Jacques (1984) 486–7; Kleijwegt (1991) 304–11. Jacques (1984) 615–7 and Weber (1993) 261 note that *praetextati* did not only come from old families and argue that less prominent families were not disadvantaged in the supplying of *praetextati*. By contrast, Jongman (1988) 328 shows that many *praetextati* were intimately connected with the upper echelons of the *ordo*.

'Most of the *pedani* must have had a political future. There is nothing to show that they were more "plebeian" in origin than any other group in the album (...)' (p. 23). This assertion has not stood up to close scrutiny. Jacques (1984) 480–1 points out that *pedani* were inferior because they lacked putative relatives in the council, and notes (521) that they were not linked to any *quinquennalicii*. Jongman (1988) 320–6 cogently shows that for purely demographic reasons, a certain number of *pedani* were required to keep a council which admitted only two new members as junior magistrates per year at the desired full strength of one hundred. Thus, *pedani* were not normally candidates for office but constituted an inferior group within the *ordo* (326). Jongman (1988) 326–8 supports this view by showing that *pedani* were more likely to bear Greek *cognomina* (see above) and less likely to be connected to top council members; he concludes, *contra* G., that 'most *pedani* were men without much future of further political advancement and office-holding' (328). Kleijwegt (1991) 279, 282 concurs. Jongman's argument is generally sound but needs further nuancing: Scheidel (forthcoming) argues that even though *pedani* can indeed be shown to be of inferior status, the evidence is more complex than previously acknowledged.

The demographic background of the *album* (p. 23) remains a controversial issue: see briefly Horstkotte (1984) 221; Jacques (1984) 484 n. 180 (ref. to G. 479 n. 165, 483 n. 179); Jongman (1988) 322–4. An inductivist model of life expectancy of councillors established by Duncan-Jones (1990) 93–6 (cf. Frier (1992) 288–9) has been criticized by Parkin (1992) 137–8, and Saller (1994) 16–18. See also Dal Cason Patriarca (1995) for a more ambitious model that aims to assess rates of political succession within this group. Scheidel (forthcoming) argues that both Duncan-Jones' and Dal Cason Patriarca's attempts are methodologically flawed and that the evidence of the *album* permits only a highly schematic demographic reconstruction which might be significantly at variance with reality.

G's interpretation of *Dig.* 50.2.7.2 (pp. 23–4) has repeatedly been rejected in more recent studies. Horstkotte (1984) 212–17 considers this text at length and concludes that it did not originate in the Severan period (217), attributing it instead to the time of Constantine (218). Therefore, it cannot be applied to the *album* (218, 224). He claims that in AD 223, the holding of office was still a means of becoming a *decurio* (218), even though it had by then become more common to join the council without first serving as a magistrate (222, 224). Jacques (1984) 592–4 also favours this alternative dating of Paul's ruling and dismisses G's interpretation for another reason as well (489). Weber (1993) 266 n. 141, 295 n. 366, also argues that this text does not testify to the attractiveness of the *ordo* under the Severans and that it does fit the Constantinian period.

G. concludes that while curial office had not yet lost its appeal for outsiders, the hereditary principle was already firmly established (p. 24). Stahl (1978) 51 follows G. with respect to the latter point. Horstkotte (1984) 222 thinks that the *ordo decurionum* of Canusium was still attractive to new members. Jacques (1984) 508–26 studies the structure of the Canusian élite; he concludes (570) that local government there, as that of Thamugadi and Thugga (569), was not monopolized by a limited group of families, and emphasizes the relative heterogeneity of the council and the opportunities to run for office; he finds no clear-cut levels of structural differentiation within the *ordo*. On access to the *ordo* and the integration of newcomers into the élite in general, see Jacques (1984) 571–661; Weber (1993) 254–90. Barja de Quiroga (1995) argues for a steady influx into the curial class from below, both by *ingenui* and freedmen.

2

INDEPENDENT FREEDMEN AND THE ECONOMY OF ROMAN ITALY UNDER THE PRINCIPATE

Freedmen in Rome and Italy were heavily involved in industrial and commercial activities and were also owners of property, both rural and urban, on a considerable scale.[1] These facts are relatively well-known, although the evidence has not been systematically collected and analysed. The surveys of Kühn and Gummerus were concerned basically with artisans and drew only on the inscriptions of Rome and other Italian centres; they need to be broadened, corrected and brought up to date.[2] Meanwhile one must bear in mind that such surveys have serious limitations, which prevent us from arriving at an accurate assessment of how the work-force was divided according to status. These limitations include the frequent absence of explicit status-indications,[3] and the unrepresentativeness of the surviving sample of inscriptions, which is biassed towards those with a special reason for having themselves commemorated, namely freedmen, and in general towards better-off artisans and traders.

My present purpose is not to establish the active involvement or numerical dominance of freedmen in this or that sector of the economy, but to try to understand the phenomenon of the successful freedman, the possessor of moderate or substantial means, in the context of the economy and

---

This paper in an earlier draft was read in August 1978 to a Triennial Conference of the Roman and Hellenic Societies in Cambridge. I have discussed the paper profitably with P. A. Brunt, M. I. Finley, G. Pucci, P. Stein, and S. M. Treggiari.

[1] I omit consideration of imperial freedmen.

[2] Kühn (1910); Gummerus (1916). One might have expected their calculations to have been challenged, since the margin of error is so wide. For a recent consideration of the question of employment in the city of Rome, see Treggiari (1980).

[3] Relatively few freedmen advertised their status with *lib.* or *l.* in the place of the mark of filiation distinguishing freeborn citizens, and indeed this became progressively less common under the Principate. Thus it is often the case that a name provides the only clue to its bearer's status. Kühn's large category of *incerti* (59.75 per cent in Rome, 83.50 per cent in the rest of Italy) attests the difficulty or impossibility of deciding, for example, whether a single name cut or scratched on an artefact belonged to a slave or a free man (freed or freeborn), or, in the more formal inscriptions, whether an individual shown with the *tria nomina* is correctly identified as freed or as freeborn. On some of these problems see, e.g., Solin (1971).

society of Italy in the period of the Principate. Examples of wealthy freedmen abound in the sources. For example, a metric inscription from the age of Augustus records how the noble Aurelius Cotta gave his || freedman Zosimus an equestrian fortune several times over, while a contemporary of his, the freedman Isidorus, left according to the elder Pliny 4,116 slaves, 3,600 teams of oxen, 257,000 other animals and sixty million sesterces in cash.[4] Numerous freedmen are known to have been benefactors of their cities, to have held the post of *sevir Augustalis* (which involved them in financial outlay), and to have provided the financial basis of their sons' public donations and political successes.[5] Some freedmen left expensive private memorials to themselves in the form of a fine sarcophagus or a monumental inscription. But the less ostentatious displays of wealth are also of interest. Even the erection of a brief inscription, typically an epitaph, cost a meaningful sum of money. It goes without saying that men of moderate wealth, whether freed or freeborn, far outnumbered millionaires.

Anyone broaching this topic inevitably finds himself in dialogue with Paul Veyne, whose deservedly influential article of 1961, 'Vie de Trimalchion', still dominates the field.[6] The article is best known for its refutation of the theory, associated especially with Rostovtzeff, that the freedmen can be regarded as a class or even a bourgeoisie, and for the brilliantly persuasive picture of Roman society which it proposes. It has the additional merit, specifically relevant to this paper, of identifying a group of independent freedmen. In taking Petronius' Trimalchio as typical Veyne has in my view delimited the group too narrowly, as if it consisted merely of a few ex-slaves who on manumission found themselves both lacking a patron and holding an ample legacy. In an Appendix I question the wisdom of leaning on the *Satyricon* as a source for the position of freedmen. There is little sign that Veyne is aware of the existence of a class of freedmen with living patrons, who conceded them a considerable measure of independence and encouraged them to accumulate wealth.[7]

---

[4] *ILS* 1949; Pliny, *HN* 33.134ff., with Brunt (1975) 624ff. Cf. Hor. *Sat.* 2.3.122, 2.5.71; Phaedrus 54.21ff. etc.
[5] *Seviri Augustales*: See the several publications of Duthoy, of which I have seen the following: (1970), with tables and bibl.; (1974). – Local politics: Gordon (1931); Garnsey (1975); D'Arms (1974), esp. 110ff.; (1976).
[6] Veyne (1961), reacting against Rostovtzeff (1957), e.g., 57.
[7] There is a hint but no more in the following passage, where I have italicized the key words: 'Mais si le patron venait à mourir *ou s'effaçait volontairement*, l'affranchi se retrouvait maître de son sort. Ainsi, à côté d'une majorité d'anciens esclaves qui restaient dans la maison de leur patron, il se reformait, à chaque génération, une catégorie d'affranchis indépendants' (227). In general the impression left by the article is that freedmen are divided between the few who became independent on the death of their master and the many who remained 'housebound' after their emancipation.

His article may nevertheless be said to have gone rather further than a number of other legal and historical studies towards explaining the phenomenon of the successful freedman.

The nature of the relationship between the freedman and his patron is fundamental. Manumission transformed a slave into a free man: that is clear. Many historians, || however, have held that freedmen, even those that were economically active, were not independent to any meaningful extent, that behind them lurked patrons exerting over them a high degree of control. Strack wrote long ago: 'Der Freigelassene war nicht frei, nicht in Italien und nicht in Griechenland.'[8] This opinion still carries much weight. Roman historians appear by and large to share the conviction that the category of independent freedmen was numerically very small and economically insignificant. The assumption seems to be that because it was open to patrons to keep their freedmen in tow, they normally did so.

This position has recently received fresh advocacy from Géza Alföldy, in an article based on a survey of inscriptions from the West giving ages of ex-slaves at death.[9] He concluded that manumission of slaves under the age of thirty and during the lifetime of the patron was massive in scale, even routine, to the extent that slaves could count on progressing to freedman status after only a very few years of servitude. Alföldy was unable to explain this on any other terms than that slaves paid handsomely for their freedom and were virtual slaves thereafter, freedman status being merely 'a modified form of slavery'.[10] There is a footnote in his article to the juristic sources and the works of various modern authorities on Roman law which are said to provide confirmation of the thesis. My reading of the legal evidence, as will be seen, produces different results.[11]

The conspicuous weaknesses of Alföldy's 'statistical-epigraphical' method have been discussed before, and best by Kurz in his critique of an earlier article, in which Alföldy's statistics led him to exaggerate the demographic significance of slaves and freedmen in Dalmatia and to conclude that owners bought slaves in order to manumit them more or less immediately.[12] I can detect no significant change in method or argument in the

---

[8] Strack (1914) 23.

[9] Alföldy (1972). His interpretation of the epigraphic evidence has been rightly criticized by Hopkins (1978a) 115 n. 30, cf. 127 n. 63; and by Harris (1980) text to nn. 8ff. I do not repeat their points or expand them here.

[10] Alföldy (1972) 119–22.

[11] Alföldy (1972) 121 n. 83. I have derived most benefit from the following studies: Buckland (1908); Lambert (1934); Treggiari (1969) 68–80. See also Watson (1967); Kaser (1971), e.g., 298–301. Schiller (1971) 24–40, is disappointing: it has the limited objective of describing the main relevant texts, and achieves little more than this.

[12] Alföldy (1961), where 126–31 clearly anticipate the article under discussion. Critique by Kurz (1963), esp. 218–22. Brief criticisms by Hopkins and Harris (n. 9).

later article. The most that Alföldy can be said to have shown is || that manumission before the age of thirty was not uncommon, at any rate in the case of ex-slaves commemorated on tombstones. But there is little reason to believe that these were typical of the slaves who were freed, or that Alföldy's analysis of the condition of freedmen is appropriate to their case.

One important category of ex-slaves freed before the age of thirty is anticipated in the Augustan *lex Aelia Sentia*, which, while fixing a minimum age of thirty for a manumitted slave and twenty for his manumittor, provided for the waiving of these limits on the furnishing of *iustae causae*. There is *iusta causa*, Gaius wrote, 'where, for instance, a man manumits before a *consilium* his natural son or daughter or his natural brother or sister or his foster-child or his children's teacher, or a slave whom he wants as *procurator* or a female slave whom he intends to marry' (1.19). But slaves manumitted *iusta causa* bear little resemblance to the freedmen described by Alföldy as virtual slaves. Even if it were to be conceded that most of them were destined to live lives of service within the household of their ex-master, and were thus technically subject like slaves to his discipline (*Dig.* 48.19.11.1), the peculiar circumstances of their manumission make it unlikely that they were prime targets for exploitation, financial or otherwise. Yet unless Gaius (who does not claim completeness) has missed out significant categories, there is only one other group of ex-slaves likely to be sizeable and to be represented among those freed before the age of thirty: those benefiting from testamentary manumission who were under thirty at the time of their master's death. But Alföldy's analysis is concerned only with manumissions *inter vivos* and cannot apply to this category at all. Indeed the assumption that slaves were normally given their freedom in the lifetime of their masters is a major defect in his argument. The legal evidence for testamentary manumission, direct and indirect, is plentiful; it includes another Augustan law, the *lex Fufia Caninia*, which was specifically designed to restrict the operation of testamentary manumission, but nevertheless left a master with the capacity to free a sizeable proportion of his slaves by will, up to one hundred slaves in the case of owners of five hundred or more. Many modern authorities regard manumission *testamento* as the most common way to liberty, and although this could not conceivably be proven, their opinions must carry some weight.[13]

The least fortunate freedmen, those whose position comes closest to that envisaged by Alföldy as the norm, are probably to be found among

[13] E.g., Buckland (1908) 546; Watson (1967) 194. – The attention given by the jurists to *manumissio testamento* is not in itself conclusive evidence of its significance; whereas the terms of a will were subject to dispute, no comparable ambiguities could arise when an owner manumitted *vindicta*. For full discussions of testamentary manumission, see Buckland (1908) chs. 21–3 and Amelotti (1966).

those who, whether manumitted *testamento* or *vindicta*, were bound to exacting or longlasting services to their former master, an heir or another, or to the payment of a considerable sum of money, or one they would find difficult to raise. Their position was still preferable to that of *statuliberi* with obligations of a similar scale, for the *statuliberi* remained slaves until they had carried out whatever conditions were laid down in the will. It would be a mistake, however, to suppose that these forms of manumission were necessarily intentionally exploitative, whether the conditions laid down were reasonably light (and the implications of the legal sources is that they often were) or less obviously so.[14] Moreover, if the master (or patron) deliberately stood in the way of the fulfilment || of the conditions, then recourse could be had to the legal authorities. It would be illegitimate to assume that this or other safeguards against a master's (or patron's) bad faith were inevitably inoperative or ineffectual.

Meanwhile, the position of slaves manumitted indirectly, usually with conditions attached, stands in contrast with that of those gaining their freedom by direct manumission and certain types of manumission imposed by the law, who were left patronless. They were in the technical parlance *libertini* or *liberti orcini*, freedmen of the deceased.[15] An *orcinus* who was also *heres* or *legatarius* had the best prospects, depending of course on the value of the inheritance or legacy: the *necessarius heres* of an insolvent testator had little to be grateful for.[16]

However, the *libertus orcinus* was not the only kind of ex-slave who escaped patronal exploitation that was worthy of the name. Another important category is accommodated, although far from clearly identified in legal terms, in recent work by Keith Hopkins, in the context of a vigorous assertion of the economic motive for manumission.[17] Hopkins argues first that the hope or promise of manumission gave a slave an incentive to do extra or better work. This is a consideration that may be supposed to have influenced in particular the master who intended to release his slave only on his death. Not surprisingly, it was ignored altogether by Alföldy, who thought in terms only of an abbreviated period of servitude proper, for slaves destined to become freedmen. Hopkins is impressed by Alföldy's arguments to the extent of conceding the frequency of manumission *inter*

---

[14] This is argued plausibly by Kupiszewski (1979). On *statuliberi* see also Buckland (1908) 286–91; Watson (1967).

[15] On freedmen *orcini* see the following texts: Gaius, *Inst.* 2.267; Ulp. 2.8; *Dig.* 26.4.3.3, 28.5.8 pr., 33.8.22 pr., 40.5.30.12, 40.5.49, 40.7.2 pr., 40.8.5, cf. 38.2.4 pr.: *nullius .. liberti*. For fideicommissary manumission, which gave the freedman considerable freedom from his patron, see Buckland (1908) 527–32.

[16] Buckland (1908) 505ff.

[17] Hopkins (1978a) 115–32: 'Why did the Romans free so many slaves?'

vivos. Moreover, in presenting a second aspect of the economic motive for manumission, namely the purchase of freedom by the slave, Hopkins appears to have had in mind only manumission in the master's lifetime. He writes: '... Roman slaves frequently, even customarily, in my view, paid substantial sums for their freedom. The prospects of becoming free kept a slave under control and hard at work, while the exaction of a market price as the cost of liberty enabled the master to buy a younger replacement.'[18] Subsequently the analysis is broadened to take in testamentary manumission.

What Hopkins fails to bring out is that purchase of freedom, as long as the funds were not provided by a third party, who played the part of *emptor* in the transaction, created a freedman who was to all intents and purposes independent of any patron: he escaped *operae*, and like the freedman father of two children (*Dig.* 38.1.37 pr.) he escaped the rule by which a patron was entitled to one half of a freedman's property on death.[19] Alföldy's belief that freedmen had both to pay well for their freedom and serve their former masters or new patrons in virtual slavery is simply mistaken. It was not even the case in the early and middle Republic, before a series of reforming praetors began to redefine the powers of a patron in respect of his freedman. The first of these praetors according to Ulpian was Rutilius Rufus, in office about 118 BC, who published a clause in his edict limiting the patron to an *actio operarum et societatis*.[20] Even after this reform, the precise details of which are obscure, a patron could in principle bring his slave to agree to surrender him all his labour in return for maintenance or as many *operae* as the freedman did not need to maintain himself. But I doubt very much whether such heavy obligations were at all common; and I find it even more difficult to believe that manumission payments were often received from slaves so placed. Payments for manumission were, one might suppose, an aspect of 'deals' made between masters and enterprising slaves. We do not know when such 'deals' began to be reflected in the law, or when jurisprudential opinion established the principle that a master who received from a slave the cost of his replacement was not entitled to further exactions. Eventually a constitution of Marcus and Verus gave a slave *suis nummis emptus* immediate manumission even in the face of opposition from his master.

Hopkins' position on this point is less clear than Alföldy's, but he does appear to hold both that freed slaves customarily paid for the gift of liberty

---

[18] Hopkins (1978a) 118.
[19] On the *servus suis nummis emptus*, see Buckland (1908) 636–46; Michel (1962) 157–67, summary at 165.
[20] *Dig.* 38.2.1.1. Discussed by Watson (1967) 228–9; Kaser (1971) 300–1; Treggiari (1969) 69ff.; Lambert pt. 2 (1934), 1.

and that *operae* were frequently stipulated as a condition of freedom.[21] His article however has the merit of showing how it was that slaves were able to buy their freedom. Following Finley, he finds the key to this in the convention by which the master 'lent' a slave *peculium*, or working capital, to enable him to engage in some business enterprise. The copious legal evidence on *peculium* leaves no doubt that the slave could treat it virtually as his own property (when it was employed in some business enterprise), and this itself implies that the master had foregone his prerogative of exercising total control over the slave, himself legally the property of his owner. As Hopkins puts it: 'The very idea that slaves could *de facto* control their own property, including their own slaves, implied independence of action. The *peculium* was the institutional expression of that freedom of action.'[22] How surprising and illogical it would have been, if a slave who had used his *peculium* with sufficient enterprise to enable him to purchase his freedom, should have found himself in his new status, as a result of a stipulation, subject to more rather than less constraint.

The legal sources indicate the kinds of role that freedmen with a considerable degree of independence could play. Freedmen were commonly employed as business agents.[23] Agency implies a relationship between social unequals which was frequently ‖ one of clientage. It does not necessarily imply, however, close supervision and control by the master or patron. That *procurator* or *actor* who worked in close proximity to the master and was kept under close rein is more appropriately described as household servant than business agent; and the juristic distinction between *procurator* and *institor*, one aspect of which was the fact that principals incurred liability for contracts negotiated with third parties by the latter, but not by the former,[24] may once have reflected the latter's greater involvement in the world of business. But the distinction became obsolete long before it was overturned by an opinion of the Severan jurist Papinian.[25]

---

[21] Hopkins (1978a) 129: 'All in all, it seems reasonable to argue that slaves' purchase of their own freedom was very common.' Cf. 131: 'On the other hand, the Romans often extended a slave's servitude into the period when he had become legally free.' I am not impressed by the arguments for the 'exploitative' nature of *operae* (130), and I suggest that we firmly reject any comparison with the Delphic manumission data (130–1), which among other things show slaves almost invariably purchasing freedom with funds the origin of which Hopkins cannot explain. Note, incidentally, that Hopkins' frequent assertion that Roman slaves paid the market price for their freedom is a speculation, if a reasonable one, derived from no other source than the Delphic documents.

[22] Hopkins (1978a) 126, anticipated by Finley (1973a) 64. I do not mean to imply in this section that only economically active freedmen benefited from sale *suis nummis* or *ut manumittatur*.

[23] Technically the Romans lacked the modern concept of agency. On agency, see Kaser (1971) 605ff., 608ff.; Stein (1959).

[24] *Dig.* 14.3.5.10. On *actiones adiectitiae qualitatis*, Kaser (1971) 605ff.   [25] *Dig.* 17.1.10.5.

With the *institor*, or business manager, and the *magister navis*, or ship-captain, we enter the world of artisans and traders familiar from the epigraphic and archaeological evidence. (It should be remembered, however, that both the self-employed and those in another's employ are represented in the inscriptions, and it is usually impossible to tell them apart.) Such men, unlike the procurators, were empowered to make contracts with third parties which bound not only themselves but also their masters – so long as in so doing they were not going beyond the terms of the specific *praepositio* with which they were charged. One implication of that rule is that they were free to conduct business on their own account outside the sphere of the *praepositio*, and the examples cited in the *Digest* show that good use was made of this freedom. Indeed the jurist Julian held that the appointment by a ship's captain of a substitute, whether or not the ship-owner (*exercitor*) knew of this, was permissible under the terms of the *actio exercitoria*; in other words, the ship-owner could still be reached by third parties.[26]

Freedmen appear in the legal sources also as *socii*, partners.[27] Partnership was in origin based on the principle of equality of associates, who were at first co-heirs of an undivided inheritance. The earliest partnerships outside the context of the family may be supposed to have been between social equals. But this tradition was gradually undermined in the course of the Republic, until the jurist Servius Sulpicius Rufus succeeded in establishing the rule, which had been resisted by conservatives such as Q. Mucius Scaevola in the previous generation, that a partner might contribute *operae* rather than *pecunia* and nonetheless share profits (and sometimes not even losses).[28] This reform must have given fresh encouragement to the formation of patron-freedman partnerships. They may be believed to have existed earlier, but not on terms so advantageous to the freedman. This is certainly true of the *societas libertatis causa* allowed by the praetor Rutilius (in c.118 BC) but impugned already by Labeo, the Augustan jurist.[29] That *societas* was a device by which a patron gained a promise of *obsequium* from a slave in return for the gift of liberty, and, if the promise was broken, an automatic partnership with him. Ulpian goes on to make the significant statement that the award of half the *bona libertorum*, which later praetors granted to patrons, corresponded to the contribution made by the freedman in his lifetime to the *patronus- ‖ socius*. We are not told why the *societas libertatis causa* fell under a cloud, but the reason is not far to seek. *Societas* was a consensual contract which by definition could not be made under duress.

[26] Pugliese (1957), at 312ff.
[27] *Societas*: *Dig.* 17.2; Gaius, *Inst.* 3.148ff.; Kaser (1971) 572ff.
[28] Gaius, *Inst.* 3.149.   [29] *Dig.* 38.2.1, cf. 38.1.36 (Lab.).

One further text, from Paulus, is of interest. It shows two co-freedmen (*colliberti*) joining together in *societas* for the pursuit of profit. Their patron was alive at the time of the formation of the partnership and was evidently uninvolved in it.[30]

Before leaving the legal sources, we might summarize the picture that they give of the condition of freedmen. The first and major impression is one of diversity. The sources show a wide range of possible relationships between patrons and freedmen. There were freedmen who won their freedom on condition that they served their masters in what were virtually household posts.[31] At the other end of the spectrum it appears that freedmen might actually be business rivals of their patrons, with the sanction of juristic authority.[32]

The position of the freedman depended by and large on the patron's attitude. It was the patron who decided the scale of the *operae* or services to be imposed on the manumitted slave, if indeed he chose to stipulate for *operae* at all. It was his interpretation of the freedman's duty of *obsequium*, respectful conduct, that prevailed. The duty of *obsequium* is never closely defined. It is expressed largely in a number of specific regulations, such as those restricting the freedman's capacity to take legal proceedings against his patron. These rules are almost entirely negative. In practice the patron was free to frame his own definition of a freedman's responsibilities to him, subject to the possibility of legal challenge. But the rules governing their relationship were moral rules, based on *fides*, and the law intervened mainly to adjust the structure of obligations and rights between the two parties when they were considered to be in serious imbalance. Unfortunately, the process of change through praetorian edict, jurisprudential judgement or legislative enactment is difficult to follow in juristic compilations that were never intended to be source-books for the historian.[33] Occasionally, too, actual conflicts of interest are settled. We have record of specific judgements favourable to freedmen, for example, that of Scaevola, who (in a case just alluded to) ruled that a freedman could practise a trade (here the clothing trade) identical with his patron's and in the same town, against the objections of the patron.[34] Ulpian's opinion that freedmen should not be prevented from engaging in any lawful trade (*negotiatione licita*) may derive from a particular dispute of this kind.[35]

---

[30] *Dig.* 17.2.71. [31] *Dig.* 40.2.13, cf. 40.4.17.1, 40.5.41.15. [32] *Dig.* 38.1.45; cf. 37.14.18.

[33] The results of change are also difficult to weigh – hence the wide disagreements among modern authorities.

[34] See n. 32.

[35] *Dig.* 37.14.2. But cf. 38.1.26 pr. (a doctor who won't let his freedmen practise, supported by Alfenus). In *Cod.Iust.* 6.13.12, Diocletian refers to *iura* of presumably earlier date according to which the freedman was not obliged to live in his patron's house. Other concessions in Kaser (1971) 301.

An example of a ruling in the patron's interest is the statement in Paul's *Sentences* that a refusal to administer a patron's affairs or to act as tutor to his sons was the mark of an ungrateful freedman.[36] In practice, actual relationships between patrons and freedmen must have diverged very widely in character. It is no more likely that patrons invariably required their freedmen to perform the services specified || in Paul's *Sentences*, than that independent freedmen typically flaunted their independence to the extent of acting as trading competitors of their patrons.

Finally, the legal evidence has put us in a better position to define the category of independent freedmen whose existence I have posited. Their characteristic feature is that they were free, and in several senses. They were juridically free, in as much as they had been emancipated from their masters. Then, they were economically free, and in two ways. In the first place, they were not tied to the land by family tradition or by personal circumstances. They could therefore invest their energies and finance in marginal activities such as commerce and industry. Secondly, they did not have patrons. Alternatively, they had patrons but were not dependent upon them, because those patrons had, as Veyne put it, 'voluntarily effaced themselves'.[37] They had purposefully withdrawn or severely limited the patronal authority that they were up to a point entitled to exert over their freedmen, by law and by convention. This description could apply even to some patrons who used freedmen as agents or managers, let alone to patrons who were their freedmen's business partners.

We come now to the issue of the identification of independent or relatively independent freedmen in the non-legal sources. The problems are severe, even if we leave on one side the initial task of separating out freed from freeborn and slaves. When faced with individual cases, scholars usually hedge their bets. Yet a series of case-studies in selected areas would yield positive results. At Pompeii for example there is information available which remains largely unexploited; with some exceptions, in particular Andreau's study of the banker Caecilius Iucundus,[38] the best studies of Pompeii have focused on the 'old' aristocracy and the official class of the city. Castren's important 'Ordo Populusque Romanus' (1975) lacks a socio-economic dimension. Yet as long ago as 1950 Lepore in an influential article indicated that most or all commercial operations geared to export and to distribution for local retailing were run by slaves and freedmen. He was primarily interested, however, in drawing out the implications for the character of the 'old' aristocracy, which he saw as the real controllers of the business life of Pompeii, and whom he labelled in consequence 'an aristocracy with both landed and commercial interests'

[36] *Dig.* 37.14.19.　[37] Veyne (1961) 225; quoted in n. 7.　[38] Andreau (1974).

('un'aristocrazia terriera e trafficante insieme').³⁹ Andreau has recently endorsed Lepore's view of the landowning class of Pompeii, and is indeed prepared to extend it to the whole city-based landowning class of Italy and the provinces. For Andreau, landowners did not disdain participating in financial and commercial operations through the mediation of freedmen whom they placed over their businesses or whom they financed.⁴⁰ These scholars appear to take it for granted that the category of independent freedmen is very small, too small to be significant.⁴¹ This may in part be a result of their ‖ concern to argue against earlier writers that the old ruling class of Pompeii was not ousted by a new moneyed class centring on freedmen and their descendants. It is interesting that Veyne, who does not approach the issue as a Pompeian specialist, and whose argument is conducted purely at a general level, is prepared to concede that independent freedmen must have been numerous; and yet for him this class consisted largely or entirely of those who had been granted testamentary manumission with an accompanying legacy. Modern accounts of the official class at Pompeii would not necessarily be undermined by a study considering the economic activities of freedmen from their point of view, and paying particular attention to the character of their relationships to patrons, not forgetting that a certain proportion of them would not have had patrons at all.

It is time to suggest some rough criteria by which independent freedmen might be identified. There are two main candidates: wealth and positions of responsibility. By wealth I mean sufficient assets to lift someone out of the mass of humanity and place him in the ranks of the propertied classes. There are isolated examples of genuinely rich freedmen.⁴² But we should also be on the lookout for moderate wealth, sufficient to finance membership of a professional association or the erection of a commemorative inscription. It has recently been suggested, indeed, that most of the artisans recorded on inscriptions were 'wealthy independent entrepreneurs and foremen'.⁴³ The truth lies somewhere between this position and the rival view that behind every freedman artisan or trader lurked a patron drawing the lion's share of the profits, exacting burdensome unpaid service, and so on.

My second index of independence, the holding of a responsible position, also requires elucidation. What I have in mind is the ownership or management of or partnership in a business, preferably a sizeable one or one that

---

[39] Lepore (1950) 159.
[40] Andreau (1973) 232, 230 and 240. See the wide-ranging discussion of Pucci (1976-7).
[41] Note for example that the article by Strack (1914) is cited by Lepore (1950) 158 with approval.
[42] See n. 4. [43] Huttunen (1974) 122.

can be seen to be profitable. Here my two indices of independence can come together.

A brief glance at several trades may serve to illustrate my points. First, the building trade, and more particularly the segment of it represented in the builder's associations of Rome and Ostia, the former having a membership of about one thousand three hundred in the second century AD, comprising both freed and freeborn citizens. A recent study of these organizations concludes that most of their members were 'employers' rather than 'employees', and that the entrance-fees and other expenses which members incurred made them 'somewhat exclusive' and guaranteed that membership was beyond the reach of many or most workers. These results could no doubt be applied, with or without adjustments, to other prestigious worker's associations or *collegia*, in Rome and other cities.[44]

The second example concerns the woollen industry. There is now a study of the Pompeian woollen industry. Its author, Moeller, may be thought to have gone too far in the attempt to resuscitate the cause of Rostovtzeff; he nevertheless shows (while exaggerating the importance of the export trade) that wool was a profitable business at Pompeii and that the key men were freedmen. How many were owners and how many managers cannot be ascertained and may not matter very much.[45] ||

Next, pottery: Arezzo was the centre of the production of fine pottery for half a century or more spanning the reign of Augustus. This was an industry with a slave workforce, where skilled workers could win manumission and run or own pottery firms. A recent study estimates that the majority of owners were freeborn not freed, but that freedmen were relatively more important in pottery industries located in South Italy. One thinks of the freedman N. Naevius Hilarus, who owned at least sixteen slave-potters at Puteoli.[46]

Finally, the brick industry at Rome. A scholar has recently put together from brickstamps a list of 150 *domini* and 355 *officinatores*.[47] His conclusions, which I find convincing, are that *officinatores*, or the men who run the brickworks, are not normally clients, especially freedmen clients, of the *domini*, or the landowners – less than a fifth of them are thus placed. They are not, in other words, foremen for a class of 'manufacturers' (who happen to include many Roman senators and equestrians, not to mention emperors); rather, they were, typically, independent contractors.

I conclude that a sizeable number of freedmen attained a position of independence or relative independence and wealth. Whether they constituted a class, or a bourgeoisie, is another matter. Veyne's critique of this notion runs along the following lines.

---

[44] Pearse (1974) ch. 5. [45] Moeller (1976). [46] Pucci (1973). [47] Helen (1975).

First, Roman civilization was fundamentally static. There was mobility, but it boils down to the fact that 'certain individuals' did well. This is what the phenomenon of the 'rise of the freedmen' amounts to.

Secondly, there was no 'economic root' in the rise of a Trimalchio, and by extension in the rise of other independent freedmen, only a 'kind of accident'. Everything depended on the chance factor of a patron's support.

Thirdly, there was no 'follow through'. Not only did freedmen and their sons have no impact on the higher orders, but they were actually absorbed into them, adopting their lifestyles (or else, in the case of the unsuccessful, they subsided into the ranks of the *plebs*). Although at first glance the freedmen were potentially a bourgeoisie, in that they were fringe people with a relatively free choice of profession, in practice they never became a bourgeoisie. Their capital, originating from the land, not in other words generated within the commercial and industrial sectors, returned in due course and inevitably to the land.

My image of Roman society and the economic role of freedmen is broadly similar to that of Veyne but by no means identical. It is also close to that of Finley, who emphasizes that slaves and freedmen carried on 'a substantial part of the urban commercial, financial and industrial activity in Rome and Italy', and sees that those active in this way 'were working independently', not only for others (masters, patrons) but also for themselves.[48]

First, the Roman economy was agrarian at base. But in the period under discussion, trading ventures, especially but not exclusively in the products of agriculture and pasturage, and loans, could be profitable, at least in the short term. The same applies, ‖ though to a lesser extent, to manufactures. Unless we grant that profits could be made in these spheres, it is difficult or impossible to understand how it was that slaves were able to buy their freedom (and not impoverish themselves completely in the process). Whether substantial fortunes could be made without the initial capital that a large legacy might provide must remain doubtful.

Secondly, there was scope therefore for the activity of an enterprising social group – if not strictly an entrepreneurial one, in the modern sense of the term.

Thirdly, freedmen and slaves formed the nucleus of the group and were its most active agents. The composition of the group was, however, broader than this, because freeborn landowners, whether of aristocratic or non-aristocratic background, often had a subsidiary interest in non-agricultural enterprises. Freedmen and slaves regularly acted as intermediaries for men of property in commercial and industrial transactions.

---

[48] Finley (1973a), citations from p. 64. On p. 78 he is cautious and undogmatic on the issues of how such freedmen gained their fortunes and how they invested them.

Fourthly, freedmen did not merely act as intermediaries. The more talented and fortunate were able to build up an independent financial position. Moreover as members of the *familia*, the social institution by which wealth and privilege is usually transmitted, they participated in the process by which the property-owning stratum was reproduced and transformed. For manumission, as well as inheritance by birth, adoption and legacy among those of the same class background, can be seen to have played a part in the wealth-transferring process.

Fifthly, it is therefore likely that there was some degree of continuity in commercial and industrial holdings, though there is no point in overstating the case. Investments that were not strictly agricultural formed part of the inherited wealth of notable families. The great warehouses and brickyards of Rome, which were owned by equestrians, senators and emperors, are conspicuous examples. It can be plausibly conjectured that some businesses owned by freedmen were passed down to their freeborn heirs, if there were any, and were not dissolved as soon as they became profitable. This is largely unexplored territory, and the evidence is difficult to handle. The potters Ateii, who had branches at Arezzo, Pisa, Lyon, and Campania, look like an instance of the accumulation and transference of industrial wealth within the wider *familia*. But without detailed information the case cannot be proven. In general, our evidence is usually insufficient in quantity or undifferentiated as to time, or both.[49]

Sixthly, while for every individual slave, legal, social, and economic advancement may have been a matter of chance, looked at in the aggregate, the prosperity of numerous individual freedmen in each generation was actually inevitable – given the points mentioned above, the profits that could be made in usury, trading and industrial ventures, the favoured position of a whole category of slaves in the *familia* of the wealthy. There is indeed a risk that by focusing attention on the turnover of persons and families involved in commercial and industrial transactions, we lose sight of the important fact that the economic system was so structured as to produce a stratum or category of positions which remained relatively stable over time.

In conclusion, the argument about the nature and proper definition of the social category of economically active freedmen which I have been discussing is to some ‖ extent about the applicability of terms and concepts which were devised for a different historical context. It should not be beyond historians of Rome to bring into service terminology which is appropriate to Roman society and which can help us identify its characteristic

---

[49] Ateii: See Pucci (1973) 286. Ostian tugboat-owners, *lenuncularii tabularii auxiliarii*, are discussed by Wilson (1935) 66; Meiggs (1960) 323; Pearse (1974) 136ff.

features, both those that it shares with other societies and those that are individual to it.

Appendix: the historicity of Trimalchio[50]

Rostovtzeff regarded him as a typical representative of the Italian urban bourgeoisie, Veyne as the representative rich freedman, MacMullen as the typical nouveau riche, Hopkins as the archetypal rich ex-slave; and so on.[51]

Was Trimalchio in any sense typical? How far and in what ways do the Trimalchio episode and its chief character resemble life?

A literary critic, Florence Dupont, has challenged 'la lecture réaliste', with arguments that imply that a text can be isolated from its social environment.[52]

The *Satyricon* is self-evidently not a sober transposition of social reality. Equally obviously, however, the work in some measure reflects the contemporary society.

Dupont is right to stress the literary context – even if her own contribution is somewhat wayward, in exaggerating the links between Petronius and the Greek tradition of the 'Banquet genre' while almost completely ignoring the *Satyricon*'s basic genre, the long tradition of Menippean satire and of satire in general which had developed in the interval. But the literary problem does have priority; we need to ask what are the conventions, if any, to which the work conforms or which it flouts? What would the ancients have said about it, how would Petronius' contemporaries have responded to it? When such questions as these can be answered, we will be in a position perhaps to establish clear and reliable criteria by which the social evidence that the work undoubtedly contains can be recognized. If, however, as seems to be the case, the literary background is so shadowy that we cannot answer the questions, then we have to acknowledge that we lack those criteria.

Where does this leave the historian? He must, in the first place, approach the text with lower expectations. Secondly, he must be careful not to assume that what is recognizable in the historical context is also representative. The details can be possible, indeed plausible; they do not have to be typical. Thirdly, given the uncertainty about the literary norms for the interpretation of the *Satyricon*, it seems that the social historian is following a correct procedure if in his quest for relevant social information he moves from the world beyond the text to Trimalchio, rather than in the

---

[50] I gratefully acknowledge help received from Drs H. Erskine-Hill and J. McKeown.

[51] Rostovtzeff (1957) 57; Veyne (1961); MacMullen (1974a) 49ff., 102ff.; Hopkins (1978a) 117 n. 36. The typicality of Trimalchio is fully investigated by D'Arms (1981).

[52] Dupont (1977), esp. 12–13.

other direction. Therein lies the best hope of establishing, for example, the ways in which freedmen, and others, obtained wealth and spent it. ||

Addendum

This paper challenges the commonly held view that freedmen remained dependent on their ex-master patrons and therefore acted, among other things, as agents for those members of the leisured class who invested in business activities but refrained from, or were barred from, involving themselves. G. argues for the existence of a class of freedmen who engaged in business on their own behalf. He is inclined in consequence to place greater emphasis than Veyne on non-agricultural investment. For a brief complementary discussion of slaves in business, see Garnsey (1982b).

In keeping with traditional perceptions, much recent work focuses on the role of freedmen as agents of members of the élite (pp. 30–5). Fabre (1981) 93–357 deals at great length with the dependence of the freedman on his patron in Republican society, arguing that manumission did not normally rupture the ties between them. See Bürge (1988) for patron-freedman links under the empire; cf. also Gardner (1989). Waldstein (1986) offers an exhaustive treatment of the services freedmen owed their patrons. Kirschenbaum (1987) 127–40, 148–60 discusses the acquisition of property through freedmen. Curchin (1987) 87–8, on Roman Spain, stresses the high level of dependence of freedmen indicated by epigraphic material. Andreau (1993) 181 refers to the fragile social position of the ordinary freedman. Eck (1978) argues that dependence on senatorial patrons might facilitate the social advancement of freedmen, who therefore profited more from lasting ties than from complete independence. On social mobility, see also Rink (1993). Los (1995) 1040 concludes that the rise of freedmen mostly depended on the status of their patrons and on their relationship with them. (But cf. Barja de Quiroga (1995) 344.) Los (1995) 1030–3 also emphasizes the role of freedmen as agents and the closeness of ties that bound them to their patrons. He thinks that Augustus' inheritance laws encouraged patrons to fund their freedmen because compulsory succession would subsequently give them access to their new wealth (1032–3). On the frequency of Roman manumission (pp. 30–1), see Wiedemann (1985); Scheidel (1997).

'Independent freedmen' (pp. 37–9) have also attracted some attention. With reference to G., Serrano Delgado (1988) 226 argues for the existence of independent freedmen in Roman Spain. (I have not seen Schulze-Oben (1989), also on Spain.) Barja de Quiroga (1991) is a study of independent freedmen, their social mobility and coherence as a successful group, focusing on Ostia. (This setting is treated at greater length by Barja de Quiroga (1992) (*non vidi*).) Barja de Quiroga (1991) 167–8, with nn. 13–14, specifically addresses the present paper; he agrees with G. that some freedmen were independent in as much as they could make their own decisions (167). Christol (1992), esp. 250, 258, discusses the case of a wealthy independent freedman in Nîmes (with reference to G.: 250 nn. 37–8). For possible traces of freedmen who acted as tenants of landowners other than their own patrons, see Los (1992a) 728-30. Independent freedmen are, however, difficult to study as a distinct category, according to Aubert (1994) 36-7: 'Freedmen are particularly likely to elude any attempt at categorization either as independent businessmen or as managers' (36).

On Trimalchio (p. 42), see, e.g., D'Arms (1981) 97-120; Andreau (1993) 175-8; Los (1995) 1011-26. Veyne (1991) 11 singles out the contribution made by the present paper.

3

ECONOMY AND SOCIETY OF MEDIOLANUM UNDER THE PRINCIPATE[1]

I

Strabo called Mediolanum (Milan) an ἀξιόλογος πόλις and classed it above all other cities in the region of Cisalpine Gaul, with the exception of Patavium (Padua). Patavium in its prime, the Augustan period, could register five hundred equestrians in a census, a number equalled only by Gades (Cadiz) among cities in the West. The presence of so many equestrians indicates a substantial population-base. Cisalpine cities as a whole impressed Strabo as being larger and richer than those of the rest of Italy.[2]

Thus, if Strabo is any guide, Mediolanum was already in his time (the beginning of the Principate), an important city, perhaps not far behind Patavium in size. Moreover, the fortunes of Mediolanum, unlike those of Patavium, were not on the wane. No contemporary of Augustus could have forecast that Mediolanum would be chosen as a seat of emperors in the fourth century. But seen in the light of the city's development in the early empire as an administrative, cultural and economic centre, this was a logical choice.

In this study of Mediolanum I discuss economic activity, aspects of social structure, and the relation between them. It does not need demonstrating in detail that the principal economic asset of Mediolanum, like that of most ancient cities, was its rural hinterland. But closer investigation of possible secondary economic activities of the city and in particular its trading links with other cities in the region and beyond is required. Strabo's assessment of the significance of Mediolanum and its subsequent history

---

[1] This is a revised draft of a paper presented in May 1974 to a seminar in Oxford under the chairmanship of Fergus Millar. I am grateful to F. Millar for the invitation to speak and to participants in the seminar for their comments. I have also benefited from the criticism of Moses Finley and Richard Gordon.

[2] Strab. C 213; 218. Strabo compares Ravenna only with the other cities 'in the marshes', and leaves Aquileia out of the comparison altogether. I have not seen estimates of the population of Mediolanum. Comum under Trajan has been assessed at up to 22,500. See Duncan-Jones (1982) 266–7. That Mediolanum outranked Comum is implied in Strab. C 213. For Aquileia's population under the Principate, see Calderini (1940) 336 (conjectures ranging from 100,000 to 800,000).

suggest that the city was not an isolated backwater, cut off from external markets, having limited potential for economic expansion.

Mediolanum was well-placed for communications and trade. It stood at the centre of an overland communications network linking, on the one hand, Piedmont and Venetia, and on the other, the Transalpine regions and the central Po valley, and beyond this the route to the south by Placentia and the via Aemilia. Moreover, while not exactly riverine, Mediolanum was in close proximity to navigable rivers. We should not, however, jump to conclusions about the extent to which the road system, or ‖ for that matter the rivers, were used for trade. In his survey of the economic geography of Cisalpine Gaul, Brunt reached the conclusion that the Po valley, for all its fertility, productivity and admirable river system, was condemned to relative isolation in the late Republic and Principate; it was too inaccessible, too far removed from important markets. Production was for local consumption on the whole; each community aimed at autarky rather than the export of a surplus.[3]

At this point it would be as well to clarify the terms of the argument and the objectives one might hope to achieve. We may take as common knowledge the constraints affecting trade and the development of markets in the ancient world: the inefficiency and cost of land transport, the risks involved in trade, especially maritime trade, the low level of demand. Our concern is rather with the extent to which commercial exchange took place within the limits set by these constraints. We cannot expect precise results, since quantitative data are not available.[4] However, it should be possible to make a provisional judgement of the extent of the economic isolation of Cisalpine Gaul on the basis of such evidence as there is.[5]

II

Literary sources of the early Empire did not regard the area as self-contained. Pliny wrote (with tantalizing vagueness) of the accessibility of Gallia Transpadana to 'all the products of the sea'; he was referring to the Augustan *Regio* XI, the central and upper Po valley.[6] Strabo knew of two items of export which had captured a large share of the most important

---

[3] Brunt (1971) 172–84.

[4] A bold attempt to circumvent this problem was made by A. H. M. Jones. He suggested that trade and industry contributed no more than 5 per cent of the imperial revenues and of the overall wealth of the empire in the late period. In my view the argument cannot stand, and in any case cannot apply to the early empire. See Jones (1964) 464ff.

[5] For a more optimistic account than Brunt's of Cisapline trade, which utilizes the archaeological evidence, see Baldacci (1967–8) 7ff.

[6] Pliny, *HN* 3. 123: 'Transpadana appellatur ab eo regio undecima, tota in mediterraneo, cui maria cuncta fructuoso alveo inportat'.

market, Rome: Rome was 'for the most part' fed from Cisalpine pork, and 'most Italian households' wore clothes made of coarse Ligurian wool. The same author mentions the 'costly carpets and covers', and 'clothes of all kinds', as well as other unnamed products, which were sent to Rome from Patavium. These were luxury goods for a more limited clientèle. But high prices were paid, and Patavium prospered accordingly. Strabo's characterization of the city as not only populous but also skilled at crafts suggests that the textile industry was at the least an important sideline. The soft wool of Mutina and the Scultenna valley, which Strabo also knew, was not produced purely for home consumption either in his day or three centuries later, when Diocletian fixed prices for a number of woollen garments made in Mutina (and for imitations made in the Phrygian town of Laodicea), and rates for the weavers of these articles. The fame of the wools of Altinum and Parma extended beyond the region; they are ranked above or just below Apulian wool by writers living after Strabo. Altinum was a minor centre for the production of woollen clothing in the late Empire, as is attested by the edict of Diocletian. Agricultural products, principally wine and oil from the region of Aquileia, Eastern Venetia, Histria, and further afield, were sent across the Alps into Illyricum and the Danubian region in exchange for slaves, hides and cattle. The trade in wine is alluded to by writers as far apart in time as Strabo and Herodian, while that in oil and possibly wine is documented for the intervening period by finds of amphorae.[7] Otherwise, the best known non-literary evidence for Transalpine trade comes from the Magdalensberg in Noricum in the form of inscriptions, which date from the late Republic to the early decades of the empire, and attest the movement of Norican metalware south into Italy and beyond: 393 large plates purchased by a Roman, 550 rings by a man from Volubilis in Mauretania, this gives an indication of the scale of the operation and the kind of goods that might be moved with profit. Further west, the transport of Arretine ware and other manufactures across the Alps into the Valais and thence to the military camps on the Rhine and Danube can be followed in the early part of the first century AD, but fades out thereafter.[8]

What is presented here is something more than an undifferentiated list of goods exported, imported and in transit. The sources sometimes indicate that goods were traded in quantity or, indirectly, with profit. The

---

[7] Strab. C 213; 218; Martial 14.143; 155; Columella, *Rust.* 7.2. 3; Herodian 8.2. 3; 4. 5; Lauffer (1971) 19.13; 21; 23–6; 20.3–4; 13; 21, 1a; 22, 16–18; 25, 1a; 2 (Mutina); 21. 2; 25. 4 (Altinum); Baldacci (1967–8) 7ff.

[8] Egger (1961); Wells (1973) 39; Ulbert (1959), e.g. 33ff.; and see n. 35 below. Evidence (non-quantifiable) for the use of Transalpine routes for trade is furnished by the existence of customs stations at numerous points in the Alpine region. See de Laet (1949) 144ff., esp. 158ff.; 175ff.

persistence of trade in a product over an extended period of time, which might be taken as one index of profitability, is exemplified by the fine garment production of Mutina and the export of wine (and probably oil) across the Alps in the Eastern sector.[9] Again, it can be safely assumed that the flow of metalware from Noricum did not stop at the time that the evidence for this traffic ceases to be available, that is, when the commercial establishment at the Magdalensberg was moved to nearby Virunum under Claudius. On the other hand, the conveyance of *terra sigillata* originating in Arretium over the central Alpine passes must have halted as soon as the Transalpine potteries came into large-scale production. It made no difference that Gallic and especially Rhenish pottery were inferior products.

The eclipse of Arretine pottery illustrates the crippling effect that bad transport facilities could have on trade over a distance. Remoteness from the market might be by itself a decisive factor. Once the Histrian oil industry attained a certain level of || development, it was inevitable that Apulian oil would be excluded from north Italy and that oil from southern Spain would fail to establish itself in the same area.[10] Histria was, similarly, suitably situated to serve Noricum and the provinces to the east of Noricum; the Alpine barrier is at its lowest in the Eastern sector, reaching heights of only 783 metres at the Saifnitz or Tarvis pass leading to Virunum (near Klagenfurt) and the Drave, and 520 metres at the Birnbaum Wald pass on the route to Emona (Ljubljana) and the Save.[11] Conversely, clothing fashioned in Patavium had further to travel to the Roman market than the Apulian product (but not the Asian), and was never likely to compete successfully with local textile industries across the Alps. This, together with the low level of demand for what were essentially luxury items, may sufficiently explain the decline of the industry – if, indeed, we can be sure that Patavine textiles did decline.[12] It is worth emphasizing that, the factor

---

[9] Whereas Strabo refers to both wine and oil as objects of trade, Herodian mentions specifically only the former. References to Pannonian wine do not begin until the late third century; yet Italian wine was still being imported (in exchange for cereals) into Pannonia in the late fourth century. See Mócsy (1974) 298–9, with refs. As for the importance of the trade, Brunt (1971) 708, regards the export of wine to the north as 'substantial'. Oil was not in Pannonia the staple that it was in Italy and Mediterranean lands, because of the competition which animal fats provided; but the army (and not merely the officer class) doubtless needed it in quantity.

[10] See Baldacci (1967–8) 15ff.; 44ff., for the evidence.

[11] For comparison, note that the easiest route across the Apennines between Dertona in the north and Beneventum in the south is taken by the via Flaminia, which nonetheless rises to a height of 581 metres at the Scheggia pass.

[12] The evidence for the decline of the city and its textile industry is meagre. Chilver acknowledges that the latter does not disappear altogether from the record (such as it is), and that Mela could still call the city 'opulentissima'. See Chilver (1941) 54–5, 164–5, citing Martial 14.143; Mela 2.2. 59.

of distance apart, there was no special problem involved in transporting wool and woollen goods within the Po valley or out of it. Waterways were at hand or not far away – thus, for example, Patavium was linked with a good harbour by a navigable river. Moreover, the cost of transporting such products by road was not high. A bale of wool costing 150 denarii per pound could be carried overland for 100 miles for less than one per cent of its value. This observation of Jones, derived from Diocletian's price edict, is less often quoted than his calculation that cereals would have doubled in price for every 100 miles they were hauled.[13] As for the cheap woollens of Liguria (of which we hear nothing after Strabo), the short journey to Rome from a Ligurian port gave them a comparative advantage over potential competitors.

This brings us to the important issue of the stature of the maritime ports that served north Italy. It has been argued that the trade relations between the Po valley, and north Italy in general, and the outside world must have been negligible, because of the apparent absence of a significant commercial port at the mouth of the Po or on the Tyrrhenian sea.

What has seemed to make untenable the notion of Genua as a centre for trade is the fact that any commodities reaching it from the hinterland would have come by road. But evidence has already been cited which indicates that some commodities might be, and were, moved profitably by land. In the case of Genua, Dertona, forty miles away by the via Postumia, could be reached by an easy pass.[14] Dertona was in Strabo's words a notable city, a centre of communications with Aemilia and the upper Po valley. An inscription from Dertona concerning a certain C. Marius Aelianus, II juryman at Rome, magistrate and priest of Dertona, magistrate of Vercellae across the Po, and priest and decurion of Genua, is a sign that Genua was by no means cut off from the area beyond the mountains.[15] I will argue that men such as he point to the existence of economic as well as social ties binding together the major population centres in north Italy. Another kind of evidence is provided by the amphorae, originating in Spain, which carried mainly oil to a number of destinations, mainly in Liguria and the upper Po valley, but also farther afield.[16]

The paucity of inscriptions from Genua has also been considered telling evidence for the insignificance of the city. But a glance at the twenty-odd inscriptions in the Corpus – a laughable number – shows that a whole body of evidence has vanished without trace. The inscriptions that survive

---

[13] Jones (1960) 186; (1964) 841ff. We do not possess freight charges for wine or oil.
[14] The via Postumia rises gradually from Dertona (114 m.) to the Passo di Giovi (472 m.) and descends over c.twelve miles to the coast.
[15] Strab. C 217; *CIL* v 7373.
[16] See Baldacci (1967–8) 44. Findspots include on the one hand, Libarna, Tortona, Nizza, Torino, Aosta in the west, and on the other, Concordia, Aquileia and Pola in the east.

are all private dedications. They mention no occupations, no buildings, no magistracies. The only indication that there was municipal organization at Genua comes from elsewhere. Marius Aelianus, whose stone was found at Dertona, was a decurion and magistrate of Genua – the only one known. Moreover, the extant inscriptions, few as they are, indirectly confirm Strabo's description of Genua as the emporium of Liguria, where wood, wool, hides and honey from the hills were exchanged for Italian oil and wine:[17] there is hardly a name on an inscription which does not point to the servile origins or connections of the bearer. Whatever the dimensions of the city, it had a large foreign element. This is what one would expect of an Italian port of respectable size.

Pliny apparently thought of the river Po as a considerable trade route: this is implied by his assertion that the eleventh region of Italy, Gallia Transpadana, though entirely landlocked, was accessible to 'all the products of the sea', and the immediately following disclosure that the Po was navigable as far as Augusta Taurinorum (Turin).[18] The river was presumably used for the conveyance of Rhodian wine or Apulian oil in the late Republic, or Histrian oil and fish-sauce in the early Empire, to places in the upper valley and beyond.[19]

Ravenna, connected with the Po delta by a canal, is the most likely candidate for the position of entrepôt at the mouth of the river. The city is known principally as the home of the imperial fleet in the Adriatic. It has produced no inscriptions of merchant shippers involved in an export trade; nor however is there any record of the activities of those engaged in supplying perhaps five thousand marines with food and equipment.[20] The epigraphical evidence is not a reliable guide to the composition of the population. If it were, it would have to be believed that marines, retired veterans, *fabri* and *centonarii* constituted the bulk of the residents of this Venice of the ancient world; it would be a legitimate deduction that Ravenna did not experience normal municipal government ‖ (a deduction made by some scholars),[21] and that building and repair of ships were not major concerns of the city.[22] Ravenna has proved vulnerable to the sea and

---

[17] Strab. C 202. If Genua was indeed the emporium for all Liguria, it would have drawn products from the whole area up to the river Po. For the inscriptions, see *CIL* v, 7749ff., and p. 885. Municipal life is indicated in v, 7153 and 7373.

[18] Pliny, *HN* 3.123. The passage follows an extended, eulogistic description of the river and its tributaries.

[19] Evidence in Baldacci (1967–8) 16ff. [20] Starr (1941) 16.

[21] 'Venice': Strab. C 213. Local government: *CIL* xi, p. 6 (Bormann); cf. Chilver (1941) 19; Calderini (1953) 177 n. 5; Degrassi (1967) 285ff.

[22] Associations of *fabri navales* are recorded at Ostia, Pisa and Narbo, but not at Ravenna, where only a *collegium fabrorum* is known, e.g. *CIL* xi, 126. For the solitary *faber navalis*, see xi, 139.

to marauders down the ages, and we are in no position to make a firm statement about its stature as a commercial centre. There were, of course, a number of other outlets on the Adriatic coast. Patavium, for instance, had its own harbour. The remains are still visible of Aquileia's substantial riverine port on the Natiso, where Strabo saw large merchant ships at anchor.[23] Aquileia was the natural clearing house for Venetia and transit station for goods passing through the Eastern zone of north Italy.

This discussion has not produced any firm results; it would have been unrealistic to expect this, given the lack of detailed evidence. However, in my view, sufficient data has been presented to show that the economic relations between Cisalpine Gaul and the outside world were more extensive than has sometimes been supposed.[24]

III

Varro is the only author who refers to products of Mediolanum and its territory. He transmits the elder Cato's praise of the Insubrians for their output of sides of pork and for the massive dimensions and immobility of their sows. It is from Varro too that we learn incidentally that the people of Mediolanum trained their vines on maples. To judge from the general comments of Polybius, Strabo and Pliny on Cisalpine or Transpadane Gaul, it may be assumed that the territory of Mediolanum produced cereals, pork, pitch, wool and wine.[25] In the case of some of these items production over and above local needs would have been necessary to meet the cost of imported commodities, particularly oil, a staple.[26]

There is a complete lacuna in the literary sources with respect to industrial activity.[27] Strabo called Patavium a populous centre noted for its skilled craftsmen. One wonders whether he or a later writer could have referred to Mediolanum in identical terms. A number of inscriptions refer to the association of *fabri* and *centonarii*, which dated probably from the early second century AD and consisted of twelve || centuries;[28] only the

---

[23] Strab. C 214.
[24] Baldacci has on the whole succeeded in steering a middle course between, on the one hand, overstressing the isolation of the Po valley, and, on the other, exaggerating the extent of its commercial contacts (in comparison, e.g., with those of southern Spain). I have reservations concerning his chronological account of the rise and decline of Cisalpine agricultural and industrial production.
[25] Varro, *Rust.* 1.8; 2.4. 10; Polyb. 2.15. 2ff.; Pliny, *HN* 18.127; Strab. C 218.
[26] The evidence is conveniently assembled in Baldacci (1967–8) 16ff.
[27] On industry, see Chilver (1941) 163ff.; cf. Brunt (1971) 181–2.
[28] See e.g. *CIL* v, 5738; 5869. If the company of *fabri* and *centonarii* was founded under Trajan, the former inscription belongs to the late Antonine period and the latter to the

corresponding organization at Ravenna was of comparable size. The presence of so many artisans need not imply any more than that Mediolanum was a centre of petty commodity production. On the other hand, some members of the *fabri* and *centonarii* succeeded in accumulating sufficient wealth from their trade to enable them or their sons to hold local office.[29] Supposing for the moment that the men in question were *centonarii* rather than *fabri*, their inscriptions, together with a number of others referring to traders in woollen or linen goods (from as far apart as Apulia and Gallia Belgica), would suggest a textile industry of some proportions.[30] This is to some degree confirmed by the fact that an imperial wool factory, one of the five in Italy, was located in Mediolanum in the late Empire.

Precise information as to the nature of the activities of the *fabri* is lacking. (Shipbuilding may have been a special line of the *fabri* of Ravenna.) Inscriptions from Mediolanum mention also a 'collegium aerar. col.', consisting of precisely twelve centuries. Mommsen supposed this to be the *fabri* and *centonarii* under another name; he read 'collegium aerar(ii) col(oniae)', and offered the interpretation that the company was subsidized by the city treasury. Waltzing held the two companies to be separate, believing that the second consisted of bronze-workers, *aerarii*. No other company of this kind is attested, small or large, but this may not be a decisive consideration, as there is much that is individual about the institutions of Mediolanum.[31] The matter must be left in the balance. Even if Mommsen is right to identify the two associations, it remains possible that a considerable number of the *fabri* were metalworkers. There is very little record of the working of metals which must have gone on in the cities of Lombardy and Piedmont. Mediolanum was well placed to work the gold, silver, copper and iron of the sub-Alpine districts to the north-west and the iron in the mountains to the north of Bergomum. But the only clear evidence for metalworking at Mediolanum is an inscription of AD 242 which shows that the city was a centre of arms-manufacture.[32] This industry may have been established as early as the reign of Augustus in conjunction with

---

middle of the third century. The dating of most of the inscriptions from Mediolanum and its territory is uncertain. Those cited in the rest of this paper are, with few exceptions, roughly datable between the end of the Julio-Claudian period and the middle of the third century. See Ucelli (1967–8) 109ff.

[29] *CIL* v, 5612; 5738; cf. 5658.

[30] *CIL* v, 5925; 5929; cf. 5923, 5926, 5928, 5932; with 5919, 5927, Pais 855. The *centonarii* were apparently makers of cheap woollens.

[31] *CIL* v, 5847, 5892. These inscriptions belong to the period when the city had colonial status, but the transformation of the city from *municipium* to *colonia* might have been accomplished under any of the emperors from Hadrian to Caracalla. See Calderini (1953) 253ff.

[32] *CIL* XIII, 6763; cf. VIII, 7036.

the subjugation of the Alpine tribes. Mediolanum probably served as a Roman base and supply depot in those wars.

One inscription commemorating a trader is of special interest. The heirs of a member of the corporation of Transalpine-Cisalpine traders erected a stone in his honour at Mediolanum. The corporation is attested in inscriptions from Lugdunum || (Lyon) and Aventicum (Avenches).[33] The trader of Mediolanum was patron of the company of sailors of Comum. He may therefore be supposed to have used Lake Como and the Splügen pass leading by way of Curia (Chur) in Raetia to the Rhineland. The most direct route to Lugdunum from Mediolanum climbed the valley of the Duria to Augusta Praetoria (Aosta) and proceeded over the Little St Bernard pass in the Graian Alps. A short steep route led from Augusta Praetoria over the Pennine Alps by the Great St Bernard pass into the Valais, thence to a number of centres, including Aventicum. It was this pass that Julius Caesar attempted to clear in 57 BC for the express purpose of reducing the risk and the cost of the commercial traffic 'accustomed' to take that route.[34] Dedications to gods from traders have been found on or near the top of the pass. One trader was a slave-dealer (*mango*);[35] and the Aventicum inscription referring to the company of Transalpine-Cisalpine traders shows that a section of the company were slave-dealers (*venalicii*). The inscription probably dates from the second century AD. It is known also that in the period after the reduction of the Salassi under Augustus a quantity of Italian *sigillata* was taken over the Great St Bernard to Vidy near Lausanne, which served as a distribution point.[36] After the Augustan period there is little information on the quantity of goods that crossed the Alps to and from Lombardy, or on the balance of trade. But the traffic existed, it was presumably profitable to those engaged in it, and its southern base appears to have been Mediolanum.

Evidence for economic contacts between Mediolanum and other north Italian cities is less explicit but still worth assembling. In the first place, a group of citizens of Mediolanum who are known to have been honoured by other cities deserve scrutiny. The background of the award of honours is not given on the relevant inscriptions, and a number of explanations might in principle apply. The individual concerned might have been a propertyowner in the other city or its territory; he might have won recognition in

---

[33] *CIL* v, 5911; cf. XIII, 2029; *A E* 1952, 205, with Reynolds (1969). See also Baldacci (1967-8) 47ff. (who puts forward the view that the association was completely dominated by non-Italians).

[34] Caes. *B Gall.* 3.1, 2.

[35] *NS* 1892, p. 68 = *Inscr. It.* XI, 1, p. 65. I have seen no recent discussion on coins from the Great St Bernard. See *NSA* 1892, 76–7. One scholar put the number at one hundred, over four centuries. See Gruaz (1910).

[36] Cf. n. 8 above.

the region as a leading politician, man of means and benefactor; he might have had ties of blood or marriage with members of the aristocracy of another city. The monumental inscription set up by the people of Vercellae for the younger Pliny and found at Fecchio might have been an expression of gratitude for services rendered.[37] Another possibility, however, in the case of those citizens of Mediolanum who are honoured abroad, is that business activities lie behind the honour or office. Thus the patronage exercised by the Transalpine-Cisalpine trader over the association of sailors of Comum is likely to have arisen out of his use of the lake for trade. Links with towns at some distance from Mediolanum, and multiple links, imply a background of commercial ventures. There is Audasius Acmazon, *sevir Augustalis* of Mediolanum and II Forum Popili (Forlimpopoli), far down the Via Aemilia near Ariminum (Rimini); or Atilius Eros, *sevir Augustalis* of Dertona and Libarna, whose stone was found at Ticinum on the north side of the Po. The latter case has no direct relevance to Mediolanum, but it should be noted that the contacts of Eros brought him within striking distance of that city, the neighbour of Ticinum to the north, and also of Genua, south of Libarna by about twenty-five miles. Acmazon and Eros were freedmen. Men of this status may be supposed to have played a special role in the forging of commercial links between the towns of north Italy.[38] The status of our Transalpine-Cisalpine trader is unknown (his name is lost), but the sailors of Comum included a *sevir senior* of Mediolanum, a freedman, and a freedman of Comum, Romatius Trophimus, was *sevir Augustalis* of Comum and *sevir* of Mediolanum.[39]

Other citizens of Mediolanum known to have been honoured away from their city were freeborn, and the question arises whether their cases should be interpreted differently. There is a temptation to assume that they were landowners rather than businessmen or traders, just because of their higher social standing. Scholarly passions were aroused when a *duovir* of Pompeii, P. Paquius Proculus, was labelled a baker (wrongly as it turned out).[40] So we might be inclined to class as a simple landowner a certain M. Aemilius Coelius Coelianus, decurion of Mediolanum and decurion also of Novaria, a town thirty miles to the west beyond the Ticinus. On the

[37] *CIL* v, 5667.   [38] *CIL* v, 5749; 6425.
[39] *AE* 1932, 73; *CIL* v, 5303. A brief discussion of some of the texts illustrating contacts between Mediolanum and neighbouring cities is presented in Tibiletti (1967). The article is relatively inaccessible and I give the conclusions here: (1) The links with Comum and Laus Pompeia were particularly close. (2) The explanation of the contacts lies, first, in the geographical proximity of Mediolanum and those cities, secondly, in the case of Comum, in its political domination by Mediolanum until the age of Caesar, and thirdly, in the central position occupied by Mediolanum in the network of communications linking Rome with the north and with the eastern and western sections of the Po valley.
[40] Della Corte (1926).

other hand, this man was not born into an established aristocratic family. His father Coelius Valerius was no more than a *sevir* at Mediolanum and perhaps a *centonarius* as well, for it was the *centonarii* who celebrated him with a monument.[41] Another borderline case is L. Valerius Secundinus, son of Secundinus (apparently a Celt), a *sevir iunior* of Mediolanum and *sevir* of Vercellae. This town lies about forty-five miles from Mediolanum, beyond Novaria and on the road to Augusta Praetoria and the Alpine passes, and the man in question is found worshipping Hercules at the god's popular shrine at Laus Pompeia. One of Hercules' functions was to guide the trader.[42] Vercellae made Marius Aelianus (the only known magistrate of Genua) a municipal magistrate, no mere *sevir*. Aelianus is unlikely to have sat at home on his estates or to have confined his financial ventures to the city of his origin, Dertona.[43]

It is convenient to refer here to a number of inscriptions showing citizens and officials of Mediolanum as, apparently, property-owners beyond their own city-territory. The territory of Comum was particularly subject to such intrusions, and the few cases known of citizens of Comum in possession of land belonging to the territory of Mediolanum fall a long way short of restoring the balance.[44] It is noticeable also that while a number of citizens of Mediolanum held posts of honour in other cities, very few outsiders are recorded as having been honoured by the authorities of Mediolanum. My tentative inference is that the two groups of inscriptions I have just been considering are an index of the economic strength of Mediolanum and in general of its dominant position in the western sector of Transpadane Gaul.

That it *was* the most important city in the region seems indisputable, despite the relative silence of the sources. There are only a few explicit references to Mediolanum as a seat of justice, education and administration. But one can refer to the judicial activities of the 'proconsul' Calpurnius Piso under Augustus (involving an advocate of neighbouring Novaria), Pliny's revelation that the children of his town of Comum went to school at Mediolanum, and the inscriptions of Ulbius Gaianus, *praefectus vehiculorum* for Transpadana and part of Noricum, which were set up at his two headquarters, Mediolanum and Virunum. There is no difficulty in establishing the primacy of Mediolanum from the mid-third century. The stationing of Gallienus' central cavalry corps there in AD 258 was a crucial move. Thereafter, the city was continuously held or fought for by emperors and usurpers into the period of the Tetrarchy. I suspect, however, that in earlier days officials such as the *legatus Augusti pro praetore regionis*

---

[41] *CIL* v, 5658.   [42] *CIL* v, 6351.   [43] *CIL* v, 7373.
[44] E.g. *CIL* v, 5518 (Gavirate); 5739 (Caponago); and see Sartori (1967–8).

Transpadanae, who appeared first under Trajan, and the Antonine and Severan *iuridici regionis Transpadanae* were also based at Mediolanum.[45] In general, we can say that the same factors which facilitated the growth of the city's economy – its productive and substantial territory, labour resources and favourable position for communications and trade – made it likely, or inevitable, that the city would become the administrative centre of the region. Naturally the presence of Roman functionaries with their entourages, at least in times of peace, and to a lesser degree that of educators, must have made a marked contribution to the development of the economy.

IV

Having assembled evidence, such as it is, for the economy of Mediolanum, and having attempted to assess the importance of the city in the region as a whole, I turn now to an examination of the financial interests and family backgrounds of the governing class. This subject has interest in itself, but it is also closely relevant to an inquiry into the nature of the economy of the city. The leading citizens were wealthy men, and one would expect the source or sources of wealth of the city to be reflected in their own economic activities.

First, the landowners. Somewhat less than half the known magistrates and priests of Mediolanum (I exclude for the moment the various kinds of *sevir*) are recorded on inscriptions found in the countryside, and presumably on or near their own properties, in most cases. Sometimes the existence of large *praedia* seems excluded by the nature of the terrain. Rezzonico, seat of the *duovir* and military tribune Minicius Exoratus, hemmed in by a massive mountain range on the west side of Lake Como, is an example;[46] one thinks also of Angera, Besozzo, Leggiuno, Brebbia by Maggiore, or Stabbio south of Lugano. Fruit and vines might be profitably grown here (a *vilicus* is recorded at Brebbia), but not on a large scale. Luxury villas, or at least summer chalets, are more appropriate to these regions than *villae rusticae*. It is unnecessary to believe that their owners were resident all the year round and had abandoned the city in the manner of Mansuelli's typical north Italian proprietor.[47]

The structure of agriculture was not markedly different south of the lake-country, in the moraine and the upper plain. There is little sign of a

---

[45] Suet. *Rhet.* 6; Pliny, *Ep.* 4. 13. 3; *ILS* 4193; cf. *CIL* III, 4802. Other officials: e.g. *ILS* 1040, 1187, 1347.

[46] *CIL* v, 5239.

[47] *CIL* v, 5500 (*vilicus*). For the conception of the model Italian city, a considerable part of the population of which, including the landowners, inhabited the countryside, see Mansuelli (1961a), (1961b), esp. 338ff.

race of country squires presiding over flourishing market towns. Villages in this area appear to have been underdeveloped, serving primarily as religious centres. There is little sign of social or political organization; a body of *iuvenes* is recorded at Modicium (Monza), but this is exceptional.[48] Tombs are uniformly modest and few precious objects have been found. There is an abundance of Celtic names of both places and people. Chilver writes that the process of Romanization in Cisalpine Gaul was largely complete by the middle of the second century BC.[49] But Romanization was slow among the Insubres. The countryside bears few marks of centuriation and could not have received a large influx of colonists from the south. Estates in the upper plain are likely to have been of small or moderate size. *Saltus* are the exception. As Brunt has observed,[50] forest and marshlands could only have been exploited profitably in fairly large units by men with substantial capital. He had in mind mainly the lower plain, the zone of the *fontanili*. This area (which was divided between Mediolanum and its neighbours Ticinum and Laus Pompeia) posed severe drainage problems and was subject in its lower reaches to flooding. One wonders how far it was exploited at all – there is a singular dearth of inscriptions. The harnessing of the *fontanili* for irrigation and the institution of comprehensive drainage schemes are developments dating from the eleventh century. The Pavia-Milano canal was constructed about 1400. The two *saltus* inscriptions, at Summa Lombardo and Valle Guidino, the latter a prayer for the safety of Verginius Rufus from his *saltuarius*, are from the upper plain in areas now deforested.[51] Outside the *saltus* relatively small farms practising *cultura promiscua* are likely to have predominated, as they appear to have done ever since. The richer landowners might of course have owned a number of these estates in several locations.

Away from the shores and environs of the lakes virtually no villas have been found predating the fourth century. This throws doubt on the hypothesis of Mansuelli that north Italian landowners typically lived on their properties, or at least on the applicability of this thesis to Mediolanum. This conclusion is reinforced by the apparent backwardness of villages and the probable fragmentation of the holdings of the richer landowners, implying that owner-absenteeism was common.[52]

Moreover, the landowning class does not appear to have been small and exclusive. It included men of recently accumulated and not very

---

[48] *CIL* v, 5742.   [49] Chilver (1941) 80.   [50] Brunt (1971) 196.   [51] *CIL* v, 5548, 5702.
[52] Some villas will no doubt be unearthed in the course of time. But one may wonder whether villas will ever prove to have been as conspicuous a feature of the countryside as they were in Emilia and in a pocket of Venetia. Mansuelli formulated his theory on the basis of research undertaken in those regions. For the archaeological evidence from the territory of Mediolanum, see Bertolone (1939). This must be supplemented by more recent works such as Garzetti (1968).

considerable wealth, of undistinguished parentage and doubtful Latinity. As an example the decurion Aemilius Coelius Coelianus might be cited; he was the son of a *sevir* of Mediolanum who was perhaps a *centonarius* (his stone was found at Tavernerio, where he presumably owned property). Others are the decurion Atilius Mocetius, *sevir iunior* and legionary veteran (property-owner at Meda), and two *pontifices*, Atilius Tertullinus and Bericricenius Valentinus, both officials of the company of *fabri* and *centonarii*, who are celebrated in inscriptions found at Caponago and Seprio respectively.[53] In addition, a number of freedmen *seviri Augustales* crop up in rural centres such as Monza, Seprio, Cantù, as well as at lake resorts such as Angera.[54] The commitment of such men to estate-management is debatable. It is a pure assumption that freedmen landowners had transferred all their assets into rural property and put an end to their former economic activities, which were located presumably in the world of finance, commerce and industry, for the most part.[55]

For that matter, rural proprietors of better birth need not have been only, or even primarily, landowners. C. Gemelius Valerianus, in company with his wife and three children, made an offering to Mercury 'master and preserver of profits' ('lucrorum potenti et conservatori'). This avowed businessman, whose inscription was found at Fontanetto, south-west of Maggiore in the territory of Novaria, held the posts of quattuorvir with aedilician powers and prefect with judicial authority in Mediolanum.[56] A municipal magistrate of Augusta Praetoria (Aosta), P. Vinesius Firmus, acknowledged his business interests with equal frankness in his epitaph, which reads; 'Dum vixi quaesi/Cessavi perdere numquam/Mors intercessit/Nunc ab utroque vaco'.[57] These inscriptions invite comparison with the celebrated mosaic inscription from Pompeii 'salve lucru(m)', which is usually thought of as the slogan of a new and vulgar freedman class. Firmus, however, need not have been even a freedman's son,[58] while Valerianus was probably of Celtic origin.[59] ||

---

[53] *CIL* v, 5658, 5713, 5738, 5612.   [54] *CIL* v, 5749, 5611, 5675, 5455, 5465.
[55] I am aware that legacies from wealthy patrons formed the basis of the fortunes of some freedmen.
[56] *CIL* v, 6596 (AD 196?).
[57] *CIL* v, 6842. The same sentiment is expressed in similar language in v, 3415 (Verona, a freedman), and 7040 (a man of status unknown, born in Aquileia, brought up in Emona and ending his days at Turin).
[58] This despite the indirect imputation of M. L. Gordon, whose article 'The freedman's son in municipal life' ends with a citation of the last lines of Firmus' epitaph. See Gordon (1931).
[59] This is an inference from the *cognomen* Valerianus, which points to descent from a Valerius, a popular name among the Celts of north Italy and Gaul. By contrast, Marius Aelianus of Dertona (*CIL* v, 7373) may well have had a slave ancestor, for he bears a *cognomen* of imperial origin, and his wife Iulia Thetis has both an imperial nomen and a Greek name.

V

Mansuelli envisages a rift between the countryside, which he sees as the refuge of inherited wealth and good birth, and the city, where new wealth and low birth held sway.[60] The epigraphical and archaeological evidence from the countryside does not appear to support his conception of the social background and life-style of the landowners of Mediolanum. It remains to consider the composition of the governing class as a whole.

One alternative, that Mediolanum was ruled by a narrow, land-based oligarchy, might seem to be supported by the existence of the junior sevirate. This brand of sevirate is thought to have been a cut above the ordinary sevirate (an office apparently open to freedmen as well as the freeborn), and also the posts of *sevir senior* and *sevir et Augustalis*, both freedman-dominated. Lily Ross Taylor ascribed to the *seviri iuniores* equestrian rank and a leading role in the training of the *iuvenes*, while Chilver found that 'the bulk' of the *iuniores* were 'men of good family without suspicion of native or freedman ancestry'.[61] The fact that only four of the more than thirty recorded *iuniores* advanced into the local council or held municipal office might suggest that curial rank was jealously guarded at Mediolanum.

The argument is without foundation. The family backgrounds of the *iuniores* taken as a whole are unimpressive. When a father of a *iunior* is named, he invariably had held no office; the only exception was himself a *iunior* and a member of the company of *dendrophori*.[62] Two other *iuniores* with full-grown sons show no mark of distinction apart from the sevirate, and the son of one of them achieved no more elevated rank than that of private in the praetorian guard.[63] The brother of another *iunior* bears the Celtic name Vervicius and was merely a legionary soldier.[64] Other *iuniores* include Campilius Virillio, Valerius Virillio (son of Vradsarius son of Sacco), Novellius Taluppius, and Cominius Atilianus (husband of Surilla the daughter of Cintullus).[65] There is also a sprinkling of freedmen's sons in their ranks. One of the four successful *iuniores*, an equestrian, was son of a freedman *sevir senior et Augustalis* and honorary decurion. He is the only known *iunior* with equestrian rank; there is nothing to be said for crediting the rest of them with a status that they do not claim for themselves.[66]

---

[60] See n. 47 above.   [61] Taylor (1924); Chilver (1941) 199ff.   [62] *CIL* v, 5902.
[63] *CIL* v, 5884, 5525.   [64] *CIL* v, 5830 (pre-Flavian).   [65] *CIL* v, 5853, 5896, 5555, 5676.
[66] *CIL* v, 6349 (equestrian); 5841 (*cognomen* Augustalis); 5908, 5906, 5768 (the last two are known only as *curator* and *quaestor*, respectively, of the *aerarium*. A *iunior* identifies himself as a freedman and was married to a woman of Greek name (5855); another has as father a man with the suspect name L. Iulius L. f. Amandus (5867); a third is named C. Spurius Valens (5883).

The junior sevirate was a mechanism for giving new men a first taste of public life. Most known *iuniores* were Celts. But there is little sign among them of tribal leaders from rural communities dependent on Mediolanum, like the *principes* who were drawn into the political life of Brixia or Tergeste. Only five of the inscriptions of *iuniores*, of || whom only two are certainly men of Celtic origin, have a rural provenance.[67] Thus L. Valerius Virillio, whose family is commemorated in a city inscription, is not to be seen as a native chieftain who had preserved his property and his pride in an enclave of the city's territory.[68] We may conjecture that he represented a class of immigrants from the countryside who made a modest fortune *after* establishing their residence in the city.

The failure of the *iuniores* in politics is evidence for their mediocrity, not for the exclusiveness of the *ordo decurionum*. The wealthiest, most talented and most adaptable of them could make the grade. The same is true of the ordinary sevirs, who contribute five decurions or magistrates from a smaller sample. Two of them have been encountered already, Aemilius Coelius Coelianus and the veteran Mocetius, landowners but small men. Another was Coelius Baro of Brebbia, whose wife, a Celt, shared his own ethnic background.[69]

With the pontificate, we move a little higher up the political hierarchy, but no higher up the social scale. This post, held in honour in most Italian cities, was at Mediolanum well within the reach of parvenus. There is some overlap with the sevirate and junior sevirate;[70] the pontificate for most of its holders (eight out of twelve) was apparently a terminal post;[71] and among the majority who made no further progress are two officials of the company of *fabri* and *centonarii*, one of them Bericricenius.[72] Certainly the son of another pontifex was *vir egregius*, and several rose to important positions in politics.[73] However, the backgrounds of two of them should be noted: Atusius Glycerus, *duovir* and equestrian, and Valerius Petronianus, priest of the youth, pleader and five times ambassador for his city without cost, all by the age of twenty-three. The name Glycerus indicates both that its bearer was of Eastern immigrant or servile origins, and that he was unashamed of the fact.[74] Petronianus was son of Eutychianus, a freedman *sevir Augustalis*.

On the subject of the decurions and municipal magistrates there is little that can be said. We have less than thirty names in all. Some new names

---

[67] *CIL* v, 5472, 5525, 5555, 5613, 5676. [68] *CIL* v, 5896.
[69] *CIL* v, 5503, 5658, 5713, 5775, 5890. [70] *CIL* v, 5445, 5503, 5900.
[71] *CIL* v, 5515, 5541, 5612, 5738, 5852, 5866 (*pontif. et cur. aer.*), 5900, 6345.
[72] *CIL* v, 5612, 5738.
[73] *CIL* v, 5239, 5503, 5849 cf. 5848; 5515 cf. 5517 (*v.e.*); 5445, 5894 (decurion).
[74] For the principle invoked here, see Garnsey (1975) 173.

have turned up since Mommsen studied the inscriptions and came to the paradoxical conclusion that Mediolanum was, like Ravenna, denied the full complement of municipal offices, because of its very importance.[75] Ex-*seviri* and *ex-pontifices* are found at all levels, even at the top. Ranged against them are a few magistrates who cite no office below the duovirate or its equivalent. The most striking of the latter is the impressive Q.Albinius Ouf. Secundinus Q.f.Q.nep.Q.pron. Mestrius Aebutius Tullianus, equestrian, *duovir*, sent to overhaul the finances of Parma probably by the last of the Severan emperors.[76] || He is also the most distinguished of the known municipal equestrians, who include his contemporaries or near-contemporaries Glycerus, Mascarpius a freedman's son, the son of a *pontifex*, and an office-bearer in the company of *fabri* and *centonarii*, also in the third century.[77] I suspect that a higher survival rate of inscriptions would not contradict the impression conveyed by those that are extant, of the openness of the governing class at Mediolanum, in the second and early third centuries.

How is the openness of the local aristocracy (supposing that this can be accepted at least as a working hypothesis) to be explained? Even a relatively closed order would have had to replace a considerable proportion of its members in each generation, for biological and economic reasons. In addition, a steady stream of municipal magnates from Mediolanum are likely to have moved into higher careers – it is mere chance that so few of them are known. Finding a patron should not have been a great problem in a city that was virtually a provincial capital and the residence or base of Roman functionaries. Other vacancies would have opened up as men gave up local politics to retire to the countryside. Yet, for what it is worth, Pliny the younger refers in his letters to individuals who rejected the imperial service or the Roman senate, or who were irregular in attendance in Rome, but not to local men who had abjured their responsibilities as civic leaders; while, to judge from the sample that we have (and its small size must be emphasized), few of the landowners of Mediolanum could be said to have abandoned local politics because of resentment at falling social standards within the curial class. Be that as it may, there was apparently a considerable turnover in personnel within the *ordo*.[78]

---

[75] *CIL* v, p. 634 (Mommsen); cf. xi, p. 6 (Bormann). For bibliography and refs. to the higher magistrates, see Calderini (1953) 252ff.

[76] *CIL* xi, 1230.

[77] Municipal equestrians: *CIL* v, 5847, 6349, 5869. Other equestrians: 5517, 5729, 5864, 5966.

[78] Known senators from Mediolanum include Novellius Torquatus (Pliny, *HN* 14.144), Didius Iulianus (Dio 74.11, 2, with Barnes (1970)), and Verginius Rufus (cf. Pliny, *Ep.* 2.1, 8). Other possible senators or friends of senators include Vibius Severus (Pliny, *Ep.* 4.28), Atilius Crescens (Pliny, *Ep.* 6.8), and the consular Caepio Hispo (*CIL* v, 5813). Many more senatorial families are known from some other north Italian towns, notably Brixia and Verona.

Replacements were not hard to find. The manpower resources of the city and its territory were ample, as army recruiters knew well throughout the period of the Principate; the city attracted new men from all backgrounds, Celts, freedmen, immigrants; and its governing class admitted the most talented, wealthy and ambitious of them. They did so not just out of necessity, in order to maintain an *ordo plenus*, but because there was little social stigma attached to uninherited wealth or lack of pedigree, and because they too were involved in the pursuit of profit. All this implies (for there is no proof) the existence of a strong and diversified economy. ‖

Addendum

This paper is a case-study of an individual Roman city and explores the diversity of investments of the local élite even in what could be taken to be a landlocked and therefore purely agricultural environment. G. argues that although investment opportunities in non-agricultural sectors were limited, there was some room for uninherited wealth and resultant social mobility.

Boffo (1977) collects evidence of navigation on the Po (p. 50). Noè (1974) discusses (epigraphic) evidence of wool and textile production in Cisalpine Gaul: see 929–30 on Milan (p. 00). Abramenko (1993) 299 asserts that Mediolanum was important for the north-south trade (pp. 52–3) which stimulated manufacture (300); cf. 300 n. 456 on professional *collegia* (pp. 51–2). See Baldacci (1977) on Mediolanum and Comum (cf. p. 54). Abramenko (1993) 297 observes that the *ordo decurionum* of Mediolanum would rarely admit freedmen because enough eligible freeborn landowners (cf. p. 58) were available; moreover, numerous freeborn individuals became *seviri* and *Augustales* (298). However, LeGlay (1990) 629 n. 27 contrasts the lack of freedmen decurions in North Africa with the presence of freedmen among the *iuvenes* of Mediolanum (p. 59). According to Abramenko (1993) 305–6, agriculture was the basis of curial wealth, especially in the western Transpadana. For a discussion of local élites in the *regiones X* and *XI*, see 296–310. For comparative purposes, see Bandelli (1983), on the élite of Aquileia, and Breuer (forthcoming), on the élites of Brixia and Verona. On the archaeology of Roman Milan, see most recently Ceresa Mori (1995), with further references.

4

URBAN PROPERTY INVESTMENT IN ROMAN SOCIETY

When historians of the Roman economy write of investments in land, they normally have in mind rural property. The role of investment in urban property in the economy is seldom discussed. Moreover, what little has been said on the subject suggests that its significance is inadequately understood.

The standard works on economic history might be expected to place urban property firmly in its economic context. Tenney Frank recognizes the following sources of income for wealthy Romans in the late Republic: commerce and trade, provincial investment and money-lending (Pompey, Brutus, Atticus), managing and enlarging an inheritance (Atticus, his landowning and industrial concerns, *inter alia*), dealing in real estate, the legal profession, acting, and provincial government.[1] Urban rents are not on the list. Rostovtzeff writes of the local aristocracy of Italian cities in the first century BC in the following terms: 'Most of them were landowners, some were owners of houses let at rent, of various shops; some carried on money-lending and banking operations.'[2] Here acknowledgement is made of the relevance of urban property to the matter of the sources of wealth of the propertied class. But the reference is an isolated one. When, for example, Rostovtzeff enumerates those investments supposedly favoured by the new rich, the items mentioned are rural property, money-lending and Italian industry. Either it is by a mere oversight that urban property is omitted here, or we must conclude that in Rostovtzeff's view urban property was not taken at all seriously as an economic investment. For that matter, I know of no work of economic history which attempts to assess the scale of the urban investment of the Roman or Italian rich, or to estimate what proportion of their income came from this source.

We have some knowledge of the financial interests of at least a few members of the Roman propertied class, and it is of interest to see how the available information has been handled. I discuss || here, *exempli gratia*, two leading Romans of the late Republic, Atticus and Cicero.

---

[1] Frank (1933) 394–6.   [2] Rostovtzeff (1957) 31; 17.

Several texts illuminate Atticus' attitude to property, both rural and urban, and reveal that his holdings in each were extensive. To facilitate the interpretation of these texts one may usefully distinguish several possible functions of urban property. A city residence or country villa might be viewed primarily as an item of consumption, a source of status or of political power. One need only refer to *De Officiis* 1.138 on the kind of house a man of rank should have, and to Cicero's own adventures in house-purchase which led to his taking up residence on the Palatine deeply in debt (*Fam.* 5.6.2). Atticus was not attracted by this aspect of property, which we might call its non-economic use. Nepos his biographer thought it noteworthy that a man with such wealth should have showed so little interest in buying or building: his house on the Quirinal, inherited rather than purchased, was tastefully, not luxuriously, ordered, and subjected to no unnecessary remodelling. And he goes on to assert that Atticus 'owned no gardens, no sumptuous villa in the suburbs or on the coast' (*Att.* 13.1; 14.3). Next, urban property might be seen as an economic investment, and in two distinct senses: it might be valued chiefly for its capacity to yield revenue, or as a capital asset. Atticus was primarily concerned with the revenue-earning aspect of property, rural or urban. Cicero did not bother to notify Atticus about a property at Lanuvium which had come on to the market, because it was not a productive investment (*Att.* 9.9.4);[3] while Nepos claims that Atticus did not accumulate country estates: in Italy he had but two, one at Arretium and another at Nomentum. He continues with the bold, and erroneous, assertion: 'his entire monetary income was derived from his possessions in Epirus and his urban holdings' (*Att.* 14.3). Nepos was obviously unaware of the multiplicity of Atticus' financial concerns. At the same time, there is no reason for doubting that urban rents made a substantial contribution to his income.

Neither Cicero nor Nepos suggests that Atticus speculated in property. Speculation is, typically, the purchase or sale of land or a commodity with the object of realizing a profit from fluctuations in its price. Damasippus, who subdivided pleasure-grounds on the Tiber bank for redevelopment, and Crassus, who purchased || houses gutted by fire at knockdown prices and sent in his slave architects and builders to construct replacements, are well-known representatives of what must have been a fairly populous band of property-speculators.[4] Martial's Tongilianus may perhaps be conceded the status of a fringe member of the group: 'You bought your house for 200,000, Tongilianus. A disaster such as happens all too often in this city snatched it from you. 10,000,000 in contributions came in. Don't you think, Tongilianus, that you may have given the impression that you set fire to

---

[3] The precise meaning of this sentence remains obscure.   [4] *Att.* 12.33; Plut. *Cras.* 2.4.

your own house?' (3.5.2).[5] Atticus' attitude to property might be called that of a 'conservative investor' rather than 'speculator'. This distinction between speculation and conservative investment seems to me valid, even if the two categories overlap to some extent in practice.

It is instructive to see how the subject of urban investment has been treated in relation to Atticus.

Salvioli regarded investment in urban property as speculative, discussing it briefly beside usury in a chapter entitled 'le capital mobilier'.[6] His two prime examples of housing-speculators were – Atticus and Crassus. The chapter that follows, 'les placements fonciers', does not discuss capital investment in land in general, but only investment in rural property.

The conceptual confusion recurs in Feger's article on Atticus. In a short section on 'Landwirtschaft', Atticus' suburban house, the two Italian estates, the ranch in Epirus, are all registered. Feger goes on to mention Atticus' concern with profitability, and to refer to Nepos' statement on his sources of income, which, in Feger's words, 'identifies revenues from his properties as his only source of wealth'. Nepos, as we saw, writes of property in Epirus *and in the city* (*urbanis possessionibus*). We might be excused for supposing, on the basis of Feger's version of this text and the preceding discussion, that the reference in Nepos was to *rural* properties. Feger goes on to assert, in a section headed 'Spekulation und Geldverleih', that Atticus speculated in property. The two texts cited show no more than that Atticus was interested in purchasing a house either in the city or in the country (*Att.* 1.6.1; 4.8.1).[7]

Urban rents do not appear among the sources of wealth attributed to Atticus by Frank. He refers to Nepos, but has not noticed the crucial clause. Frank may have been following Nepos less closely than a modern biographer of Atticus, Byrne. She notes Nepos' statement on the revenues of Atticus, dismisses it as 'incorrect', and has nothing more to say of the urban holdings.[8]

In discussing the income of Cicero, Frank juxtaposes two texts, *Philippics* 2.40 and *Paradoxa Stoicorum* 49. The first of these is used as the basis of the argument that Cicero's income came to about 600,000 sesterces annually, while the second is cited for Cicero's opinion there expressed that an income of these dimensions would enable one to live a

---

[5] Cf. Juv. 3.212ff. Other examples of intentional demolition, varied in context and motive, include Strab. 5.3.7; Hor, *Ep.* 1.1.100; *Dig.* 19.2.30; 39.2.45. I make no attempt to provide here a comprehensive analysis of the subject of speculation.

[6] Salvioli (1906) 31ff.; 61ff. See e.g. 54: 'La spéculation édilitaire, qu'Atticus a également pratiqué...'

[7] Feger (1956) 516–17.   [8] Frank (1933) 394; Byrne (1920) 13.

life of luxury.[9] However, Cicero says in the next breath that his own estates brought in only 100,000 sesterces. One wonders, therefore, whether the passage in the *Philippics* has also been misread. This proves to be the case. What Cicero there claims is that he has received some 20,000,000 sesterces in legacies from friends and kinsmen; it is Frank's deduction that Cicero's annual income over thirty years would have been more than 600,000 sesterces (and his assumption, equally erroneous, that the money came exclusively from clients at law).[10] It surely needs no demonstrating that Cicero did not have such a sum of money to dispose of annually from the beginning to the end of his legal and political career. Moreover, even if Frank had been able to show that Cicero was equipped to live lavishly throughout his active public life, it does not follow that he did so. Cicero is not likely to have regarded the legacies as a source of regular spending-money. The bulk of them probably consisted of immovable property, and were best left in this form. *Some* of the property made over to him would have been productive and furnished him with income. Thus the shops at Puteoli left him by Cluvius the banker brought in 80,000 sesterces a year despite their dilapidated state. But part of the legacy consisted of *horti* and other unspecified property, which could only be designated *possessiones voluptuariae*.[11] Incidentally, this was one legacy from which Cicero derived little benefit, as it arrived in the second-last year of his life.

In addition to *Paradoxa Stoicorum* 49, there are passages in letters which contribute information on Cicero's income. It is known that from the time of his marriage to Terentia shortly before 77 BC Cicero had the use of an annual income of 80,000 sesterces || in rent from apartment blocks, *insulae*, in Rome.[12] This figure is more reliable than the 100,000 sesterces from rural properties (if indeed *praedia* stands here for *praedia rustica*), which derives from a highly rhetorical passage. (The figure of 20,000,000 sesterces has been rejected by some scholars on the same grounds.) But an income of 100,000 sesterces from country estates may not be very wide of the mark. This level of income presupposes a holding in productive land worth somewhere between one and two million sesterces, depending on the kind of farming carried out.[13] Carcopino, who was not prone to underrate the wealth of Cicero, opted for the lower figure,

[9] Frank (1933) 393–5. For the influence of Tenney Frank on later scholars, see e.g. Smutny (1951) 54, on the 600,000: 'this amount, as Frank points out, approximately equals Cicero's own income'.
[10] Observed by Smutny (1951) 53.
[11] *Att.* 13.46.2; 14.9.1, 10.3, 11.2; cf. 12.25.1: *voluptuarias possessiones*.
[12] *Att.* 12.32.2, 7.1, 24.1; 16.1.5.
[13] E.g. 100,000 sesterces might represent a return of 10 per cent on an investment of 1,000,000 sesterces. But the capital outlay might be somewhat greater, for 10 per cent is an unusually high yield. See Duncan-Jones (1982) 33ff.

on other grounds.[14] (It might, I suppose, be charged that Carcopino's dislike of the man may have led him to exaggerate the value of Cicero's non-productive property as against his productive property.) The numerous texts which relate to Cicero's financial standing and dealings do not prepare us for a much higher figure. It therefore seems a safe conjecture that urban property contributed almost as much to Cicero's income as country estates. We might have been prepared for this significant result by *De Officiis* 2.88, where the choice between urban and rural rents, *vectigalia*, is put on the same level as that between *gloria* and *divitiae*, or *bona valetudo* and *voluptas*, or *vires* and *celeritas*.

There is some evidence, then, that the subject of urban property investment has been mishandled. Why should this have been so?

There appears to have been a reluctance among scholars to concede that the typical Roman aristocrat regarded the activity of the *rentier* as respectable. Writers of agricultural treatises and moral discourses have reinforced this belief by giving the impression that involvement in only a very few income-producing activities was countenanced. Thus, for example, in *De Officiis*. 1.150-1 only agriculture, trade (under certain conditions) and the liberal arts are designated honourable revenue-earning occupations. Such passages must be recognized for what they are, statements of an antiquated value-system with only limited relevance to contemporary economic behaviour.[15]

The conceptual confusion referred to earlier has played its part. The category of speculation has been broadened to include the activity of the *rentier*; and speculation is viewed as the characteristic activity of the capitalist, whose outlook is || branded as unmistakably plebeian.[16]

Again, there are relatively few texts that bear on urban property, and their numbers are reduced markedly if we discard those relating primarily to non-economic aspects of house-ownership. This in itself might feed the supposition that Romans did not regard urban property as a serious investment. But the paucity of texts might be explicable on other grounds. As I have already implied, ownership of productive rural property was the cornerstone of the ideology of the ruling class. A senator writing for a public audience if not for posterity would not fight shy of identifying himself or a peer as a rural landowner. But residential rents were a proper subject mainly for private correspondence with agents or friends. It is because Martial thought nothing of divulging confidences that we know of the

[14] Carcopino (1951) I, 54: the bulk of Cicero's productive land was near Arpinum, this land was roughly of equal value to the Tusculan, and the latter was worth about 1,000,000 sesterces.
[15] This statement is controversial and will have to be defended in detail in another place.
[16] Salvioli (1906) 36-7.

finances of the mysterious Afer: 3,200,000 out on loan, 3,000,000 coming in from apartment-houses and country estates (*ex insulis fundisque*), and 600,000 from grazing (Mart. 4.37). There was nothing degrading about being a *rentier*, but this was thought of as a purely private affair, having no relevance to a man's public image or political stance.

Finally, the message of a number of literary texts seems to be that urban property brought in a higher return than rural property, but was in two respects less secure: it was more vulnerable to damage or destruction, not the land itself, but the capital additions required to make it revenue-earning; and its greater destructibility rendered it more liable to suffer sudden loss of market value. There is an explicit text in Aulus Gellius (*NA* 15.1). A member of a rhetorician's entourage looks down on a fire from the Esquiline and comments: 'The returns from urban property are great, but the risks are far, far greater. If there were some remedy, something to prevent the houses of Rome burning so readily, I assure you I would have given up my estates in the countryside and purchased urban property.' On the basis of this and other passages a generalization might be formulated to the effect that the greater profitability and insecurity of urban as compared with rural property investment diverted aristocratic funds from the urban to the rural sphere.

But could such a generalization be defended? Its validity would have to be tested with reference to Republican Rome, Imperial ‖ Rome, and the cities of the empire. The outcome of the investigation (which cannot be undertaken here) is not as predictable as may seem.

Is the thesis valid for the late Republic? What indications are there that the average senator or equestrian was deterred from investing in *insulae* by considerations of risk? And how great were those risks? The house built with walls of wattle work of which Vitruvius writes was highly inflammable, a real death-trap, but its loss would have been borne lightly by a wealthy owner. In any case, rich men were more likely to invest money in a more solid structure with concrete walls. This was the typical multi-storied tenement house of Cicero's day, and though less durable than one built of brick, was officially judged to have a life-span of eighty years (Vitr. 2.8.8; 17; 20). Cicero's sang-froid in the face of his collapsed and cracking buildings is notorious (*Att.* 14.9.1; 11.2).[17] Can we assume that it was also unusual?

Is the thesis valid for Imperial Rome, and in particular for the new Rome constructed by Nero and other emperors out of materials superior to those used in the lifetime of Vitruvius and earlier? The Ostian evidence is relevant. Ostia became virtually a suburb of Rome, and was

---

[17] These properties were at Puteoli.

architecturally a Rome in miniature. The Ostian *insulae* were secure and lucrative investments. They were well-planned, brick-faced and vaulted. Most had shops on the ground floor. A high proportion of Ostians lived in them. Rents must have been an important constituent of Ostia's gross city income.[18]

Is the thesis valid for the cities? When the inquiry is extended beyond the capital, as it must be, archaeological evidence leaves no doubt that many house-owners put their property to productive use. Rooms or apartments were rented to lodgers, houses or parts of houses were made available for commercial enterprises, in some of which the house-owners appear to have participated directly. At Volubilis in Mauretania, the economic functions of urban property can be appreciated at a glance, thanks to the excellent publication of Etienne. The houses of the north-east quarter, which date from the first part of the third century, are ample, even sumptuous. Ten of the twenty-three have oil-producing establishments, seven have bakeries. There are a great many shops: only two houses have none, and one of them has an apartment for || rent. House number nineteen is left, very rich in mosaics, and owned, according to Etienne, by 'un propriétaire éloigné de toute préoccupation de lucre'.[19] It would be safer to say that the man did not wish commercial activity to interfere with his domestic tranquillity; for how can we be sure that he did not own buildings elsewhere which housed commercial or industrial operations? Unfortunately, names and statuses cannot be assigned to any of the house-owners. We might be tempted to suppose that the higher an individual stood in the social hierarchy, the less deeply he was involved in commercial operations. This would probably be a mistaken assumption, as is suggested by an analogy from another African town, whose economy was also basically agrarian. Of the three most luxurious houses in Timgad, Algeria, in the early third century, the one with most shops, and the only one with shops communicating with the house-interior, was owned by M. Plotius Faustus, equestrian army officer, local magistrate and priest.[20] It is of course only at Pompeii, where the names of a large number of

---

[18] Provided, of course, that the owners were citizens of Ostia and the profits did not go to outsiders. Meiggs (1960) 235ff.; Packer (1971); Boethius (1960) 128ff.

[19] Etienne (1960).

[20] Boeswillwald, Cagnat, Ballu (1905) 325–6; *CIL* VIII 2395, 2399; 17904–5; *ILS* 5579; *BCTH* 1932–3, pp. 185–6 (Plotius Faustus). We are in no position to calculate the returns coming to house-owners in Africa. If Faustus had invested 400,000 sesterces, the equestrian census, in rural land, he might have received 24,000 sesterces per annum at 6 per cent. His shops might have been worth 12,000 sesterces per annum (i.e. less than 1,000 sesterces per room, which seems a low estimate). The ratio 2 : 1 between income from rural and urban sectors might be a significant result for an agricultural town. For some rents in late Republican Rome see Yavetz (1958) 504; cf. *Dig.* 19.2.7–8, 30 pr.

house-owners and prominent persons are known, that a division between 'politicians' and 'businessmen' can be seen to be artificial. It is strange that no satisfactory analysis of the economic behaviour of the richer and more important Pompeians has yet been made. A first step might be to assemble all the information relating to the income-producing activities of urban proprietors. One fact that would immediately become apparent is that only a small minority of the better quality houses so far excavated were untouched by any degree of commercial enterprise.[21]

To sum up the argument so far: neglect of the subject of urban property investment can be explained but not justified. There is room for a study of the relative levels of investment in urban and rural property, and the relative contribution made by these and other forms of investment to the income of the wealthy. The literary sources have not been fully exploited and may serve as a starting-point. We should, however, be prepared to extend the inquiry to include cities where, thanks to the archaeologists, private housing can be studied more profitably than at Rome. An investigation of this kind would not dethrone agriculture, but would reveal that investment and income patterns were very varied, and that by no means all those prominent in politics and society, ‖ in Rome and the cities, would have been able, or would have wanted, to state with the younger Pliny, *sum quidem prope totus in praediis* (*Ep.* 3.19.8).

I will conclude by placing the argument in a wider context, that of the economy as a whole.

Though they seldom make it explicit, historians writing about the sources of wealth of the aristocracy have some kind of conceptual scheme of the workings of the economy. In emphasizing the predominance of rural property as a source of income, they are, indirectly, making a statement about the balance of trade between the rural and urban sectors of the economy. They are stressing the flow of goods from the rural to the urban sector. The cities are viewed as markets for agricultural produce. There was also a trickle of goods, consumer goods, back to the countryside from the cities. But on the whole, rural landowners pocketed the returns from sales of agricultural produce either directly in their capacity as agricultural producers, or indirectly through the rents they charged producers. I doubt whether anybody would dispute this as a general account of the balance of trade between town and country in a primitive economy.

---

[21] Basic reference-works include Overbeck (1875); Maiuri (1942) 97ff.; Della Corte (1954). This is not the place to undertake a critique of Maiuri's influential theory, the essence of which is that the Pompeian aristocracy was forced to invest in commerce and industry as a result of its losses in the earthquake of AD 62. I find little concrete evidence to support this argument.

But it is also necessary to recognize that there were income-generating transactions taking place in the 'internal' urban economy, as a result of the division of labour within the cities, that is to say, in consequence of the fact that urban residents were providing employment for one another. Property-owners participated indirectly in those activities. For example, they took a rake-off from transactions between private producers and retailers on the one hand, and retailers and urban consumers on the other, through rents charged on premises. Again, as producers themselves – one thinks of the oil-manufacturers of Volubilis, or Veranius Hypsaeus the Pompeian fuller and magistrate[22] – they took part in and drew profits directly from the commercial life of the city.

The purpose of this chapter then, has been not to deny the importance of the flow of income from the rural sector, but to focus more closely on income-generating activities that took place within the cities. Ownership of urban property provided access to, and in some cases control over, these activities. This other source of income should not be ignored or defined out as of marginal significance, unless it can be shown that the Roman aristocracy and the aristocracy of the cities as a class turned their backs on it.

Appendix: demolition of houses and the law

The evidence that the Roman authorities placed restrictions on house-demolition is familiar but confusing. It consists of legal enactments that are often brief and uninformative, or decidedly ambiguous, and of extracts from juristic commentaries which focus on strictly legal points and in large part ignore the social, economic and even political background. In practical terms this means that it is seldom possible to probe in any depth into the attitude of the political authorities, the activities they are seeking to curb, and the impact of such activities on the community.

The municipal charters may be considered first. A clause in the late-Republican charter of Tarentum ran as follows:

> nei quis in oppido quod eius municipi erit aedificium detegito neive demolito neive disturbato nisei quod non deterius restiturus erit nisei de s(enatus) s(ententia). sei quis adversus ea faxit, quanti id aedificium fuerit, tantam pequniam municipio dare damnas esto, eiusque pequniae quei volet petitio esto.

[22] Hypsaeus: Maiuri (1942) 165–6; Overbeck (1875) 345, fig. 192; Della Corte (1954) 46. Of course many owners of bakeries, dye-works, fulleries, and so on, would have been merely *rentiers*.

In other words, anyone who unroofed or pulled down a building was liable to a fine equal to the value of the building, unless restoration was made to a state no worse than before. At Spanish Urso, the Caesarian colony, a security was forfeited if rebuilding did not take place, while the Flavian law for Malaga required restoration of the building concerned within the following year.[23] It is hard not to believe that some such regulation was published at Rome in the late Republic.

The charters are silent as to the motives of either legislators or those whose activities were being legislated against. The unroofing of a building (*detegere*) suggests the practice of *distractio*, which in this context means the breaking up of a building with a view to salvaging the materials;[24] demolition that was not followed by rebuilding might in theory have been aimed at forcing up the prices of lands and rents.[25] The legislators, for their part, might || have been principally interested in preserving the physical aspect of the city. This may be implied in the stipulation that a building should be replaced by a structure 'no worse' (*non deterius*). A subsidiary motive might conceivably have been to keep the stock of residential housing at its existing level.[26] But all this is conjecture; the texts themselves do not fill in, or even hint at, the background of the legislation.

The so-called Senatus Consultum Hosidianum of AD 45 is somewhat more explicit.[27] The inspiration for the decree came from the emperor Claudius himself.[28] Eleven years later its main points are summarized in the S. C. Volusianum issued by Nero's senate in settling a case involving housing in an abandoned community in the territory of Mutina. The Claudian decree, as restated, emended and interpreted, remained the basic

---

[23] Lex Tar. 32ff.; lex Urs. 75; lex Malac. 62. Texts in *FIRA* I, pp. 168; 184; 214.

[24] See note 40 below.

[25] Clearly not every wrecker who did not immediately rebuild can properly be termed a land hoarder. Delay in rebuilding was inevitable if builders and architects proved unavailable, or materials were not to hand, or cash was short and credit tight. Housing was no doubt an extremely volatile industry. Probably only monopolists like Crassus with his slave-builders and limitless resources were unaffected by its instability. It may be that in Spanish colonies, where, as the charters show, permission to demolish had to be obtained, a petitioner had to satisfy the council that he could rebuild without delay.

[26] Phillips (1973) 88–91, goes too far in arguing that the prescriptions of the charters were designed to protect the inhabitants of cheap, sub-standard housing against redevelopment and the inevitable higher rents. This interpretation is linked with the strange thesis that the charters ruled out demolition altogether, but were circumvented by the (unregulated) practice of demolishing after sale. The weak points are the construction placed on the words *non deterius restiturus erit* and *se reaedificaturum*, and the manipulation of Strab. 5.3.7 (p. 87). His rejection of a humanitarian purpose behind the S. C. Hosidianum is at least paradoxical (p. 94, quoted n. 39 below).

[27] *FIRA* I no. 45, p. 288.

[28] Note *auctore divo Claudio* in the S. C. Volusianum, *FIRA* I no. 45, p. 289 l.26, the language of the prolegomenon of the Claudian decree, and the archaic dative *pace* (1.10).

statement of the Roman authorities on the subject of the demolition of houses until the Severan period at least.

Several differences between the decree and the charters are evident. The range of the decree is wider; it applies to Rome and apparently also to Italy, both rural and urban.[29] The decree is concerned with house-demolition following sale. A profit motive is supplied for the first time; moreover, the phrase *negotiandi causa* may even imply that the decree was directed against regular trafficking in buildings, rather than merely single acts of demolition for profit. The penalty is higher: the buyer forfeits double the price of the house, the seller is reprimanded, and the sale is voided.[30] In the final clause exemption is given to house-owners who sell off parts of a house while intending to retain the bulk of it in their possession, provided that they do not make a regular business of it (*dum non negotiationis causa*).[31]

The prolegomenon contains a bitter denunciation of 'this most cruel form of profiteering', which leaves behind a scene of destruction more appropriate to an age of war than of peace.

The language seemed to de Pachtere too strong to have been employed against professional wreckers of houses.[32] He held that Claudius was in fact attacking creditors who took over the property of bankrupted farmers and turned it over to ranching instead of agriculture, and that the decree was nothing less than an attempt to arrest the decline of agriculture and the depopulation of the countryside.

---

[29] This might be inferred from the reference to Italy in the opening clause, the mention of *villae* as well as *domus*, and the location of the houses whose demolition is discussed in the Neronian decree. But I do not agree with Phillips (1973) 95 that the charters and decrees 'in the main concerned different types of property', i.e. *domus* and *villae* (*rusticae*) respectively. (This is the supposition that underpins the thesis that the two sets of legislation had different objectives.) Note 'tectis urbis nostrae', emphatically placed and more specific than 'totius Italiae aeternitati', which can easily degenerate into a mere slogan. 'Exemplo suo' in the following clause I take as a reference to specific building or public works undertaken by Claudius in the first years of his reign. Claudius goes on to profess concern for the preservation (*custodia*) of public and private buildings.

[30] On the penalty see Arangio-Ruiz (1936) 518, with reference to *Dig.* 39.2.48.

[31] I translate *mutare* as 'sell', not 'change'; cf. Plaut. *Capt.* 27–9; Virg. *Ecl.* 4.38; Hor. *Sat.* 1.4.29; 2.7.109; Sall. *Jug.* 44.5; etc. Contrast, e.g. Hor. *Ep.* 1.1.100; Nepos, *Att.* 13.2 ('nihil commutavit'). Remodelling is not here excluded, but rather the disposing of part of a house for pecuniary advantage; cf. in the Neronian decree, *neve quis negotiandi causa eorum quid emeret venderetve*, where *eorum quid* may be the equivalent of *aliquas partes earum*, and refer to parts of houses. (A prohibition against buying and selling houses for profit makes no sense to me.) Against, Daube (1957). See *Dig.* 18.1.52, preserving the wording of the Neronian decree, with the roughly contemporaneous 39.2.48: *si quis ad demoliendum negotiandi causa vendidisse domum partemve domus fuerit convictus*.

[32] De Pachtere (1912).

This theory, which won wide acceptance, is not supported by the text of the decree.[33] There is no reference in it to agriculture. The emperor's preoccupation throughout is with buildings, in the first place urban buildings.[34] In addition, one may wonder how a decree outlawing trafficking in buildings could have affected absentee-landlords and *latifondisti*, who would have escaped its jurisdiction simply by leaving farmhouses intact.

On a superficial reading of the text, Claudius was protesting at the despoliation of his cities for profit. This might indeed be a sufficient explanation of his anger. All emperors were concerned about the physical aspect of the cities, Rome above all.[35] Fine buildings were thought to enhance, and decrepit ones to tarnish, the image of a reign. Both the Claudian decree and the Neronian decree complain that the unsightliness of ruined buildings has presented a direct challenge to the ruler.

There is just a possibility that Claudius was aware that profiteering of this sort might have a further consequence. The words he uses to describe it, *cruentissimo genere negotiationis*, might allude obliquely to the plight of Rome's tenants. In this connection it is worth noting that Claudius, unlike many emperors, did not sacrifice residential areas to wasteful and grandiose building projects; he did not, in effect, aggravate Rome's perpetual housing shortage. His public works policy was primarily utilitarian; it aimed at bettering living conditions in Rome through reduction of the risk of flooding, and improvement of supplies of food and water.[36] We need not believe that Nero inherited any of his predecessor's humanitarianism;[37] yet his senate in AD 56 might have accurately interpreted Claudius' intentions, in requiring Celsilla to show that the buildings she owned and wished to demolish in the ghost town of Campi Macri were uninhabited, uninhabitable, and that no one could conceivably be desirous of living in them.[38]

The argument from 'cruentissimo' is not of course conclusive – the most that I would claim is that it merits consideration. Meanwhile we should be

---

[33] E.g. Charlesworth (1934) 695; Scramuzza (1940) 173. Against de Pachtere I have seen only Phillips (1973) 92–3, with whom I am in general agreement, having reached similar conclusions by independent investigation. But see note 29 above.

[34] See note 29 above.

[35] Augustus set the pattern. See Suet. *Aug.* 29. On the municipal level, cf. Dio's plan to beautify Prusa, not appreciated by the poorer classes. See *Or.* 40.8–9; 45.12; 46.9; 47.11 and 15.

[36] Claudius' projects in and around Rome included work on the Tiber bank to prevent flooding, the harbour at Ostia, a new distribution centre and granaries, the draining of the Fucine lake, the repair of Aqua Virgo, and the construction of Aqua Claudia and Aqua Anio Novus. See Blake (1959) 25ff.

[37] Mart. *Spect.* 1.2.7–8: *Hic, ubi miramur velocia munera thermas/abstulerat miseris tecta superbus.*

[38] *FIRA* I p. 290, 11. 36ff.: *eaque aedificia longa vetustate dilaberentur neque refecta usui essent futura, quia neque habitaret in iis quisquam nec vellet in deserta ac ruentia commigrare.*

on our guard lest we exaggerate the extent of Claudius' sympathy for the plight of the poor. For example, the decree is not a manifestation of hostility to the practice of pulling down slum dwellings prior to replacing them with better quality and more profitable *insulae*. It was the spectacle of houses left in ruins by wreckers which roused Claudius to anger, and the wreckers are accused simply of making money out of their destruction (*diruendo*).[39] The assumption, made here as in later texts, that demolition was a profitable enterprise,[40] together with the emphasis given to aesthetic considerations,[41] indicate that the destruction of sub-standard housing was not at issue.

Similarly, though we may suspect that the house-wreckers included speculators who kept land idle with the purpose of forcing up its market price and the level of rents, there is no hint of this in any of the texts. Explicit reference is made only to the short-term profits obtainable from demolition. Either hoarding was not a serious problem, or the authorities were unwilling or unable to attack it directly and effectively. The Romans were not known for any bias against *rentiers* or profiteers, or in general for protecting the poor against exploitation by the rich.

In the last resort, the texts must be allowed to speak for themselves. The municipal charters apart, they show that money was being made out of dismantling houses for the purpose of salvaging materials, and that the emperors intervened with the aim of preserving the aspect of their cities. This may not be a complete explanation of the legislative and judicial activity we have been considering, but it is as much as can be discerned with certainty.[42]

---

[39] Cf. Phillips (1973) 94: 'It affected better class property rather than slums and was concerned with appearances, not with the social necessity of providing housing for the poor.'
[40] The attractiveness of marble to wreckers is brought out as early as the reign of Vespasian: *Negotiandi causa aedificia demoliri et marmora detrahere edicto divi Vespasiani et senatus consulto vetitum est.* See *Cod.Iust.* 8.10.2. In *Dig.* 30.41.1, reference is made to a S.C. of AD 122, an amendment to the earlier decrees: 'ea quae aedibus iuncta sunt legari non possent'. Para. 2 shows that marble and columns are at stake. In para. 3 the transference of materials from one house to another is permitted, where the same man owns both houses and intends to retain them (*possessoribus*) ... *id est non distracturis*. See paras. 5, 7–9, 12 for other amendments. In *Dig.* 18.1.34 pr. Paulus indicates that a house might be bought for its appurtenances among which are listed marble statues and paintings.
[41] See *Cod.Iust.* 8.10.2: *sed nec dominis ita transferre licet, ut integris aedificiis depositis publicus deformetur adspectus* (AD 222); 8.10.6 pr.: *si quis post hanc legem civitate spoliata ornatum, hoc est marmora vel columnas, ad rura transtulerit, privetur ea possessiones, quam ita ornaverit.* See also MacMullen (1959). Derelict housing becomes a matter of concern to the imperial authorities for the same reasons. See *IGRR* IV 1156a = *SIG*³ 837 (AD 127); *Dig.* 17.2.52.10 (Marcus); *Cod.Iust.* 8.10.4 (Philip); 11.29.4 (Diocl./Max.); 8.10.8 (AD 377); *Dig.* 1.18.7; 39.2.7.2; 15.21.
[42] I am grateful to J. J. Nicholls for acute comments on the Claudian decree.

Addendum

This paper draws attention to the value of urban real estate and argues that it attracted investment by members of the élite. In the ancient consumer city, rentier landlords would not only rely on rents and profits from rural property but would also benefit from profit-generating activities within the city.

Frier (1977) and (1980) 21–47 discuss the rental market in the city of Rome. Frier (1980) 21 sees urban property as a field of élite investment (following G. pp. 70–1); on owners see ibid. 21–6. 'No doubt it was the case throughout the early empire that most urban property was controlled by the aristocracy' (24), but compared to agricultural estates, urban investment was 'relatively small' (25). See also Frier (1978), on Cicero's urban properties (pp. 65–7).

Rainer (1987) and Martin (1989) examine legal evidence of private building in Rome. Murga (1975), (1976b) 163–70; Rainer (1987) 284–90 deal with known laws on the demolition of buildings (pp. 71–5). Rainer (1987) 294 (with 297 n. 1) doubts the existence of similar regulations, now lost, for the capital (p. 72), and (289 n. 8) rejects G's view that the S. C. Hosidianum provided for higher fines than the provincial charters (p. 73). *Pace* G. (pp. 74–5), Camodeca (1980) 468 n. 65; Rainer (1987) 289 n. 5 argue that the S. C. Hosidianum was primarily directed against speculation rather than concerned about ruins. On the rationale for that law, see, e.g., Arias Bonnet (1982) 290–1; Sargenti (1982) 272–80; Rainer (1987) 287 (Murga (1976a) stresses aesthetic concerns).

5

AN ASSOCIATION OF BUILDERS IN LATE ANTIQUE SARDIS

I. THE DOCUMENT

This is an agreement made in AD 459 between an association of builders in Sardis and an official, called in the document *magistrianos kai ekdikos*. If, as is likely, this man is the equivalent of the *defensor civitatis* known from the early fourth century, then he was the top city official, who may also be regarded as a minor imperial functionary.[1]

According to the preamble (lines 9ff.), certain private employers, *ergodotes*, have filed complaints with the *defensor* to the effect that men who contract to do building jobs leave them unfinished and obstruct their employers in some way unspecified.

The association concedes that these practices are injurious to employers and agrees that they will be stopped, provided that employers are ready to pay for jobs (lines 20ff.).

The document then spells out procedures to be followed in certain circumstances:

First (lines 23ff.), if a job is abandoned by someone, a substitute will be furnished from within the association – provided that the man being replaced is himself a member of the association. Second (lines 31ff.), in the event of obstruction by the original craftsman or a substitute, *misthoi* (presumably 'compensation', though 'pay' is a more natural translation) will be furnished ('by us' is restored). Third (lines 39ff.), the employer, it appears, is expected to give twenty days grace to a craftsman who stops working because of illness (in other cases seven days grace is considered appropriate, lines 37ff.). But after that a substitute must be provided, if the original craftsman does not return to the job.

Finally, non-completion of the job, even after the provision of a substitute, results in a fine and the prosecution of the association (lines 43ff.); and the property of the association is pledged against full payment (lines 53ff.).

---

[1] The best version of this text is in *Sardis* VII 1.18. An English translation is available there, and a French translation in Chastagnol (1976) 331–2. See also Garnsey (1985) 159–60.

There is no other document from antiquity like this one; the three imperial inscriptional fragments from Ephesus, Pergamum and Miletus which Buckler republished together with our inscription[2] are not comparable beyond the bare fact that they concern disputes.

Buckler in fact published the first adequate text of the Sardis inscription, although it had been discovered in the middle of the eighteenth century. Thus Waltzing, whose classic three-volume work on professional associations appeared at the turn of the last century, was unaware of its existence,[3] while Persson does not refer to it in *Staat und Manufaktur* (1923). It is also absent from Gunnar Mickwitz's *Die Kartellfunktionen der Zünfte* (1936).[4] Later writers have made only brief allusions to the document.[5] Buckler glanced at it again towards the end of his life[6] and the latest version of the text, that printed in *Sardis* VII.1, includes some minor corrections that he introduced.

II. THE ASSOCIATION

The title, if we had it, might help us ascertain the character of the association. In line one, which included the title, *oikodomōn* is apparently assured from an earlier copy, but *techniton* is not. Buckler stakes a lot on this restoration. The union, he says, is a collective of crafts, only some of which are connected with building; he writes:

> Throughout the declaration, the strength of the union stands in contrast with the feebleness of the curbs imposed by the city's defensor. Why the union's power was so great is plainly shown by its title. Neither builders nor artisans is the description of a single craft; each is a collective term denoting a group of crafts, the masons, brickmakers, carpenters, cement-workers, etc. being all designated as builders, while the members of the other crafts not identified with the building trade are together embraced under the generic term 'artisans', *technitai*. Such comprehensive titles are seldom if ever found among craft unions of the first to the 3rd century, where each union bore as its title the specific name of its own particular craft. The vague nomenclature of our union seems comprehensible only on the assumption that between the 3rd and 5th centuries the Sardian unions of the building trade had become amalgamated to form a Builder's union. These changes were presumably followed by the amalgamation of those composite unions into the single body by which our agreement was negotiated. The mere size of this body, which may rank as the earliest of 'Amalgamated Societies', gave it no doubt the bargaining advantages so conspicuous in our document.[7]

---

[2] Buckler (1923) esp. 36–45, 47–50. [3] Waltzing (1896) 208–22.
[4] Persson (1923) 51–2; Mickwitz (1936) 166–7. [5] Giardina (1982) 123–6.
[6] Buckler (1953) 982–3. [7] Ibid. 983.

I do not find the bargaining advantages of the association so conspicuous. Nor do I find any internal evidence supporting Buckler's restoration or the construction that he placed on it. The singular *technites*, which occurs in the inscription several times, is simply a non-specific word for 'craftsman', as is its alternative *ergolabesas*; its use does not necessarily carry implications for the name of the association (or rather for part of that name). Retaining *techniton* in line 1, preferably with a dependent genitive such as *oikēmatōn*, does not commit us to Buckler's 'Amalgamated Society'. That this was an association of men devoted to *one craft* seems established by the reference to our *technē*, in the singular, in line 11; and the craft in question is identified in the following line as building (erga *oikodomika*). The idea that the association brought together a number of different specialists connected with the building trade is a more reasonable speculation.

Is our association a trade union? For Buckler it was: one with power to make bargains with employers over wage-rates, to operate a closed shop, having the funds to pay compensation in the event of unsatisfactory work.

The institution he had in mind is unlikely to have existed at this time and in this trade.[8] To take up simply this latter point: historically, building has been one of the most difficult trades in which to establish trade unionism. This is partly because of the physical conditions in which, perforce, building work is done. When workers are scattered in small groups on different sites within a geographical area, there tends to be a low level of solidarity, and, more importantly, there are considerable organizational difficulties facing those who try to form them into trade unions. The collection of subscriptions, the keeping of records, the holding of meetings – all are rendered much more difficult when you have a peripatetic group to deal with. Another factor is the high proportion of unskilled workers employed in the building trade. Because much building work is basically only labouring, there is plenty of scope for casual labour – and these workers are notoriously difficult to organize and keep as members.

It is more likely that the men who produced our documents were not ordinary labourers, but master builders – presumably doubling up as building contractors – who employed them and undertook the doing of building work, presumably by *locatio conductio operis*. Such an association might have had both the funds and the control over its members suggested by the text.

If we are looking for modern comparisons, then we might consider traders' associations, the motor traders association, or the law society, or

---

[8] See esp. Giardina (1982) 123–6.

whatever – these are élite groups which come together for certain professional purposes, and are qualitatively different from industrial trade unions.

Is our association better compared to a medieval guild?[9] It is hardly necessary to point out that analogies with medieval craft organizations (in Latin *officia* or *mesteria*, usually), in the absence of similar municipal government and economic ideas, might be as false as analogies with modern trade unions in the absence of modern industry. Moreoever, guilds of wage workers (or journeymen) existed as well as guilds of masters, in the medieval period. If there is a comparison, it is with a guild of *masters*, such as the Fellowship of Masons of London in the fourteenth century: Membership was expensive. After paying the basic quarterage and a small recreation fee, money had to be found for livery and dining expenses, while the fines for those in default in one way or another were heavy.

However, the search for comparative material must begin in the Graeco-Roman world in the period of the Principate. A study of the composition of the *collegia fabrum tignariorum* of both Rome and Ostia reveals that their members were the élite of those engaged in the building trade.[10] They were men of some means, who could afford an entry fee, a regular subscription, and from time to time additional expenditures for purposes public or private. Like the professional associations of the Principate, the association of builders of Sardis was first and foremost, it can be assumed, a social community. As one scholar has written of the earlier *collegia*:

> The benefits of membership were essentially those of personal pleasure and privilege – the sharing of banquets and handouts, the provision of a decent burial, and, on a more abstract level, the sense of belonging to a small and distinct 'community', which played a larger role in the life, political and social, of the whole community outside, than most of the members would have played in an individual capacity.[11]

Something similar can be said, as it happens, of the medieval guilds which, as Connaert demonstrated in a fundamental article,[12] were essentially clubs or associations formed for social and religious purposes; some of them developed specific professional aims, but only relatively late. To return to the Graeco-Roman world: Waltzing has yet to be refuted in his claim that the professional colleges of the Principate did not exist to promote or protect the professional interests of their members. But they clearly *did* change in character in the *late* Empire, and we must now try to define and explain their transformation, with special reference to our

---

[9] On medieval guilds, see the overview by Reynolds (1977) 80–4, 164–8, cf. 127–8, 181–5, and, in greater detail, Connaert (1948). I have consulted Salzman (1952) with profit; Knoop and Jones (1967). I am grateful to Dr Susan Reynolds for bibliographic advice.
[10] Pearse (1974).   [11] Ibid. 121.   [12] Connaert (1948).

college at Sardis. We are given in the inscription only a partial view of the college. We see it accepting a code of conduct under threat of fine and prosecution by the public authorities. The agreement was drawn up specifically to satisfy consumer interests, to provide employers with guarantees that any contracts made with association members would be honoured. Nothing specific is said about the internal organization of the college, nor about the nature of the involvement of the college, if any, in the business relationships of its individual members and employers. In respect of these matters we can do no more than make some speculative inferences.

First, on the matter of internal organization: the college is clearly committed to enforcing a degree of discipline on its members, simply to ensure that the terms of the agreement made with the *defensor* are carried out. One must suppose, post 459, if not before, the existence of regulations governing the choice of substitute craftsmen, stipulating the circumstances under which withdrawal from a job was legitimate, stating penalties for rule-breaking, and so on. One must assume the existence of a body of officials with power to supervise the ordinary membership. The second issue, the involvement of the college as such in professional activities, is more problematic. A key question is that of pay or wages: how was this settled, and did the association have a role to play? Lines 23ff. contain a reference to pay, *misthoi*. The builders agree to complete a job, so long as the employer is ready to furnish the *sunaresantas misthous*. Buckler (1923) translated: 'the wages mutually agreed upon', and commented:

> The wages are ostensibly fixed by the several contracts between individual artisans and employers (see lines 35ff.), and of 'union', 'standard', or 'minimum' rates there is no mention. Since however, an employer can enjoy the benefit of the agreement only if he deals exclusively with members of the union (lines 28-9, 33-4), he has to pay them the wages it permits them to accept. Thus a strict 'union agreement' such as ours is a tacit adoption of 'union' rates of pay.

Thirty years later, Buckler gave this speculation the status of fact, retranslating the key words 'so long as the employer is ready to give us the wages regarded by us as satisfactory'.[13] 'The aorist *sunaresantas*', he says, 'indicates a prior fixing of the wages, not a wage-scale established by the employer on the occasion of his particular contract.' In other words, the employer must have 'accepted the wage rates fixed by the union'.[14] But the clause is quite ambiguous; we simply cannot know on the basis of this document how the level of *misthoi* was arrived at. Lines 35-7, however, make clear that an agreement or contract (*sumphonon*) was made with the

[13] Buckler (1953) 983.   [14] Ibid.

individual worker; and this suggests that the employer had greater power to fix the precise wage rate than is conceded by Buckler.

It is not beyond the realms of possibility (though I am sceptical) that there was something like an agreed scale of pay, with variations according to the particular skill of an individual craftsman – the document is silent on this as on related matters. This is essentially the argument I have been advancing, that the document is simply a code of conduct, and anything that we want to deduce beyond that is essentially speculative.

III. THE CONTEXT

Having sounded this cautionary note I will now try to place the inscription in its historical context.

According to the traditional view, which goes back at least as far as Waltzing, the late empire witnessed an attempt by the government to impose on tradesmen compulsory collegialism, and hereditary membership of the *collegia*. Waltzing is rightly critical of the position that membership of a college was necessary for practice of a craft, either in theory or in practice. He did hold, however, that all corporations were hereditarily attached to some public service from the time of Constantine – this to ensure that important public functions were performed and essential supplies furnished.[15]

Mickwitz added an important new dimension to the standard account when he advanced the thesis that Korporationzwang or Zunftzwang, the regimentation and state control of the colleges, opened the way for their transformation into monopolistic bodies. More generally, he believed that Zunftzwang was a precondition for the involvement of the colleges in economic life. Previously the existence of the professional associations had been justified by social, religious and political ends; now, however, they developed a new and explicit economic function, the monopolistic fixing of prices on the market. Why did this major development, which he dated to the middle of the fifth century, come about? The government was unable to impose obligations on the colleges of tradesmen without at the same time awarding privileges, and in some cases it even granted monopoly rights. This, coupled with a labour shortage associated with a decline in slavery, created the new syndicalist spirit.[16] Lellia Cracco Ruggini has drawn attention to the *riottosità*, the volatility or rebelliousness of the

---

[15] Waltzing (1896) 208–22.

[16] See also De Robertis (1955). De Robertis qualified Mickwitz's argument, concluding that the latter had greatly exaggerated the supposed regulation of the economy and society of the later Roman empire.

corporati from the fourth century onwards, adding the observation that the most 'punchy' of the *collegiati* were actually the workers in state factories, or *fabricenses*, and others whose colleges were controlled by the state to a significant degree.[17] However, can one use the building industry to illustrate and confirm any or all of these doctrines and assertions?

Under the Principate, emperors did not try to produce craftsmen and labourers for building projects from their own households. They drew instead upon the services of independent tradesmen, some of whom were certainly members of building associations. There is very little to suggest that they used the services of building *collegia* qua *collegia*. Callistratus has a sentence in the *Digest* (50.6.6.12) indicating that building workers were expected to aid the state and the cities by constructing public buildings; Ulpian also says (50.6.6.4) that the repair of public buildings was a *munus publicum*. But it is not clear in either case that the colleges were themselves employed as sources of skilled craftsmen or labourers. The building *collegia*, in particular the *collegium fabrorum* which is ubiquitous in the West, is usually assumed to have had one corporate function, but that had nothing to do with building – putting out fires.

Did things change, as they are said to have done, in the late empire? Our inscription appears to register little change.

First, membership is apparently voluntary, for the existence of builders who are not 'of us' is acknowledged, at least in principle.

Second, the inscription indicates that some work, probably a significant amount of work, is done for private employers or contractors.

Third, one clause may refer obliquely to liturgies: 'should the man undertaking the work have any plea on which he declines it for some reason of his own either private *or public*, . . .' If a liturgy is meant, however, it is self-evidently one borne by the craftsman in his own person.

Fourth, there is no reference to any liturgy undertaken by the college qua college. I do not rule out that there were such liturgies; one obvious possibility is the collection from members of the tax on tradesmen, the *collatio lustralis* or *chrusarguron*.

Fifth, as we have seen, there is no proof that the association of builders intervened in the wage-bargaining between employers and workers.

This association, then, was not, like the arms factory in Sardis, run by the state; nor did it primarily serve the state, prior to the agreement of AD 459. Moreover, no extension of state control is envisaged in the document. In one sense, then, the agreement changed little. The most that can be said is that it set in motion a development which might conceivably have terminated in monopolistic price-fixing in the interests of an organized group

[17] Cracco Ruggini (1971), esp. 167–8.

of tradesmen. By agreeing to conform to certain minimum standards, the association was encouraging the public to deal with them, and so increasing its chances of dominating the building trade in the city. Buckler was one of those who believed that the Sardians were *already* operating in a syndicalist spirit; and he cited a cluster of imperial constitutions to strengthen his case, as if they reflect a similar situation. The earliest of these constitutions is dated to AD 473 from the reign or Leo, and bans monopolies (*Cod.Iust.* 4.59.1). If Leo gave a definition of monopoly and provided examples, these were contained in the missing first part of the constitution. The background, however, is clear. Monopoly rights had been conferred by imperial rescript (ultimately secured through the intervention of a high official); they are now withdrawn and declared invalid, presumably because they had been abused. Next, in a constitution of 483 (*Cod.Iust.* 4.59.2.1), Zeno addresses to the prefect of the city of Constantinople an order against those responsible for provisioning the capital (several examples are given) and against price-fixing among such trades. It is not until the next clause that building is specifically mentioned – as follows:

> Building artisans and men undertaking such work ... must likewise be prevented from making among themselves agreements intended to restrain anyone from completing a piece of work entrusted to another man ... and every man shall have the right to complete without fear or injury of any kind, a piece of work begun by another when abandoned by him.

The constitution goes on in the final clause to restate the emperor's opposition to monopolies and to threaten the leaders, *primates*, of the several essential trades with heavy fines if they conspire to raise prices above accepted or acceptable levels.

The preface and clauses two and three, in which alone monopolies and price-fixing are specified, do not appear to have been aimed at builders. When builders are mentioned by name, in clause one, they are charged, curiously, with nothing more than organized intimidation of any worker trying to complete a job left unfinished, presumably by one of them.

Finally the Justinianic Code preserves a long and comprehensive constitution on building from the same emperor, Zeno (*Cod.Iust.* 8.10.12.9); this is also addressed to the prefect of Constantinople, and concludes with a wordy complaint against certain offences:

> Your magnificence will see to it that no man undertaking work and no artisan who has begun a piece of work shall abandon it unfinished, but the same man who began it, if he received the wages, must be compelled to complete the work, or else to pay for the injury thereby inflicted on the

person building and for all damage resulting from the non-completion of the work . . . No workman of the same craft must be hindered from completing work begun by another, for this we know is boldly done by men undertaking work and by artisans to the detriment of persons building houses; these men neither deliver a finished product to the persons for whom they began to work, nor permit others to complete the same, but contrive thus to inflict intolerable loss upon those erecting the houses. Any man declining to complete what another began for the mere reason that another began it shall himself be subject to a penalty similar to that of the man who abandoned the work.

The offences, then, are those of the constitution of 483: unfinished work and intimidation. Conspiracy to intimidate is a new complaint since the Sardis document, which envisages only obstruction by an individual workman. But if this is the only novelty, then the building industry even in the capital city had not advanced very far along the road to the closed shop, monopolistic price-fixing or collective bargaining with employers. The builders of Constantinople were no more operating a closed shop than the builders of Sardis a generation earlier – hence the need for intimidation. If they were trying to establish a closed shop they appear to have had a very limited conception of the uses to which this weapon could be put.

To sum up: the Sardis inscription does not reflect the iron regime supposedly established by Diocletian and his successors. Nor does the inscription show a body of tradesmen asserting itself corporately with a view to advancing the financial interests of its members. To this extent Ruggini is wrong to place it among the texts held to illustrate the crankiness, *riottosità*, of late imperial *collegia*. Finally, building is not the industry one would go to *first* to find confirmation of Mickwitz's thesis. That thesis is applicable, if at all, only in a toned-down version; we might want to say that pressure exerted on the Sardian builders from outside created at least the potential for collective action by their association in the economic sphere.

It is necessary, in my opinion, to liberate ourselves from the twin notions of *Zunftzwang* and *riottosità*, and begin again.

This is a trade in which there has been conspicuous malpractice. Builders have gone from job to job, taking pay, but not finishing the work. The going sick clause (clause five) is interesting in this connection. It does not say straightforwardly that a craftsman is to be allowed twenty days off for illness, after which time a substitute has to be provided. It says this:

Should the artisan happen to fall ill, the employer shall wait 20 days, and if after such indulgence for 20 days the man should get well, *but neglect to work at that time*, another man shall take his place on the terms stipulated by us as to the man who has begged off.

In other words, the clause is aimed at the practice of using sickness as a pretext for throwing up a job. Sickness as a *legitimate* reason for abandoning a job would come under an earlier clause (see lines 23ff.). Three factors help to explain this state of affairs:

First, the character of the building trade. This is not a traditional, family-ordered trade. Its organization is fluid enough to let in a lot of 'cowboys'.

Second, skilled craftsmen are in short supply, now as always in antiquity.

Third, business is good.

It is this last factor which I wish to take up now. The Harvard excavations have revealed expansion and prosperity in the Western part of Sardis.[18] The area was completely transformed in late antiquity.

The Builders inscription to my mind reflects the very favourable employment opportunities open to those in the building trade in late antique Sardis. If business had not been good, then *economic* sanctions could have been expected to do their work, forcing the builders to put their house in order. But business *was* good, and the move to discipline the industry came from outside. The political authorities intervened. Even so, they pulled their punches.

The inscription and the archaeological evidence fit together very nicely. Moreover, they combine with evidence concerning other regions of the empire to suggest that the traditional picture of urban decline is a gross distortion of the truth. The thesis of decline is the product of an over-concentration on the literary sources and a neglect of archaeology, or a misinterpretation of archaeological evidence – I have in mind the common assumption that a reduction in the intra-mural area of a city implies a reduction in the area of habitation and demographic decline.

Some parts of the empire fared better than others. Asia Minor and North Africa saw considerable urban prosperity – there is hardly an African city that did not visibly expand in late antiquity – whereas Thrace, Macedonia, Gaul did not.[19]

A more subtle objection is that while large cities may have attained a certain level of prosperity – Sardis, Ephesus, Antioch, Nicaea – this would have been achieved at the expense of the small. There is no need to be seduced by this argument, even if it can never be refuted, except perhaps in the case of North Africa.

The more fundamental question, however, concerns the nature of urban economic life, the basis of the prosperity of cities in late antiquity. Were the cities dependent on wealthy outsiders, governors or occasionally

---

[18] Hanfmann and Waldbaum (1975); Foss (1976).
[19] This is not the place for an exhaustive bibliography, but see Claude (1969); Lepelley (1979–81); Patlagean (1977) 156–235. The contribution of archaeology was neglected in Jones (1964), e.g., 712–66, but not in Jones (1937).

emperors, or a few local men, for injections of capital? Were their traders involved in moving goods that represented for the most part taxes or requisitions? Were their artisans producing largely for the state and private patrons? That picture is surely a caricature: I find it hard to credit that the Sardian craftsmen-shopkeepers who produced metal goods, glassware and jewelry in abundance along the North wall of the gymnasium were cut off from the market; and I see the builders of Sardis as the nucleus of a group of artisans who were both moderately well-off, and for all practical purposes, independent.

That means, among other things, that there existed also a group of consumers whose personal expenses were a source of revenue for others, who increased demand and the level of economic activity, and stimulated production for the market.

Moreover, the construction industry can be considered as a creator rather than simply a distributer of wealth, inasmuch as it did not simply serve rich consumers, whether individuals or institutions (in having villas, churches or decorative public buildings constructed), but laid down a material infrastructure which served as the basis of further production (for example, roads, workshops, places of exchange, brick-factories).

It remains the case that the fundamental source of urban wealth was the land.[20]

[20] I delivered versions of this paper at seminars in London, Cambridge and Aix-en-Provence. I am very grateful to the participants of these seminars for their criticism, and to Brian Napier who discussed with me the problems raised by this inscription from the perspective of a specialist of labour legislation.

PART II
PEASANTS

6

PEASANTS IN ANCIENT ROMAN SOCIETY

I present in this paper a summary view of the condition of the peasantry under the Romans rather than case studies of particular peasant communities. I have two reasons for doing so. Firstly, because regional differences within the Roman empire were so extensive, the most reliable generalizations that can be made about peasants concern the effects on them of the policies and actions of ruling groups, both imperial and local. Secondly, given the largely static technological conditions which prevailed in the Roman world, we can assume that these policies and actions constituted the most significant source of change in social and economic circumstances on the land.

This is not intended as a comparative study. Nevertheless I will make some attempt to apply to the ancient world (for this purpose it seems appropriate to consider Greece as well as Rome) recent theories on the proper classification of societies and economies. Thus we will consider briefly the applicability of current definitions of 'peasant society' and 'peasant economy' to the Graeco-Roman world.

To judge from the relevant literature,[1] any attempt to apply the label 'peasant economy' to the ancient world would be misguided. It is assumed that Rome is to be classed as a slave state. Many Greek states are ruled out of consideration for the same reason. All Greek states fail to meet a requirement of size. Democratic Athens possesses the additional disqualification of having had a peasantry that can hardly be termed an oppressed class.

PEASANT POWER

Let us take this last point first. The peasants of Attica, and I am interested in the smallholders rather than the better-off farmers who might have hoplite status, had an active part to play in the political life of the Athenian

---

[1] In the term peasants, I include small freeholders, tenant-farmers and agricultural labourers. I discuss in detail here only the situation of freeholders. I wish to acknowledge my debt to Moses Finley.

state.[2] We may believe that they were drawn upon to some degree for service in the Council of 500, a body with important functions in administration and the legislative process, that they served as jurors in the public law-courts, and above all, that they joined in the meetings of a sovereign assembly.

The power of the assembly at Athens is indisputable. Athenian citizens were fully capable, for example, of dethroning and fining their leading statesman and general, Pericles, for pursuing a war strategy that they judged to be injurious to their interests. But are we to suppose that the peasants of Attica were present on that occasion solely because it was war-time, and they had obeyed Pericles' instructions to abandon their properties in the event of a Spartan invasion that would destroy their crops? Were the men of the deme Acharnai, to judge from Aristophanes and Thucydides the most vocal element of the peasantry, on hand in more normal conditions?

The idea of peasants moving back and forth between their farms and the assembly does not fit our preconceptions concerning the way peasants behave.[3] In Aristotle's 'agricultural democracy', the smallholders cannot 'often' attend the assembly because they have to work for their livelihood. However, Aristotle (whose preference was for a constitution that would disfranchise them altogether) assumes that they will exercise the power of electing magistrates and calling them to count, even if modesty and poverty prevent them from following a magisterial career and therefore from challenging the aristocratic monopoly of office (Arist. *Pol.* 1318b 6ff.). Now, one of the characteristic features of Athenian democracy was the institution of pay for offices and jury-service, and in the fourth century, for attendance at the assembly. As Aristotle acknowledges with disapproval in another passage, pay accords leisure to the poor (*Pol.* 1293a 5ff.). It is therefore distinctly likely that the farmers of Attica engaged in political activity rather more extensively than Aristotle would have liked. In any case, certain other features of the Athenian constitution made it more or less inevitable that they would participate to some extent: in particular, the quorum of 6,000 for important meetings of the assembly (this figure to be set against a constituency of about 35,000), and a council of 500 chosen by lot each year from male citizens qualified in age, a council on which none could serve more than twice in a lifetime. Finally, the peasants had a stake in a government which gave them a share in the material benefits of empire. The acquisition of land abroad must have

---

[2] On the hoplite census, see Jones (1957) 14, 135. For an introduction to Athenian democracy, see Finley (1973b).

[3] Farmers at furthest remove from the city would have had about forty kilometres to travel. See the map in Gomme (1933).

given a considerable number of them the opportunity of adding to their meagre resources, while sons would have found profitable employment in the Athenian fleet.

Democratic Athens is the great exception. Athens in the Roman Empire, || in, for example, the second century AD, was a totally different society. An oligarchy of wealthy and pedigreed families dominated the political scene and owned most of Attica, even if in scattered plots rather than concentrated holdings, or *latifundia*. The most prominent Athenian was the sophist Herodes Atticus. We cannot put a figure on his enormous wealth nor map out his extensive properties in Attica and beyond, but no aristocrat of the classical age could have possessed more than a fraction of his resources. This was a world in which peasant proprietors were being steadily transformed into tenant farmers, agricultural labourers, and unemployed and underemployed urban residents, throughout the area under Roman control (Finley (1973a) 99ff.; Day (1942) ch. 5).

A brief consideration of the role of the peasant in society and politics in Republican Rome will serve to confirm the uniqueness of classical Athens. Soldier-peasants had won for Rome its empire, first in Italy, later overseas, and they formed the bulk of the electorate. But there is little sign that aristocratic power was limited in any measurable degree. The oligarchic structure of the constitution and the institution of patronage, an effective method of social selection and control, denied peasants any influence in society and politics. As possible concessions to the peasants one might cite the distribution of land under the government's colonial policy, the exemption of Roman citizens in Italy from direct taxes after 167 BC, or the employment of slaves rather than dispossessed peasants on large aristocratic estates. None of this amounts to much. The granting of land normally at some remove from Rome, and often in hostile country, to landless citizens cost the ruling classes nothing and in fact served their own interests and those of the state (as I shall argue below). The absence of a direct tax (in Italy) made subsistence farming a viable proposition, in principle; but the position of the subsistence peasant would hardly have been affected by the abolition of the *tributum* following the exceedingly lucrative wars in the East and in Spain: the tax was levied only occasionally, at a rate of 0.01 per cent, and probably not on poorer farmers. Finally, it is arguable that the decision to use slaves on the *latifundia* was based on the economic advantages of using slave-labour at a time when slaves were plentiful and relatively cheap, rather than on any political risks that might have been involved in the downgrading of a traditionally free peasantry. The fundamental fact is that Roman peasants had been forced to make, and would continue to make, enormous sacrifices for the cause of Roman militarism, and that the aristocracy responded by enforcing harsh debt laws, turning them off the land, and blocking their reinstatement onto the land. The aristocratic opposition to land reform is particularly significant, in view of the fact that the original reformers, led by Tiberius Gracchus, in seeking to revive the peasantry, had in mind not only humanitarian considerations, but also the current military needs of the state, which was short of manpower. As the recruitment laws stood, landless peasants could not be used as cannon fodder. Thus, in accelerating the demise of the free peasantry, the aristocracy was hastening the collapse of the peasant army. This demonstrates the lack of || foresight of the senatorial oligarchy – but also the impotence of the peasantry.[4]

The Romans, of course, had a peasant cult. Writers from the elder Cato to Virgil and beyond harked back to a golden age when peasants set the moral tone of society, and *bonus agricola* and *bonus vir* were synonymous terms. But the promulgation of this myth coincided with the displacement of peasant-farmers and the growth of *latifundia*, and cannot be regarded as an indicator of peasant power. The idealization of the peasant patriarch was then, as in the twentieth century, primarily an expression of the nationalist ideology of the ruling class of a militarist state.

SLAVES AND PEASANTS

In classical Athens slaves made up perhaps 30 per cent of the population. They were employed in all sections of the economy, including agriculture, wherever the unit of production was larger than the family, that is, the householder and his sons. Slavery as an institution underpinned the political dominance of the ruling class.[5] At the same time, we can hardly dismiss as of little importance the fact that the majority of the inhabitants of Attica were small peasant proprietors who depended in large part on their families for labour (Finley (1959) 56ff.). Rather than term Athens a 'slave society' or 'peasant society', it may be more accurate and informative to say that two different modes of agricultural production coexisted within the one society.

The proper classification of Roman society is a complex problem. What after all is meant by 'Roman society'? Is the reference to the whole area covered by the Roman Empire, including, for example, the great agrarian provinces of Egypt and Africa where agricultural slavery was virtually non-existent? Tenancy was the most common method of production in the empire taken as a whole. Indeed there are no good grounds for believing

---

[4] The basic reference work for topics in the social and economic history of the Roman Republic is by Brunt (1971).
[5] On Greek slavery see Finley (1959).

that agricultural slavery was dominant, or even widely distributed, in any province outside Italy and Sicily. For these reasons alone we should reject the Marxist thesis recently revived by Perry Anderson, that the ultimate responsibility for the collapse of the Western Empire is attributable to the slave system of production, the internal contradictions of which led the economy to disintegrate from within (Anderson (1974) ch. 4).

Alternatively, if by 'Roman society' we mean Italy, we must decide which period we have in mind. It is generally accepted that the slave system of production was in decline as early as the first century AD, so that in the most recent discussion of Roman peasants we read the following: 'What seems to emerge is a picture of largely slave-manned estates run as businesses until some time around the turn of the first to the second century AD. Thereafter, though the concentration of property in the hands of fewer, richer landowners continued, the balance of the work force tipped back towards freemen, both as tenants and labourers' (MacMullen (1974b) 254–5). The matter cannot be given full discussion here, but the following observations may be offered. First, large properties are securely attested as dominant only in the south and some areas of central Italy during the late II Republic and early Empire. Second, the expropriation of peasant-farmers did not lead inevitably to the absorption of their farms into large holdings.[6] Third, in some parts of Italy, particularly the north, the indigenous population was an alternative to slaves as a labour-force. Fourth, the small freeholder was by no means eclipsed, especially in the northern part of the peninsula.[7] Finally, as peasant properties were taken over by wealthy landowners in areas relatively close to the capital, others were created further afield as part of the long-range imperialist strategy of the Roman state.

Thus it is by no means established that the large estate manned by slaves working under the supervision of a slave bailiff was the most typical unit of cultivation, even in the late Republic when slaves are conjectured to have totalled three million, or about two fifths of the population of Italy (Brunt (1971) 124). Conversely, it is impossible to substantiate the claim that the balance between servile labour and free labour on the land was radically altered in the course of the first centuries of the Empire. The various

---

[6] At Veleia near Parma, where thanks to an inscription of Trajan's reign (AD 97–117) the values (and by inference, the approximate sizes) of over 300 estates are known, the more considerable landlords owned a number of properties, many of which were small enough to be worked by single families. Evidently not all landlords were interested in taking advantage of economies of scale. How far they understood this concept is a debatable point.

[7] See the evidence cited in Chilver (1941) 145ff.; Jones (1962), (1963); Kahane, Threipland and Ward-Perkins (1968); White (1970) 384ff.; Duncan-Jones (1982) 323ff.

explanations that have been offered for this supposed development are necessarily conjectural; some of them are also quite implausible, including the following: deficient productivity of slave-labour, inability of the slave-population to reproduce itself, changing economic attitudes among the upper-classes.[8]

Of the several themes introduced in this opening section which merit further discussion, the last mentioned raises the most interesting possibilities. The absorption of small farms by large landowners bears all the marks of being a 'natural' or inexorable trend. At the same time, the Roman authorities appear to have been engaged in the deliberate policy of setting up a 'new' stock of peasant proprietors on small allotments. This apparent inconsistency deserves investigation.

NEW PEASANTS FOR OLD

It is hard for subsistence farmers to survive and remain independent. Their margins are narrow. There is an easy slide into debt; small proprietors are readily converted into tenants of rich money-lending landowners.

Under the Romans, taxation[9] (from which Italy was no longer exempt from the end of the third century AD), compulsory liturgies and requisitions made the situation of smallholders more precarious. Yet their survival into the late Empire is well-attested, especially in the eastern provinces. In Egypt, the granary of the Roman world, the Romans inherited the administrative machine built by the Ptolemies. It was an oppressive order, characterized by heavy taxation and bureaucratic brutality. But some peasant-farmers retained their holdings, even in the fourth century and later (Jones (1964) 773ff.), when the trend towards larger concentrations of land in the hands of fewer, more powerful, men became marked. In Syria and the interior of Asia Minor, some autonomous or semi-autonomous communities of villagers held their own. Libanius, a leading citizen of Antioch, writing in the second half of the fourth century, knew of villages owned by one master, and others in the possession of many; the latter paid taxes || direct to the tax-collectors, an indication of independence (Lib. 47. 4ff.) There are other references in the works of Libanius to villages in the territory of Antioch that were prosperous and independent of the economy of the city (Lib. 46. 230). He might have had in mind, for example, those lying on the limestone plateau to the east and southeast of the city. There the archaeological remains reveal an area of expanding

---

[8] For these views see, respectively, Schtajerman (1964) 34–5; Anderson (1974) 77–8; Brockmeyer (1968) 289.

[9] On taxation see Jones (1964) 769ff, (1974) ch. 4, 8.

olive-production and steady population growth throughout the period from the second to the sixth century. Some communities are dominated by, or associated with, the well-apportioned mansions of wealthy resident proprietors, and their inhabitants presumably worked as tenants or labourers on their estates. In other villages of later growth, however, such as Bamuqqa, Qirqbize and Behyo, the remains of modest villas, each furnished with its olive-press, suggest the presence of independent cultivators.[10]

One should not exaggerate the independence of the small freeholders in late Roman Syria. Passages of Libanius and his near-contemporary John Chrysostom indicate how vulnerable their position could be. In the fourth and fifth centuries many of them appear to have held out only with the aid of powerful protectors in the form of large landowners or military garrisons, which kept the tax-collectors at bay, though at a price. Initially the price was the payment of commodities or money, but clearly the hold of such peasants on their property was precarious. In fifth-century Gaul, if we can accept the testimony of Salvian, bishop of Marseilles, peasants exchanged their property-rights for the security of protection.[11]

Nor should the numbers of the smallholders be overestimated. The society of the olive-growers of the limestone plateau appears an isolated and insignificant phenomenon when set against the dominant pattern of large properties and poor dependent hamlets in the Antiochene plain, the fertile valleys of the Orontes and Afrin, and the plains of Beroea and Chalcis.

But the situation of the smallholders of Bamuqqa, Qirqbize and Behyo needs to be further explored. Peasants cannot set up olive plantations without capital both to cover initial expenses and to tide them over during the ten to twelve years in which the trees are not productive. It has been suggested that these men were *métayers* like the *mugharasi* of the contemporary Near East, contracting with private landlords to plant out olive trees on uncultivated land in return for proprietary rights over a portion of the trees (and the land), when they began to yield a full crop.[12] It is conceivable, however, that the land was ultimately imperial and not private property, let or sublet to peasant-farmers on favourable terms, also on condition that it was brought into cultivation.[13] In the latter case, the nearest comparison is with some African *métayers* known from inscriptions of the second century, who introduced olive trees and vines onto marginal land on the fringe of imperial estates, and received in return the

---

[10] Tchalenko (1953) 383ff.; cf. the short account in Liebeschuetz (1972) 61ff.
[11] On rural patronage see Lib. 47, with Harmand (1955); cf. Salvian, *de Gubernatione Dei* 5.38ff. For the plight of Syrian peasants see also John Chrysostom, *Homilies on Matthew* 61.
[12] Tchalenko (1953) 414ff.; Latron (1936) 65ff.; cf. Despois (1940) 419ff.
[13] I have in mind state land leased, as was normal in this period, in perpetuity. See below.

right to possess the land and enjoy its produce, alienate or transmit it to heirs.[14] The absence of reference to either arrangement in late Roman documents suggests we should give serious consideration to a third alternative. The olive-growers of the plateau were perhaps members of a substantial class of peasant || farmers who certainly benefited from land-grants bestowed by the state. Each year, over the Empire as a whole, thousands of newly discharged veterans received perhaps 20 *iugera* or 12.5 acres of arable, on condition that a son followed them into the legions. Their land was also for the most part marginal or uncultivated, but they held it with full proprietary rights, and it bore no taxes (Jones (1964) 636). Were the olive-growers *mugharasi*, imperial *coloni*, or veterans? Their status, the nature of their tenures, and the character of their relationship to the large landowners are unknown. But under the conditions prevailing in the late Empire, only the veteran-farmers had reasonable prospects for survival, because their land was tax-free. It is hard to make a meaningful distinction between other smallholders and tenant-farmers,[15] in a situation where the mass of the rural population of the empire was losing such independence as it had earlier possessed.

Here, then, is the situation to be identified and explained. Conditions did not favour the survival of a free peasantry. The Roman state and its leaders as individual landowners and creditors hastened rather than arrested its decline, by weighing it down with taxation and military burdens, and by encroaching on its holdings. At the same time, however, a 'peasantry of obligation' was being created by act of state. For the new peasants, the allocation of land and security of tenure were conditional on the pursuit of worthy goals or the fulfilment of specific services for the state.

The creation of 'new peasants for old' was a policy forged in the initial period of conquest, in the course of which Rome won control of the Italian peninsula. It was then applied to a greater or lesser extent in the overseas provinces as they fell under Roman sway. These developments may now be briefly surveyed.

The allotment of land taken from enemy powers and rebel communities to groups of colonists and to individuals was a characteristic feature of Roman expansionist policy from an early stage. A similar policy was developed contemporaneously and independently by Alexander the Great and the kings who succeeded to parts of his empire (Griffith (1935) 147ff.). Alexander, who is regularly dismissed as a conqueror with no interest in and no plan for securing his conquests, put Greek mercenaries

[14] See Haywood (1938) 94ff.; 100ff.; Leschi et al. (1952) 97ff.; and below. The *lex Hadriana* was preceded by a *lex Manciana*, of which the scope and historical context are obscure.

[15] In any case, Roman legal categories never made much impact in rural areas in the interior of provinces where tribal society remained firmly entrenched.

or Macedonian veterans together with natives in a substantial number of cities and garrison-towns in strategic points in the far-flung eastern provinces of his empire. Again, the Successor kingdom of the Seleucids established soldier settlers, whose land-grants were conditional on their fulfilment of military obligations, in numerous communities in North Syria, Asia Minor and east of the Tigris.[16]

The immediate purpose of the Roman settlements was, similarly, strategic defence. But they also took the pressure off aristocratic landholders, who were building up their properties in more secure areas, particularly in the 'home provinces', at the expense of peasant proprietors. With the exception of those who participated in the small seaboard garrison-colonies || (300 colonists in each settlement), the settlers were not excused military service, while their children would be recruited in the next generation and make possible a further wave of expansion. There was no humanitarian inspiration, therefore, behind these colonies. They served the interests of the state and of the wealthy landowners and war-lords who directed it.

Confirmation of this can be found in the size of allotments. Ten *iugera*, or about six acres, might just produce sufficient wheat to keep alive a family of four (Brunt (1971) 194). Recorded land-grants to Roman citizens range from two *iugera* to (exceptionally) ten. Thus the first Roman inhabitants of Modena (Mutina) and Parma received five and eight *iugera* respectively. The figures may seem questionable, but they form a coherent picture, and are consistent with the traditions that the mythical founder of Rome, Romulus, gave two *iugera* to each of the original settlers, and the early yeomen farmers of Rome made do with seven *iugera*. We have to suppose that farmers supplemented their meagre resources by working as tenants or labourers on neighbouring farms, and put animals to pasture on unassigned state domain – which was often in plentiful supply, especially in the early days of a colony. It is clear that the authorities in Rome saw themselves as establishing communities of subsistence farmers, not rich peasants who might move into a higher census class and upset the political balance at Rome.

In this first period of colonization, which ran from about 338 BC to 177 BC, settlers in so called 'Latin' colonies received larger lots than their counterparts in Roman colonies – allotments of 15, 20, 30 and 50 *iugera* are recorded, the largest at Bologna and also at Aquileia, where 3,000 foot-soldiers benefited. The anomaly is to be explained by the fact that Latin colonies were unpopular. Those Roman citizens who participated in them

---

[16] Note, for example, that the first citizens of Antioch, 5,300 in number, were Athenian soldiers who had been previously settled at nearby Antigonus. See Downey (1961) 81.

forfeited their Roman status.[17] Non-commissioned officers and cavalrymen did better than footsoldiers at Aquileia, receiving respectively 100 and 140 *iugera*. The Roman aristocracy could not construct a community that was designed to have an independent existence without introducing a social hierarchy that conformed to their tastes. We do not know whether social and economic differentiation was allowed to develop by a more natural process in the early Roman colonies, which were technically not independent of Rome. A class structure might have been imposed on them as well.

The general impression to be derived of Italy during this extended period of conquest is one of fluidity, with land changing hands under the supervision of Roman officials or through the actions of wealthy private individuals, and the emergence of a social hierarchy also shaped by the Roman aristocracy. Ownership of land was crucial. Much of the land was acquired by senators and equestrians, who were, respectively, the political rulers of Rome, and the class of financiers and businessmen who were closely linked with the senatorial order by social, economic and political ties. Some land was held by docile supporters of the imperial power in the subject 'allied' cities, who were permitted to enjoy moderate or considerable wealth in return for quiescent acceptance of Roman rule. Most of what remained was carved up into allotments and assigned to soldiers, landless peasants, || and tribesmen. The beneficiaries represented in the main groups that had suffered from the war policy of the Roman state and the encroachment of large landowners, and they stood a good chance of suffering again.

By 177 BC the Italian peninsula had been more or less subjugated and there was no longer a pressing military need for colonies.[18] But the social and economic need for the distribution of land remained and was intensified. Accordingly, the disposition and use of unallotted state land – now in finite supply, much of it appropriated by wealthy landowners or rented to them – became a pressing political issue. The senate succeeded in heading off most of the proposals for land distribution. Three agrarian laws that were passed and implemented, those of Tiberius Gracchus (133 BC) and Julius Caesar (two, in 59 BC) are worth a brief comparison in terms of their scope and purpose. Gracchus merely set a limit on the amount of state domain (*ager publicus*) that any individual could work, of 500 *iugera*, plus 250 for each child, up to a total of 1,000 *iugera* (600 acres); the rest was earmarked for the poor. A few hundred families, basically dispossessed

---

[17] On Roman colonization in the Republic, see Salmon (1969); Brunt (1971).
[18] A few colonies were nonetheless founded in the period of the late Republic. See Salmon (1969) ch. 5.

peasants, may have benefited from the work of his Land Commission. In contrast, Caesar's two laws secured some of the best land in Italy, the *ager Campanus*, for 50,000 settlers, at least half of whom were land-hungry veterans recruited from the rural proletariat who had fought for Caesar's political ally Pompey, and were depending on him for rewards. Both the Gracchan and the Caesarian legislation were passed irregularly. But whereas Gracchus had caught the nobility by surprise by his obstinacy and his willingness to break with constitutional convention, Caesar used brute force against what was by now organized opposition. His victory presaged the end of the Republic. Henceforth the distribution of land and the patronage of the poor would be in the hands of dynasts. There is no doubt that the peasantry benefited by the change. In the last century of the Republic they had gained little or nothing; such advances as were made by individuals were nullified by recurring civil wars and chronic instability. Thus, for example, the colonies established by Sulla to reward his veterans merely replaced one group of peasant proprietors by another. Caesar in his legislation of 59 BC had not followed Sulla in expropriating the poor, but much of his work must have been undone by the two decades of civil strife that followed his death. In his brief career as dictator, however, he set in motion a vast programme of colonization abroad, setting a precedent that the emperors would follow. The next stage in the history of Roman colonization is linked, as was the first, with a policy of imperialist expansion.

The enforced social mobility that characterized Italy during the period of conquest has parallels in a number of provinces, mainly in the west, where the Romans encountered less advanced systems of social organization than their own and where pacification was a long process. Africa is a clear example. Exploitation of Africa's agricultural resources by Roman absentee landowners and Italian immigrants, who filled the vacuum left by the vanquished Carthaginian empire and the Numidian kingdom, proceeded against a background of military advance at the expense of the native Berber ‖ tribes, whether nomads, semi-nomads, transhumants or sedentary farmers (Rachet (1970)). The whole land was at the disposal of the Romans and one of the consequences is still visible today: centuriation. Centuriation is a gridded system of land-partition, imposed on a countryside as a preliminary to settling a farming population (Bradford (1957a) ch. 4). It is attested outside North Africa, for example, in Italy, Dalmatia, Pannonia and Gaul, but the Tunisian system is the most grandiose in conception and scale. Roman land-surveyors turned a large part of the country into a giant chess-board. A centuriation system is often centred on a colony, and colonies and cities of a quasi-military character were numerous in the North African provinces, intruding regularly into tribal territory and acting as a forward defence line against the nomads of the desert. In other parts of the Empire, particularly in the east, visible signs of conquest are less apparent. Where the Romans met an advanced culture and a social formation with roots deep in the past, there was no question of imposing an agricultural system from without and an alien pattern of landowning. The complex structure of Ptolemaic Egypt, for example, was carried over into the Empire without basic change; neither centuriation nor colonies are to be found in imperial Egypt.

As one might expect, Africa was an area where *latifundia*, imperial and private, were unusually common and extensive. A law reveals that imperial estates in roughly the area occupied by modern Tunisia covered 29,777 centuries, or 15,052 square kilometres in AD 422, about one sixth of the country.[19] But my interest at present is in the smallholders who received property under the imperial '*politique d'assignation*' in Africa (D'Escurac-Doisy (1967)).

The largest group were military personnel. From Augustus on, Rome had a professional army. Soldiers of the imperial army, in contrast to the armed citizen peasants, who made Rome the mistress of the Mediterranean, needed no initial property qualification and were guaranteed land or money on discharge after twenty or twenty-five years' service. Those who participated in the subjugation of the tribes in the interior of Tunisia and eastern Algeria were settled in large part in newly-founded cities such as Ammaedara, Thelepte, Cillium, Theveste, Madauros, Thamugadi, Diana Veteranorum, Cuicul and Sitifis, in the period from Vespasian to Trajan (AD 69–117). The military character of these cities is evident from their situation. Noteworthy, for example, is the triangle of three military colonies, Ammaedara, Madauros and Theveste, which hemmed in the unstable Musulamii on what was left of their tribal territory. Cities such as these provided a regular flow of recruits into the second-century army. That army, however, had a different character. Now permanently stationed at Lambaesis in the interior of Numidia, it drew recruits locally, and an increasing number of them were of camp origin. In other words they were sons of legionaries, born to Berber women, and their legitimacy and citizen status were made conditional on their entering the armed forces. As veterans they usually settled as farmers in the military zone in communities often promoted to city status in the || course of time. (The old military colony was phased out from the early second century.) In the later Empire the frontier was guarded by *limitanei*, soldier-farmers who held their land on condition that they defended their section of the *limes*. Barbarian *laeti* or *foederati* were settled on similar terms in frontier areas,

---

[19] *Cod. Theod.* 11.28.13, with Lepelley (1967).

especially in the Rhineland and the Danubian provinces where unsettled conditions had left land vacant. The presence of the *limitanei* and *foederati* is an index of the changed structure and disposition of the army of the late Empire (which now consisted of mobile forces stationed in centres away from the frontiers), and of its weakness.[20]

We know little about the size of veteran allotments under the early Empire.[21] The availability of land was one factor, its quality might have been another – certainly the veterans of the Rhine frontier, the remains of whose regularly-spaced villas have been unearthed near Trier (Wightman (1970) 151, 155), could expect higher productivity from their land than their counterparts in the sub-Sahara region in Tripolitania (Libya) or Numidia (Eastern Algeria). The rank-and-file soldier of the fourth century army received about 20 tax-free *iugera* (12.5 acres) of arable. The literary sources show that the allotment was regularly carved out of abandoned land in frontier areas (Jones (1964) 636). One may wonder whether a farm of this size was a viable proposition anywhere without tax exemption, and, we may add, without regular income coming to the family in the form of military pay.[22] The veteran farmers were a favoured class, one which the poorer sections of the population might do well to join, at least in relatively settled conditions.[23] But they were on the whole small men. Promotion through the ranks brought more substantial privileges and greater rewards but was open only to a small minority.

Land was also assigned to tribesmen.[24] Tribes that stood in the way of the Roman advance, if they were not exterminated (the African Nasamones, the Thracian Getae), enslaved (the Salassi of the Aosta valley, the Statielli of Liguria), or pushed back (over the Alps, into the Sahara), were split up, deported and settled far from home (in Italy, the Picentes of Asculum, the Ligurian Apuani) or pinned down in circumscribed areas that were all that remained to them of formerly extensive lands (in Africa, the Musulamii, Nicives, Numidae), there to learn the skills of sedentary farming on mediocre or undeveloped land. Many of them probably ended up as labourers on large estates. It should be remembered that the agricultural work-force in Africa was largely free.

[20] On the army of the late Roman Empire see Jones (1964) 607ff. On soldiers as farmers, see MacMullen (1963) ch. 1.
[21] One source for the early Principate, *Corpus Agrimensorum Romanorum*, ed. C. Thulin, 162ff., mentions farms of $66^2/_3$ *iugera* or 40 acres, but there is no way of telling whether land-grants were regularly set at this level.
[22] See Mócsy (1974) 239, in connection with veteran settlements near the Danube.
[23] For a short account of the privileges of veterans, see Garnsey (1970) 245ff.
[24] We do not know what rights over the land were conceded to the tribesmen. On the Roman treatment of the Berber tribes, see Syme (1951); Burian (1964); Rachet (1970).

Finally we come to the beneficiaries of the law of Hadrian 'concerning virgin soil and fields that have remained untilled for ten consecutive years', known from African inscriptions.[25] Some have thought that the dispensation (which afforded full rights of possession and tax-exemption for an initial period) was inspired by a desire to 'improve the lot of the peasantry', and was applied throughout the Empire. There was always an essentially practical motive behind any Roman *beneficium*, and here it was obviously the extension of the cultivated area and the raising of productivity. The long-term prospects of these farmers would have varied according to their backgrounds and material resources (about which the inscriptions give us very few clues). Any who were already property-owners in their own right, with a little capital, might have been able to widen the gap that separated them from the mass of tenant-farmers and agricultural labourers of Africa. But an ordinary landless peasant who endeavoured to take advantage of the law would have been a debtor from the start, with only a slight chance of establishing his financial independence. It is difficult to assess the wider significance of Hadrian's measure; we lack detailed knowledge of Hadrian's agricultural policy throughout the empire. It is known that he had the general aim of bringing abandoned or uncultivated land into production. In Egypt he lowered rents on deserted or damaged property belonging to the state, without, however, offering the farmers enhanced rights over the land.[26] Secondly, the 'Hadrianic cultivators' of Africa may have been a short-lived, as well as a local, phenomenon. In the fourth and fifth centuries imperial legislation returned time and time again to the subject of deserted and uncultivated land. But the laws were addressed principally to the large landowners, who alone were able to take up state land offered on perpetual or emphyteutic lease with favourable terms (in brief, exemption from a whole range of exactions and burdens).[27] There is no evidence that any of these benefits were passed on to the farmers who worked the estates. The laws do not comment on the contract of *mugharasa*, or any equivalent institution, and it is anybody's guess how far it operated, if at all, in the Roman period. As I have already indicated, the olive-growers of the Antiochene hinterland of unknown status and origin, who appear from the archaeological evidence to have been relatively independent, make no impact on the legal sources – unless they happen to have been veterans, or just possibly tenant-farmers who were also small freeholders and in a situation preferable to that of the mass of

---

[25] See note 14 above. The quotation that follows is from Piganiol (1965) 135.
[26] For Egypt, see Westermann (1925); Piganiol (1965).
[27] For a short account of such leases see Jones (1964) 417–19, 788–9. The device of *epibole*, by which landowners were forced to assume responsibility for uncultivated land in their area, is another concern of the laws.

coloni. In general, the laws were interested only in those *coloni* who ran away from the estate to which they were bound,[28] and in those freeholders who evaded the tax-collector. Thus, while it would be unwise to stake too much on the silence of the sources, the fact remains that the only substantial class of peasant proprietors for which there is documentary evidence in the late Empire consists of military men.[29]

The survival of the Empire depended ultimately on the capacity of successive governments to draw sufficient tax-revenue and military manpower from the agricultural population. The rulers of the eastern Roman empire, after losing Syria and Armenia to the Arabs in the first half of the seventh century, solved the problem by establishing and encouraging two classes of peasant proprietors, of which one bore the lion's share of taxation and the other contributed and supported the soldiery. The system collapsed in the course of the tenth century, through the encroachments of large landowners, which emperors either encouraged or could not prevent (Ostrogorsky (1966); Toynbee (1973) 122ff.). The freeholder of the Republic and Empire up to the early seventh century was always, similarly, a 'peasant of obligation', looked to for the performance of certain specific functions. But maintaining || the integrity of peasant tenures was not a priority for the Roman political élite, always dominated by wealthy landowners. Moreover, government policy contributed to the advance of the large landowners – heavy taxation drove peasants into the arms of powerful patrons who gave them protection while absorbing their holdings. The consequences were inevitable: diminished revenues and a crisis in recruitment. There was no way out, short of breaking up the large estates of private landholders. The rulers of the roughly contemporaneous Chinese Empire achieved this (Elvin (1973)), but no late Roman emperor had the requisite power or the will. The programme of resettlement and land distribution undertaken by the Roman government in the west was on too small a scale to cope with recruitment problems, let alone the heavy cost of maintaining an administrative superstructure and militia in an over-extended empire. ||

Addendum

Research on labour in the ancient world has long been preoccupied with slavery, with a side-line on farm-tenancy and the 'colonate'. Inspired by peasant studies

---

[28] On the tied colonate see Jones (1964) 795ff.
[29] I exclude from consideration the poorest *curiales* or city councillors, who might own as little as 25 *iugera* of land, on the grounds that they were required by law to be absentee landlords. Veterans who took up trade and business rather than landowning also disqualify themselves. See *Cod. Theod.* 12.1.33; 12.18.2; 7.20.3.

of more recent periods, this paper focuses instead on peasants in general. G. deals with the political economy of the peasantry of Athens and Rome, arguing that elements of a peasant society and a slave society coexisted within Athens, and advances the notion of a cycle, whereby peasants were drafted into the army and were later returned to the land as farmers, as the underlying mechanism of Roman imperial expansion.

This study touches on various more general aspects of Greek and Roman society that cannot be followed up here in any detail. Greek peasants (pp. 91-4) have been the focus of work by Gallant (1991) and Burford (1993); see also Sallares (1991). Greek rural life between farming and fighting is discussed by Foxhall (1993). On political participation (pp. 91-2), see, e.g., Carter (1986) 76-98. The role of the free peasant-citizen in the making of Athenian political institutions and culture – what G. calls the 'great exception' (p. 93) – is examined by Wood (1988) and more fully by Hanson (1995) (cf. Cartledge (1995)).

On Roman peasants (p. 93 and passim), see Frayn (1979); Evans (1980a) (a much-needed critique of the former consensus, now outdated, on the decline of the free rural population of Roman Italy) and (1980b) (on the peasant economy); cf. also Evans (1991). The question of the decline or survival of the Italian peasantry (p. 95) is also discussed by Bringmann (1985) and De Neeve (1984b). De Ligt (1990) (1991) (1993) 106-98 argues for an integration of peasants into systems of market exchange. On ancient peasants in general, see also Zoepffel (1988); Kolendo (1993). The residence patterns of Roman peasants (cf. pp. 99-100) are discussed in chapter 7. On the 'colonate' (p. 105), see Krause (1987) 88-155; Marcone (1988); Panitschek (1990); Rosafio (1991) 127-216; Vera (1992-3); Sirks (1993); and cf. below, chapter 9, on late antiquity.

7

WHERE DID ITALIAN PEASANTS LIVE?

I

Until recently this was a question that was not asked. It was not asked because there was a prior question that *was* asked, and that received a negative answer: Did peasant proprietors survive in significant numbers in the late Republic or early Empire?[1]

The consensus of opinion has been that they were always to be found, but that they were relatively few. As the traditional rural economy of which they had been the characteristic feature gave way under the impact of new economic forces, they became a residual phenomenon. Moreover, this development had already occurred by the late second century BC.[2]

It is to be noted that peasant proprietors, small farmers working the land they owned, rather than free cultivators as a whole, have usually been the object of inquiry. The roles of tenancy in the late Republic and of wage labour in all periods have rarely been positively evaluated. Again, the idea that small owner-cultivators, tenant-farmers and day-labourers were overlapping categories in ancient Italy has been little developed in the scholarly literature.[3]

---

[1] This article is a version of a paper read to the Cambridge Philological Society on 22 February 1979. I am grateful to P. A. Brunt, M. H. Crawford, R. P. Duncan-Jones, M. W. Frederiksen and to members present at the meeting for helpful comments, to G. B. D. Jones for discussing with me the Apulian evidence, and to G. Barker, J. Lloyd and D. Webley for allowing me to see their report on the Molise survey in advance of publication. The debt I owe to earlier writing on the subject of Roman agrarian history is obvious.

[2] Full documentation cannot be attempted here. Heitland (1921) 182 refers once to the survival of peasant-farmers, in a gloss on Varro *Rust.* 1.17.2. In Toynbee (1965) the massive argumentation for the eclipse of peasant proprietors quite overshadows the qualifications introduced (251–2; ch.VI: Annex v 563–7, showing familiarity with much of the archaeological evidence which might have persuaded him to modify his conclusions). The review of Toynbee by Gabba (1976) endorses Toynbee's views, at least with reference to Central and Southern Italy. No change of basic position is detectable in Gabba (1977), esp. 271,273–4,283. See also the different approach but similar conclusions of Staerman (1969), e.g. 5.

[3] For Heitland (1921) the terms 'small farmer', 'peasant farmer', 'peasant proprietor' are synonymous. On p. 157 he correlates private tenancies with a shortage of free labour,

The literary sources for Roman agrarian history are largely responsible for these prevailing attitudes. They have long monopolized the attention of ancient historians, despite their more or less obvious inadequacies.[4] The supposed rout of the free peasantry in the second century BC is grounded in the accounts of the Gracchan crisis of Appian and Plutarch and the even briefer generalizations of Sallust. On the other side we now have studies of military manpower resources and recruitment practices (based ultimately of course on literary sources) which show that the rural districts contributed the bulk of the very considerable number of recruits enrolled in the army in the first century BC as well as in the second,[5] and assert that the class of free cultivators from which they came formed the majority of the inhabitants of Italy throughout this period.[6]

The proportion of slave to free cultivators in every period must be a matter for conjecture. Scholars will also continue to arrive at different assessments of the extent of the decline of small landowners and of free agricultural labour in general, the degree to which colonial settlements and land assignations compensated for that decline, and the dimensions of the increase in the proportion of free farmers (tenants rather than small owners) after the reign of Augustus, contemporaneously with a putative fall in slave numbers. But I ll believe it can now be convincingly argued that the free labouring class as a whole was much larger than has usually been thought and, correspondingly, that the role of slave labour in Italian agriculture has been overestimated.

In addition to the general historical sources, the agricultural writers can be seen to have contributed to the underestimation of the role of free labour and the lack of interest in the world of the free cultivator. The very accessibility of the slave-estate in their works – with the notorious

---

which he appears to see as an early imperial phenomenon (cf. 161). He notes references to tenancy in *pro Caecina* (190) and in Varro (183), and other references in various speeches of Cicero to tenants of state land in Campania (177; 198) and Sicily (194), but concludes too conservatively that tenant farmers 'were no exception at this time, though perhaps not a numerous class' (195). One is left with the strong impression that Heitland is unwilling or unable to rise above the texts of Varro and the others, which, as he regularly complains, are marked by serious omissions. Thus, valuable insights (such as the blending of free and slave labour on the slave-estate, 171) are left undeveloped. On individual points his discussion has been improved upon but only relatively recently. See e.g. on private tenancies work by Brunt (1962) 71 and Finley (1976). On tenancies of *ager publicus* see Gabba (1977) building on major articles by G. Tibiletti published in *Athenaeum* between 1948 and 1950, and *idem* (1955). For slave-*coloni*, who are well attested under the Empire but might also have to be reckoned with in the Republican period, see Staerman and Trofimova (1975) 43–50.

[4] These are best discussed by Frederiksen (1970–1).
[5] Brunt (1962), (1971); Hopkins (1978a); adumbrated by Gabba (1976) 24.
[6] Hopkins (1978a) 67–9.

exception of the *Georgics* in which Virgil managed never to hint at the existence of a slave work-force in agriculture – has I suspect played a part. More importantly, the aims of the agronomists, which led them to focus on those aspects of contemporary farming practice which could (and, in their opinion, should) be changed, ruled out consideration of traditional 'peasant' farming. It is this, not the supposed isolation of the slave-estate from its environment, which explains their neglect of the related topic of the nature of the rural community that lay beyond the limits of the villa-system. There is nothing in Cato, Varro or Columella to justify the view that the slave-estate was virtually a self-contained unit, and this can be refuted by judicious citation from the texts themselves.[7] In fact one can show with reference to the treatises in question that what might be called the slave and peasant systems of production not only coexisted – in the sense that the free labouring class, consisting of the overlapping categories of freeholders, tenant-farmers and the landless poor, made a major contribution of labour on as well as off the slave estate – but were also to an important extent interdependent in terms of labour.[8]

But no amount of reinterpretation can conceal the limitations of the literary sources. We should therefore ask how, if at all, the gaps in our knowledge can be filled, and in particular how the role of archaeology should be assessed. That it has some contribution to make is beyond dispute. For example, field archaeology has shown that free cultivators were more important in certain times and places than was once supposed. Those who derived their picture of Southern Etruria from the literary sources, and particularly from a famous anecdote of Plutarch (*Ti. Gracch.* 8), might well have been surprised by the results of the surveys conducted in that region in the last two decades, revealing small-unit farms as a major feature in Republican and early Imperial times.[9] Again, archaeological evidence has given rural Samnium, traditionally regarded as a culturally backward and underpopulated region, a rather more civilized and vigorous look. The old view reaffirmed by Salmon derives from the very sketchy literary sources – Salmon's 'deprived mountain dwellers' are precisely Livy's *montani atque agrestes*.[10] Now we have a full report of an archaeological survey of the Biferno valley, Molise, on the borders of Samnium.[11] In both the upper and lower valley was found 'a dense pattern of rural

---

[7] Modern interpreters of the agronomists have similarly tended to neglect peasants and the peasant community, whether or not they have believed that the Catonian ideal of autarky was actually realized in the slave estate. No challenge to this way of thinking was provided by the traditional archaeologist, with his preference for uncovering fine public buildings on urban sites and luxury villas in suburban or rural areas.

[8] Garnsey (1980) [= chapter 8].   [9] See the summary by Potter (1979) 1–18.

[10] Salmon (1967) 77; Livy 9.13.7.   [11] Barker, Lloyd and Webley (1978) cf. Barker (1977).

classical settlement', comparable with that identified in Southern Etruria. How much of this might have been inferred from the literary sources? The authors' own comment will suffice: ||

> In some respects therefore the archeological record of classical settlement in the lower Biferno valley corroborates the documentary tradition. On the one hand, the survey evidence and the sources both suggest an arable landscape with few major centres but high rural population densities. On the other hand, whereas the classical authors could only allow us to generalize about shepherd communities in the upper valley and mixed farming in the lower valley, the project has discovered a complex mosaic of settlement that could not be inferred from the sources.

Until relatively recently, the work of archaeologists could be ignored by historians more or less with impunity. W. E. Heitland's classic *Agricola, A study of agriculture and rustic life in the Greco-Roman world from the point of view of labour* (1921), was written as far as I can see entirely from the literary sources. Heitland was not a narrow scholar: his concluding pages discuss the doctrines of Leninite Bolshevism on wage labour and the peasantry, an appendix brings together citations from literature on modern Italy and some other countries, and among the headings in the bibliographical section are Medieval and Modern Conditions, and Special American Section. The truth is that if Heitland had been interested in rural habitation patterns, he would have received very little guidance from earlier and contemporary scholarship, from the several studies of the institutions and status of rural communities[12] or the largely descriptive work on centuriation systems.

Nowadays the historian runs greater risks if he omits to consider archaeological evidence or nods in the direction of archaeology without assimilating its findings. Nicolet's detailed discussion of the rural economy in his excellent new history of the Republic makes brief reference to the field surveys conducted in Apulia and Etruria, and cites, apparently with approval, their conclusion that 'la plupart des exploitations demeuraient fondées sur la polyculture et étaient d'ailleurs de taille assez réduite'. But this sentence is not integrated with the rest of the discussion, which soon reverts to the familiar literary evidence.[13]

On the other side, one can rehearse the usual criticisms levelled at archaeology and archaeologists:[14] the chronological vagueness of much of the published evidence; the inability of archaeologists to identify the status of smallholdings (tenancies or owner-cultivated farms?); the difficulties they experience in trying to fit field-systems to farmsteads and calculate

---

[12] See e.g. Kornemann (1905) 72. [13] Nicolet (1977) 106, cf. 109.
[14] See, briefly, Brunt (1971) 352-3 on S. Etruria.

their size. To take up only this last point: although Nicolet's verdict that 'most enterprises were relatively small' ('de taille assez réduite') is imprecise, has the archaeologist told us more, or can he tell us more? Jones assigned a maximum of ten *iugera* (six acres, 2.5 hectares) to each of six sites on the Monte Forco ridge in the Ager Capenas north of Rome, but the field reports from Southern Etruria are otherwise, I believe, empty of such information.[15] Bradford's preliminary reports on the Tavoliere in Northern Apulia[16] – he published no full report – merely whet the appetite with || their brief reference to internal sub-divisions within the system of centuriation. Bradford deduced from the vestiges of centuriation in the territory of Pola that the original colonists had received allotments of fifty *iugera* (thirty acres, 12.5 hectares), or one quarter of a century.[17] Information of this kind is available in other areas as well, but has been inadequately reported. Indeed the most serious complaint against the archaeologists is that they have not reported their surveys in sufficient detail,[18] and of course that the number of surveys they have conducted is still too few. But this is only another way of saying that historians rely on them for vital data that can be derived from no other source.

To sum up the discussion to this point: recent work by historians and archaeologists has indicated that the traditional 'peasant' agriculture was more resilient in late Republican Italy than has been supposed, or, at least, that free cultivators of whatever status and condition continued to make an important contribution of labour both on and off the slave-estate. In the light of these findings, the matter of the residential base of free agricultural workers, the extent to which they lived in towns or in scattered farms and villages, takes on added significance. The very least that can be said is that this is an issue that can hardly now be neglected by students of the economy and organization of the slave-estate. Finally, agrarian history must draw on archaeological as well as literary evidence where it is available. There is no branch of this topic where archaeology has nothing to contribute, and in any inquiry into rural settlement patterns it must be conceded a role of special significance.

It would however be unrealistic to end this introductory section without issuing a warning concerning the inadequacy of all the ancient sources – literary, epigraphical and archaeological – when it comes to the task of

---

[15] Jones (1963) 147. Comments such as those of Duncan (1958) 97 n.74 are, however, of a similar order: 'The density of Roman sites is approximately 3 per sq. km.'
[16] Bradford (1949), (1950).
[17] Bradford (1957a) 177; cf. 168–9 with Plate 39 (Padova, Cesena, etc.).
[18] This charge can certainly not be levelled at Trousset (1977). This is the most successful attempt I have seen to fit together the evidence for centuriation and habitation. See further n.78.

revealing and analyzing the broad significance of rural settlement patterns. In this matter we must turn to comparative evidence for enlightenment, and it is with evidence of this kind that I introduce the main theme of this paper.

II

'Commuting' peasants and the 'agro towns' where they live, geographically separated from the land they work, are typical features of Mediterranean regions today, Southern Italy and Sicily included. In Northern Italy and most of Central Italy large concentrations and substantial villages or towns are unusual, while dispersed settlement in the form of small villages, hamlets and open farmsteads, prevails.[19]

Contemporary anthropological studies, notably those of Silverman on an Umbrian village and Davis on a community in the Metaponto,[20] confirm the contrast and show that more is at stake than simply patterns of settlement: there are profound differences in land tenure arrangements, owner-cultivator relationships, inheritance systems and family structure. In an article[21] Silverman || has schematized the major differences between North and South (strictly, in her analysis, Centre and South), thus: in the Deep South, constituting most of Abruzzi, Molese and Lucania, the interior hills of Campania, scattered parts of Apulia and most of Calabria, she finds:

(1) farms are typically small, irregular and scattered;
(2) they are worked by peasants living some distance away, in agro-towns, with the countryside left virtually uninhabited;
(3) cultivators are isolated both from owners (who are genuine absentees) and from each other; hired labour rather than exchange labour is the norm;
(4) property is continually circulating;
(5) the nuclear as opposed to the extended family is preferred.

In Central Italy, that is, Emilia, Tuscany, Umbria, Marche and parts of Abruzzi, she found:

(1) mezzadria or share contracts of one form or another predominate;
(2) landlords and cultivators are closely linked in patron-client relationships;
(3) the characteristic community consists of, on the one hand, separated but interdependent town centres, typically the residences of landlords, and, on the other hand, dispersed countryside settlements where the cultivators live, on or near the land;

---

[19] For the general picture see e.g. Dovring (1960). On the agro-town see e.g. Blok (1968) with bibliography.
[20] Silverman (1975); Davis (1973). Cf. Carlyle (1962).   [21] Silverman (1968).

(4) the preferred family type is the extended family, which satisfies most of its labour needs from within, and has resort when necessary to work-exchange with neighbours;
(5) continuity in control of landholdings is regularly achieved and the break up of farms is unusual, despite the legal recognition of partible inheritance.

The main lesson to be derived from these studies by historians of antiquity is that the rural settlement pattern in ancient as well as modern Italy can be expected to be correlated with a whole complex of factors, including mode of cultivation, system of tenure, material resources of cultivators, demographic conditions, physical environment, social order and public policy. How far our sources, including archaeology, can enlighten us on such matters is another question. The literary and epigraphical sources in general are sadly deficient, and it is fairly clear that archaeology cannot illuminate such matters as tenure systems, social order and public policy.

Beyond making possible this general observation, the benefits that the comparative method can bring us in this case are dubious. For example, while it is likely enough that settlement patterns differed markedly between and within regions in ancient as in modern Italy, it does not follow that a North/South or Centre/South division holds good for ancient Italy.[22] A distinction between urbanized and under-urbanized regions may prove more apposite. In the regions of Etruscan, Greek and Punic colonization (and some areas such as Latium or || Umbria influenced by the Etruscans), cities and an urban pattern of culture were well-established in pre-Roman times. Much of the rest of Italy was characterized by a *pagus-vicus* structure, where *pagus* has the sense of a rural division containing within it both isolated farmsteads and small population centres or *vici*, one or more of which might have emerged as a central place of refuge, a cult-centre or an economic focus.

Just as the North-South contrast is of doubtful relevance to ancient Italy, so it should not be assumed that any particular aspect of the modern contrast can be transplanted to the ancient context. This applies, among other things, to the agro-town and its correlates, a virtually uninhabited countryside and a peasantry alienated from the land. There is a risk that 'agro town'[23] and 'commuting peasant' will become part of the everyday vocabulary of historians of antiquity, before these concepts have been

[22] The great prosperity of the North in modern times in relation to the South and even Central Italy has no analogue in the ancient world, being largely a consequence of the Industrial Revolution, and to a lesser degree, medieval developments.
[23] Hopkins (1978b) 68: 'Village populations were sometimes synoecized, perhaps forcibly, into towns... Turning villages into agro-towns probably contributed little of itself to economic growth.'

properly understood and their applicability tested. It is difficult to resist the accumulated force of the historical geographer's speculations on the origins of modern forms of settlement,[24] and the 'then as now' comparisons of historians and archaeologists concerning the life-style of cultivators.[25]

John Bradford is one archaeologist who saw the reality of change in the landscape of Italy. His *Ancient landscapes*, the first major contribution I have seen on the subject of rural settlement in ancient Italy, contains the following suggestive passage, which I quote *in extenso*. The context is a brief discussion of the system of field-partition, centuriation, or *limitatio*, in the territory of Pola, on the Istrian peninsula at the top of the Adriatic:

> The sites of scattered 'villas' have given an indication of the manner in which the land was farmed during the Roman period. There are a few (very few) isolated farms today, and most of the land is tilled by peasants who live in the large villages and make long daily journeys in carts to their fields, starting at dawn and returning at dusk. The same thing happens throughout much of Southern Europe. But, as we were able to prove in Apulia, this was not always the chief basis of rural life, for there we excavated a series of small Roman farms, far from village or town, set at short intervals along the centuriated roads. In Apulia these daily long-distance journeys are common enough still, but small unfortified farms of single families are at last returning in numbers to this landscape which enjoys a newly found security. The needs of defence and protection in a compact village, and the very different structure of society in feudal nuclei from the Dark Ages onwards has, one may think, probably profoundly recast the peopling of the centuriated landscape behind Pola. From the far-reaching effects, this and other regions like it have not yet emancipated themselves. There is a strong case for systematic fieldwork on the ground in fresh search of the small and large Roman farms which should be found along the roads . . . It is certainly upon such problems – to discover how the ancient landscape really 'worked' – that || archaeology needs to concentrate as soon as the formal mapping of the traces is complete.[26]

The movement of country-dwelling peasants to new rural communities, or *città contadine*, for reasons of security, which reached a peak in the eleventh and twelfth centuries, is one development which breaks the tenuous thread of continuity through the ages.[27] Bradford, however, also raises the

---

[24] Dovring (1960) 23: 'The agro-town of Medieval Europe probably has its roots in the city of antiquity.'

[25] See e.g. Heitland (1921) 51; Toynbee (1965) 246; Scullard (1967) 63; Duncan-Jones (1982) 260; Kahane, Threipland and Ward-Perkins (1968) 70–1.

[26] Bradford (1957a) 176–7.

[27] For this development in the Ager Veientanus, see Kahane, Threipland and Ward-Perkins (1968) 164–79. At p. 165 they write: 'The pattern is clear and consistent. It was no longer safe to live in the old villas and farms of the open countryside, and one by one these were abandoned in favour of the nearest easily fortifiable site.'

issue of continuity between pre-Roman and Roman periods, a more central concern of this paper, and a matter requiring detailed investigation.

The urbanized/under-urbanized (or pre-urban) distinction already introduced may serve as a starting-point for a discussion designed to investigate the extent to which the free agricultural population lived in dispersed communities and farmsteads. It is a distinction employed effectively for example by Frederiksen, who in a recent article contrasts that part of Italy which was organized in cities, 'the Hellenized areas of the south, parts of Etruria, and a few places elsewhere', with those areas in which 'a large part of the Italian population lived outside walled cities, dispersed in small *vici* or in isolated *villae*'.[28] The question I wish to ask is how far it is true that even in the apparently urbanized regions of Italy the free rural workforce lived in cities. In other words, should we be prepared to accept that a distinction between nucleated and dispersed settlement coincides with the urbanized/pre-urban distinction that has been posited; and further, that the first of these distinctions remained genuine and valid during the Roman period?

III

We may usefully study this question first in relation to Southern Etruria,[29] perhaps the best known of the so-called urbanized areas.

Veii in Southern Etruria has been characterized as a city that in the Etruscan period maintained a centralized control over its territory and concentrated its population within its walls. Scullard was tempted to generalize from Veii on the basis of early reports of the British archaeologists. 'The fields', he writers, 'were largely tended by men who lived in the cities, if the evidence from around Veii may be taken as typical of at least Southern Etruria.'[30] How much of the territory of Veii, an area of about 115 square kilometres, and extending to the North as much as fifteen kilometres from the city, could be cultivated effectively from under these conditions is the pertinent question. In any case, the final report on the ager Veientanus reveals altered conceptions. The existence is now recognized in 'outlying areas' of 'small, open farms, no larger than would have

---

[28] Frederiksen (1976) 342–3, referring to the last centuries of the republic and 'well into the empire'. Cf. Gabba (1977) 273, contrasting Etruria, Umbria and the Greek colonies with the rest of Central and Southern Italy. For a summary account of pre-Roman urbanization in Italy, see Pallottino (1970–71) 11–14. For the under-urbanized or pre-urban area, see La Regina (1970–71); Gabba (1972); Laffi (1974).

[29] For North Etruria see the summary discussions of Torelli (1970–1), (1976). For a report on the ager Cosanus see Dyson (1978).

[30] Scullard (1967).

been occupied by the members of a single family'. Otherwise the land was farmed from the city: 'Besides the individual farmsteads, there are also large areas which were probably worked by farmers who followed the time-honoured Italian practice of living in the city and of travelling, often considerable distances, out to their fields each day.'[31] Meanwhile it had become clear that Veii could no longer be regarded as typical. The villages, fortified or not, that were missing in the ager Veientanus, were found in quantity in nearby Faliscan territory. In the agro Falisco, the town of Falerii was merely *primus inter pares*, ringed by a series of settlements, of which three of the closer ones (that is, lying within ten kilometres of Falerii) were sizeable.[32] Neither Veii nor Falerii was unique among cities of the region. Vulci and Tarquinia, for example, dominated their hinterlands in the Veian manner, whereas decentralized settlement was a feature of the Fiora valley leading up to Lake Bolsena or the ager Capenas with its five nucleated settlements including Capena itself.[33]

In short, this was an area organized in cities, and cities on average only about twenty-five kilometres apart. Yet the countryside was inhabited. Ward-Perkins sums up in this fashion: 'The preferred system of the Etruscans ... rested essentially on the city as centre of a territory wherein the population – *modo Romano* – lived dispersed in the open countryside.'[34]

As for the question of what if anything changed under Roman rule, this quotation signals the answer. Continuity between pre-Roman and Roman times is a theme of the report on the ager Veientanus: 'One will probably not go far wrong in stating that during the two centuries after the Roman conquest there was an intensification of settlement within the ager Veientanus, but no major change within the broad pattern.' And, covering as well the period of the Principate: 'Such open settlement has at all periods been an index of stable living conditions, and a beginning had already been made in this direction in Etruscan times. The establishment of the pax Romana greatly accelerated the process ... The early empire saw an intensification of, but no fundamental change in, the circumstances already prevailing in the second and first centuries BC.'[35] Moreover, there are indications that the expansion of rural settlement definitely altered the balance between city and country; in both the ager Veientanus and the ager Capenas the city became less a residential and more an administrative centre. Augustus sought to prop up the cities with benefactions in the form

---

[31] Kahane, Threipland and Ward-Perkins (1968) 70–1.
[32] Frederiksen and Ward-Parkins (1957).
[33] Brief discussion in Ward-Perkins (1970). [34] Ward-Perkins (1970) 295.
[35] Kahane, Threipland and Ward-Perkins (1968) 146, 148. In Veian inscriptions of imperial date mention is made of both *municipes intramurani* (*CIL* XI 3797, AD 1) and *municipes extramurani* (*CIL* XI 3798 = *ILS* 6581, Augustan).

of new public buildings and the gift of higher status (examples include Veii, Caere and Lucus Feroniae). At the same time, however, he was carrying through Caesar's plan to settle veterans in the countryside.[36] If we can trust the Liber Coloniarum viritane assignations had been made in various parts of South Etruria in the period from the Gracchi to the second triumvirate.[37] It is likely, however, that the expanded rural settlement of the Republican period was on the whole a spontaneous process, checked only by periods of insecurity.[38] It was the urban development which deserves to be called artificial and impermanent. A comment from the Faliscan report can be applied generally to the whole region: 'By comparison with the enduring facts and needs of rustic life the relative sophistication of the Roman cities and villas was a transient phenomenon. Even in Roman times many outlying communities must have kept to a way of life that ‖ differed only in superficial details from that of their Faliscan precursors.'[39]

We still await a comprehensive account of rural Campania, an area where cities were of ancient origin and relatively frequent.[40] Basic problems await solution, such as the origin and the character of the *pagi* which are so prominent after the reduction of Capua in 211 BC.[41] But whether they are old and tribal or a recent, Roman creation, their rural base is not open to doubt. The inscriptions attesting their existence and activity, archaeological finds and the evidence furnished by the historical sources, especially Livy,[42] combine to prove the reality of dispersed settlement in Campania. There is more than a suggestion in the literary sources that the subjection of Capua in the course of the Hannibalic War was a major turning-point in the history of that town and Campania as a whole, but even that is problematic. One leading authority denies that there is 'any reason to suppose that any great change was effected in agriculture after the Romans defeated Capua; the fertile plain of Campania was dotted with small agricultural settlements in later periods as in earlier ones'.[43] What then occurred in 211 BC? In that year it was resolved in the Roman senate that Capua be punished for its role in the war by being reduced to an *aratorum sedes*, a mere dwelling place and population centre, as Livy

[36] On Augustan developments see, briefly, Potter (1979) 111–15.
[37] The evidence is summarized in Brunt (1971) 351–2.
[38] For the civil war period see Jones (1973). Jones stresses the impermanence of the veteran settlements in this period.
[39] Frederiksen and Ward-Perkins (1957) 183.
[40] Frederiksen (1959) remains basic, but does not concern itself except in passing with the ager Campanus. Johannowsky (1970–1) is summary and impressionistic. Of earlier works, Heurgon (1971) is not much concerned with agrarian history.
[41] See the doubts expressed by Frederiksen (1976) 351.
[42] See Frederiksen (1976) 342 n.7; add Strabo 5.4.2.   [43] Frederiksen (1959) 123.

puts it (26.16.7–9); or, in Cicero's formulation (he is referring to, but not necessarily quoting from, extant documentary evidence),[44] 'receptaculum aratorum, nundinas rusticorum, cellam atque horreum Campani agri' (*Leg. Agr.* 2.89). The senate's purpose was to demote a powerful city, which it saw as a competitor to Rome, to the status of a rural village, and to deny it the functions and main characteristics of a city (*res publica*), in particular those of a political nature. It is interesting that Rullus' plan to establish a colony at Capua in 63 BC would have involved the *expulsion* of the *aratores* from the city, according to Cicero (2.76). His Rullan speeches have been called compulsory reading for 'all politicians who aspire to become proficient in the art of misrepresentation'.[45] Here the question at issue is not just whether Rullus' colony if implemented would have radically altered the social structure and pattern of life in Capua, but whether we should even accept the implication that the senate had introduced revolutionary change in 211 BC (and, moreover, that the 'new' social framework had remained unaltered in the succeeding 150 years). Recent research has asserted 'the permanence and vitality of Capuan traditions', in the social, economic and political spheres.[46] The consequences of this theory for the history and life-style of the free agricultural work-force of Campania, insofar as this survived,[47] remain to be explored. Meanwhile we are entitled to doubt that the countryside was emptied of farmers and produce by order of the Roman senate in 211 BC, and remained empty thereafter until a colony was finally established in Capua by Caesar in 58 BC. Capua was probably a *sedes aratorum* only in the minds of Roman senators seeking vengeance in the midst of a terrible war, not in actuality. And if the senators' intentions *had* been carried out, the new Capua would have been an anomaly among cities. ‖

It would of course be going too far to deny any agricultural workers an urban base, in Campania or anywhere else. In the small houses and shops of Pompeii (not only in the more opulent residences) a quantity of agricultural tools and equipment has been found, and this led Frederiksen to infer that large numbers of Pompeians were agricultural workers 'either owning small lots themselves, or else as farm-labourers, *operarii* or *mercenarii*'.[48]

---

[44] In the previous sentence Cicero might be paraphrasing a s.c.: 'Itaque hoc perscriptum in monumentis veteribus reperietis, ut esset urbs, quae res eas quibus ager Campanus coleretur, suppeditare posset, ut esset locus comportandis condendisque fructibus, ut aratores cultu agrorum defessi urbis domiciliis uterentur, idcirco illa aedificia non esse deleta' (2.88).
[45] Holmes (1923) 249 n.2.   [46] Frederiksen (1959) 122.
[47] The best known literary reference is Cic. *Leg. Agr.* 2.84 (63 BC). These small farmers can be assumed to have been tenants and labourers on both *ager privatus* and *ager publicus*. See Brunt (1971) 312–19 for the ager Campanus in the late Republic.
[48] Frederiksen (1970–1) 351–5.

Both are feasible alternatives. First, slave-estates needed free labour, and were commonly placed within easy reach of the cities, as they were at Pompeii, and as Cato advised. Recently extensive vineyards (extensive for an intra-mural area) presumably worked by slaves have been found in the area north of the stadium *within* the city walls.[49] Second, small-unit farming with the cultivator producing food for subsistence and a small surplus for the market was a viable proposition near urban centres, and must have been a common feature of the suburban landscape. What does not seem to me probable is that the tools found in Pompeii were regularly carried by commuting cultivators far from the town. Dispersed settlement, as suggested above, had long been a feature of the Campanian countryside, and in some areas, particularly in the south, it expanded in the period of Roman control.

In the 'Deep South' a rather different kind (or different kinds) of city is found, of which exemplars are Arpi in Northern Apulia, Rudiae in Calabria and Tarentum and Metapontum in the gulf of Taranto. They are large and sprawling – the city area of Arpi measured a remarkable 3.25 miles across – and their necropoleis lie within the city walls. But all these cities had extensive territories beyond the walls, marked by numerous smaller and larger settlements.[50] In the case of at least some of the cities of Magna Graecia it is helpful to think of the polis not as confined to one urban centre, but as fragmented into villages and farms, which between them controlled the agricultural resources of the territory. The tradition of a mighty Sybaris dominant over twenty-five cities is consistent with this concept of the polis, for which the Greek settlements in the Black Sea region provide useful parallels.[51] The Roman period saw decline in many areas of the South.[52] Both urban centres and rural territories were affected, and there was little appreciable change in the *manner* in which the population was distributed. In what follows, however, I argue, with special reference to North Apulia, that state-sponsored settlement, in the

---

[49] Jashemski (1973).

[50] Bradford (1957b). For Apulia in the fourth and third centuries Torelli writes of 'centri periferici' in which 'vediamo emergere gruppi di tipo intermedio, forse piccoli proprietari'. He finds some grounds for comparing these communities with the *vici* of the tribal areas of Central Italy, and continues: 'e infatti, alcuni di questi centri minori, anche se presentano dimensioni e tratti monumentali, paragonabili alle città, restano pur sempre strutturalmente una pura e semplice aggregazione di case'. See Torelli (1970–1) 439–40.

For Tarentum, see e.g. Stazio (1968).

[51] Sartori (1970–1) 47. The parallel with the Black Sea region is brought up in the discussion of that paper by both D. Condurachi and A. Wasowicz. See for more detail Wasowicz (1968), (1969).

[52] The extent and the character of decline in the South has been much discussed and disputed. See e.g. Kahrstedt (1960); Brunt (1971) 353–75; Small, ed. (1977) 97–101.

form of the assignation of land to colonists either outside or within a colonial setting, had the effect of stimulating dispersed settlement.

The Tavoliere, an extensive plain in Northern Apulia, offers an excellent chance of evaluating the purpose and the practice of Roman colonization.[53] Several systems of centuriation are clearly identifiable, at Troia (Aecae), Lucera (Luceria, two sets), Ordona (Herdonia, two sets), Ascoli Satriano (Asculum, two sets superimposed), and Ergitium. Aerial photographs have exposed not only the basic outline of the various grids, but frequently also the actual uses to which the land was put. A comprehensive survey of the whole system or individual systems might be expected to produce valuable data on field divisions and perhaps even a plausible conjecture concerning the relative part played by each crop. At the present time analysis of the available data is not far enough advanced to make possible full and accurate assertions about any section of the system. For example, we can deduce that the system lying to the East of Lucera is a very early one,[54] probably to be associated with the foundation of the Latin colony in 314 BC, but it is not known at present whether the viticulture which is associated with a later period goes back to that date.

East of Lucera a series of farms have been identified (and one *villa rustica* excavated), practising mixed arable farming centring on the production of cash crops, vines as well as olives. The farm-units appear to have been small (although we await confirmation of the figure of ten *iugera* that has been mentioned in second-hand reports of field-work undertaken first by Bradford and later by Jones).[55] The farms lie as much as eight to ten kilometres from the town. Without undertaking elaborate calculations based either on modern surveys or on Columella,[56] we can legitimately express doubts as to whether such farms could have been worked efficiently from the city.

Of course, small farmers do not always behave rationally or in accordance with the prescriptions laid out for them by geographers or bureaucrats. *Piccoli proprietari* recently returned to this area following the

---

[53] In writing this section I have benefited greatly from information provided by Professor Barri Jones. Published work on the Tavoliere includes Bradford (1949), (1950) and Delano Smith (1966).

On the practical side of colony-foundation the *gromatici* are singularly uninformative. 'As far as I know, no author tells us to what extent it was either expected or customary for colonists to reside on the land allotted to them. Hyginus Gromaticus talks about escorting them to the lands they had received by lot' (Professor O. A. W. Dilke, personal communication). See in general Hinrichs (1974).

[54] This system was laid out 'per decumanos solos', a practice applied in other early Latin colonies, e.g. Cales (334 BC), Alba Fucens (303 BC), Cosa (273 BC).

[55] Frederiksen (1976) 344; Toynbee (1965) II 563–5.

[56] Davis (1973) 99 and App. IV; Duncan-Jones (1982) 327–33 (Columella).

enactment of land reforms; but before long they boarded up their cabins and moved away to the city to resume the way of life with which they were familiar. Their predecessors in ancient times appear to have held out longer; one excavated farmstead had been lived in until the reign of Tiberius (after which time it was used as a storeroom).

The analogy with modern times and with the behaviour of contemporary peasants may well be seriously misleading, if it tempts us to explain the decline of the Roman farms in terms of the pull of the city and an alternative life-style, involving among other things a reduced commitment to farming. The collapse of the Lucera grid and the other systems of centuriation was in the end inevitable just because intensive mixed farming is atypical of a region which is naturally suited to a dual economy based on wheat farmed extensively and stock-raising.

This raises the issue of the policy which underlay settlement programmes such as this. What we are witnessing in the Tavoliere is the radical transformation of an existing pattern of land utilization by order of the authorities in Rome. Moreover, the cost of the scheme must have been considerable. As small men with no capital resources of their own, dumped in a strange place, were in no position to build up a farm of the kind we are considering, we must envisage state subsidies on a substantial scale.[57]

The establishment of a colony, or the dispatch of a group of settlers outside the context of a specific colonial foundation, was a major enterprise, taking normally two to three years. A large number of people had to be collected, moved, fed, equipped, established, and cushioned against one season or more of ‖ non-production. The sources are sparing in the information they provide concerning costs. From Livy (40.38.6) we learn that in 180 BC 40,000 Ligures Apuani with wives and children were moved down to Samnium at a cost to the public treasury of 150,000 units of silver. A special coin issue shows that nine million denarii were apparently set aside for expenditure on the foundation of Narbo in Gaul, probably in 118 BC.[58] Plutarch (*Ti. Gracch.* 14) says that Tiberius Gracchus proposed a law to the effect that the money of Attalus of Pergamum be spent on his land distribution schemes. It would be very interesting to know if any farms in the Tavoliere benefited from this bill (which can be assumed to have passed). The colony of Luceria dates to 314 BC, but the strategic importance of the site, on the northern borders of Samnium, means that numerous phases of redevelopment or resettlement are likely. Pottery

---

[57] Despite the possible implications of App. *B Civ.* 1.18 it is highly improbable that many of the (? Gracchan) colonists in Apulia moved into fully equipped and functioning farms.

[58] Information from Michael Crawford.

finds had raised the possibility that some of the Lucera farms were part of a Gracchan settlement. More recently a *cippus* found to the West of Luceria (about thirty kilometres from the city and probably within its territory) shows Gracchan commissioners present in the area and apparently assigning land. The date is probably 130 BC.[59] It is no longer reasonable to doubt that the Gracchan commissioners were responsible for much of the centuriation that can be witnessed in the Tavoliere, though they undoubtedly built upon already existing systems. But my concern at present is with the extent of the state's commitment to these operations. The Roman authorities were not setting up basic subsistence farms, but, at considerable cost, small unit enterprises capable of producing a surplus for the market. As indicated earlier, in the present state of our knowledge, very little can be said about the character of the farms established in the area after the capture of Luceria (and perhaps also after the Hannibalic wars, when Herdonia, Aecae and Arpi at least were deprived of substantial tracts of territory). It is not too much to suggest that the founders of the original colony of Luceria appreciated that its survival depended upon the viability of the farms allotted to the settlers. Viability and prosperity would have become in subsequent foundations ends in themselves, as the stability of the area became more assured.

That the Roman state was frequently much less generous to its colonists, particularly those of Roman status, is a major problem to which there is no easy solution. One factor to be borne in mind is the evident need to provide incentives to men who were surrendering their citizenship and being sent to an often distant, unfamiliar and dangerous place. Livy tells us that many voters at Rome had wanted the town of Luceria wiped out, not only because of the bitter memory of persistent and sometimes treacherous anti-Roman conduct on the part of its citizens, but also because of 'the remoteness of the place, which made them shrink from condemning fellow-citizens to an exile so far from home and surrounded by such hostile tribes' (9.26).

To sum up, in the South, as in Etruria, the distribution of land, whether to groups of individuals or within the context of a formal colonial foundation, had || at least the short-term effect of encouraging settlement in the countryside. I have no doubt that such land-allocation as was carried out in the ager Campanus both before 211 BC and between that date and the end of the Republic had a similar consequence.[60]

---

[59] Date conjectured from pottery finds: see refs. in n.55; *A E* 1973 322 (cippus). See now Pani (1977).

[60] I have in mind, for example, the colonies established on Campanian land in 194 BC (Livy 34.45), and such redistribution of land as officials of the Roman state were able to achieve in 173 BC and 165 BC. See Toynbee (1965) II 232–3.

IV

We may now consider the effect of Roman rule on settlement patterns in those parts of Italy in which urban life was little developed, focusing initially on settlement officially sponsored by the Roman state, its character and consequences.

Once again it is necessary to mention the practice of allotting land *viritim*, as a time-honoured way of disposing of newly conquered land.[61] The relation of the settlers to any particular nucleated settlement was often not an issue. They themselves, with or without the aid of an individual Roman magistrate acting in a personal capacity, were left to form their own villages and assembly points, or to revive those that had existed previously. In this way the character of the region was maintained. The population had always lived in villages and scattered farms; only the personnel had changed. To my mind this policy of viritane allotment in areas designed from the point of view of the Roman government purely for agrarian settlement, creates a presumption in favour of the view which is here advanced, that colonists participating in a formal colonial scheme were expected to establish a rural base.

La Regina[62] may have been the first to question whether the intramural areas of some colonial cities in Italy were sufficiently large to hold more than a proportion of the original colonists and their families. He had in mind two Latin colonies, Alba Fucens, where the city area was about thirty-four hectares and the colonists numbered 6,000 and their families, and Aesernia, founded in the land of the Samnite Pentri with 400 square kilometres of territory and a city area of only a little over ten hectares. The number of colonists at Aesernia is not recorded, but no Latin colony where figures are known received fewer than 2,000 colonists plus their families, and in this town living space was found for an unknown number of Samnite *incolae*.[63] Tozzi has taken the argument further in his discussion of Cremona.[64] Cremona and Placentia each received 6,000 families in 218 BC. The two cities barely held out against the rebellious Gauls and had to be supplemented with a further 6,000 colonists between them in 190 BC. Working from the figure of 6,000 families (about 24,000 people) and a city area of about twenty-five hectares, Tozzi calculates that about two-thirds of the colonists at Cremona lived outside the city proper. He notes further[65] that over 400 square kilometres of Cremona's territory were

---

[61] See Taylor (1960) 35–100. Taylor regards the institution of new tribes in rural areas – made up of viritane allotments without walled towns – as the *first* solution to conquered land (47–8).
[62] La Regina (1970–1) 451–2.   [63] Inscription published by La Regina (1970–1) 452.
[64] Tozzi (1972) 16–17.   [65] Tozzi (1972) 18–21.

centuriated in the first instance, or early in the colony's history (it may be that 190 BC and the following years is a more likely date for this operation than 218 BC). If the centuriated area was fully || occupied, then some farms would have lain as many as fifteen miles from the city. Any city-based farmer would have had a long way to walk to and from his place of work (supposing he did not possess a mule) and as a result would probably have had to farm extensively rather than intensively. In other words, he would have grown staple crops requiring a low labour input, particularly cereals, and primarily for domestic consumption. It is fair to ask whether colonists at Cremona could conceivably have submitted to such a regime and the Roman government have deliberately established farming of this kind on a large scale in the rich valley of the Po.

There are some counter-arguments. The calculation of reasonable living space is highly problematic (it might be argued); it is right that we should be told what a tolerable population density is thought to be and how any figure for this has been arrived at. Again, it cannot just be assumed that all the land marked out for allotment was actually allotted and occupied. Next, one may challenge the assertions concerning the distance peasants might be prepared to travel and the effect of this on their use of the land. Finally, one might seek to impugn the figure of 6,000 colonists with families.

The final objection is surely a desperate last throw. One cannot dispose of it altogether, but unless a number of texts are to be discarded, then it must be accepted that the Romans were capable of carrying out operations on this scale and from time to time actually did so.[66] The argument over the geographical relation of settlement to farm and the implications for land use is necessarily inconclusive[67] and cannot be considered apart from other matters (including those about to be raised in response to the other objections). One difficulty is that this argument inevitably involves an analogy with the modern world. If any comparison between ancient and modern is appropriate, then it seems to me to lie between the farmer-colonists of the Roman age and the *piccoli proprietari* of the modern reform schemes, and it supports the supposition that the former were intended to farm intensively and not to commute over long distances. How far and for how long any original directives were respected is another matter. The second

---

[66] See e.g. Brunt (1971) 56.

[67] Davis (1977) 45 states that the relation between settlement and land system is under-researched, and indicates that intensive farming is not *invariably* correlated with rural residence. In other words, there are always exceptions. Similarly, Carlyle (1962) 40 writes: 'All over the South he (sc. the peasant) lives in the agricultural towns and goes out from them to cultivate his land, which may be anything from 5 to 10 miles away'. But the various observers do not furnish identical figures; and mules, where possessed, presumably make a difference.

objection, over the extent to which centuriated land was occupied, may have some force in other contexts, but it fails in the case of Cremona, for the following reason: if the 6,000 colonists each received twenty-five *iugera* (fifteen acres, 6.25 hectares), as their counterparts did at Placentia, then over 400 square kilometres were assigned. This roughly tallies with the amount of land marked out for distribution. Now, a considerable number of nucleated settlements formed along the lines of centuriation, often at points of intersection between kardo and decumanus. Tozzi showed by the use of toponomastic, epigraphical and archaeological evidence, that many of these places had a Roman ancestor, whether at the level of village, hamlet, cult-centre or farm.[68] The point can be sharpened in the following way. The evidence often provides no more than a rough date from the imperial period for the existence of a community or farm which had a medieval and/or modern successor; it does not indicate conclusively an original or early pattern of settlement. Such a pattern is however demonstrable where a series of sites can be located on the system of centuriation which are regularly spaced and close together. Such series are in fact detectable on the Cremona system. Finally, although Tozzi's estimate of the population density of the city-area may be conjectural and is not defended by argument, the most recent and comprehensive discussions of this subject show that his figure of 320 persons per hectare is a relatively high one.[69] The further his figure is lowered, the stronger his case becomes.

To establish the case for dispersed settlement in the ager Cremonensis, I have employed a set of arguments which are not necessarily equally cogent in other instances. Without further detailed investigation (always supposing this might be fruitful), I can claim only the status of plausible hypothesis for my general theory that colonists participating in a formal colonial scheme, as well as settlers receiving allotments *viritim*, were expected to establish a rural base.

Other modifications or concessions, however, might have to be made. The first involves a recognition of the possibility of deviation from the principles, formal or informal, which might have guided the founders of a colony.[70] In particular it should be remembered that colonies, especially in the fourth and third centuries BC, were strategic outposts (*propugnacula*

---

[68] Tozzi (1972) 30–3. Some evidence for *vici* in North Italy is collected by Ruggini (1961) 527–30.

[69] For N. Africa, see Lézine (1969), who arrives at figures of less than 150 people per hectare both for Carthage and for lesser towns with smaller areas of streets and monuments. See also Duncan-Jones (1982) 259–77.

[70] The most obvious and radical form of deviation was the abandonment of a colony. See e.g. Livy 39.23 (Buxentum and Sipontum). It was difficult to get volunteers for some colonies. See Livy 9.26.4; 10.21.10. Many other colonies needed an additional draft of settlers.

imperii), vital for Rome's hold on Italy. As such they might in times of crisis have to serve the function of a simple garrison town, rather than merely a potential place of refuge. Cremona was one of a number of cities (Luceria was another) which assumed this role during the Hannibalic War. On the other hand, the intention was, I believe, for colonial cities to be or evolve into administrative centres, the domicile of the larger landowners, not primarily that of cultivators. In relatively settled conditions that is what they became. Italy was on the whole peaceful from about the middle of the third century BC, apart from obvious interruptions caused by the Hannibalic and civil wars. Moreover, the practice of disposing of land in viritane allotments in newly conquered and therefore potentially hostile areas, without establishing centres of defence and political organization, is distinctly problematic, unless we accept that dispersed settlement could be viewed as a way of controlling an area on which the hold of the ruling power was unsure.

Secondly, one must allow for the urban residence of some farmers whose allotments were located close to the city. I have already cited the case of the urban-based agricultural workers of Pompeii. The Molise survey shows that the small farms located in the vicinity of Larinum, as opposed to those lower down the Biferno valley, survived in the Late Republic and early Principate.[71] They may of course have fallen into the hands of the wealthy townsmen. However, Virgil's old Corycian who farmed his few *iugera* 'under the towers of Oebalia's citadel' (that is, Tarentum), serves to remind us that market-gardening was not exclusively a preserve of the rich (Virg. *G.* 4.125–48). But was he a resident of that city? Simylus, the 'exigui cultor rusticus agri' of the *Moretum*, lived in the country and marketed his produce in the town.[72] It is very curious that whereas we have both literary and archaeological evidence for the residence of small farmers in the countryside in the vicinity of Rome,[73] no

---

[71] For Pompeii, see above; for the Molise, see Barker, Lloyd and Webley (1978).
[72] Sed populi proventus erat, nonisque diebus
Venalis umero fasces portabat in urbem:
Inde domum cervice levis, gravis aere redibat.
Vix unquam urbani comitatus merce macelli.   (ll. 78–81)
[73] App. *B Civ* 1. 13–14 shows that Tiberius Gracchus had crucial support among the *rural* population. The archaeological evidence is presented by the various surveys conducted in the area North of Rome (see nn.15, 25, 32). The promised report on the Grottarossa allotments, beside the Via Flaminia between Rome and the Prima Porta (Kahane, Threipland and Ward-Perkins (1968) 148), might provide information relevant to the point in question; it is apparently seen as an aspect of the establishment of open farming in Roman ager Veientanus. Of the settlements in the area of Sutrium, much further from Rome (i.e. about fifty km.), Duncan (1958) 97 writes: 'There are only two of the larger sites which could have been the centres of estates of any size ... The number of sites to the square kilometre was very close to the number of buildings that there are today ...

source to my knowledge furnishes information on the free Rome-based labour force who must have hired themselves out to large landowners to take in the harvest and do other seasonal work on the slave-estate.

Finally,[74] one must assume that colonists of relatively high status, such as *equites* and centurions, often lived in the city. They will have received larger allotments than rank-and-file colonists in every colony,[75] and will have been in a position to put the management of their estates in other hands. They formed the political and social élite of the foundation. There is indeed at least in theory a possibility that all colonists were city-residents where the basic allocation of land was sufficient to enable them to hire tenant-farmers. Of the fifty *iugera* (thirty acres, 12.5 hectares) distributed to participants in the Latin colony of Bononia (189 BC) Brunt writes: 'These were generous allotments, more than enough for peasant holdings; and it might be surmised that the settlers were expected to employ Gauls as labourers or rent out part of the land to them as tenants.'[76] Elsewhere he acknowledges that this could only have been a marginal phenomenon, since in the great majority of colonies the settlers appear to have received 'peasant holdings'.[77] But need it be assumed, either that such colonists opted for urban residence more or less automatically, or that Roman governments saw themselves as sponsoring a class of absentee landlords in such cities? In any case, the implication of Brunt's thesis appears to be that the domicile of the cultivators was rural, while the city was the seat of the landowners.

In one case, but one case only, can the Roman authorities be said to have had it in mind to establish a city of cultivators. That was Capua, in 211 BC. I have already argued that Capua probably never was transformed into a *sedes aratorum*, and if it had been, would have been an anomaly among cities and can on no account serve as a model for the Roman or Latin *colonia*.

A *colonia* was, as the name indicates, a settlement of cultivators. That does not itself show that they lived on the land. On the evidence thus far

and it is quite likely that the type of farming practised was also similar in nature. This consists, in the main, of groups of small vineyards, alternating with fields of corn and plots of vegetables with occasional flocks of goats or sheep and a few cattle.'

[74] Blok (1968) 46 adds another motive for maintaining urban rather than rural domicile: he observes that in the modern context the scattering of holdings, the variety of supplementary jobs, the instability of contracts all make it sensible for peasants to live in a city and travel to work on the land. The relevance of this observation to the ancient world is to me dubious.

[75] Directly attested at Aquileia, Livy 40.34.2 (181 BC).

[76] Brunt (1971) 191. Bononia measured about sixty hectares within the walls and received 3,000 colonists with families, perhaps 12,000 people in all. A density of 200 people per hectare is not impossible, though high by North African standards. See Lézine (1969).

[77] Brunt (1971) 297, with reference to the first century BC.

presented, I am inclined to believe that they were expected to do so. One consequence appears to be that the foundation of colonies in areas where cities were unfamiliar was not incompatible with the maintenance of a rural settlement pattern based on *vici* and *pagi*. Within the centuriated area, a network of villages, hamlets and farmhouses grew up to coexist with and compete with whatever survived of the old.[78] The existence of settlements of one kind or another off the main lines of centuriation in the territory of Cremona and securely dated to the Roman or pre-Roman period suggests the survival of Celtic communities in pockets, despite the complete absence of Celtic place-names in the region.[79]

Meanwhile, beyond the limits of the system of centuriation, the basic structure || of the rural community does not appear to have been tampered with. To put the matter into perspective, it is necessary to add that *limitatio* affected only a fraction of the territories of the cities concerned – at Cremona, after the refoundation of the city under the second triumvirate, about 550 square kilometres out of about 1,400; at Brescia, some 800 square kilometres out of a massive 6,000 (and Brescia was only a colony under Augustus); and so on. In general, where the territory of cities was very extensive, as especially in Cisalpina, it was obviously quite impossible for the inhabitants to live chiefly in the civic centres.

Dispersion *modo Romano*, then, however arrogantly it rode over a preexisting pattern of settlement, was of very limited extent. Moreover, it is not unreasonable to suggest that it actually cushioned the outlying areas from the blow of urbanization. The process of subordination of countryside to city was inevitable; yet the vitality of the village was only gradually sapped. The *pagi* of the Appennine peoples, like their counterparts in the Celtic strongholds of North Italy, maintained a relatively high level of autonomy for a surprisingly long period.[80]

The Late Republic witnessed the phenomenon of the promotion to municipal status of selected *vici*, and, in areas of viritane assignation, of

---

[78] In a different context Trousset has analysed a somewhat similar phenomenon. In the area east of El Jem he identified two forms of 'habitat rural antique'. The first, Republican in date and reviving at the end of antiquity, 'est représentée par des petites bourgades', the second is imperial and dispersed 'soit en nébuleuse autour des sites précédents, soit sous la forme d'un habitat intercalaire à espacement assez constant pour ponctuer régulièrement le damier des centuries. Ces établissements sont fréquemment situés au centre ou à l'angle d'une centurie, les plus importants à l'intersection des diverses maîtresses'. See Trousset (1977) 203.

[79] E.g. Betriacum (Calvatone), Acerrae (Pizzighettone). One must assume a measure of assimilation of Gallic with immigrant families in both country and town. For the Gallic character of the population of Placentia, see Cic. *Pis.* 53. The toponomastic survey, accompanied by an interesting map of Celtic place-names, is by Bernardi (1976).

[80] Gabba (1972); Laffi (1974).

certain *fora* and *conciliabula*. However, with Gabba,[81] I do not believe that the so-called municipalization of Italy, culminating in the period from the Social war to Augustus, was in itself a cause of a decline in the rural population. The new or refurbished cities of this period in the centre and south (Gabba contrasts those of the north) were to some extent artificial creations;[82] they did not attract the rural population and did not accelerate the depopulation of the countryside.

The main causes of change in the rural areas are too well known to require more than brief mention here: war and civil disruption, the expansion of the holdings of the wealthy and the investment of the wealthy to some extent in new modes of production. Of these factors, the expansion of the properties of the wealthy is a permanent feature of the rural scene, providing the link between Republican and Imperial agrarian history. There is no reason to expect that any deceleration of the process of absorption of small by large occurred under the empire, especially as no action was taken in the form of settlement schemes to hold back the process.

What, however, happened when the rich expanded their properties? The Molise survey illustrates one possibility, the Veian survey another.[83] Until at least the Social war, the upper and lower Biferno valley was densely populated by farmers, often working properties only a few hundred metres apart, engaged in intensive polycultural farming – involving cereals, vine, olive, fruit, stock in the lower valley, and cereals, legumes, stock in the upper valley. The lower valley 'farmsteads' gave way to larger 'villas' at some stage; this could in principle have occurred at any time between the middle of the first century BC and the middle of the second century BC. If the new enterprises were all- || year-round sheep stations, which is one possibility under consideration at the moment, their arrival would have involved the displacement of small farmers – if they had not already disappeared.

The territory of Veii, on the other hand, experienced a multiplication of farm sites in the first 150 years of the Empire, and the newer foundations were mostly of small or moderate size. Some concentration of estates was surely occurring during this period, but if so it was not characterized by consolidation. Peasant proprietors were not being displaced; they were perhaps being transformed into tenants.

---

[81] Gabba (1972).
[82] The thesis should not be pressed too hard. To some extent there was a natural development of city centres, based among other factors on emulation of Rome. In La Regina (1970), it is stressed that municipal status was normally awarded to communities where 'la condizione urbana' had already manifested itself.
[83] Barker, Lloyd and Webley (1978); Kahane, Threipland and Ward-Perkins (1968).

There is of course no point in trying to estimate the relative importance of what might be called the Molise and Veii solutions in Italy as a whole, although, for what it is worth, it is conventional wisdom that the early empire saw an expansion of tenant-farming, and some see this as one side of a related phenomenon, the fragmentation of large estates. These are matters requiring further investigation. Another issue, which is closely related to the subject of this paper, is the extent to which tenant-farmers were, or were permitted by their contracts to be, absentees, or commuters. *Coloni urbani* certainly existed – Columella warned his readers against them – but there is no way of telling how prevalent they were.[84] Any landowner who looked for a steady return from his property and had invested considerable capital in it would not have been satisfied with a *colonus urbanus* as manager or labourer. Furthermore, any trend toward the downgrading of the material and legal situation of the tenant-farmer would have worked in the direction of reducing his freedom to move, not just from country to town, but from a particular estate.

V

A resident of one of the rural centres or hamlets of Samnium is depicted on a funerary relief from Aesernia. His name is Lucius Calidius Eroticus. He has come in to the town and is seen paying his bill for a bed at an inn, a flagon of wine, and a girl. He is wearing a countryman's cloak and leading a mule. The well-attested role of the ancient city as regional market, religious and recreational centre is important if indirect evidence of a populated countryside.[85]

The establishment of civic centres for *populi* organized in *vici* and *pagi* did not break the primeval relationship between the Italian peasant and the land; nor did state-sponsored settlement schemes of the Republican period and Augustan Principate. The emergence of 'investment agriculture' marked by the introduction of slaves as a permanent labour-force, the recruitment policies of an imperialist state, and the destruction and insecurity that accompanied the Hannibalic and civil wars, took their toll of the free peasantry; but their effect on the relation of the peasant to the soil was less general and more short-lived than has been thought. What none of these phenomena achieved was brought || about by the prolonged instability of the Middle Ages. The peasantry abandoned the country for

---

[84] Columella, *Rust.* 1.7.3. The *colonus urbanus* is characterized as one 'qui per familiam mavult agrum quam per se colere'. Columella apparently does not visualize a case where a tenant-farmer does not utilize slaves (*familia*) and is nevertheless *urbanus*.

[85] *CIL* IX 2689, utilized by MacMullen (1970) 338–9 (with Figure 1). I do not know why he assigns the inscription to Pompeii.

the relative security of the town. Where town-dwelling became customary, peasants became attached to it,[86] however inconvenient.

The agro-town, the essential feature of which is the separation and alienation of the peasantry from the land, was not in my view an ancient phenomenon. In ancient Italy, the movement of agricultural workers took place in two directions, from an urban base, from a rural base.

Addendum

Following up on the previous paper, G. tries to identify the habitation patterns of Roman Italian peasants. He rejects the application of the concept of the 'agro-city' to the Roman period and argues that the majority of peasants lived spread out over the countryside.

Since 1979, the results of a considerable number of field surveys have been published. For reviews of recent research, see, e.g., Patterson (1987) 134-44; Barker (1991); Curti, Dench and Patterson (1996). Barker and Lloyd, eds. (1991) is a good collection of pertinent studies (cf. Mattingly (1993)); see also Christie, ed. (1995). Potter (1987) 94-124 gives a general account of the countryside of Roman Italy.

Most surveys have produced little tangible evidence of genuine peasants in the form of small farmsteads (p. 111). Thus, the sites reported by Jones (1963) still remain the classic example. On small (peasant) farmsteads, see briefly Lloyd (1991) 236-7; Rasmussen (1991) 112; Barker (1995a) 225, 235-6. Rathbone (1981) 17 stresses the need 'to recreate from other sources the peasantry who left no archaeological record', and attributes dismal rates of recovering small farmsteads to the use of poor building materials and low standards of living. This pessimism is shared by Garnsey and Saller (1987) 76; Foxhall (1990) 108; Scheidel (1994a) 11 (with further references). Alcock (1993) 53 argues that it *is* possible to discover small sites. However, difficulties of interpretation persist: see Alcock, Cherry and Davis (1994) 163, on the problem of distinguishing continuously occupied small sites from seasonal bases; cf. also Wightman and Hayes (1994b) 45.

In his study of the *ager Cosanus*, Rathbone (1981) repeatedly draws on the present paper. He tries to show that because the upper-class villa-owners in this area would not hold more than 20 per cent of the land (21), most of the colonists must have lived in the countryside (17); the city was too small to accommodate their numbers (17 n. 30) (cf. pp. 123-6). *Contra*: Celuzza and Regoli (1982) 60. Attolini et al. (1991) 144 maintain that when Cosa was founded in 273 BC, most colonists lived inside the walls, but imply that the situation was different in the mid-second century BC foundation of Heba (144-5). G's argument from numbers resurfaces in Lloyd (1991) 234, who notes that early imperial Veii had not more than 2-3,000 residents and was too small to house everyone who farmed

---

[86] It is nevertheless perhaps an extravagance to speak of the 'spiritual urbanization' of the peasantry of the Middle Ages. The remark is cited by White (1962) 67.

the territory; hence, the multitude of finds leaves 'little doubt that the isolated farm was a very significant element in the local settlement pattern'. At the same time, he reminds us that the known small sites need not have been contemporaneous or occupied all year round. On the dispersal of 'small' farmsteads under the early empire, see Gualteri and de Polignac (1991) 197–8 (Lucania); Rasmussen (1991) (Tuscania). In his most recent summing up the state of research on rural Italy, Barker (1995b) 3 makes the general point that 'the classical rural population was abundant, and tended to live in dispersed rather than nucleated settlements, especially in the lowland areas extensively cultivated today', whereas in the Middle Ages, the population was smaller and clustered in nucleated settlements.

Some researchers invoke the concept of the 'agro-town' that has been challenged by G. (esp. pp. 113–14, 131). Wightman and Hayes (1994a) 36 claim that the original 4,000 settlers sent to Interamna 'must be imagined as living in the town and farming their plots from there', mainly for reasons of security in a hostile environment. If that was the case, they calculate that even if every colonist was allotted only six *iugera* of land, some of them would have to commute six to eight kilometres to reach their fields (36). This could be taken to corroborate G's argument in favour of denucleated settlement or at least helps to explain subsequent developments: thus, settlement became more dispersed during the late Republic and early empire (39). For that period, Wightman and Hayes (1994b) 45 reckon with eight to ten farmsteads per 100 hectares. Small (1991) 217 notes that the fertile area around Gravina was thinly populated under the Republic and considers the possibility that grain-farmers would commute from 'agro-towns': 'This theory can be supported to some extent by analogy with the medieval and post-medieval practice, but we cannot as yet prove it for the Roman period.' In a survey in the Brindisi region, Yntema (1993) 201 finds no trace of smallholdings and deems it 'perhaps more plausible to assume that the majority of small farmers continued to live (. . .) in the settlement of Ovia itself' (202) in a close parallel to medieval and early modern conditions (202, restated 216). On the countryside of Roman Sicily, see Wilson (1990) 189–236, esp. 221–2 on field surveys. He finds a spreading of settlements into the countryside from the late second century BC onwards and refers to the continuous growth of the 'agro-towns' in the valleys throughout the empire (232). In times of peace, the provincials lived in 'agro-towns', having moved from the hills into the valleys (155). Despite his confident application of the term 'agro-town', Wilson (1990) 232 acknowledges that the precise function of these settlements is still to a large extent unclear; they might have been market centres, possibly also administrative centres. Belvedere (1995) adds nothing. None of these scholars makes use of the present paper, and they fail to consider the possibility that 'agro-towns' may be of more recent origin. For evidence suggestive of the existence of farm labourers (slaves?) who lived in the city and worked in the countryside, see Kolendo (1985) 114–17 (on Pompeii) (p. 119).

Residence on the land would enable peasants to farm their fields more intensively. In this respect, G's argument links up with the 'alternative model' of

WHERE DID ITALIAN PEASANTS LIVE? 133

ancient Mediterranean farming developed in the 1980s which advocates a more optimistic view of agricultural productivity (see below, bibliographical supplement to chapter 11). Rural residence also facilitated food-gathering, a practice explored by Frayn (1979) 57–72; Evans (1980b) 137–9 (cf. Gallant (1991) 115–21 on Greece).

For comparative purposes, see Osborne (1985) 15–63 and (1987) 53–74; Roy (1988); Langdon (1991); Lohmann (1993), on rural residence in Attica. On field surveys of ancient Greece, see Alcock (1993) 33–92; cf. Davis (1996).

8

NON-SLAVE LABOUR IN THE ROMAN WORLD[1]

The Roman lawyer Gaius wrote that the fundamental social division was that between slave and free (*Inst.* 1.9). This doctrine is unexceptionable, but it does not advance us far towards an understanding of the structure of society or the character of the labour force. Moreover, it must not be taken to imply that the slave-free division was clear-cut. Among workers there were numerous groups or categories of those whose positions, defined not in purely juridical terms, but in terms of obligations, privileges and degree of subjection to another's power, fell somewhere between the chattel slaves of the ranches and mines and the free peasant proprietors and self-employed artisans.[2] For present purposes we may relegate to the background those intermediate groups whose situations were not significantly better than those of the bulk of the servile labour force: for example, the tied *coloni* of the late empire (described as *servi glebae* in *Cod.Iust.* 11.52.1), and debt bondsmen, who existed in every period, not least the late Republic (Varro, *Rust.* 1.17.2) and early Empire (Columella, *Rust.* 1.3.12).

The classification of some groups of workers is by no means a straightforward procedure. Finley, reviving a thesis of Fustel de Coulanges, has suggested that a significant proportion of the free tenant-farmers of the Principate (and late Republic) were *de facto* bondsmen. Again, the position of the freedmen, an important element in the urban labour force, was ambiguous. The legal position was clear: manumission transformed a slave into a free man. But social convention sanctioned by law placed the master-turned-patron in a position to exercise a substantial degree of control over the ex-slave. 'Der Freigelassene war nicht frei, nicht in

---

[1] A basic selection of works on topics covered here might include Gummerus (1906), (1916); Heitland (1921); Loane (1938); Macqueron (1958); De Robertis (1963), with the review by Nörr (1965); Schtajerman (1964); Toynbee (1965); Mossé (1966); Brockmeyer (1968); Treggiari (1969); Brunt (1971); Martin (1971); Burford (1972); Finley (1973a); Staerman and Trofimova (1975); Hopkins (1978a).

Other articles and monographs I have used with profit include Frederiksen (1970–1); Pucci (1973); Helen (1975); Pearse (1974); Finley (1976); Skydsgaard (1976).

[2] Cf. Finley (1960).

Italien und nicht in Griechenland.' These words sum up the views of many scholars today.[3] Thirdly, some ancient authorities, including the classical lawyers, were prone to assimilate *mercennarii*, or salaried workers, and slaves, especially in the context of the *familia*.

It can be agreed that tenant-farmers, freedmen employees and hired labourers were heterogeneous groups who occupy no fixed point on the continuum, but a broad central band which at one extremity penetrates an indeterminate area 'between slave and free'. This, however, need not inhibit us from building our discussion around the non-slave labourers and tenant-farmers in addition to the smallholders – where the defining characteristic of the smallholder is that he was an owner-cultivator whose basic labour resource was his family. Again, in the urban context, free salaried workers or labourers, managers and overseers, as well as self-employed artisans, come within the scope of our inquiry.

The great majority of the population living under Roman rule worked the land || and were directly dependent on it for their livelihood. I am therefore giving rural labour most space in what follows.

The primacy of agriculture is reflected in the prevailing ideology, which was that of the land-owning aristocracy. 'Of all revenue-producing activities', wrote Cicero, 'none is finer, more productive, more agreeable, more worthy of a free man than agriculture' (*Off.* 1.150–1). From other texts of Cicero it emerges that farm labour as such, not merely farm ownership, nor even the active supervision of farming operations on the part of the owner, could be the object of moral approval. In *Cato Major* the sweaty workers who earn praise are great Roman statesmen and generals of the past. It was Virgil and, to a lesser degree, the other agricultural writers, who put the independent small farmer in the centre of the picture.

No other type of worker is honoured in the (upper-class) literature. We can accept that craftsmen could be proud of their skills and convinced of the worth of their enterprise, but for Cicero the crafts (and even more so wage-labour) were virtually servile occupations. Some have thought that he was influenced by the predominance of slaves in crafts, and that agriculture was regarded as a worthy occupation for free men in part because farmers were traditionally free. In my view the origin of the cult of the peasant patriarch and the related doctrine of the dignity of agricultural labour lies elsewhere; I will come back to this topic. Meanwhile I must try to make at least a preliminary statement about the relative importance of servile labour on one hand, and free labour on the other.

At the risk of dogmatism, I would suggest that slave labour was never dominant in agriculture outside Italy and Sicily. There is some indication

[3] Strack (1914) 23. But see my concluding section.

that slave-labour was common in parts of Greece and in Tripolitania.[4] In the remainder of Africa Proconsularis and in Numidia the evidence points to the use of free indigenous labour, notably on the extensive imperial domains. Slave labour was even less in evidence in the other principal grain-producing region of the empire, Egypt, and elsewhere appears to have been scattered and relatively insignificant. As to Italy, according to a *communis opinio* the slave system was in decline as early as the first century AD. It seems to me unlikely that the balance between servile and free labour on the land was radically altered in the early empire, although some decline in the numbers and economic importance of slaves can be conceded. However, one may wonder whether too much has been made of the role of slaves in agriculture in the second and first centuries BC, the hey-day of the slave system, when the total slave population in Italy reached two to three million (out of six to seven and a half million).[5] In this connection I would make the following remarks:

(1) The employment of slave labour on large properties (which are sometimes given the name *latifundia* by writers of the mid-first century AD) is securely attested as prominent only in some areas of Italy, particularly in the south and centre, in the late Republic and early empire.

(2) The rural free at all times heavily outnumbered rural slaves,[6] particularly one might suppose in the north, where slavery is attested only sporadically and the || indigenous population was numerous. In such regions free men are likely to have provided an alternative to slaves as a permanent labour force on large properties, while remaining dominant on small.

(3) The speed and extent of the decline of small-unit production, whether in the form of peasant holdings or tenancies, should not be exaggerated.[7] For the late Republic the testimony of Varro is important. He writes of the 'plerique pauperculi', who 'ipsi colunt ... cum sua progenie' (*Rust.* 1.17.2). Confirmation of their existence is provided by largely archaeological evidence from areas such as Southern Etruria, Northern Apulia, the Molise and North Italy.[8]

---

[4] For Greece, see e.g. Hopkins (1978a) 133–71 (Delphi); for North Africa, see briefly Garnsey (1978) 236–8.

[5] Different estimates in Beloch (1886), 418 (two million out of six) and Brunt (1971), 124 (three million out of seven and a half).

[6] See Hopkins (1978a) 67–9.

[7] For a bold statement of this view see Frederiksen (1970–1), reacting against, e.g., Toynbee (1965). Hopkins (1978a) 55–6, has provided 'speculative figures' to illustrate the scale of peasant-displacement; and see n. 10 below.

[8] The Southern Etruria evidence has been summarized by Potter (1979). For North Apulia (the Tavoliere) see the preliminary report of Bradford (1950). On the Molise, Barker, Lloyd and Webley (1978). For North Italy see e.g. Bradford (1957a) 156–78 (especially on subdivisions within the centuriated systems).

(4) The Varro passage might in principle embrace not just owners but also tenants,[9] those for example who held what were in effect permanent leases and like the peasant of Maktar (*CIL* VIII 1 1824 = *ILS* 7457) might talk as if the fields they worked were their own (*ruri meo*). Varro is writing here of labour, not ownership. Similarly, the archaeological evidence does not discriminate between owners and tenants. But there is ample evidence for the assignation of smallholdings either in viritane grants or in the context of colonization schemes in Italy under the Republic, and in both Italy and the provinces from the dictatorship of Caesar into the Principate. The settlement of these new proprietors counterbalanced to some degree the displacement of the old.[10]

(5) Slavery coexisted with at least one other form of dependent labour, debt bondage. The abolition of *nexum*, traditionally dated to 326 BC, did not put a stop to it, because Roman law always permitted the creditor with the authority of the court to arrest, hold and put to work the insolvent debtor. The existence of debt bondage in the late Republic is implicit in the complaint of followers of Catiline that they had lost both their property and their freedom (Sall. *Cat.* 33), and is not ruled out by Varro's sentence on *obaerarii*.[11] For the early Empire Columella's reference to citizens in bondage (*nexu*) who cultivated large estates is unambiguous (*Rust.* 1.3.12).

(6) Free wage-labour was always needed to supplement a permanent servile labour-force on the slave-estates.

Some of these points may be given further consideration, in the context of a discussion of the nature of the free rural labour-force.

We begin with the peasant proprietors, who stand at the top of the hierarchy of workers in agriculture. As already indicated, the Romans had a myth of the peasant. They even developed concurrently a doctrine of the dignity of agricultural labour. This phenomenon is not to be explained with reference to any supposed influence of the peasantry in society and politics.[12] I do not believe that the 'peasant patriarch' idealized in the elder Cato or in Virgil set the moral tone of society or provided crucial political and military leadership in early Rome. It is hardly credible that the

[9] The usual interpretation of Varro's *pauperculi*, that they are freeholders exclusively, may go back to Heitland's tentative '*ipsi* suggests peasant owners' ((1921) 180 n. 6).

[10] Figures, more or less speculative, are furnished by Brunt (1971) 342–4 and Hopkins (1978a) 66. See also Garnsey (1976) [= chapter 6].

[11] Can we assume that Varro was consciously excluding contemporary Italy when he said that *obaerarii* existed still in numbers in Asia, Egypt and Illyricum? And if so, was he right? Professor Brunt, who gives a positive answer to my first question, has suggested to me that Varro was writing in a period in which we might expect heavy enrolment of debt bondsmen into the army to have taken place.

[12] For a different view see Hopkins (1978a) 108–15.

owner-cultivator of a four-*iugera* farm, as T. Quinctius Cincinnatus is said to have been, saved the state as dictator in the middle of the fifth century BC (Plin. *HN* 18.20); while if M. Atilius Regulus owned merely || seven *iugera* of land (Val. Max. 4.4.6) he would never have risen to the consulship and led a Roman army against the Carthaginians. The leadership of the Roman state was always in the hands of a restricted aristocracy which controlled most of the land and showed a consistent reluctance to allow their social inferiors to farm above subsistence level. This did not change in the course of the Republic. Indeed the emergence and promotion of the myth of the peasant patriarch came at a time when the process of peasant displacement and the concentration of estates in the hands of the rich was speeding up.

Cato, the first to our knowledge to promulgate the myth, provides the clue, when he glosses his equation of good man and good farmer with the comment that farmers made the best soldiers (*Agr.* Pref. 4). The Roman army was built around the peasant proprietor. This made good sense, because he could usually be relied on to fight for his land; he was by nature conservative; and above all he was relatively easy to exploit and manipulate.

The cult of the peasant had its origins in the expansionist and militarist character of the Roman state. It did not so much reflect 'peasant power' as the indispensability of the peasant farmer as soldier and, we should add with Varro (*Rust.* 3.1.4), as producer. Our concern is with the role of the freeholders as producer. In what follows I outline an argument to the effect that freeholders characteristically worked other land in addition to their own. The consequences for the rural economy as a whole are sketched in a later section.

The first point relates to the size of smallholdings. Estimates of the minimum size of a holding necessary to support an average family range from about six *iugera* (3.5 acres, 1.5 hectares) to about twenty *iugera*. According to one tradition, the *heredium* allocated to the original inhabitants of Rome was two *iugera* (Varro, *Rust.* 1.10.2). That allotments of two to ten *iugera* were common is supported by the literary sources and to some extent by archaeology. The only way to make sense of such figures (and they should not be rejected out of hand) is to suppose that farmers supplemented their incomes by cultivating or putting animals to pasture on unassigned state domain (or in early Rome, clan land), by serving as tenants and labourers on neighbouring properties, or by working as craftsmen and labourers in towns and villages. This supposition is confirmed by other considerations, in particular the nature of the farming calendar, insofar as it can be reconstructed. Grain crops and olives, which were main crops in Roman Italy, require a relatively low labour input. For long periods of the year, the winter months in the case of cereals, there was little work to be done on the farm, and the farmer was free to look for ways of adding to his income. Even in the busy seasons, the ploughing or the harvesting, a peasant family might have labour to spare after its own work was done. Intensive farming required more labour; but smallholders might be expected to have gone in normally for extensive farming, since they lacked the capital resources to make an initial investment, or to protect themselves against the vagaries of the market, or even perhaps to hire additional labour in the peak periods of the year. In addition, intensive farming was virtually out of the question where the smallholder (or tenant-farmer) was not resident on the property. Any peasants domiciled in towns would have been available in slack seasons for short-term employment in local industry, or free to try their hand at a craft.[13]

This section has suggested that no firm lines of demarcation existed between the freeholder and the other categories of free workers. One might add in this connection that distinctions would have existed within the class of freeholders between those, the better off, who were able to take a tenancy rather than resort to hiring themselves out, and the very poor, whom economic compulsion drove to sell their labour. The difference between the position of the latter and that of the poor tenant-farmer who was not also an owner-cultivator was one of form rather than substance.

Tenant-farmers were always a significant feature of the rural economy in Italy as well as in the provinces. A study of the composition of this class provides confirmation of the theory just outlined, that the several categories which make up the free rural labour force were separated by fluid boundaries which were frequently crossed. In this respect the ambiguity of the word *colonus*, which means either 'tenant' or 'farmer', is a fair reflection of real conditions. The category of tenant-farmers is in fact not only heterogeneous, but also far too broad for our purposes. It takes in rich as well as poor. In the period of the late Empire the wealthy found it advantageous to take up imperial land on perpetual or emphyteutic lease with favourable terms. Under the Principate, emperors are known to have made available tracts of abandoned or virgin land on similar conditions in North Africa particularly in the second and early third centuries; it can virtually be assumed that only men with some resources would have found it feasible to take up the offer. The *conductores* who leased imperial properties in five-year periods are likely to have been prosperous men, likewise lessees of moderate-sized or relatively substantial private estates who had sufficient resources of their own to install slaves or hire free labour. Our concern is rather with men of more modest means, who sublet from

---

[13] On peasant domicile, Garnsey (1979) [= chapter 7].

contractors or leased directly from the owner, farming with equipment (and slaves) provided by the latter, or by means of their own meagre resources.

A hierarchy can be discerned in the ranks of tenant-farmers thus delimited. A peasant proprietor with a little capital to spare might take a short-term tenancy in order to increase his income, purchase more land and improve his position in society. At the other end of the scale might be found ex-owners working land that once was theirs, and other landless men who saw the taking of a tenancy as a way of gaining some measure of financial independence. It can be assumed that a great many tenancies were taken by small men, farming largely for subsistence and relying on the labour of the family.

What were their prospects? Their material position as farmers working at the subsistence level on a short lease would probably have been rather worse than that ‖ of peasant proprietors.[14] In Italy, where before the time of Diocletian land was not taxed, they had to pay rent (or a share of the harvest); elsewhere they had to foot the bill for rents and taxes. Tenants on imperial estates in North Africa contributed one-third of the crop, while in Egypt they might have had to surrender one-half. In view of their narrow margins, we might expect indebtedness to have been normal among tenants, and this expectation is confirmed by the large number of legal texts referring to *reliqua colonorum*, tenants' arrears, among the assets of an estate. The references to *reliqua colonorum* do not invariably point to bad debts, but they must often do so.

The letters of Pliny provide further evidence that tenants got into difficulties. In one letter he refers to tenants who had lost hope of ever paying the rent (*Ep.* 9.37). Finley observes that these same tenants, whose position was so impossible that they had resorted to consuming the harvest, nevertheless stayed put.[15] His explanation that they were *de facto* bondsmen appears to be basically correct. But there is one puzzle. Evidence from elsewhere suggests that peasants who felt themselves to be in desperate straits could not be counted on not to leave. Petitioning *coloni* of imperial estates sometimes threatened to leave the estates, and the threat was no doubt from time to time carried out. Egyptian peasants, the most exploited in the empire, were certainly capable of running away, in this as in all periods. Even in the late empire, when the state was

---

[14] I confess there is danger of overemphasizing the effect of economic pressures on free peasants, and of underestimating their resilience and ability to maintain their family fortunes. That the *general* trend was against them seems to me undeniable. In particular, their position could not but have been undermined by the steadily increasing fiscal burden in the late Empire.

[15] Finley (1973a) 115–16. In general, my views on the position of tenants and the decline of slavery are close to his.

co-operating with landlords in tying their labour force to the land, *coloni* frequently absconded. Pliny's tenants, it appears, did not want to run away. The explanation, I suggest, is that they had ties with the neighbourhood, often as cultivators of nearby property. Pliny's situation now comes into sharper focus. Columella's preferred tenants were *indigenae, rustici, assidui* (*Rust.* 1.7.4). In other words, in his and no doubt in others' eyes, the most satisfactory tenants were experienced farmers, in particular freeholders, domiciled in the neighbourhood. Such men were, understandably, in short supply. We are not entitled to infer that there was a general labour shortage in the regions where Pliny owned land, or in Italy as a whole, only that desirable tenants were scarce.

Whatever is decided about the condition of tenants in the early Empire – and any conclusion to be accurate would have to reflect the diverse situations of tenant-farmers, regional variations and temporal differences – there remains a clear contrast between the free tenant of the late Republic and early Empire, who entered a contractual relation with a landlord for a short term and was then legally entitled to go elsewhere, and the serf-like tenant of the late Empire, bound to the soil as were his heirs. In my view, the solution of the notorious problems of the rise of the colonate lies in the peculiar conditions of the late third and fourth centuries, in particular the increasingly oppressive tax burden, and any attempt to trace a continuous trend from Principate to late Empire across the great divide of the third century is doomed to failure.

The matter of the transition from a slave system to tenancy is equally contentious. Even the basic chronology of the development is in dispute, some ‖ regarding the beginning of the Principate as the turning-point, others the end of the first century AD, still others the middle of the second century or later.[16] The issue of the slave-supply is crucial. It is regularly stated that the supply of slaves dwindled after the reign of Augustus and that landowners were in consequence forced to lease more of their land to tenant-farmers. It still seems to be necessary to insist that the truth of this statement cannot be established with reference to the sources. We are told more of tenancy under the Empire than under the Republic, but this may be quite by chance. Cicero and Horace, as well as the younger Pliny, used tenants. Columella had more to say on tenants than had Cato or Varro. But those writers mentioned them nonetheless, Columella's treatise is a good deal longer than either of theirs, and after the section on tenancy in his first book we hear only of slaves. In fact if all the available literary sources are utilized, including Justinian's *Digest*, the case for the survival

---

[16] Respectively, Hopkins (1978a) 95; MacMullen (1974b) 254–5; Staerman and Trofimova (1975); various Marxist writers cited in Schtajerman (1964) 1–21.

of slaves in numbers after the first century AD is considerably strengthened. The lawyers of the second and early third centuries imply that slave labour was important in Italy in their time.

In my view the decline of agricultural slavery is a much longer and slower process than is usually thought. It is by no means certain that the cessation or slow-down of territorial expansion from the time of Augustus had a drastic effect on the supply of slaves. The slave-trade, which was well-organized and freely crossed the imperial frontiers, was always a very important source of slaves. In addition, breeding was a very significant source of supply. It is a myth that a slave population cannot reproduce itself. It is another myth that imperial Romans were disinclined to breed slaves (cf. Colum, *Rust.* 1.8.19). Nor am I impressed by the argument for decline from rising slave-prices. Jones's calculation, on which it rests, that 'a slave in the second century cost eight to ten times his annual keep as against a year or a year and a quarter's keep in fourth-century Athens' is based on grossly insufficient data.[17] In any case, if slaves did become more expensive, the aristocracy of the imperial period had greater buying power than their counterparts under the Republic. Moreover, sizeable aggregations of slaves continued to be employed on great estates in Italy and Sicily in the fourth and fifth centuries – Melania the younger is said to have had 24,000 slaves on her estates near Rome alone. If these figures are at all reliable (and they may not be), then the slaveholdings of only 80 to 125 Melanias would have equalled the total conjectured slave population of Italy in the time of Augustus.[18]

Meanwhile, there are sufficient references in early imperial texts to the supervision of a slave work-force by free tenants, to suggest that the alternative for a landowner lay between two different ways of *managing* estates (through slave bailiffs and free tenants) rather than between two systems of labour, slave and free, as it is commonly represented.

It is quite uncertain whether a third alternative was commonly resorted to, that is, the installation of slaves as managers of quasi-tenancies.[19] This practice, already attested at the close of the Republic, and an increase in free tenancies have been associated by some with a process of fragmentation of estates. All these supposed || developments are very dubious. While we can be sure that the concentration of property continued inexorably among the rich, we do not know how this affected farm-unit size and methods of organization and production.

---

[17] Jones (1956) 194.

[18] See n.5 for estimates of slave-population. Melania's slaves: *Vita Mel.* (Latin) 18: sixty hamlets (*villulae*) each with 400 slaves. Cf. Palladius, *Historia Lausiaca* 5 : 8,000 manumitted.

[19] Despite Schtajerman (1964) 97–8, 103–6, and Brockmeyer (1971).

My general conclusion is that in the present state of knowledge any statement about 'trends' between the late Republic and middle Empire which tries to take account of all the evidence will be so guarded and full of qualifications as to be almost useless. Predictably, I am unimpressed by explanations that have been offered for these inadequately understood phenomena, such as Brockmeyer's that a trend towards tenancy under the Principate is to be explained in terms of changing economic attitudes among landowners – the assumption being that the less interested a landowner was in his estate, the more likely he was to turn to tenancy.[20] I do not see how this theory could be established, and I do not find it plausible. Similarly, I do not accept the argument for decline from the alleged unprofitability of slave-run and slave-worked estates.[21] Slave-estates could be profitable, as indeed could tenancies, given adequate supervision by the owner. Hence my belief that there was a genuine choice for a landlord throughout this period between 'direct' exploitation of an estate through slaves under a slave-bailiff, and the lease of land to a tenant, who might operate with slaves, provided by himself or the landowner.

We come finally to those at the bottom of the scale, the day-wage labourers in the setting of the slave-estate. Varro writing in the mid-first century BC says that all farm work is done by slaves or free men or both (*Rust.* 1.17.2). He divides the free work-force into small farmers, hired labourers (*mercennarii*) and debt-labourers (*obaerarii*). He indicates that the heavier or more important jobs ('res maiores') like the vintage or haymaking are performed by hired labourers. He goes on to endorse this practice (this time citing the storing of the products of the vintage, and harvesting, as examples of the 'opera rustica maiora'), and to recommend that hired labour be used instead of slaves on farms in insalubrious locations, apparently as the permanent labour-force. None of the agricultural writers has any specific information or advice to give on labour for ploughing. As that was a heavy operation, a landowner who followed Varro's prescriptions would probably have hired labourers for this purpose.

Cato a century earlier had told potential landowners, among other things, to buy a farm in an area where the labour supply was plentiful ('operariorum copia siet', *Agr.* 1.1.3), and he elsewhere stresses that good relations with the neighbourhood hold the key to ease of selling, letting out work and hiring labourers (4). He provides a full résumé of conditions that should be written into contracts for operations like the gathering and milling of olives (144–5). And he allows for the hiring of skilled workers like builders, lime burners and blacksmiths (14, 16, 21). Both

---

[20] Brockmeyer (1968) 181.
[21] A thesis of Schtajerman (1964), justly impugned by Brockmeyer (1968) e.g. 60.

these Republican writers assume that a sizeable pool of free labour was not only desirable but also available. The inevitable fluctuations in labour-supply and labour-costs are reflected in one or two places in the literary sources (e.g. Plin. *HN* 18.300), but it seems that no major reallocation of jobs was caused thereby. ||

What emerges very clearly from the writers on agriculture, and has not been brought out by their interpreters,[22] is the essential part played by free labour in the economy of the slave-estate. There is no way of measuring the comparative costs of hired and slave labour. But it can be said with confidence that hired workers formed a significant part of the total supply of labour. They were not permanent employees, but we must bear in mind the seasonality and irregularity of agricultural work in a simple economy in a dry farming zone. Moreover, the seasonal operations reserved for hired labourers were, or included, the vital operations of the farming year.

Itinerant workers are seldom mentioned in the sources. Suetonius (*Vesp.* 1.4) retails a story about Vespasian's grandfather, allegedly a labour contractor who brought workers down every year from Umbria to the Sabine country. The peasant of Maktar in Tunisia performed a job of this nature for nine years, after having served twelve years himself as a member of a gang of harvesters (*CIL* VIII 11824). *Turmae messorum* consisting of sedentary farmers, transhumants, semi-nomads regularly brought in the harvests in Numidia and the Medjerda valley south-west of Carthage.

In Italy hired labour came mainly from the neighbourhood. Passages of Cato already cited establish this for his period, while passing over the source of workers. I take it as certain that in all periods a substantial proportion of free workers were cultivators of small farms, either their own or another's, taking work to supplement a meagre income. There was also exchange labour on a short-term basis and for particular jobs (cf. Apul. *Apol.* 17). Cato may be alluding to this in a passage referring to 'help' that one might receive from neighbours in building by the furnishing of materials, animals and labour ('operae') (*Agr.* 4). No explicit mention is made here of services in return. This is not necessarily significant, given the context and brevity of the passage. On the other hand, one can imagine that such informal arrangements between neighbours could, when the parties

---

[22] With the exception of Hopkins (1978a) 9, who alludes briefly to 'the interdependence of rich men and of free peasants, many of whom owned some land and also worked as part tenants or as labourers on the land of the rich', scholars imply or say outright that free labour was peripheral. Heitland (1921) 173 writes of 'emergency labour', and White (1970) 366, 448, believes that free labour was significant only in the time of the elder Cato. A similar issue exercises medieval agrarian historians. See Postan (1954); Kosminsky (1956) ch. 6.

were unequal, slide easily into an exchange of labour for patronal services of a financial or legal kind. The next step in the process, the furnishing of obligatory labour services, is not attested (except in Egypt) outside the imperial estates in the province of Africa Proconsularis in the second century AD (*CIL* VIII 10570; 25902), though this may be purely fortuitous.

Unemployed and under-employed residents of cities and towns can be expected to have made a contribution to the free rural work-force. We can accept that many large slave-estates were placed near urban centres. Cato advised the purchaser of a farm to choose a site near a sizeable town ('oppidum validum'). He may have had in mind labour needs as well as markets (4). It has recently been suggested that many Pompeians were employed in agriculture, on the basis of the impressive number and range of tools and farm implements found in houses in Pompeii. These and other urban-based workers would have included owner-cultivators and tenant-farmers. It is reasonable to believe that in some areas of Italy, especially where || urban centres were relatively close together, a proportion of cultivators lived in the town and travelled to and from their farms each day.

The free wage-labourers on the large estates, then, were a mixed heterogeneous group. It would obviously be erroneous to claim that a 'labouring class' existed or was emerging when freeholders, tenant-farmers, and the landless poor of the rural districts and urban centres all made major contributions of labour, and in all cases on a temporary basis. Further, we have to suppose that landowners secured such free workers as they needed by informal, regular arrangements with neighbouring farmers and contractors of labour, not through the mechanism of an extensive labour market.

The more fundamental point concerns the relationship of the slave and peasant systems of production. The growth of the former at the expense of the latter is one of the best known facts of Roman history. But the extent of their interdependence has not been noted, nor has recognition been given to the dilemma this posed for the slave system. Large landowners needed a stable labour force near their estates. Smallholders were the preferred source of labour. Yet the relationship was not between equals, and the independence of the smallholder was precarious. If he became insolvent and had to surrender his land to his powerful neighbour, the latter might find his labour problems aggravated. A system of free tenancies was an interim solution, but no more than that, for free tenants operated in unpromising conditions. The free peasantry was never eradicated in the Roman world, but the future lay largely with a dependent labour system, and this was consistent with the logic of the system of agricultural slavery.

Cicero follows Greek writers in condemning the banausic crafts (and even more so wage-labour) as sordid and unworthy of a free man. A comment in

Livy is more characteristically Roman: craftsmen are the least qualified of all for soldiering (8.20.4).

The sources for industry, upper-class attitudes apart, are largely epigraphical and archaeological. The evidence is inevitably fragmented. Most Rome-based workers appear only as individuals, or rather, names cut or scratched on stone, clay lamp or lead pipe; some stone inscriptions place them in the context of the family. Apart from one inscription recording members of a single decury of the main builders' association of Rome, no list of ordinary members of any Rome-based trade or craft survives. Only at Pompeii do diverse sources come together sufficient in quantity and quality to tempt an enterprising scholar to essay judgements on the organization of an industry (the wool trade), the size and status of the work-force, the status of managers and owners, and the importance of the industry in the life of the city.[23] Otherwise, the best we can do is compile lists of personnel involved in particular industries which operated on a considerable scale, on the basis of chance finds of || artefacts marked or stamped with their makers' names. A few pottery firms at Arezzo employed over thirty men, a relatively large number in the Roman context.[24]

Again, evidence is selective. Most of the single-worker inscriptions on stone were probably set up by the better-off craftsmen. It is likely also that the proportion of freeborn to freedman artisans recorded is unrealistically low, because of the greater status-consciousness of the latter; slaves hardly ever appear. Similarly, the *collegia*-inscriptions from Rome and Ostia give us only (a sample of) the élite of those in the building trade. Conversely, while the names of producers may survive on artefacts, those of employers are only sometimes detectable.

A notorious problem is inferring status from nomenclature in the absence of explicit status-indications. The more informal inscriptions can degenerate into mere scratches or graffiti. Where a single name can be read, is it better understood as the name of a slave or the last of a freedman's (two or three) names? In the more formal inscriptions, notably epitaphs, it is freedmen and the freeborn who are easily confused.

The list of recorded artisans compiled long ago by Kühn is the basis of most work on the status of the industrial work-force.[25] Kühn was a cautious scholar: some 59.75 per cent of home-based artisans in his list he pronounced to be of uncertain status (*incerti*), likewise no fewer than 83.50 per cent of those from the rest of Italy. Gummerus[26] distributed the *incerti*

---

[23] Moeller (1976). While I welcome the author's bold approach, I find many of his interpretations unconvincing.
[24] But the average number of slaves working in the ninety-odd pottery firms that can be identified is ten to twenty. See Pucci (1973) 266–8.
[25] Kühn (1910).   [26] Gummerus (1916).

between freedmen and the freeborn (*ingenui*), and arrived at the following results: two-thirds of recorded artisans at Rome were freedmen, and about half of those from elsewhere; 27 per cent (Rome) and 46.25 per cent (elsewhere) were *ingenui*; the figures for slaves were 6.25 per cent and 1.75 per cent. I have not seen any doubts expressed over these results, although the margin of error is wide.

Kühn's basic figures for *ingenui*, 2.25 per cent (Rome) and 4.75 per cent (elsewhere), obviously require adjustment. Self-employed artisans are under-represented in the sample though they probably prevailed; unskilled free workers, also numerically significant, are omitted altogether. Both groups included *ingenui*, particularly the latter. The demand for skilled workers was met by the importation of slaves from abroad or the training of slaves bred in the household (*vernae*). *Ingenui* who were not born into a craft had little prospect of acquiring the skills necessary to compete with slaves. Most of them were forced back on to seasonal or part-time work, on building sites or on the docks. There was also agriculture. A continuum existed between agricultural and industrial employment. Most displaced peasants kept themselves alive by picking up casual labour in town and country. Finally, mining attracted some free labour.[27]

Freedmen make up 31.75 per cent of Kühn's sample of Rome-based workers. This is surely proof, if proof is needed, that the figure of 6.25 per cent for slave-craftsmen is a gross distortion. The freedman-craftsmen were the most successful members of a distinctly larger group of slave-craftsmen. Of somewhat over 450 recorded potters at Arezzo rather fewer than 10 per cent were freedmen, and the remainder were slaves. In the rest of Italy slaves predominate, though by a less wide margin.[28]

The role of freedmen in industry requires clarification. In particular, are those who ran or controlled a profitable business to be seen as mainly foremen and agents, or independent entrepreneurs? I suspect that the category of independent freedmen was larger than is usually supposed. *Libertini orcini*, ex-slaves manumitted by will, often with legacies, were not an insignificant group. But one can also envisage a class of freedmen with living patrons, who might have been kept in tow, but were in practice given a considerable measure of freedom, encouraged to accumulate wealth, and allowed to transmit it to heirs. The phenomenon of wealthy freedmen in responsible positions casts doubt on the value of the manager/owner dichotomy.[29]

Dependent freedmen should be sought, rather, among teams of craftsmen in the employ of another (a freedman, perhaps), and in small-scale

---

[27] See e.g. Mrozek (1977), esp. 102–7.   [28] Pucci (1973) 288–91.

[29] These arguments are developed in Garnsey (1981) [= chapter 2].

manufacture, where freedmen and *ingenui* of libertine origin were well-represented.

This last observation has interesting implications. The use of skilled slaves was not wholly detrimental to free labour if it guaranteed a steady influx of manumitted slaves and their freeborn sons into the ranks of the self-employed artisans. In this way the slave-system can be said, paradoxically, actually to have propped up the free artisanate. But the main reason for the survival of free artisans was the high premium placed by the rich on social and political as distinct from economic goals. Their support as clients was valued above the increased *profits* that might have accrued from taking over and expanding their enterprises.[30] ||

Addendum

The third in a series of articles on the Roman peasantry (see chapters 6 and 7), this paper deals with the location of free labour in the Roman economy. It focuses on farm-tenancy and temporary wage-labour in agriculture and on the relationship between free labour and chattel slavery. This paper affirms, for the first time in the field of ancient history, the fact (already acknowledged by anthropologists and students of more recent peasant societies) that the main components of the rural labour-force – owner-occupiers, farm-tenants and wage-labourers – constitute three overlapping categories. It is also stressed, against previous undifferentiated appraisals of the nature of the villa-system, that the Roman slave-estate was not, and could not afford to be, self-sufficient in labour.

In practice, the separation of slave and free was not always clear-cut (pp. 134–5): on debt-bondage, see Lo Cascio (1982), and for the survival of *nexum* beyond the fourth century BC, see Hölkeskamp (1987) 160 and n. 137. Foxhall (1990) discusses dependent tenants in general, with an emphasis on comparative material (cf. also van Dommelen (1993)). Roman evidence for rural patronage and dependence is scarce: Garnsey and Woolf (1989). The view that the majority of the rural population was always made up of free farmers, whether as owner-occupiers or as tenants, and that their decline during the late Republic had been exaggerated (pp. 136–7), is also supported by Evans (1980a). The argument that since agricultural plots were often small, many peasants had to work other people's land to supplement their income and to make use of their surplus labour (pp. 138–9), has been elaborated by Rathbone (1981) 19, and also endorsed by Pleket (1990) 94–5, 112 n. 80. For a discussion of fluctuations in the labour supply of ancient Greek peasant households that also applies to the Roman world, see Gallant (1991).

The concept of a hierarchy of farm-tenants from wealthy managers to poor peasants (p. 140) was briefly addressed by Corbier (1981) 434, adopted from the present paper by De Neeve (1984a) 15, 174, and more recently developed by

[30] Skydsgaard (1976).

Foxhall (1990) 104–11 and especially by Scheidel (1992a), (1994a) 29–117; see also Lo Cascio (1993) 297–302. On wealthy tenants, see De Neeve (1984a) 83–6; Scheidel (1994a), esp. 71. The fundamental study of the historical development and economic background of Roman farm-tenancy is now De Neeve (1984a); see also Capogrossi Colognesi (1986); Rosafio (1991); Lo Cascio (1993); Scheidel (1992a), (1993a), (1993b), (1994a). On the important evidence of tenancy in the letters of Pliny the Younger, see Kehoe (1988b), (1989), (1993). Johne et al. (1983) is useful only as a comprehensive compilation of references. The difference between *locatio conductio*-style farm-tenancy of Republic and Principate and the colonate of the later Roman Empire (p. 141) is now commonly acknowledged; recent work on the latter is extensively referred to by Sirks (1993). The decline of plantation slavery in relation to farm-tenancy was a drawn-out affair that cannot be traced with any precision (pp. 141–2); further scepticism as to the validity of this concept has been voiced by Garnsey and Saller (1987) 71–3. The importance of slave-breeding (p. 142) has been examined in greater detail by Bradley (1987b) and further emphasized by Scheidel (1997).

That in the early Empire, tenants would supervise a slave work-force is taken to 'suggest that the alternative for a landowner lay between two different ways of *managing* estates (through bailiffs and free tenants) rather than two systems of labour, slave and free, as it is commonly represented' (p. 142). This previously unacknowledged point (for restatements see Garnsey (1982a) 344; Garnsey and Saller (1982) 34) has gradually gained acceptance (e.g., Wiedemann (1981) 138; Avram (1985) 94) and has been substantiated through a re-assessment of Colum. *Rust.* 1.7, a commonly misunderstood passage which can be shown to address slavery and tenancy as different types of management, by Scheidel (1993a), (1994a) 83–117. The suggestion that *servi quasi coloni* would also act as managers rather than labourers (p. 142) has been developed by Scheidel (1993b), (1994a) 131–42 (and see 142–8 on freedmen tenants; cf. Scheidel (1990)). On the extent of the overlapping of slavery and tenancy, see Scheidel (1996b).

The paper stresses the dependence of slave-staffed estates on temporary outside labour when demand for labour peaked, especially during the harvest (pp. 143–5). This point is followed up by Rathbone (1981), who through schematic calculations estimates that casual labour of harvesters would account for a sizeable proportion of the total annual labour requirement of a large villa specializing in wine or olives (13). He also shows an estate which exclusively relied on internal slave labour to be less profitable than one that brought in temporary labour from outside (14): 'The villa system was more economic because it carried no surplus labour . . . because it exploited the underemployment of the neighbouring free peasantry' (15). This underlines the interdependence of slave and free labour; slavery did not merely expand at the expense of the peasants but also depended on their input and provided additional income to the survivors (p. 145). The villa economy and peasant smallholders can thus be seen as 'complementary modes of agricultural production' (Rathbone (1981) 15). This relationship has been independently established by Backhaus (1981), and has also been addressed by Corbier (1981); Scheidel (1989) (on Columella);

D'Arms (1990) 396 (based on the present paper); Scheidel (1994a) 158–60 (in general). The most comprehensive discussion of agricultural wage-labour is provided by Scheidel (1994a) 151–224. On free labour in Roman villages, see Kudlien (1984); on wage-labour in Varro, see Dumont (1986); for hired labour in Roman agriculture, see Maróti (1989); and cf. Mrozek (1989) for ancient wage-labour in general: the last two studies are of a rather antiquarian nature. (Cf. also Curchin (1986), on Spain.) For casual labour on large estates in Roman Egypt, see Rathbone (1991) 148–66. While it is likely that many temporary agricultural wage-labourers were peasants (p. 144; Scheidel (1994a) 160–76), it proves very difficult to determine their status on the basis of the sources: Scheidel (1994a) 176–200. Some were migrant labourers (op. cit. 169–70), others may have come from cities (op. cit. 167–8, 199). A recent radical proposal to see most Roman wage-labourers as hired slaves put forward by Bürge (1990) has met with opposition: see Möller (1993); Scheidel (1994a) 153–202.

The significance of urban free labour was stressed by Brunt (1980). Free-born labourers may be underrepresented in the (mostly epigraphic) evidence, all the more so as status indicators are often absent from the documentation (p. 146); on this issue, cf. now Joshel (1992). The final suggestion that urban slavery, through the regular manumission of skilled slaves, may have 'propped up' the free artisanate deserves further attention (p. 148). On the question of the regularity of manumission, see Wiedemann (1985).

9

PROLEGOMENON TO A STUDY OF THE LAND IN THE LATER ROMAN EMPIRE

I. INTRODUCTION

This paper focuses on broad structural developments affecting the agricultural economy of the Roman world in late antiquity, with special reference to levels of production and productivity. My general aim is to encourage or provoke economic historians of antiquity into taking a greater interest in the subject than they have done in recent years. In particular, I would welcome the considered thoughts of our honorand on the subject. Harry Pleket has recently published full and illuminating studies of the land in the early Empire, but he has not, as far as I am aware, applied the full armoury of his intellectual skills to the study of late antique agriculture.[1]

I favour a broad approach because I think this is the best way of setting up a dialogue with historians of other periods, and, in particular those historians with a comparative bent. Ancient historians should be making a contribution to comparative historical scholarship.

I would like to make it more difficult for comparative historians to pass over Roman history altogether, or, insofar as they recognize the existence of Roman history, to leap from the Principate to the early Middle Ages, passing over, in the process, a whole period of history, one which happens to be quite as long as the period of the Principate. I want at the same time to challenge the tendency of comparativists to adopt without much question the traditional view of late antiquity as a period of decline.

Broad interpretations of the late Roman empire are not exactly novel. Ever since the 1780s, it has been almost *de rigueur* for a self-respecting historian of late antiquity to pronounce on the causes of the decline and fall of the Roman empire. However, such explanations have rarely put the economy, and in particular, the agricultural economy, in the centre of the stage, where it belongs. And in any case, the methodologies used in many

---

[1] Pleket (1990), (1993). Synthetic accounts are rare: I have benefited in particular from that of Vera (1986). The discussion that follows should be read in conjunction with a forthcoming chapter in *CAH* 2nd edn XIII on the countryside in late antiquity by C. R. Whittaker and P. Garnsey, which is more detailed and explores matters passed over here.

such studies have reduced their effectiveness and persuasiveness. I am thinking, for example, of studies which are heavily reliant on literary sources while giving archaeology short shrift. More recently there has been a flirtation with quantification. Both these characteristics are visible in the work of a truly great historian of antiquity, A. H. M. Jones, especially in his monumental *Later Roman Empire*.

On the archaeological front, the archaeology of cities (and lesser agglomerations) is now forcing a revision of older theories of urban decline, with important implications for the health of the rural economy. More recently, field surveys are providing an additional challenge to inherited, cherished assumptions.

As for quantification: there is a strong case for saying that quantification is not a tool that is available to the ancient historian. This is simply because detailed evidence relevant to economic history, for example, for the way in which wealth was accumulated, invested and consumed, does not exist. Some figures have come down to us from antiquity, and these can be exploited insofar as their reliability can be accepted. However, they have not always been used legitimately, even by giants in the world of scholarship such as Jones, and this has added to the already considerable problems facing the student of late antiquity. A ground-clearing operation such as that in which I am presently engaged cannot avoid scrutinizing some of Jones' more influential calculations.

For what I am engaged in at the moment is preliminary exploration, as is reflected in the wording of my title. At the present time it may be impossible to reach general conclusions about the economic condition of late antique society that are persuasive and in tune with the evidence. But at the least we can begin questioning established orthodoxies and investigating the usefulness of methodologies old and new.

II. AGRICULTURE AS A SOURCE OF WEALTH

In this as in all periods of antiquity, most production and wealth was generated on the land. As Jones noted, taxes on agriculture and the rural population paid for virtually the whole apparatus of the state (court, civil service and army).[2]

However, Jones went on to suggest that agriculture contributed all but 5 per cent of the imperial revenues and the overall wealth of the empire. This figure is arrived at by a comparison of the contributions made by the city of ‖ Edessa in Western Mesopotamia to the *collatio lustralis*, commonly called the 'trade tax' (an invention of the reign of Constantine) in the late

[2] Jones (1964) 465ff.

fifth century, with the returns in the *land tax* from the Egyptian towns of Heracleopolis and Oxyrhynchus in the sixth century.

When I raised objections to this argument in a paper to Arnaldo Momigliano's seminar in the Warburg Institute in 1978, he remarked that Jones' argument was so obviously flawed that he saw no point in refuting it. I disagree. To start with, I learned a lot in deciding what I thought was wrong with the argument.[3]

What is the comparison between Edessa and the Egyptian towns worth? We have, on the one hand, two urban centres with extensive and fertile rural territories in the richest province of the empire, and, on the other, a trading city, wealthy but apparently in decline since Jovian's cession of Nisibis to the Persians had cut the caravan route from the East. A second objection concerns the nature of the *collatio lustralis*. The label 'trade tax' is misleading. The tax was not imposed only on traders and manufacturers – it fell equally on usurers and prostitutes. Again, it was by no means charged against all trading activities, since tolls, sales taxes, and above all, customs duties, did not come within its range, but were collected separately.

There are other, fundamental criticisms. To infer the relative importance to the economy of agriculture from its contribution to tax revenue requires, first, that the rate of taxation in each section of the economy was equal, and second, that the extent of state ownership, and hence the scope of a taxable private sector, was equivalent in agriculture, on the one hand, and in commerce and industry, on the other.

With respect to the first of these questions: we do not know whether the so-called 'traders' of Syria and Egyptian peasants paid taxes at a comparable rate. That the Edessans complained about their tax-burden tells us nothing about the level at which they were taxed. It is not in fact known at what rate the *collatio lustralis* was paid at Edessa or anywhere else. If, as may be suspected, peasants were more heavily taxed, especially in Egypt, than merchants and artisans, this may not have been merely because of any supposed greater potential that they possessed as revenue-earners. Traders are less easily taxed than cultivators; trade, in particular internal trade, has many outlets, especially in 'primitive' economies. Handicraft industry is no different in this respect. ||

Secondly, we do not know the extent of state ownership, and thus the extent of a taxable private sector, in each area of the economy. I have the impression, first, that state intervention in commerce and industry is a striking feature of the late Roman economy, and second, that the

---

[3] The first scholar to question the validity of the argument in print was Pleket (1983) 132. See also Garnsey and Saller (1987) 46–7.

countryside experienced a concentration of landed wealth in the hands of the few, and not an advance of imperial ownership at the expense of the private landlord.

The main point is that any estimate of the value to the state of the agricultural, manufacturing and commercial sectors must take account not only of income from taxation, but also of such savings as accrued to the state through its independence of the commercial market and of private merchants and shippers. It may not be worth attempting a calculation of this sort, for none of the items are quantifiable. Thus I return to my starting-point, our inability to back up with figures any assertion concerning the ancient economy.

So far I have been underlining some of the constraints under which the economic historian of antiquity is operating. It does not follow that any attempt to characterize the late Roman economy and isolate developments within it would be useless. We can be sure that agriculture provided the lion's share of the empire's wealth. This means that the performance of the agricultural sector is the key to the state of the economy as a whole. Can we say what is happening in agriculture in late antiquity?

III. A DECLINE IN PRODUCTION?

'It is generally agreed', writes Jones, 'that there was a decline in agriculture in the later Roman Empire; but little attempt has been made to estimate how serious it was, and on its causes debate has been inconclusive, whether it was due to the general exhaustion of the soil, to shortage of agricultural manpower, or, as contemporaries believed, partly to barbarian invasions and depredations, but predominantly to overtaxation.' At the end of his discussion, Jones states that 'a considerable and growing proportion of the land was abandoned'; he estimates the area abandoned as 'probably no more than say 20 per cent', and identifies high tax rates as the main cause.[4]

The consequences of accepting the figure of 20 per cent or thereabouts are serious. Supposing productivity, i.e., yields per unit area, remained the same, then there would be 20 per cent less food available for consumption – which entails a significantly lower standard of living for the same number of people, or a significant reduction in the numbers of consumers who could ΙΙ be supported at the same level. There were no 'grain mountains' (or 'olive oil mountains') in late Roman society. Poverty and uncertainty were the lot of the mass of the population, at the best of times. This was, incidentally, Fernand Braudel's judgement on the Mediterranean of the historical period up to the sixteenth century.

[4] Jones (1964) 812.

Now Jones does suggest that the land abandoned was mostly of poor quality – which leaves open the possibility that the downturn in food production was less severe than at first sight. And poor land would surely be abandoned first, if there was any choice in the matter. He issued two other caveats: that land was apparently still in high demand and still fetched good prices and that new areas were opened up, most conspicuously in Syria east of Antioch and of adjacent cities. These admissions and the misinterpretation of a crucial text render the figure of 20 per cent useless.

I will come to that text in the moment. Let me first ask whether in principle one can hope to substitute another, in my view more realistic figure. That would be to indulge in idle speculation, all the more idle in my view, because the point has yet to be established that there was a decline in production over the empire as a whole. And that proposition could only be investigated by means of an empire-wide survey. In place of such a survey, which would be premature in the existing state of the evidence, I will confine myself to illustrations from three groups of provinces or regions. These appear to me to have rather different characteristics, which is part of the logic behind my selection. This will also turn out to be my main observation, that the picture of agricultural production is mixed and complex. This is not a very exciting conclusion, perhaps, but still an improvement on a bland generalization about decline.

My groups of provinces are:

(1) North Africa and Syria
(2) Palestine, Greece and Sicily
(3) The frontier provinces of the North and North-West.

1. *North Africa and Syria*

These happen to be the areas from which Jones' figure of 20 per cent *agri deserti* is derived. A great deal hinges on one text. That is a law of the emperor Honorius dated to 422 and directed at North Africa (*Cod.Theod.* 11.28.13). In this law, Honorius wrote off *agri deserti* of the *res privata*, that is, imperial property, in the province of Africa Proconsularis and the neighbouring province of Byzacena: in the former, it would appear that over a third was abandoned, in the latter, more than one half. This law provides the only dramatic case of desertion and depopulation in the list produced by Jones; without North Africa, the figure for *agri deserti* would be nowhere near 20 per cent. The following considerations are apposite:[5]

---

[5] I am greatly indebted in what follows to the discussions of Lepelley (1967), and Whittaker (1976) 138–9, 159–61.

(1) Imperial estates alone are the subject of the law. Land in the hands of individuals and cities is not mentioned. The figures of one-third and one-half abandoned land are calculated on the basis of perhaps one-sixth of the total area.

(2) There is an interesting correspondence between the amount of abandoned land in the law of Honorius and the amount of uncultivated land in present-day Tunisia and Eastern Algeria (the area covered by the two ancient provinces); around four-ninths of the land is not under cultivation.

(3) This makes one wonder about the character and previous history of the land written off for tax purposes by Honorius. First, its character. The imperial estates in North Africa were immense and exceedingly diverse. They took in mountain slopes, forests and bushland, while in Byzacena, in the interior of Tunisia, they included areas of sterile steppe. In short, much of the land being written off by Honorius was not so much abandoned as never brought into regular cultivation. Second, the previous history of the land. Let us suppose that the land was accurately described as abandoned, in the sense of having gone out of cultivation. When had such land ceased to be cultivated? The statistic in the Code does not admit a distinction between, on the one hand, land that had recently gone out of cultivation due to permanent abandonment (and how could permanence of abandonment be established?), and, on the other, land that had some time before gone out of cultivation – just as it does not distinguish between land never farmed and at some time farmed. This point leads to the next.

(4) The law of Honorius comes at the end of a long succession of imperial legislation, and will not be the last of its kind. Its primary objective was actually to encourage the cultivation of imperial land. Honorius was offering a long-term tenancy, an emphyteutic contract, to anyone willing to take over uncultivated land on the imperial estates. About three centuries previously the emperor Hadrian had taken a similar initiative: he had tried to find cultivators of marginal land by offering similar terms.[6] The terms offered by Honorius and by Hadrian were favourable: volunteer cultivators would acquire permanent possession and the right to transmit the land to ΙΙ their heirs. Nor did this policy lapse after Hadrian. Honorius' law suggests that some land – it is not stated how much – had been let on such terms relatively recently. The administrators of the *res privata*, that is the imperial properties, are being ordered to revamp the scheme and find farmers to take on the land. The object of laws of this kind is transparent: they are one aspect of a policy of raising production levels and increasing tax revenues and the efficiency of the tax system. As such, they tell us more

---

[6] For the lex Hadriana and the earlier lex Manciana see e.g. Whittaker (1976) 159–61; Whittaker (1978) 355–61; Kehoe (1988a), e.g. 22ff., 37ff.; Kolendo (1991) 47–74.

about the government's obsession with tax revenues than about the true extent of cultivated land.

(5) Finally, the law as read by Jones is out of line with a whole range of other sources.[7] In the first place, literary sources from Lactantius, in the time of Constantine, through the *Expositio Totius Mundi* of the mid-fourth century, to Augustine (late fourth and early fifth centuries) testify to a prosperous countryside. Then, the archaeological evidence for the numbers, size and fabric of cities, and for trade in agricultural produce again implies prosperity, a prosperity grounded on an essentially agrarian economy. The newer art of field survey adds confirmation for selected regions, such as the Tunisian High Steppe; there in the words of the archaeologist Bruce Hitchner, the 'balanced specialization in both oleoculture and stock-raising to meet the resource requirements of the Roman central state and local urban markets' was sustained until the early sixth century.[8] Finally, Domenico Vera can find no evidence of decadence in North African agriculture in late antiquity: his work revolves around the legal and epigraphic sources and makes a strong case for the prevalence of emphyteutic leases in African agriculture, and by implication for the success of laws such as that of Honorius.[9]

Let us now glance at the case of Syria. This illustrates the point, not necessarily valid only for Syria, that a reduction of cultivation in one area might be compensated for or more than compensated for by an expansion of cultivation in another. Syrian *agri deserti* is attested in two texts, the *Misopogon of* the emperor Julian, for Antioch, and a letter of Theodoret, for Cyrrhus. In *Misopogon*, Julian writes that he has assigned tax-free to the council of Antioch nearly 3,000 *iuga* of cultivated land; this amounted to perhaps about 5 per cent of the total rural territory of that city. Then in 451, about ninety years later, Theodoret, bishop of Cyrrhus, writes in a letter to an official that in a certain category of land 2,500 out of 15,000 *iuga* were bad; this would have amounted to more than 16 per cent of the 15,000, and 4 per cent of the || around 62,000 *iuga* that made up the total territory of the city of Cyrrhus.[10]

On the other hand, the archaeologist Tchalenko found that there was considerable development of agriculture and of villages on the limestone plateau to the East and South-West of Antioch, and inferred the practice of monoculture in olives from the second to the seventh century, and an expansion of wheat growing in areas to the east, from the fourth to the sixth. Jones, whose discussion otherwise omits the evidence of archaeology

---

[7] Briefly, Macmullen (1988) 29ff.; in detail, Lepelley (1979-81).
[8] Hitchner (1994) 39-40.   [9] Vera (1992).
[10] Julian *Mis.* 370D-371A; Theodoret *Ep.* 42, 47.

altogether, makes brief reference to this work but without bringing it into confrontation with the texts relating to *agri deserti*. One wonders what those isolated texts are worth (and the grumbles about hard times from sources such as Libanius), when some sections the Syrian economy at least can be seen to have been booming from the third to the sixth century AD. Some of Tchalenko's interpretations have been revised: for example his picture of uninterrupted prosperity in the region through to the seventh century is now seen as overoptimistic. This does not matter much for our present purposes (though the conclusion that the area witnessed not so much monoculture of olives as polyculture of a prosperous peasantry is relevant to the next section of my paper). Meanwhile the suggestion that the whole phenomenon was a highly successful experiment in the breaking up of imperial property for cultivation in accordance with emphyteutic tenancy agreements, is attractive.[11]

This matter of government initiative and the needs of the central state provides a convenient point of transition to my next group of provinces. And in the case of some members of this group, we have a rather precise turning-point in their history.

2. Palestine, Greece and Sicily

Let us take first Palestine.[12] Constantine became a Christian in 312. One of the consequences was a new era for Palestine. An obscure province became the Holy Land. Lavish endowments were made by emperors, empresses, and aristocratic men and women, and pilgrims and tourists flooded in. The main impact was felt in the urban economy, most obviously in the construction industry. However, demands were made, and life was brought, to the rural economy, and not just to the immediate hinterlands of Jerusalem and the major cities, but also in villages like Shivtah in the arid Negev, which practised run-off agriculture in dammed and terraced wadis. ‖ In time the bubble burst, and it was an economically depressed region that received the Arab invaders.

A second precise date is 330, the inauguration of a second imperial capital, in Constantinople, that is, the creation of a vast centre of consumption, which in no time was making heavy demands on the agricultural resources of the whole region. This was the origin of the mid-fourth-century boom in Thrace, interrupted only by the arrival of the Visigoths in the last quarter of the century; but the region recovered after the departure of Alaric and his Visigoths for the West, and resumed its services to the capital city.[13]

---

[11] Tchalenko (1953); Kennedy (1985) 157–62; Tate (1989).
[12] Kedar (1957); Avi-Yonah (1958). [13] Velkov (1962).

A similar origin may perhaps be attributed to the somewhat mysterious repopulation of the countryside of Greece from the first part of the fourth century, exposed recently by archaeological land-survey in places such as Aetolia, the Argolid, South-west Boeotia, Southern Euboea, Northern Keos, Lakonia, Megalopolis, Melos, Messenia, Nemea and Panakton. The pattern is repeating. A landscape that was full in the Classical and early Hellenistic era emptied thereafter, and remained relatively deserted, for around five centuries. In the late empire, site numbers gradually return over three or more centuries to something like their former count. This might in principle signal more intensive land-use and a demographic upturn, or a redistribution of population to the benefit of the countryside. Susan Alcock has publicized this work in a bold new work of synthesis. Nothing is clear-cut in the historical interpretation of archaeological evidence, and an imaginative reconstruction of long-term trends such as Alcock's is not going to please everyone. But something is happening in the countryside of Greece, and whatever it is, it is not *agri deserti*.[14]

Sicily, as seen through the eyes of Domenica Vera, is a case-study of the repopulation of the countryside, associated with the concentration of large estates, but at the same time their breaking up into parcels for cultivation by *coloni*.[15] It is moreover a regional phenomenon, affecting North Africa and Central and South Italy as well as Sicily. The stimulus for this development is provided by the continuing needs of the city of Rome for basic commodities, and the agency is the interest of the Roman aristocracy in increasing their investments. The process begins in Sicily, in the second half of the third century, interestingly, in compensation for a downturn in African imports into Rome, and is revived in the mid-fourth || century when the grain ships of Egypt are diverted from Rome to Constantinople. My only point of doubt is whether Sicily really belonged to a free market zone wherein rich Romans could cash in more or less at will, exploiting a monopolistic position in the capital city. I wonder whether Sicily was in fact outside the *annona* system of state-organized supply. Was not the expansion of senatorial investments in Sicily and elsewhere made possible by a state-supervised leasing of *res privata*, and did not a desire for increased tax-revenue, in kind or cash, underlie the whole operation?

3. Frontier provinces

In general, one might expect farming to have been most vulnerable, and *agri deserti* most prevalent, in frontier provinces – genuine frontier

---

[14] Briefly, MacMullen (1988) 34, 229–30 n. 126; in detail, Alcock (1993), reviewed by de Ligt (1994); see also Bintliff and Snodgrass (1988) 178–9, 211ff.
[15] Vera (1988).

provinces, not provinces like Syria, which was technically a frontier province, but was relatively free from disruption in the period in question, or Italy, only really disturbed in the time of Visigothic invasion, as was North Africa when the Vandals arrived. For areas thoroughly disrupted by recurring war and barbarian invasion we have to turn away, in fact, from those parts of the empire from which Jones drew his evidence for *agri deserti*, to the Northern provinces. How important was the phenomenon of abandoned land in the Northern frontier areas?

A preliminary observation is that Britain should not be grouped with the other North-West and Northern provinces bordering on the Rhine and Danube. Late third and fourth century Britain was in general prosperous and relatively tranquil, suffering only sporadic and superficial disruption as a result of usurpation and the raiding of Picts and Saxons. In this period the advance of farming onto the damp, heavy soils of valley-bottoms, initiated in an earlier period accelerated, while technological innovations permitted the full development of what had been marginal into optimal agricultural land.[16]

In contrast, the archaeological evidence for North Gaul appears to show population decrease in some areas, the desertion or diminution of some villages or *vici*, a decrease in the number of occupied villas, and so on. This summary of the conclusions of Edith Wightman does need to be qualified in the light of recent work, for example, by Lewit, arguing for a net expansion of site numbers in the Western provinces, though not in Northern Gaul and Germany, and by Whittaker who in his recent work on the frontiers talks of 'population growth' in Lower Saxony and the Low Countries.[17] As for the Northern Balkan provinces, Velkov has assembled the evidence for the || 'incessant incursions of barbarians' and the damage done to village life and agriculture in those regions. It is worth repeating, however, that the late fourth century difficulties followed a mid-fourth century expansion and that Thrace never lost its role as a major supplier of Constantinople.[18]

Influenced by these examples, we might formulate some arguments against permanent depopulation and land-abandonment in the period and places under consideration. I put forward two such arguments for consideration:

First, there were persistent imperial initiatives to resettle land, typically with barbarians, precisely in the zones of maximum disruption, and not always on land that had previously seen cultivation. It is arguable that

---

[16] Jones (1981); Fulford (1989). For Italy, see Hannestad (1962).
[17] Wightman (1985); Lewit (1991); Whittaker (1994) 215. See also Van Ossel (1992).
[18] Velkov (1962).

barbarian settlement made a significant contribution to the preservation of the Roman empire from an economic point of view. The barbarians provided a workforce the cost of producing which did not fall on the economy. Moreover, these were not nomads without agricultural knowledge or skills, whether we are talking of fourth century Alamanni in the upper and middle Rhine, or Visigoths and Ostrogoths in the Danube region. The ethnic composition and legal status of the farming population in frontier areas may well have changed (as is indicated for example by Velkov for the Eastern Danubian provinces), but the land was still being cultivated. In time, of course, central government lost political control and fiscal access to these frontier areas, which became something like 'satrapies' dominated by local warlords.[19]

Secondly, there is a danger of overestimating the extent of the disruption caused by barbarian activity and insecurity in general. There was no scorched earth policy, but rather, pillaging and plunder. The deleterious consequences for agriculture therefore need not have been *permanent*. Evelyne Patlagean summarizes judiciously the evidence for the regions most exposed to invasions in the Eastern empire, namely Thrace, the Persian frontiers, and the Syrian and Arabian steppes.[20] She finds that rural populations tended to retreat into walled cities, villages and fortified strongholds rather than abandon the countryside altogether; the exodus of the peasantry, in other words, was temporary or provisional rather than permanent. As to Thrace, following Velkov, she argues that there was no genuine depopulation and no large-scale transformation of the Thracian countryside until the invasions of the Slavs in the middle of the sixth century – a finding which is confirmed by the continued recruitment of numerous rural Thracians into the army. The corresponding moment of transition in Syria came in the seventh century.

To sum up the argument so far: the picture of agricultural production in the empire is mixed. Some land went out of cultivation, other land was opened up for the first time or rejuvenated. Neither of these developments, the one negative, the other positive, were necessarily permanent in the areas in question. Even if the balance was in favour of *agri deserti*, and this cannot be shown, it was not as heavily weighted in this direction as has been thought.

And we still have to consider the matter of productivity on the remaining arable. The loss of land that was largely marginal and unproductive

---

[19] See Whittaker (1994) ch. 7. The evidence for barbarian settlement is summarized in de Ste. Croix (1981) 509–17.
[20] Patlagean (1977) 303ff.

might not have diminished total food stocks by much. If landowners worked their better land more intensively, then we might actually expect rising productivity to have made up any losses in production totals. Is there any evidence for rising productivity, and what might have been the cause or causes?

IV. RISING PRODUCTIVITY?

We may approach this question indirectly, asking how in principle higher productivity might have been obtained under late Roman conditions. I will briefly consider four possibilities: technological progress; intensification; changes in the organization of labour; and increased taxation.

First, technological progress. It is normally supposed that traditional agricultural methods were only improved on in modest ways after the third century BC in the Mediterranean region.[21] This view is broadly correct, except that it overlooks or underrates the development of new crops, such as new kinds of wheat, and the vine and the olive.[22] One might of course argue, as Robert Sallares does, that relative progress of this kind, where a comparatively backward region makes up ground, petered out in the late empire, simply because 'the potential of the new crops had been fully exploited'.[23] But this is based on the premise that there was no significant expansion of farming onto marginal or virgin land in the late empire, and the archaeological evidence in addition to the prevalence of emphyteutic leases tells against this.

Moving to temperate Europe: there was no stagnation in late Roman Britain, though there might have been in Gaul, from which British farmers appear to have borrowed new crops and techniques. Martin Jones writes of a period of innovation, enterprise and progress from the late third century, especially visible in the sphere of arable production, particularly in the extensive use of metal in ploughs and harvesting equipment. He writes of a 'new lowland agriculture', characterized by the production of breadwheat in the clays and clay loams of valley-bottoms.[24]

Second, intensification. This term has been used to apply to a variety of farming strategies designed to extract more return from the soil. It might involve, for example, a switch from a subsistence crop to one more designed for marketing, or increased labour-inputs aimed at reducing the competition of weeds and building up soil-fertility. Intensification is implied, for example, in the expansion of the production of a highly marketable commodity, olive oil, east of Antioch, and in the specialized production of

[21] Finley (1965). [22] Sallares (1991) 14. [23] Sallares (1991) 15. [24] See n. 16 for refs.

bread-wheat in the valley bottoms of Britain. This is a crop which cannot be grown successfully in such an environment without a high labour input.

A further example of intensification might be the movement of population back onto the land as is thought to have occurred in Achaia. Alcock associated this with the development of the colonate. Whether this is right or not, it does provoke speculation around the question: did the system or systems of labour characteristic of the late empire lead to higher productivity?

Third, changes in labour systems. The labour system especially associated with the later Roman Empire is tied tenancy, the colonate, notwithstanding the fact that slavery still carried on in some quarters. De Martino has recently complained that scholars are preoccupied with the legal status of *coloni* and the origin of the institution, and neglect the economic condition of *coloni*; they write, he says, as if *coloni* existed in isolation from the realities of economic life.[25] His intervention is timely. There has certainly been much less interest in the economic significance of the transition from free tenancy to tied tenancy, that is, the colonate, than in the economic significance of the transition from slavery to tenancy. One notes however the assumption of several authors – for example, Vera for Sicily and Alcock for Greece – that tied tenancy implies the extraction of ‖ higher returns from the land, because of the greater degree of control and supervision that it entailed. This recalls the argument of Finley, and others, for the efficiency and profitability of slavery arising from the extreme exploitability of slaves.[26]

There is some doubt in my mind as to how far the implied analogy between slaves and tied tenants can be taken. Were *coloni* physically as well as legally, slaves to the soil? Let us, however, assume for the sake of the argument that *coloni* were in some sense immobile and made up the permanent labour force on the properties in question.

In 1980 I argued, with reference to an earlier historical period, that the most profitable system of labour was one in which a small, permanent labour force was supplemented by casual labour at peak periods of the agricultural year. I added that such a practice was feasible in Graeco-Roman society, even where the permanent force was made up of slaves, because the slave economy coexisted with the peasant economy, and in the latter, proprietors, tenants and wage-labourers were overlapping categories. Dominic Rathbone proceeded to confirm this hypothesis with numerical models, and has recently demonstrated in an important monograph that the Appianus estate in Egypt was organized in such a way in the mid-third century AD.[27]

---

[25] De Martino (1991) 327–8. [26] Finley (1985) ch. 3; Hopkins (1978a) ch. 1.
[27] Garnsey (1980); Rathbone (1981), (1991).

I am not going to speculate on how many estate-owners were as productivity-conscious and profit-conscious as the management of the Appianus estate. My point is a different and a more general one. It is that a late Roman estate completely dependent on a tied labour-force would have been just as unprofitable as a late Republican 'slave estate' which tried to be self-sufficient in terms of labour. In fact, the latter never existed – there never was a fully self-sufficient slave estate, while economic logic is against the existence of the former, a fully self-sufficient colonate estate.

Those estates did best in the late empire, I would conjecture, which could draw on an ample supply of extra labourers from off the estate to supplement a nucleus of permanent workers. This implies a vigorous village life and a free peasantry, or at the least a peasantry that was not physically affixed to their tenancies. We have good evidence from Libanius and other literary sources that both villages and free peasants survived in Syria.[28] Meanwhile, archaeologists are increasingly talking of the survival, increase, ubiquity of villages and other sub-urban agglomerations in Gaul, Sicily and sundry other provinces of the empire.[29] They were there all the time, as it were, but archaeologists and historians had not noticed them, being preoccupied with, on the one hand cities, and on the other hand, villas. In the same way, speculation as to the status of the inhabitants of the villages has hardly even begun. I submit that these villages, and villagers, hold the key to the economic success or otherwise of the colonate.[30]

Finally, the effect of higher rates of taxation on productivity should be considered. It is a thesis of Hopkins, enunciated in relation to the period of the Principate, that conquest and the imposition of tribute forced provincials to raise the level of agricultural productivity. The size of the surplus had to be increased in order to meet demands that were new or higher than those imposed by earlier authorities. The matter is disputed: Whittaker and Shaw independently argue that tax might depress rather than stimulate production.[31] Hopkins' proposition is not one that Jones would have wanted to apply to the late Roman period, and Hopkins does not himself try to relate his thesis to late antiquity. It was Jones who expounded most systematically the theory that taxes substantially increased, and continued to increase, in the late empire. In addition, for Jones, it was above all the mounting tax burden that depressed agriculture and led to the abandonment of land and depopulation in the countryside. In addition, it was the

---

[28] Liebeschuetz (1972) 61–72.
[29] On *vici*, see e.g. Whittaker (1990); de Ligt (1991) 33–42.
[30] Brenner (1976), applied by de Ste. Croix (1981) 83 to the colonate, emphasizes that pre-industrial labour systems (he has serfdom in mind in particular) were exploitative of the work-force; the issue with which I am here concerned is the effect of (putative) higher levels of exploitation on agricultural productivity.
[31] Hopkins (1980); Whittaker (1978) 331ff.; Shaw (1983) 149ff.

view of Finley that the late imperial world failed to raise production and productivity to meet the challenge of higher taxation levels.[32]

That taxes were higher in the late than early empire is plausible, whatever may be thought of Jones' methodology, and again a few isolated references are made to carry a great deal of weight. It is likely enough that a substantially larger court, bureaucracy and army made increased tax demands on the population, particularly the farming population, of the empire.[33] But it is not clear how this can be connected with developments on the land. Take the case of Greece. How do we relate the imposition of a land tax, following the reduction of Greece to the status of a || province at the beginning of the Principate, to the relative emptiness of the landscape of Roman Greece? How do we relate the supposed higher tax rates of the late empire, and the inexorable rise in those rates, to the apparent repopulation of the same landscape in that period?

Did taxation stimulate or depress production? On the one hand, neither proposition is always true, and each might have plausibility in particular circumstances; on the other hand, taxation may only be one of several contributing factors to a rise in productivity, and we shall never know how these factors should be ranked. Those factors might include, as a backdrop, settled conditions, encouraging active engagement and investment in farming, and, not unrelated, the existence or growth of demand for an agricultural surplus.

CONCLUSION

This was a large subject, as is indicated by all that I have omitted, and by the summary way in which I have dealt with the matters I did include. A sceptic might go further than this, and say that it simply is a waste of time to try to generalize about the economic and demographic condition of 'the empire' (a huge expanse of territory taking in large tracts of three continents) in 'late antiquity' (a period of two-to-three hundred years), especially in view of the meagre evidence at our disposal. I sympathize with this position. But earlier scholars have not been deterred by the formidable scale of the undertaking, and it has not stopped them propounding theories of general decline and depopulation. Their views need to be critically examined, and there needs to be a debate on methodology, on more fruitful and less fruitful ways to proceed. The size of the task has not been, and should not be, a disincentive; but in attempting it we should above all give due consideration to spatial and temporal differences, that is to say, we must be attentive to regional contrasts, and to the ebb and flow of rural life, in this as in other historical epochs. ||

[32] Jones (1964), (1974) chs. 2, 8; Finley (1981) 193–5.
[33] But see Whittaker (1980); Carrié (1993).

10

MOUNTAIN ECONOMIES IN SOUTHERN EUROPE

THOUGHTS ON THE EARLY HISTORY,
CONTINUITY AND INDIVIDUALITY
OF MEDITERRANEAN UPLAND
PASTORALISM[1]

INTRODUCTION

The perspective of this paper is historical rather than ethnological. This is necessarily the case given my area of specialization (antiquity and early Middle Ages) and the relative paucity of information bearing on Mediterranean mountain societies before documentary evidence becomes available, in the Middle Ages or later. (This is not to say that medieval documents, consisting typically of the records of large, ecclesiastical landholdings (e.g. Wickham (1982); Rowland (1982)), are of the stuff to produce studies comparable with E. Le Roy Ladurie's 'Montaillou'). However, students of antiquity no longer passively accept the deficiencies of the conventional source material, which is for the most part literary and city-oriented, issuing from a civilization centred on the lowlands, coasts and islands of the Mediterranean region. Archaeology, through the utilization of new techniques such as carbon-dating, pollen analysis, zoo-archaeology and dendrochronology (Bottema (1974); Kuniholm and Striker (1983); Payne (1985)), improved methods of field survey and excavation (Barker, Lloyd and Webley (1978), Lloyd and Barker (1981)), and, not least, methods, theories and information gleaned from the social and life sciences (cf. Halstead (1984)), can now establish a firmer outline of the chronology and changing character of human and environmental development in the Mediterranean. In addition, historians and archaeologists are now learning to use modern or recent quantitative data for climatic behaviour and agricultural performance to construct agroclimatological models of past

[1] In writing this paper I have benefited in particular from the assistance of Robin Donkin, Paul Halstead, James Lewthwaite, John Patterson, Oliver Rackham and Jonathan Thompson. I am grateful also to Graeme Barker and Chris Wickham for making work available in advance of publication, and to Carmine Ampolo for sending me material unavailable in the United Kingdom.

Mediterranean societies (Garnsey, Gallant and Rathbone (1984)). Also important is the development of ethnoarchaeology, the study of the archaeology created by modern or recent societies, of hunter-gatherers or nomadic or transhumant pastoralists, with a view to identifying and characterizing comparable societies in the past from the archaeological record (Barker (1989)). Unfortunately the emergence of ethnoarchaeology is proceeding *pari passu* with a diminution in quantity and quality of the raw material on which its progress depends – in the case that concerns us, the traditional mountain communities of the Mediterranean, which are fast declining under the impact of economic forces. The need to catch these societies before they disappear should be brought home to anthropologists, as well as to historians and archaeologists. Despite a few successful || studies (Campbell (1964); Koster (1977); Ravis-Giordani (1983)) this is an underexploited area of scholarship – in contrast with the study of Alpine, and in particular Andean mountain societies (e.g. Netting (1972); (1982), Rhoades and Thompson (1975); Murra (1975); Lehmann (1982)), or for that matter, Mediterranean peasant societies (Davis (1973); Forbes (1982)). In what follows I pursue certain broad themes relating to the historical development of man's interest in and exploitation of what was and still is, for most inhabitants of the Mediterranean, a peripheral and inhospitable world.

THE MARGINALITY OF THE MOUNTAINS

Strabo, a Greek geographer patronized by the emperor Augustus, wrote with distaste of the mountain peoples of the Iberian peninsula who lived on goat's meat, ate acorn bread for two thirds of the year, drank beer not wine, used butter not olive oil and exchanged by barter (3.3.7).

Strabo reveals the prejudices – and some of the dietary preferences – of the cultured urban élite of Mediterranean antiquity. In the literature of antiquity mountains are the haunt of the uncivilized and savage, whether men or beasts. Civilization is centred on the 'polis' or 'civitas'; it does not extend much beyond the lowlands, where in the main the permanent communities of the Graeco-Roman world were to be found. When the Romans, the supreme conquering nation of the ancient world, extended their advance into the interior of the Iberian peninsula or the backblocks of France, for example, the prerequisite and symbol of their success was the abandonment by the conquered tribes of their hill-top refuges and their resettlement as communities of farmers in the plain, preferably within the territory and juridical and fiscal control of an urban centre.

Goods were exchanged with the inhabitants of the mountains. Strabo knew that the Carretanians on the Celtic side of the Pyrenees gained useful revenues from their excellent hams (3.4.11), that the Ligurians brought down to Genua flocks, hides, honey and timber, taking back olive oil and Italian wine, their own wine being harsh and flavoured with pitch; their preferred beverages, however, were milk and a drink made of barley (4.6.2). Strabo no doubt represents a general view when he states that the mountain peoples were forced into exchange relationships with the people of the plain because of the poverty of their own territory, and that their natural instinct was to plunder. The mountains were the home of brigands. In any case there is no hint in Strabo that the inhabitants of the plains were interested in any direct exploitation of the resources of the mountains. We note for example the detail that the Ligurian uplanders pastured their flocks in the coastal districts as well as in the mountains, but Strabo does not identify any plain-based pastoral industry which used the pastures of the Ligurian alps: Strabo, then, knew of the operation in Liguria of 'transhumance inverse', migration of livestock proceeding from a mountain base (a practice of || modern Ligurian shepherds, cf. Lamboglia (1921)) but not apparently of 'transhumance normale', migration initiating from the plain. Strabo, a most casual collector and dispenser of information, was less than well-informed on this score.

Still, the general impression that Strabo conveys, of the marginality of the mountains from an economic point of view, is largely correct. The Mediterranean peoples have traditionally been cereal consumers on a massive scale; in antiquity perhaps 65–75 per cent of their daily food energy requirements were provided by the annual cereal crop (cf. Foxhall and Forbes (1982)). Seed crops can be grown at high elevations, up to perhaps 1500–1800 metres in Southern Europe – not however the preferred cereals of antiquity, the various primitive wheats and barleys. Potatoes and maize were unknown. But yields were low and variable, reflecting the relative unsuitability of the soils and the shortness of the growing season, which decreases as altitude increases – falling for example from around 170 days at 1,000 metres to around 95 days at 2,000 metres (Baticle (1974) 83). Early farmers made use of lower slopes for the deep-rooted walnut, chestnut, vine, fig, and to a limited extent, that is, in frost-free zones, the olive. However, insofar as the peoples of the Mediterranean lowlands were interested in the economic exploitation of the mountains in the age before hydro-electricity, tourism and the cult of health (if we leave aside minerals, in any case only sporadically present), it was summer pasture which attracted them. A characteristic feature of livestock raising in the Mediterranean region is transhumance, 'Transhumanz', 'yaylag' pastoralism (a Soviet anthropological term, where 'yaylag' is Turkish for summer highland pasture, Khazanov (1983) 23), defined as 'l'oscillation annuelle du bétail entre deux zones de pâturage que séparent des espaces consacrés à des formes d'exploitation différentes' (Arbos (1922)). In some specific historical contexts the pastoral industry has established a position of relative independence in relation to the agricultural economy. The mass of the population of the Mediterranean, however, has continued to depend for their subsistence on the products of agriculture. Agriculture in comparison with animal husbandry is both more efficient in furnishing man's calorific requirements, and more productive per unit area, given choice of area, that is, lowlands. A family of six must consume about 115 sheep of carcass weight twenty kilograms or about 130 sheep of fifteen kilograms if mutton is to be their main source of food energy (Dahl and Hjort (1976) 220); such a family would have to run about 360 live sheep and control a grazing area of about 3.6 square kilometres (Halstead (1981) 314, (1984) ch. 7.3). For a largely lowland population of limited land resources, pure pastoralism was no alternative to agriculture as a way of life.

WAS THERE A SPECIFICALLY MEDITERRANEAN FORM OF PASTORALISM?

The best known and most conspicuous examples of Mediterranean transhumance in past history are perhaps the 'Mesta' of Castile, and the 'Dogana della Mena delle Pecore di Puglia'. The 'Mesta' ran for five and one half centuries from || its establishment by the court in 1273 and involved at its height in the early sixteenth century the movement of four to five million sheep (Klein (1920)). The 'Dogana' governed the movements of sheep (amounting to around five and one half million at its peak in the late seventeenth century) in the Central and Southern Apennines from its inauguration by Alfonso I of Aragon in 1447 until its abolition in 1806 (Sprengel (1971)). In the Balkans it is the transhumant or seminomadic 'Vlachs' and 'Sarakatsani' who have attracted most attention among historians and anthropologists (Wiegand (1894); Wace and Thompson (1914); Campbell (1964); Hammond (1976); Winnifrith (1983)).

For early evidence of a developed pastoral industry in Italy, we can go back to classical Roman times to Varro, a Roman senator, antiquarian, and composer of three books on *Res rusticae* in the mid-first century BC, that is, a generation before Strabo. Varro knew of rich Romans who owned transhumant flocks of sheep in Italy. Indeed he was one of them, sending a substantial flock, presumably all or most of the 800 sheep that are attributed to him, the distance of around 250 kilometres between the Tavoliere, the great plain of Puglia, and the mountains near Reate east of Rome. The origins of what has been called 'horizontal or Mediterranean' transhumance practised by Varro and his friends and in later ages by Roman emperors is much debated (Skydsgaard (1974); Pasquinucci (1979)). Rome's conquest of Samnium had removed the main political barrier to the long-distance movement of livestock in Italy by the early third century BC. But there may not have been any substantial investment in long-distance transhumance for another century, that is to say, until suitable conditions for its development were created with the establishment of peace in Italy following the Carthaginian invasion and occupation of the South, the large-scale confiscation of land from Italian supporters of Hannibal that followed his retreat, and the enrichment of Roman magnates in the wars in Spain, the Eastern Mediterranean and North Africa (Toynbee (1965); Brunt (1971); Frayn (1984)). By this account, then, long-distance transhumant pastoralism 'took off' in Italy in the course of the second century BC, a century before the lifetime of Varro.

Some would give Italian long-distance transhumance a longer history. Not Franciosa, who in a lengthy treatment of the subject put forward the view that in the pre-Roman period political conditions, in particular territorial conflicts, made possible only a simple form of livestock raising in the Apennines, 'quella stanziale con movimenti localizzati tra le vallate e i sovrincombenti rilievi montuosi' (Franciosa (1951) 52). A recent, authoritative treatment, however, makes the following generalized statement in support of a pre-Roman origin for long-distance stock movement:

> Tanto più che nella maggior parte delle aree annesse, l'economia pastorale aveva grande importanza e la transumanza doveva essere stata praticata da epoca pre- e protostorica, con spostamenti stagionali di raggio più o meno ‖ esteso, verosimilmente regolati in tempo di pace da accordi e consuetudini che permettevano alle comunità di pianura e di montagna di sfruttare i rispettivi pascoli complementari. (Pasquinucci (1979) 93-4)

The evidence on which this statement is based is essentially archaeological: it consists of excavated artefacts and faunal samples and the implications of site locations. The presence of hill-top sites, shrines to Hercules and statuettes of the same god, or for that matter *fibulae* (clasps) in scattered sites of the Abruzzi and in the approaches to the mountains in proximity to drove roads, does point to their use for the passage of flocks (Barker (1973), (1975); La Regina (1970-1); (1975), di Niro (1977); J. Patterson (1985)). However, it would be unwise to ascribe to pastoralism a continuous, trouble-free history. Franciosa's intuition concerning the unstable political situation in pre-Roman times carries weight. One might add that the defeat of the main Samnite forces, and the colonization of key points in enemy territory such as Isernia and Benevento, are unlikely to have produced tranquillity overnight in the conquered area. Again, caution is advisable in estimating the scale of pastoralism in the context of what was probably an underpopulated society practising a relatively primitive mixed farming economy. A statement such as the following needs to be tested in the light of the demographic and economic setting of the mountain communities concerned and their neighbours:

> Che il carico di bestiame (sc. in età preromana) fosse consistente e richiedesse vaste estensioni pascolive, si può intuire anche dal fatto che lana e pelli erano indispensabili per l'abbigliamento e l'armamento. (Pasquinucci (1984))

In the Balkan peninsula also, the early history of transhumant pastoralism is obscure and controversial. Evidence is in fact notoriously thin even for the classical period of Greek history (Georgoudi (1976)). This has not prevented scholars from surmising that pastoralism, transhumant or semi-nomadic, has been a constant feature of the North-west Balkan peninsula throughout history – and prehistory; and even that the present-day shepherds are direct descendants of their presumed predecessors in pre-classical Greece (Hoeg (1925)).

Whatever the truth about long-range transhumant pastoralism in the context of pre-Roman Italy, there is no difficulty in admitting the presence in this period of the kind of pastoralism envisaged by Franciosa (above), that is to say, a modest form of transhumance which involved the movement of flocks over short distances from pastures in the plain to others on high ground, or vice versa. It is to be noted that its existence is explicitly accepted by Pasquinucci in the passage quoted above ('con spostamenti stagionali di raggio più o meno esteso'), if only in passing, while elsewhere brief reference is made to 'piccola' as opposed to 'grande' transhumance. ||

Similarly, for the Roman period, it would be a mistake to assert that long-distance transhumant pastoralism displaced earlier forms of animal husbandry, or that Varro and classical Romans knew and practised no other. For classical as for pre-classical Italy it is safe to postulate the coexistence of several patterns of animal husbandry. The enterprises of Roman aristocrats and emperors (Corbier (1983)) are simply the most conspicuous, and it is not surprising that they have monopolized the attention of historians of antiquity, rather as the 'Mesta' and 'Dogana' have caught the eye of students of the medieval and early modern periods at the expense of smaller-scale pastoral movements. In the Biferno valley (Molise), the site of a recent extensive archaeological field survey, villagers at the valley head apparently drove their flocks a few miles into the lower valley in a descent of about 500 metres. This same valley in its upper reaches is crossed by major north-south transhumant tracks joining Apulia and the Abruzzi. The Roman writer Columella, whose *De re rustica* in ten books appeared in the middle of the first century AD, that is, about one hundred years after Varro's work, actually manages to ignore transhumance movements altogether in describing what appears to be entirely a farm-based animal husbandry. Varro himself gives most of his attention to the raising of stock at or near the farm. He does advise the pasturing of cattle 'in wooded land' (*in nemoribus*), adding 'and those which spend the winter along the coast are driven in summer into the leafy mountains' (2.2.8); and he observes that mules, a speciality of his home district Reate, 'are driven into the mountains in summer' (2.8.5). But it is not to be supposed that in either case the destination of the animals was distant rather than local upland ranges. Meanwhile in the case of sheep, Varro contrasts the flocks of the home farm (*uillatici greges*) with those who use the 'glades and woody pastures' (*saltus et siluestres loci*) (2.2.8), self-evidently not a description of high mountains. Similarly, herdsmen are divided into those who work the *calles* (Latin for tracks, 'tratturi'), and those who come back to the farm every day (2.10.1). The *calles* in question need not be the long-distance 'tratturi'.

In sum, there is a case for saying that a form of long-distance transhumance developed in the Mediterranean which was distinctive to the region, and that it evolved, in Italy anyway, when an élite possessed the resources in cash and in land to run sizeable flocks between properties in their possession or under their control. Varro certainly owned land around Reate; presumably it was for this reason that his sheep travelled all the way to the Reatine mountains instead of pasturing for a fee in some equally suitable terrain further south and closer to their base, which was Apulia (2 pr. 6). It does not follow, however, that this was the typical Mediterranean form of pastoralism. To this extent the terminological distinction sometimes employed between 'horizontal or Mediterranean' and 'vertical or Alpine' transhumance is a barrier to understanding. When scholars refer to the former, they evidently have in mind the seasonal movement of livestock, typically sheep but also goats, over long distances. But we have identified another form of stock movement, namely short-range transhumance, which is equally 'Mediterranean' and more accurately described as 'vertical' than 'horizontal'. In any case, 'horizontal' must be shorthand for 'vertical plus horizontal'. However far the flock travels along range-roads to reach the seasonal pastures, winter or summer, that are their destination, the 'raison d'être' of such stock migration is 'vertical' movement between lower and higher ecological zones. To add to the confusion, there are writers who choose not to refer to the 'vertical' movement of livestock in an Alpine setting (monticazione, alpeggio, alpinage) as 'transhumance'. Blache in his classic *L'homme et la montagne* claims that transhumance in France is practised only in the southern part of the Alpine chain and the Pyrenees; the North French Alps and Switzerland are excluded, because there is no migration from plain (or 'Mittelland') to mountains, which are left to the 'montagnards' and inhabitants of the valleys to exploit (Blache

(1933)). Blache was apparently unaware of a pattern of sheep-raising which established itself in Switzerland subsequent to the First World War, involving the transport of the flock in summer from the Mittelland to the mountains. Gubler-Gross, in his recent dissertation on transhumance in modern Switzerland, focuses almost entirely on this phenomenon, to the exclusion, in the manner of Blache, of the traditional seasonal movement of cattle between valley and lower mountain slope and upland meadow (Gubler-Gross (1962)). Yet the Alpine districts were turning away from cereal cultivation towards extensive livestock raising, involving cattle, from the eleventh century, in a development which took five or more centuries to complete. There are other apparent illogicalities in the literature of pastoralism; one is the refusal in some quarters to apply the label 'pastoralism' to any system of animal husbandry in which agricultural activities are a not negligible element (Delano Smith (1979) 239). In our case, there is a need to apply a less restrictive definition of transhumance, one which for example takes in short-range as well as long-range stock movements and can therefore embrace animals other than small ruminants.

One by-product of the adoption of a single model with two-dimensional variations, would be the restoration of the concept of 'verticality' to the central position that it must occupy in the analysis of any pastoral system which utilizes mountains. One can then proceed to draw distinctions between Mediterranean and Alpine (and Andean) verticality. The essential difference between Mediterranean and Alpine pastoral movements becomes clear if we ask why they were undertaken. Briefly, Central and Southern Italians, and other Mediteranean peoples, take their sheep to the mountains when, and because, there is no more food for them on the parched plains. Alpine farmers, on the other hand, drive their cattle to the high grasslands in the same, somewhat abbreviated, summer season, in order to free the lower fields for the production of forage crops and hay for consumption by the cattle after their autumn return and stabling. Meanwhile, ‖ in parallel with transhumant pasturing, some of the middle and high grasslands are set aside for haymaking, since high altitude grass is thought to be beneficial to the animals. Haymaking is not generally feasible in the Mediterranean uplands.

CLIMATIC DETERMINISM – AND ITS LIMITS

Having accepted the coexistence of different forms of pastoralism in the Mediterranean, we should next recognize the possibility of discontinuities in the historical development of pastoralism. The case for continuity is normally put in terms of the climatic and ecological constraints on man's existence and survival in a Mediterranean setting. The argument is a traditional one; it has been accepted without question by generations of scholars. The picture of historical reality which it implies has been challenged and the primacy of social, economic and political factors asserted only recently (Lewthwaite (1981), (1984)). In Andean scholarship the converse has occurred: Murra's explanation of verticality in terms of superstructural factors (verticality is seen as essentially a mechanism of control) (Murra (1975)) is being countered by rival explanations emphasizing the environmental constraints on production in mountain zones (Guillet (1981)).

The case for environmental constraints on man's operations in the Mediterranean region can be put simply. In the Mediterranean, plant growth is inhibited by cold, especially in the uplands (the lowlands generally experience a mild winter), and by aridity. Spring growth can represent as much as 85 per cent of the growth of the year, as has been demonstrated in stations in the 'Murge' in South Italy and the 'los Pedroches' plateau north of the Sierra Morena in Spain (Baticle (1974) 26). Outside the (untypical) irrigated meadows and marshes, the (typical) summer drought dries up the natural pastures of the lowlands and forces the livestock into the mountains, where the snows have melted to expose fresh pastures. The seasonal movement of stock is confined in large part to the smaller ruminants, especially sheep, often the goat, occasionally the pig. Sheep and goats are light and mobile, can cope with steep and rough terrain, and can live off the poorer pastures, the 'maquis' and 'garriga', which are common on Mediterranean slopes and uplands.

This, the conventional picture of Mediterranean pastoralism, needs to be refined to make allowance for regional variations in climatic and vegetational conditions, which affect for example the length and severity of the summer drought. Its main weakness, however, is its limited usefulness as a tool to explain the shape that animal husbandry has taken in the Mediterranean throughout history. For example, it would be quite mistaken to seek to explain the phenomenon of the aragonese 'Dogana' or for that matter the quantitatively much less significant enterprises of classical Romans with reference to a supposed iron law of climate and geography. Blache writes: 'Aux origines de la transhumance on trouve moins l'ingéniosité humaine que les lois de la nature vivante' (Blache (1933)). For Franciosa, transhumance is 'una consequenza del clima ... con una causalità puramente geografica' (Franciosa (1951) 11, cf. 17). This is at best a halftruth – as in fact Franciosa appears to concede later when he states that transhumance represents 'un adattamento costruttivo alle condizioni fisiche ... e non meno a quelle sociali e igieniche (di instabilità, di insicurezza, di malaria)' (p. 51). Transhumance was not 'naturale', 'un fenomeno geografico': it was man-made, the product of social, economic and political conditions specific to particular historical periods.

This is particularly true in the case of extensive pastoralism, or long-range transhumance. One requirement for its institution, or expansion, is the economic and political weakness of local agriculture often following a period of warfare, as in classical Rome and medieval Spain; another is the existence of an outlet for the products of pastoralism, in antiquity and the Middle Ages principally wool, in the modern period more commonly cheese and meat. The size of the industry was determined above all by the strength and stability of market demand. In the last hundred years, the fortunes of Sardinian pastoralism have been closely related to the fluctuating demand for Sardinian cheese in Italy and other countries, including North America; while Roquefort sustains Corsican pastoralism at its relatively high level of significance. The estimates (or assumptions) of scholars of antiquity concerning the size and importance of Italian transhumance in the Republican and Imperial period are invariably exaggerated because they are not based on a realistic assessment of the size of the market, and on an understanding of the economy of extensive pastoralism in general. 'Mesta' and 'Dogana', which responded to a Europe-wide demand for wool for textiles, would have far outstripped the pastoral industry of the classical Roman period.

In the second place, political conditions affected the health of the pastoral industry. The end of the Roman Empire may have ushered in a period of uncertainty for pastoralism in the Apennines (Wickham (1982) 50, (1983) 34), although the organizational capacity of Lombardian or Frankish governments is not to be discounted altogether. In the same period insecurity in Sardinia and Corsica, because it was concentrated in the littoral and lowland areas, had the paradoxical effect of stimulating pastoralism in the less vulnerable interior of those islands in the early Middle Ages (Lewthwaite (1984)). At the other extreme, 'Mesta' and 'Dogana' were implemented by powerful political authorities, which, spurred on by the prospect of lucrative tax revenues, were able to control the economy of extensive regions in Spain and Italy, respectively. The parallel with Andean verticality as interpreted by Murra does not need stressing (Murra (1975); D'Altroy and Earle (1985) 189). In classical Rome, pastoral enterprises were regulated but not institutionalized: a less elaborate apparatus of control and a less dirigist ideology combined with strictly limited marketing possibilities to produce a smaller scale pastoral industry. ‖

THE CREATION OF MOUNTAIN PASTURE

We have been considering the role that man has himself played in shaping the historical development of pastoralism. But this has an aspect thus far untreated. The physical environment imposes constraints on human behaviour. Yet man has shown himself capable of transforming his natural surroundings. In particular, the geographical conditions under which long-distance transhumance could flourish are in some important respects man-made.

Transhumance by definition involves stock movements between two sets of seasonal pastures, in the plain and in the mountains. But we need to ask what pasture was available in the mountains.

Natural grassland is relatively rare in the Mediterranean. This is not because the mountains are everywhere too low. It is true that we are dealing with mountains that rarely top 3,000 metres, mere ant-hills from the perspective of an Andean or Himalayan geographer. However, the lack of height is offset by the phenomenon of 'Massenerhebung', the compression of zones of climate and vegetation on small mountains relative to altitude, compared with the interior of big mountain ranges. The natural upper limit of woodland in South Greek mountains, for example, is about 1,800–1,900 metres, as is indicated by relict trees in cliffs. Thus on Parnassus and Cretan Ida a zone of 500–600 metres separates treeline from (more or less permanent) snowline. If natural grassland is rare in Greece, the reason is not so much the lack of altitude as the hard limestone and marble rock which inhibits the formation of suitable soils (O. Rackham, personal communication).

However, man has lowered the treeline and created an artificial, pseudo-alpine meadow. The pastures thus formed are frequently low in mineral and protein content and also very liable to the summer drought, which, in the traditional model of transhumant pastoralism, is a feature of the lowlands (Baticle (1974)). The irregularity of the mountain climate in Sardinia means that insofar as transhumance takes place (and most sheep are not transhumant), the flocks are driven not up to escape the summer drought but down to avoid the winter cold (Le Lannou (1941)).

The deforestation which created the middle-altitude pastures is usually attributed to organized pastoralism. 'In Spain after the Reconquest, deforestation became the accepted policy of the pastoralists, especially after 1273 when the Mesta of Castile was established, first along the drove roads, and then in the pastures ... With their Spanish experience, the Aragonese did the same thing in Southern Italy after 1300' (Houston (1964) 114). 'Trees were not tolerated on or near the grazing lands because, it was held, their roots absorbed too much moisture from the soil and so reduced the grass cover. Whole forests were cut down by or as a result of Dogana pressures' (Delano Smith (1979) 246). Clearance of high woodland is thought to have accelerated markedly in the nineteenth century. We read that it was in this period that half the woods that covered the ‖ slopes of the Gran Sasso and other high mountains in the Abruzzi were destroyed (Franciosa (1951) 71).

Was antiquity too a period of significant tree-clearance in the mountains? Woods can be cut down (or burned) more than once; they come back when pastoralism is in retreat. For this reason wildwood is on the increase in the Mediterranean mountains today. It is thus in theory possible that deforestation was carried out to the same extent in Italy in the Roman period as in the high Middle Ages – although the probability of this seems slim in view of the relatively small scale of Roman pastoralism. In the Balkans the problem is rather different: we know that Greece was well-wooded in antiquity, especially in the Pindus range in the North-west – this is confirmed by the palynological evidence, where it is available in sufficient quantity and quality (Bottema (1974); Halstead (1981), (1984)). And as we saw we have virtually no information about uplands pastoralism in ancient Greece. But it would be rash to state that woodland cover in antiquity was such as to preclude transhumance altogether. This means among other things that the continuous existence of pastoral transhumance in the Greek mountains cannot be ruled out, even if we are not inclined to accept particular continuity theories, such as those that find the origins of today's 'Sarakatsani' in antiquity (Hoeg (1925)), or ascribe the emergence of Doric and Northwest Greek dialects to the infiltration into settled early archaic Greek communities of transhumant or nomadic shepherds established in the Greek mountains (Kirsten (1983)).

CONCLUSION

Geographical facts do not account for long-range transhumance, or even for the existence of a pastoral industry at all. They rather govern the form, or more accurately, forms, that pastoralism can take in a Mediterranean setting, whether as a partner with agriculture and arboriculture in the mixed farm characteristic of the traditional peasant economy, or as a semi-independent, relatively specialized industry operating over an extended area, or as something in between. Of these two 'pure' forms the first has strong grounds for being considered indigenous to the Mediterranean region and a more or less permanent feature of the landscape. In it the pastoral element is underdeveloped and engaged in a symbiotic association with the other sectors. It is also mixed in character, involving bovines for traction, swine for meat and ovicaprines for clothing and milk products – not normally for meat, for sheep are less efficient converters of plant food into meat than pigs and have other uses. The fodder shortage of the summer months when vegetational growth ceases varies in scale and severity with local climatic conditions. It is met, or alleviated, by the combination of several remedies. The first is the use of stubble, fallow and wasteland for grazing, typically by sheep, which in the process return manure to the soil. Sheep manure is both qualitatively superior and ample – a modern sheep is capable of producing 500 kilograms of manure ‖ per annum (Baticle (1974) 34) – and in some contexts has been regarded as the sheep's main asset. The second food resource for animals in the lean season is arboreal. An observer of Umbrian agriculture at the turn of the eighteenth century describes the careful exploitation by the peasants of foliage as well as all kinds of vegetable growth:

> Le paysan met à profit toute l'herbe qu'il peut faucher sur le bord des fossées, toutes les feuilles qu'il peut arracher à la vigne ou aux peupliers, toutes les plantes parasites qu'il peut trier entre ses blés et toute la paille qu'il peut hacher et mêler aux fourrages vertes; il va souvent jusqu'à dépouiller en automne les arbres fruitiers de leurs feuilles, et même les figuiers, malgré l'âcreté de leur sève; il réussit enfin par cet esprit d'économie, s'il a peu de bêtes en proportion de son terrain, à en avoir beaucoup et beaucoup de fumier en proportion de son fourrage. (Desplanques (1969) 419)

But we should also bear in mind traditional forms of woodland exploitation, in particular the acorn-hog economy of Southwest Iberia or Umbria, or the chestnut-hog economy of the Tyrrhenian islands (Parsons (1962); Desplanques (1969) 420; Lewthwaite (1982)), Umbria, the Tyrrhenian islands, and most notably the SouthWest region of the Iberian peninsula (Desplanques (1969) 420; Lewthwaite (1982); Parsons (1962)). Thirdly, the broken nature of much of the landscape, particularly in the Balkan and Italian peninsulas, makes the local movement of livestock between different ecological zones desirable and feasible. Long-range transhumance in contrast is inconvenient, expensive and detrimental to agriculture in that it deprives the lowland soils of a valuable fertilizer. Its emergence is associated with historical change, whether social and demographic, or in respect of the shape or structure of political authority, or in the level and nature of consumer demand for its products. Similar factors have engineered its recent rapid decline and will set the limits of its future development. ‖

Addendum

With the aid of comparative evidence, this article attacks the position of Gabba and Pasquinucci (1979), arguing in particular against the deterministic assumption that the Mediterranean terrain and climate could only produce a single kind of transhumance. G. insists on the importance of historical context, which is essential for the differentiation between types of Italian pastoralism in different historical periods.

This line of inquiry has been extensively developed by Thompson (1989) who reinterprets the literary sources and, with reference to comparative evidence, tries to assess the quantitative and qualitative importance of pastoralism in Italy in the classical period. Halstead (1987) 79–81 discusses transhumance, arguing that wholesale removal of livestock from arable farmlands was probably not common in antiquity (with reference to Garnsey (1986b)); because of differences in the social environment, transhumance was not as widespread in Roman Italy as in later periods. Barker (1989) does not refer to either version of this paper but follows Thompson (1989) in reckoning with substantial flocks which were permanently kept in lowlands (13). Morley (1996) 151–8 deals with pastoralism and transhumance in Roman Italy: he concludes that even though small-scale pastoralism was the norm (155), long-distance transhumance took place on a considerable scale (157) prompted by the pull of the metropolitan market (156); this was confined to a limited area of Italy (158). On pastoralism in Roman Italy, see also Lo Cascio (1985–90); Buonocore (1986); and cf. Chaniotis (1995) on ancient Crete. For comparative evidence, see, e.g., Blanks (1995).

PART III

FOOD

11

GRAIN FOR ATHENS

How classical Athens was fed is not a matter of marginal importance. Nothing less than the material base of a brilliant civilization is at issue. The subject gains additional interest from the apparent fact that Athens' food needs far outstripped the capacity of its home territory to satisfy them.

However, any attempt to discover the extent of Athens' dependence on external sources of supply in any particular period is hindered by the lack of precise and detailed information pertaining to land under cultivation, population level, food consumption rate, yield, and sowing rate. Absence of data has not deterred scholars in the past from attempting to calculate the relative importance of home-produced and imported grain, and for better or for worse their conjectures underpin current conceptions not only of the food supply policy of Athens but also of Athenian foreign policy in general over several centuries. Thus the pessimistic conclusions of Gernet, Jardé and Gomme (to cite only the most influential of those twentieth-century scholars who have worked on this topic) provide basic support for the doctrine that Athens' dependence on imports for 'by far the greater part of her corn supply... led almost inevitably to naval imperialism', and also the more radical thesis that Athens relied on foreign grain as early as the turn of the seventh century BC, well before the era of 'naval imperialism'.[1] It is worth asking how || Jardé and Gomme arrived at figures which imply that Attica in the 320s BC could support between 60,000 and 70,000 residents only, or between 23 per cent and 27 per cent of the population – and presumably a lower percentage in the period preceding the Peloponnesian War in the fifth century BC. Jardé's percentage

---

[1] The quotation is from de Ste. Croix (1972) 46. His brief discussion (pp. 45–9) is as good an introduction to the subject as any. Fuller treatment in Gernet (1909); Jardé (1925); cf. also Gomme (1933) 28–33. The 'more radical thesis': Grundy (1948) 67–9, cf. 64. Rhodes (1981) 95–6, 577; and others. Against I have seen only Noonan (1973) and Bloedow (1975). It is unnecessary to explain the early wars and imperialistic ventures in terms of a search for grain to make up for a permanent shortfall in home production; and Plut. *Sol.* 24 does not indicate a permanent deficiency, nor even an absolute shortage of grain, but rather the coexistence of surplus and want in Athens. Cf. Garnsey (1983) 4; Bravo (1983) 21–3.

figure (supposing he had been interested in arriving at one) might have been considerably lower if like Gernet he had in mind a population of 500,000–600,000 for Attica in the fourth century. Gomme's great contribution was to reduce Gernet's population estimates by more or less half. Otherwise his discussion, which in any case leans on that of Jardé in all major matters, is by no means an improvement on those of his predecessors. This is hardly surprising, in view of the fact that Gomme assigned a mere four pages to the food supply problem, designed to confirm the demographic calculations which were his main concern. What is remarkable is the respect his discussion has been accorded by half a century of scholars.[2]

Gomme's figures for annual consumption are as follows: 410,000 medimnoi of home-produced grain (wheat and barley), and 1,200,000 medimnoi of imported grain (one-third from the Black Sea). The figures are based on two sources, one an Athenian inscription recording the First Fruits offered to Demeter at Eleusis in 329/8 BC (IG II^2 1672), the other a passage of Demosthenes 20 (*Against Leptines* 31–3). The First Fruits inscription gives total production figures for barley and wheat in Attica (and in dependent territories) for the year concerned, on the assumption that the contribution amounted to not less than 1/600 in the case of barley and 1/1200 in the case of wheat – the proportions operative in the late fifth century.[3] The sums are around 27,500 medimnoi of wheat and around 340,500 medimnoi of barley, following Jardé; 28,500 and 340,350 respectively, following Gomme.[4] Gomme deducts one-sixth for seed and adds 100,000 medimnoi as compensation for underestimation by Athenian farmers. And he assumes that his final figure of c.410,000 medimnoi represents the return of a normal year. Demosthenes says first that the Athenians consume more imported grain than any other people, and that as much grain comes from the Pontus as from other foreign suppliers put together. He adds, a little later, that Leukon, ruler of the Bosporan kingdom, who controls the region (or the grain?) sends about 400,000 medimnoi – a figure that could be checked in the records of the *sitophulakes*, the officials concerned with the grain market. 'Demosthenes', ‖ says Gomme, 'was a politician and so was probably not speaking the truth' (p. 32). In this case Gomme thinks that Demosthenes has deliberately underestimated the quantity of non-Pontic grain, which in his view might have been double the amount of Pontic grain reaching Athens. Before passing on to Jardé, we should note that the two crucial assumptions encountered already, that the

---

[2] Most recently, Hornblower (1983) 171–2. [3] IG I^3 78 (425/4 or about 422 or 416/15 BC).
[4] The reason for the discrepancy is unclear, since Gomme (1933) 28 does not show how he arrived at his figures. The other figures are not the totals of Jardé (1925) 48, which include Drymos and Oropos, but represent the contributions of Attica proper, as listed on pp. 38 and 40.

production level of 329/8 was normal, and that imports far exceeded home production, however plausible they might appear to be, have no basis in the texts in question, nor as far as I know in any other ancient texts. If, for the sake of the argument, we should wish to follow, in the first place, Gernet or Isager and Hansen, in their belief that the harvest of 329/8 was below average, and in the second place, Jones, in his view that the Demosthenes passage yields a figure for imports of 800,000 medimnoi, then we would receive quite a different picture from that presented by Gomme.[5]

The groundwork for Gomme's analysis was laid by Jardé's full discussion of production and yield, with special reference to the First Fruits inscription. That discussion, however, while impressive in its range, detail and criticism of earlier analyses, is ultimately disappointing. On the harvest of 329/8 he weights the argument against the position that the harvest was deficient, while taking up the superficially open-minded and unexceptionable stance that we cannot say on the basis of a single year's figures whether the harvest was good, bad or indifferent; while on the matter of the extent of arable he fuels the fire of those who are inclined to the view that Attica had poor agricultural potential, by adopting (without any positive argumentation) a low figure of 10 per cent for cultivated grain land as a proportion of the surface area of Attica, having rejected a patently unsatisfactory case for a higher figure.[6] In fact, there are clear signs that Jardé had begun to appreciate the unsatisfactory nature of his own arguments, as we shall see a little later. But it is the negative and pessimistic tenor of his discussion that has made an impact on scholars, whereas the ambiguity and self-doubt have gone unnoticed. This can be illustrated from the work of Starr, who has recently made a brief but ambitious attempt at a quantitative assessment of Attica's capacity to feed its population.[7] ||

Starr takes as his point of departure a figure of 69,000 hectares for cultivable land, which is Jardé's 68,734 rounded. This is not a beginning such as to inspire confidence.[8] Jardé produced this figure only to reject

---

[5] Gernet (1909) 296; Isager and Hansen (1975) 202; Jones (1957) 77–8. Note in particular Isager and Hansen's observation that the Athenian assembly in 329/8 fixed the price at which the wheat and barley would be sold, presumably below market rates. Apart from the evidence provided by IG II^2 1672, there is nothing in the sources relevant to the food supply of 329/8. In contrast, food shortages are firmly attested in 330/29 and 328/7 (IG II^2 360; Dem. 34.38; etc.). Tod II 196, the 'Cyrene edict' recording among other things the dispatch of 100,000 Aeginetan medimnoi (or 150,000 Attic medimnoi) of grain to Athens, is not precisely dated. I tentatively place it in 328/7.

[6] Jardé (1925) 47, 52–3. Hopper (1979) 90 returns to an argument refuted by Jardé, apparently unaware of his discussion.

[7] Starr (1977) 152–6.

[8] And not merely because although his focus is on Solonian Attica he has recourse to figures relevant to the fourth century.

it. His argument is worth close attention. The surface area of Attica was calculated by Beloch[9] at 2,527 km², including Oropos and Eleutherai, two border areas both Boeotian in origin and in Athenian possession from the late sixth to the late fifth century and for parts of the fourth. Excluding them (which Jardé does not), we arrive at a base figure of around 2,400 km² for Attica.[10] How much of this area was, first, cultivable, and second, cultivated? Jardé first considered, following Letronne, the estate of Phainippos as evidence for the extent of land under cultivation and arrived at a figure of 34,368 hectares. He then doubled this to produce a figure of 68,736 hectares of cultivable area (to take in fallow), which he said is about 27 per cent of the total area of Attica. (Excluding Oropos it is around 28.75 per cent of Attica.) The figures are worth very little. That for land actually under cultivation is arrived at by a methodology which de Ste. Croix in his study of the estate of Phainippos finds 'shocking'[11] and which Jardé himself distrusts. Yet Jardé's basic objections are not methodological but substantial. They stem from two convictions, the one that fallow was universal and hence that around 34,500 hectares of cultivated land implies 69,000 hectares of arable, the other, that this level of arable is unacceptably high. A little later, Jardé dismisses Barbagallo's estimate of a relation of cultivated area to total area of one sixth or 16.67 per cent (a cautious estimate – Barbagallo would prefer one quarter) on the grounds that it implies a cultivable area of one third, in his view too high. Jardé, as we saw, can himself do no better than fall back on a figure of 20 per cent arable (half of it cultivated) for Greece as a whole, derived from a work of Philippson published in 1892, who had himself taken it over from earlier writers.[12] If it is unclear why Starr passed over this latter figure, to which Jardé did commit himself, it is decidedly odd that he chose the former, which Jardé regarded as 'peu vraisemblable'.

So, in Starr's account, arable in Attica amounted to 69,000 hectares. Of this, one half was under cultivation in any particular year. Starr, in other words, has taken over from Jardé and built into his own analysis the assumption that a system of half-fallow was universal. This is unbelievable, especially in classical Attica where small-scale, intensive, mixed farming must have been commonplace.[13] Starr then proceeds to divide the 34,500 hectares of cultivated arable between wheat and barley using a wheat/

---

[9] Beloch (1886) 56–7. [10] See Jardé (1925) 48–52, on Letronne and Barbagallo.
[11] De Ste. Croix (1966) 111.
[12] Philippson (1892) 537. Arable in Greece is estimated at 29 per cent in Kayser and Thompson (1964).
[13] See Jardé (1925) 81–105; but the whole subject of the use of fallow in Greek agriculture needs a thorough investigation. For thetic landholding, see Jones (1957) 79–80; and for the nature of subsistence agriculture in classical Attica, see Jameson (1977–8).

barley ratio derived from the First Fruits inscription. In 329/8, he says, 39,000 medimnoi of wheat and 363,000 medimnoi of barley were produced in Attica; therefore[14] about ten times as much land was put under barley as under wheat. The methodology is flawed.[15] In particular, the year might not have been typical (and Starr himself says 'we do not know if this was a poor year', p. 155). If it was a bad year, then barley is likely to have done better than wheat, which needs more rain in the growing season.[16] Barley's share of the crop might therefore have been substantially larger than its share of the seed sown and of land cultivated. Next, working from a hypothetical maximum yield of 8 hectolitres per hectare for wheat and 16 for barley (in Jardé's account they are minimum figures), and assuming that half of the harvest went to seed and animal requirements and wastage, Starr calculates that 13,800 hl of wheat and 248,400 hl of barley were available for human consumption. Finally, he fixes grain consumption at the rate of 3 hl per man year in the case of wheat, and 3.5 hl per man year in the case of barley, and concludes that 4,600 people were fed on wheat and 71,000 on barley, a grand total of 75,000 – at most; that is, around 29 per cent of the population of 323 as estimated by Gomme.[17]

I have already commented on Starr's starting point and his barley/wheat ratio. The other weak points are the halving of gross yield and the consumption figure. Starr does not show how he arrives at his nett yield; I suspect ‖ that, following Jardé,[18] he has grossly overestimated animal feed. It is hard to believe that animals had to be fed a large proportion of the main cereal crop in the Attica of Starr and Jardé where only 10–14 per cent of the land was under cereal cultivation. Again, the consumption figure is too high: 3 hl or around 230 kg of wheat and 3.5 hl or 225 kg of barley. By recent estimates, around 2.5 hl (193 kg) and 3 hl (193 kg) would be a generous allowance.[19] We can, then, adjust Starr's estimate of the consuming

---

[14] Starr (1977) 244, n. 28 (not stated in the text).

[15] Jardé (1925) 93–8 pinpoints the same error in an earlier writer: 'il ne faut pas confondre production et surface emblavée.' His own calculation takes account of a difference in the return of wheat and barley of 1:2, but he has not considered the unequal effects of a bad season on yields. Note that, following his figures, wheat occupied 13.5 per cent of the grain land of Attica (his figure of 18 per cent includes Drymos and Oropos).

[16] See e.g. Arnon (1972) 55, on water requirements of wheat (350–400 mm October–April). Barley needs c. 100 mm less.

[17] Starr (1977) 244, n. 28. He is right to include consumption estimates for barley, because barley was a staple food of many residents of Athens and Attica. Here I side with Gallo (1983) against the *communis opinio* as expressed in Jardé (1925) 124–7, and the extreme view of Jones (1957) 77.

[18] Jardé (1925) 127 would reserve an amount equivalent to virtually the whole barley crop of 329/8 for animal feed.

[19] See now Foxhall and Forbes (1982); cf. Clark and Haswell (1970) 17. The conventional estimate of 6 medimnoi of wheat per person per year (3.15 hl at 52.5 litres per medimnos;

population to 88,300 (5,500 + 82,800). But the whole construct is a pack of cards.

Let us now return to Jardé and see how he undoes his own work of, first, killing off the idea that 329/8 might have been a bad year, and, second, establishing that only a small proportion of Attica was put under cereals. In the last footnote of the relevant chapter *Les Rendements* he discloses that 329/8 could not have been a normal year if his own conjectured normal return on wheat and barley are accepted, 8–12 hl/ha and 16–20 hl/ha respectively. By applying the lowest of these yields to the product of 329/8 he reaches the conclusion that grain land as a proportion of the surface area of Attica was a mere 5.65 per cent, an embarrassingly low figure: 'Ce rapport semble trop faible et par conséquent les chiffres de rendement trop élevés. C'est là une vérification de l'hypothèse souvent faite, mais que nous avions jugée indémonstrée, d'après laquelle la campagne agricole de 329/8 a été mauvaise.'[20] Jardé might at this point have invoked the comparative performances of Attica and Lemnos in 329/8 (*IG* ii² 1672). He had earlier done just this, and made the sound observation that the 10 per cent figure for land under cultivation as a proportion of surface area is inappropriate for Lemnos, because it produces by this calculation an unacceptably high yield figure of 33 hl/ha for wheat and barley combined. On the other hand Jardé apparently thought the figure for Attica of 8 hl/ha could stand: 'Il y a un tel écart entre ces deux chiffres, le second étant plus que quadruple du premier, que, même en accordant aux champs de Lemnos une exceptionnelle fertilité, nous devons admettre que le rapport de 10%, *s'il est exact pour l'Attique*, est trop faible pour Lemnos.'[21] ‖ Curiously, the next sentence suggests that Jardé was on the point of entertaining the hypothesis that for Attica also 10 per cent is too low, and the yield figure therefore too high: 'Certainement, en raison de ses besoins, l'Attique a dû, malgré l'extension de ses vignobles et de ses olivettes, consacrer le plus de terrain possible au blé et semer des céréales même en des cantons où les résultats étaient médiocres, et c'est là ce qui devait abaisser le rendement moyen du pays.'

At any rate Jardé could have given added weight to this hypothesis – if he had fully grasped its implications – at the end of the chapter by reintroducing the Attica-Lemnos comparison, see table 11.1, this time applying a

---

or 243.2 kg at .772 kg per litre or 2425 kcals per day) is too high. Even 5 medimnoi (2.625 hl or 202.65 kg or 2021 kcals per day) is generous as a basic allowance of wheat – Athenians may be supposed to have taken as much as 25–30 per cent of their food energy requirements from non-cereals. It should be added that the widespread Greek belief that women required less food than men (e.g. Xen. *Lac. Pol.* 1.3; Arist. *Hist.An.* 608b 14–15) will affect any population calculations based on food consumption.

[20] Jardé (1925) 60, n. 6.   [21] Jardé (1925) 53.

Table 11.1. *Attica and Lemnos: Product and estimated area under grain in 329/8 BC*

	Attica	Lemnos
WHEAT: in medimnoi	27,500	56,750
WHEAT: in volume (hl)	14,438	29,794
WHEAT: yield (hl/ha)	8	8
WHEAT: sown area (ha)	1,805	3,724
BARLEY: in medimnoi	340,500	248,525
BARLEY: in volume (hl)	178,763	130,475
BARLEY: yield (hl/ha)	16	16
BARLEY: sown area (ha)	11,173	8,155
Total area under grain (ha)	12,977	11,879
Total area (ha)	240,000	47,700
% of total area under grain	5.4	24.9

(from *IG* II^2 1672)

uniform yield at the bottom of the range which Jardé has by now decided is normal for Greece.

There seems no escape from the conclusion that Lemnos had an average or good year. To test this we could lower the yield to, for example, 4.5 hl/ha in the case of wheat and 9 hl/ha in the case of barley. This gives the result that 44.27 per cent of Lemnos was under cereals in 329/8 (6,621 + 14,497 = 21,118 ha), ‖ clearly too high a figure. The same yield figures when applied to Attica's harvest give only 9.6 per cent as the area under cereals (3,208 + 19,862 = 23,070 ha). In fact it is only by lowering the yield estimate radically that we arrive at more reasonable figures for land under cereals in Attica. Thus, for example, a yield of 2.25 hl/ha for wheat and 6 hl/ha for barley gives a total for land under wheat and barley of 36,210 ha, which is a little over 15 per cent of Attica, while yields of 2.25 and 4.25 respectively give a total of 42,060 or approx. 20 per cent of Attica; it is only by lowering yields to, for example, 1.5 and 3.6 for wheat and barley respectively, that one can produce a percentage figure for land under cultivation which is almost equivalent to that arrived at for Lemnos by applying the much higher yields of 8 and 16, respectively (24.7 per cent of Attica, 24.9 per cent of Lemnos).

Even the most determined critics of Attica's agricultural potential would stop short of classing such abysmal returns as typical for the region. In fact, the 'deficiencies' of Attica are somewhat exaggerated in the literature. The account of Cary is fairly standard. After discussing the 'ill favoured' climate and especially the low rainfall, which 'barely suffices for the cultivation of wheat', Cary continues: 'The two central plains of the Attic Cephissus (in which Athens lies) and of the Mesogaea (between Hymettus and Pentelicus) and the coastal lowlands of Thria (near Eleusis) and of Marathon, contain small areas of richer soil, but Attica as a whole is, in the words of Plato (*Critias* 111 BC), a discarnate skeleton, whose bones show through in large slabs of bare rock. Only one-quarter of Attica is estimated as cultivable and part of this is ill-suited for anything save the drought-resisting olive-tree. In the fourth century only one-third to one-quarter of the Athenian requirements in cereals was home grown (mostly barley), and from the time of Solon the importation of foreign grain into Attica was a matter of such importance as to require state regulation.'[22] Apart from Plato, no expert on Attic soils, no ancient source is referred to by Cary, and the modern authority cited in a footnote is Gomme. In fact Plato is not alone in making remarks that might be taken as disparaging about the soil of Attica – there are such comments in, among others, Thucydides, Strabo and Plutarch.[23] But as Cary himself concedes, not all of the soil of Attica is λεπτός, light or thin. Moreover, barley yields well in light soils in dry climates. Did not Theophrastus, who *did* know his crops and soils, write (*Hist. pl.* 8.8.2): 'At Athens the barley produces more meal than anywhere else, since it is an excellent land for that crop'? Philippson in his standard work on geography gets it right: 'but it is in no way true that Attica is to be classed as infertile, as is too often stated with assurance. This judgement is based on the appearance of the landscape in summer and autumn, and is coloured by the assumption of a Northerner that fertility is bound up with lush green growth. The light soil of the Athens and Eleusis plains and slopes brings very good returns of grain, oil and wine, and the plains of Marathon and especially that of Mesogeia actually have relatively rich soil with a relatively deep plough-zone.' Philippson's own judgement is that Attica could not *by itself* support a state of any substantial size, and with this we can agree.[24]

To return to the matter of the extent of arable. If, as is not unlikely, average cereal yields in Attica, at any rate for wheat, *were* a little lower than in many parts of Greece, this was not because of any general poverty of the soil, but because population pressure forced the cultivation of more marginal land than was worked in other parts of Greece, land which would have served elsewhere as pasture.[25] Jardé saw this, but for some reason did

---

[22] Cary (1949) 75-6.
[23] E.g. Thuc. 1.2; Strab. 9.1.8; Plut. *Sol.* 22; cf. Men., *Dys.* 3 (Phyle); Lucian, *Timon* 31.
[24] Philippson (1952) 783. The (fairly free) translation is mine.
[25] As observed by Osborne (1982), Appendix A: 'Greek knowledge of the Soil'. I am grateful to the author for bringing this to my notice. See also Lewis (1973), esp. Appendix C, 210-12 on *eschatia* as a land designation in Attica; also Walbank (1983a) 105, 112, corrected in (1983b) 177, n. 1.

not revise his initial low figure for cereal land under cultivation in Attica, a figure derived as we saw from nineteenth-century estimates of arable in Greece as a whole, plus a belief in universal biennial fallow. The absurdity of using figures from a relatively underpopulated Greece of about a century ago as a guide to conditions pertaining in Attica in the classical era is patent. Jardé would have done better to ask what are the implications for cultivated area of the presence of a *Grossstadt* (to borrow Philippson's term). He was writing, moreover, before Gomme had drastically revised downwards prevailing population estimates for Attica in antiquity. Gomme's own figures are probably too high.[26] That there were around 200–300,000 residents of Attica between 450 and 320, however, can perhaps be accepted as a working hypothesis. ‖

This population, moreover, included a substantial number of landowners of moderate or considerable wealth. Let us say, for the sake of the argument, that the landowning class consisted exclusively of hoplites and knights, and that there were around 10,000 members of this class in 323 – Gomme thought there were around 14,500 men of hoplite census and over between the ages of eighteen and fifty-nine, and Jones, whose estimate has not found favour, 9,000. If the 10,000 owned all the land in Attica that was cultivated in any particular year (which they did not)[27] and this amounted to 10 per cent of the surface area of Attica, then they would have cultivated on average 2.4 hectares. If one believes in a ubiquitous biennial fallow (which I do not), then each man/family owned 4.8 ha of arable, of which half was worked each year. This puts the average hoplite (and above) at or below subsistence level, in terms of his Attica-based properties. Burford Cooper thought 4–6 hectares a *basic* hoplite plot, and doubted its viability.[28] On the strength of her figure, hoplite hectarage in 323 would have amounted to a *minimum* of 40–60,000 hectares or 17–25 per cent of Attica. The results are even more striking if fifth-century figures are considered. There were about 20,000 citizen hoplites and above in 431, as many as 25,000 if Gomme is right. If 20,000 had all the arable in Attica, they would have had on average 2.4 hectares and worked 1.2 hectares with biennial fallow – which puts them below subsistence level, again in terms of their home-based property. Yet they might have been expected to own at least 80–120,000 hectares or 33–50 per cent of Attica.

[26] C. Patterson's sensible critique of Gomme in Patterson (1981) 40–81, is confined to the fifth-century population figures. She scales down his estimates for adult males for both 480 (from 35,000? to *c.*26,250?) and 431 (from 43,000? to 40,000?). See also Hansen (1981), who reduces Gomme's citizen hoplite figure of 431 from 25,000 to 18,000. For a reworking of Gomme's fourth-century figures see Hansen (1985).

[27] As Professor Michael Jameson has reminded me, there were apart from thetic properties significant public lands in Attica. See Lewis (1973) 198–9 (*c.*5 per cent of agricultural land); cf. Andreyev (1974) 43 (*c.*10 per cent).

[28] Burford-Cooper (1977–8), endorsed by Jameson (1977–8) 125, n. 13.

It should be noted in passing that in the 1961 census 30 per cent of Attica was classified as arable (22 per cent grain land, a strikingly high figure). The expansion of the built-up area (19 per cent of Attica in 1961) plus the remains of ancient terracing as revealed by aerial photography imply that cultivation in some period of antiquity was more extensive than it has been in modern times.[29]

To sum up: the conventional picture – little land under cultivation, low total product, few consumers fed, very high level of imports – which is based on the erroneous belief that 329/8 was a normal year in Attica, needs to be ‖ corrected. The estimates of land under cultivation, product and consumers supported from home production should be raised, and the estimate of grain imports lowered correspondingly. But by how much? The calculations shown in table 11.2 are offered simply *exempli gratia* as a rough indication of the range of the possible.

Note that the estimated ratio of wheat to barley hectarage is more equal than is normally assumed, and estimated yield in both crops might be considered ‖ low.[30] Any adjustment made at these points would have the effect of increasing overall product. Again, the estimated consumption rate is generous, if grain provided 75 per cent of food energy requirements for the average consumer. Increasing the rates of sowing, animal consumption and wastage would by no means restore the balance. Note also that my calculations concern Attica only. I have not taken into consideration the contribution from dependent territories, in particular those mentioned in the First Fruits inscription – the Boeotian border lands of Drymos and Oropos, Salamis, Lemnos, Imbros and Skyros. In 329/8 these areas between them produced a little more barley and just under five times more wheat than the ten tribes of Attica put together. We can assume that Athenians were able to tap a considerable proportion of the surplus of these territories as landowners and residents within them, and as consumers in Attica itself. My conclusion is that Attica was able to support perhaps 120–150,000 of its residents in the classical period, and an inner ring of dependent territories perhaps 20–25,000 more Athenians, in the classical period, under normal conditions.[31]

---

[29] Bradford (1957a) 29ff.; cf. Renfrew and Wagstaff, eds. (1982) 132: 14 per cent cultivated now, 20 per cent at some time not clearly discernible in antiquity.

[30] At one third fallow, *exempli gratia*, arable comes to 22.5 per cent, 30 per cent and 37.5 per cent of Attica, respectively. None of these figures is impossible, though the implications for other crops need working out. Tree crops, especially the vine and olive, could occupy hill slopes and poorer arable, although interplanting with cereals is both likely and attested. Legumes for human and animal feed could be grown in alternation with cereals. I envisage some use of spring/summer as well as winter cereals and legumes.

[31] I bank nothing on these figures, which are based on the assumption that Athens could take roughly 20 per cent of the crop, and that crop levels in 329/8 were normal (which in some cases they were not).

Table 11.2 *Estimates of production and consumption of home grain in Attica*

% area of Attica under grain	15	20	25
area under grain in hectares (ha)	36,000	48,000	60,000
area of wheat (ha) (at 1/4 barley)	7,200	9,600	12,000
gross wheat (at 6 hl/ha)	43,200	57,600	72,000
nett wheat (hl) (less 1/4 seed etc)	32,400	43,200	54,000
weight of wheat (kg) (1 litre = .772 kg)	2,501,280	3,335,040	4,168,800
area of barley (ha)	28,800	38,400	48,000
gross barley (at 12 hl/ha)	345,600	460,800	576,000
nett barley (less 1/4 seed etc.)	259,200	345,600	432,000
weight of barley (1 litre = .643 kg)	16,666,560	22,222,080	27,777,600
total weight (kg)	19,167,840	25,557,120	31,946,400
consumers fed (at 175 kg per person/year)	109,530	146,040	182,550

I stress normal conditions: Attica is one of the driest parts of Greece; variability of rainfall in the growing season is very high; the risk of crop-failure is pronounced, especially in the case of legumes and wheat (almost three bad years in four, more than one bad year in four, respectively, on the basis of modern rainfall statistics). In bad years, therefore, and particularly when the barley crop failed (a little over one year in twenty), Athens' order for foreign grain must have been enormous.[32]

But how much grain did Athens *regularly* import? There are two stray figures in the ancient sources, one in Strab. 7.4.6, the other in Demosthenes 20.31–3, both relevant to the fourth century. Leukon, according to Strabo, sent 2,100,000 medimnoi from Theodosia in the Bosporus to Athens. This ‖ would represent about 84,000,000 kilograms, enough to feed about

---

[32] These statistics, supplied by T. Gallant, are provisional and may require revision. For variability of rainfall in Attica, consult Gallant (1983) I, 24–6.

480,000 people. But was the grain sent in one year (and if so in a normal or an abnormal year?), or in the course of the four decades in which Leukon was king of the Bosporus; and was it sent from Theodosia as distinct from Panticapaeum, or from both ports? The discussion must be inconclusive.[33] Nor for that matter is a definitive interpretation of the Demosthenes passage possible: scholars cannot agree, even on the basic issue of the extent of the trustworthiness of the author. Attention must focus on the 400,000 medimnoi which Demosthenes says came from the Bosporus. It is the only detail for which he claims documentary support (in the records of the *sitophulakes*), and is perhaps the only detail which can be salvaged from the passage, apart from the unexceptionable claim that the Athenians consume more imported grain than any other people. In particular, no figure for non-Pontic imports can be safely derived from Demosthenes.[34] Even the 400,000 medimnoi, however, is a figure of dubious value. It cannot even be safely assumed that this represents a regular, annual import, rather than merely the amount imported in one year, which might even have been the bad year to which Demosthenes refers in the same passage. In that case it would support the limited point that Athens might have had to import as much as 400,000 medimnoi from one source (enough to feed around 90,000 people) in any particular year.

To conclude: That Athens was dependent on foreign grain is not at issue. My own (very tentative) calculations suggest that Athens in the fourth century had to find grain for perhaps one-half of its resident population from outside Attica, narrowly defined, in a normal year. My argument has been designed to show that Athens at all times – with the exception of the Peloponnesian War period when the Athenians' capacity to exploit their own territory was seriously reduced and ultimately lost (Thuc. 7.27–8) – was less dependent on foreign grain, and in particular on distant sources of grain, than is generally assumed. A second conclusion follows, if the general tenor of my argument is accepted: that Athens became dependent on grain from foreign sources later than is generally assumed. Briefly, I am inclined to the view that a serious disequilibrium between Athens' food needs and its capacity to meet them from Attica and nearby

---

[33] The Strabo text is discussed by Hopper (1979) 90–2: 52,500 medimnoi per annum from (only) Theodosia over a forty-year period. His chapter 3 'The import trade – principally corn' (71–92), is unfortunately unreliable.

[34] The statement that as much was sent to Athens from the Pontus as from other external sources comes a little earlier in the Demosthenes passage (20 [*Against Leptines*] 31) and has a different (and reduced) truth-value – though Jones (1957) 77–8 eccentrically thinks that Demosthenes saw the figure of 800,000, not that of 400,000, in the records of the *sitophulakes*. Isager and Hansen (1975) 18–19 is sound. Few have been prepared to accept at face value Demosthenes' suggestion that Athens imported twice 400,000 medimnoi.

dependencies did not develop until well into the || post-Persian war period in consequence of population growth, and that there was no food supply *problem* (thanks to Athens' control of the sea, particularly the corn route from the North, and the attractiveness of her market to suppliers) until 431 BC.[35] ||

Addendum

This paper argues that previous scholarship has tended to inflate the importance of grain imports into Athens. Based on an alternative model of grain yields in Attica, this argument has been further developed in Garnsey (1988). Garnsey (1992) [= chapter 12] returns to this issue and discusses related matters.

Demosthenes 20. 31-2 refers to the import of some 400,000 *medimnoi* of grain from the Bosporan kingdom (pp. 184-5, 193-4). Drawing on this testimony, Gallo (1984) 48-57 discusses the scale of regular grain imports from the Black Sea region and concludes that every year, 800,000 to 900,000 *medimnoi* were shipped to Athens. Garnsey here and again in (1988) 96-9 casts doubt on the representative value of this passage. He stresses that there is no way of knowing how much grain Athens imported on a regular basis (105).

Recent estimates of the amount of arable land in Attica available for cereal cultivation in any given year (pp. 185-6) have fluctuated between 10 and over 20 per cent, a range of variation of more than 100 per cent. Gallo (1984) 69 reckons with a total of 50,000 hectares of arable land, half of which lay fallow; i.e., some 10 per cent of Attica was annually used for grain production. Garnsey (1988) 92-3 estimates that 35 to 40 per cent of Attica consisted of arable land, about half of which was under cultivation in any given year. Garnsey (1988) 102 Table 7;

---

[35] This means that I am unwilling to accept the starting point of Ph. Gauthier's excellent article (1981) 5: 'Peu importe l'estimation du nombre de ses habitants; dès le ve siècle, en tout cas, le territoire civique, même augmenté des possessions d'outre-mer, ne parvenait pas à nourrir la population pendant toute l'année. Pour l'intelligence de la discussion qui suit, il faut rappeler que l'approvisionnement en grain était pour les Athéniens un souci lancinant; il suffit pour s'en convaincre de réciter la litanie des témoignages antiques.' Note however that the earliest text he can cite is Thuc. 6.20.4. He cannot of course include Hdt. 7.147, the first mention of Pontic grain ships bound for Greece, because these, *pace* Hornblower (1983) 12, were heading for Aegina and the Peloponnese. The silence of the fifth-century sources is an embarrassment for Grundy (1948) e.g. 60-1, who would like to trace Athens' dependence on foreign grain back to the age of Solon. The circumspect remarks of de Ste. Croix (1972) 379 (cf. 217 on Athens' interest in the West during the Periclean age) can be taken as a guide to the correct interpretation of other Athenian foreign policy activities in this period, including the Egyptian and Cypriot expeditions, the colony in Thurii and the cleruchies. In contrast Hornblower (1983) 40, 57, 77, 170 ff., leaning on the account of Hopper (1979) e.g. 72, finds symptoms of Athenian anxiety about her supplies of grain everywhere. The subject will receive fuller treatment in another place.

I owe thanks to Tom Gallant.

(1992) 148 [= p. 204] considers it most likely that 17.5 per cent of Attica was under grain every year, 80 per cent of which was used for barley. Sallares (1991) 80 agrees with G's raising of Jardé's figures for the amount of land under cultivation, estimating that 30 per cent was under cultivation (386), 15 per cent, or 36,000 hectares, in any given year (79). Osborne (1995) 32 assumes that around one-third of Attica was cultivated with cereals, so that allowing for some biennial fallow, 'just over one fifth of Attica (say 50,000 ha.) was sown with cereals each year'. Whitby (forthcoming) considers it 'plausible' that in principle, one-half of arable land was annually available for grain cultivation. Taking account of the land taken up by the cultivation of leguminous crops, market gardening and animal husbandry (all of which were sustained by urban demand), he estimates that 10 to 15 per cent of Attica was actually devoted to grain in any given year.

G's rejection of the widely held notion of universal biennial fallow (p. 186) is corroborated by Halstead (1987) 81-3 who argues that regular manuring and cereal/pulse rotation *may* have been common. This 'alternative model' proposed by Halstead is endorsed by Garnsey (1988) 93-4. Gallant (1991) 52-6 and Garnsey (1992) 151 [= p. 210] consider it likely that a variety of fallow/rotation systems (including triennial fallow) were in use. However, Sallares (1991) 385-6 stresses that biennial fallow was indeed a regular practice in Greece. Isager and Skydsgaard (1992) 22, 24 likewise seem to believe biennial fallow to be the norm, a view put forward somewhat more strongly by Skydsgaard (1988) 81, 83. Osborne (1995) 32 thinks biennial fallow was less than universal. Cf. also Burford (1993) 121-5.

329/8 BC was an average or good year in Lemnos but a bad year in Attica (pp. 188-9). Garnsey (1988) 100-1 returns to this issue, cogently demonstrating that in that year, yields in Attica must have been far lower than in Lemnos. Garnsey (1992) 149 [= p. 204], reckoning with a normal average yield of 625 kg of wheat/hectare and 770 kg of barley/hectare, estimates that the yields in Attica implied by IG II^2. 1672 amounted to 20 per cent of the average total for wheat and 44 per cent for barley. Osborne (1987) 46 and Gallant (1991) 177 agree that in 329/8, the grain harvest in Attica was unusually poor. G's analysis supersedes Gallo (1984) 60-5 (following Jardé), who concludes that the figures recorded in IG II^2. 1672 are close to the possible maximum (68) or at any rate indicative of the regular mean (69). On 329/8, see also Marasco (1984) 288. I have not seen Faraguna (1992). Stroud (forthcoming) objects to the idea that 329/8 was a bad year on methodological grounds; in particular he denies the validity of the comparison of Attica and Lemnos. Cf. Sallares (1991) 478 n. 70, who raises doubts about the feasibility of a direct comparison between Attica and Lemnos but nevertheless agrees with G. that 329/8 was a bad year, attributing this poor performance to drought (393-4). He concludes that 'if the information from the inscription is related to the proportion of Attica that is devoted to agriculture today (. . .), productivity per area unit would be so low, even assuming that yields were low on average anyway, that it is an inevitable conclusion that the harvest recorded on the inscription was that of a below average year' (394). On the importance of Lemnos, Imbros and Skyros for the production of grain and as strategic stations of the grain ships, see Salomon (1995) 191–206 (*non vidi*, cited by Stroud (forthcoming), who presents comparative data on the productivity of these islands). Furthermore, Stroud (forthcoming) objects to generalizing inferences drawn from a combination of *IG* II² 1672 and *IG* I³. 78 because the procedure of collecting the *aparche* may have changed between c.425/15 and 329/8 BC, and also because of the possible impact of cheating on the reported amounts (on cheating cf. also Ober (1985) 23–4; on the *aparche* in general, see Isager and Skydsgaard (1992) 169–73).

As a 'working hypothesis', G. puts the number of residents in Attica between 450 and 320 BC at 200,000 to 300,000 (p. 191). Since then, the question of the size of the Athenian population, above all in the age of Alexander, has continued to generate debate. Garnsey (1988) 90 prefers somewhat lower population figures, ranging from a maximum of 250,000 in the 430s BC to between 120,000 to 150,000 in 323/2 BC, compared to 200,000 in the mid-fourth century. In the same study, he puts the number of residents in the fourth century BC at between 150,000 to 200,000, assigning 150,000 to the beginning and the end of that period. Total population size is usually extrapolated from the number of adult male citizens. Hansen (1985) makes a case for c.25,000 adult male citizens in 350 BC and 30,000 in 322 BC. In this context, he refers to the present paper as 'by far the best treatment of the problem' (96 n. 77) but considers it impossible to calculate population numbers from estimates of grain consumption (24–5, endorsed by Stroud (forthcoming)). Gallo (1984) 70, 111 n. 137 believes that 110–120,000 free persons lived in Attica but implausibly implies that slaves outnumbered the free (cf. 69, 79–80). Marasco (1984) 287 refers to 21,000 adult male citizens in the late fourth century BC. Osborne (1985) 42–6 briefly discusses the size of the population of Attica, reckoning with 20–21,000 adult male citizens in the fourth century BC (45). Osborne (1987) 46 puts the total population of Attica at 150,000, made up of 60–80,000 citizens, 20,000 foreigners and 50,000 slaves. Hansen (1988) 7–13 discusses the estimates of G. and Osborne; he himself reckons with 133–186,000 free and 66–93,000 slave residents in Attica, or a total of 200–250,000, in the fourth century BC (12), compared to over 300,000 under Pericles, at a time when there were 60,000 adult male citizens (12, 28). For the most recent restatement of his views, see Hansen (1994) against Sekunda (1992) who unconvincingly argues for 20–21,000 adult male citizens in 323/2 BC; on his controversy with E. Ruschenbusch, who favours a similarly low figure, see Hansen (1989). Hansen (1994) 310 concludes that 'at least 30,000 and perhaps several thousand more' adult male citizens existed in 323/2 BC. Oliver (1995) 9–38 (ch. 2: 'The population and agriculture of Attica') returns to this issue. He proposes a figure of 25,000 adult male citizens in c.320 BC (10–19) in reaction to Hansen's higher estimate (see above). Reckoning with 80–90,000 citizens, 25,000 metics and 50,000 slaves, he puts the total population at that time at about 160–180,000 residents (18–19). He also thinks that it shrank during subsequent generations (19–29): somewhat arbitrarily reducing the number of adult citizens to 22–23,000, the number of metics to 17–19,000 and that of slaves to 40,000, he arrives at a total of 130–140,000 residents in the early Hellenistic period (25–9).

On the other hand, Whitby (forthcoming) finds G's estimates 'significantly too low'. Arguing for the presence of over 30,000, perhaps as many as 35,000, adult male citizens in the third quarter of the fourth century BC, he puts the total citizen population at 120–140,000. Adding 30,000 metics ('a pure guess') and 100,000 slaves (at the peak of the slave system [which may however have predated the period under review]), he gives 250–300,000 residents in the mid-fourth century BC. It is interesting to see how Oliver and Whitby draw on precisely the same ancient sources yet arrive at significantly divergent results. In much the same way as previous contributions, these most recent estimates above all highlight the lack of scholarly consensus in the face of considerable and possibly ineradicable margins of error.

Concerning the schematic estimates of local production and consumption of grain in Attica (p. 193), Rhodes (1993) 769 refers to a computational error disclosed by J. M. M. Helm in his unpublished Durham BA thesis of 1986/7 (personal communication, P. J. Rhodes 20 June 1996). The affected values, namely, the final four figures in the first column of numbers (for 15 per cent under grain), have accordingly been changed in the text reprinted here. The reference to the area of wheat amounting to one-*fifth* of the area under barley has been corrected to one-*fourth*. None of these corrections have any bearing on the overall argument unless the total area under cultivation is put at a significantly lower level, as does Whitby (forthcoming) (see above), who however seems unaware of these errors. Garnsey (1988) 102–4 with Table 7 and Figure 1 presents a model indicating that Attica's agriculture could have supported a population density of 55 residents per square kilometre, or about 120–150,000 persons. (This revised model – 102 Table 7 – is more complex than the present tabulation, involving as it does three different estimates for each of seven independent variables. Fully exploited, this configuration would yield $3^7 = 2,187$ possible results from which mean, median and mode need to be derived.) Sallares (1991) 79, who finds himself in broad agreement with G., presents his own schematic calculations (see above on the percentage of arable), reckoning with possible average yields per hectare of 400, 500 or 600 kg of grain. In his view, 84,000 to 124,000 people could have been fed by local grain, a range that falls short of G's figures. A lower degree of local supply is also implied by Whitby (forthcoming): see above for his estimate of the percentage of the arable land in Attica.

G. appreciates the extent of variability in grain yields (p. 193 and n. 32). Ruschenbusch (1988) presents comparative evidence on Greek grain yields from 1921 to 1938 in order to demonstrate considerable annual deviation from the mean. He maintains that data from at least ten years in a row are required to establish a realistic mean, whereas evidence from only one or two years is worthless (141). Stroud (forthcoming) makes the same point. According to Sallares (1991) 394, 'a continuous run of data for twenty or thirty years would be needed to obtain statistically significant results for total production'.

In the fourth century BC, local grain could support one-half of the resident population in a normal year (p. 194). Garnsey (1988) 105, based on his estimate that 120–150,000 people could be supported by local production, stresses that there were always imports, but argues that even when the population peaked before 431 BC, Attica, except in the event of crop failure, never had to import more than half of its grain. Attica, he holds, always produced less grain than was required to feed all its residents, even when there were as few as 150,000 of them (137). Herz (1989) 138 agrees that 120–150,000 people could be supported in a normal year. (Gallo (1984) 72, 79–80 adheres to the earlier view: local production could feed only 66,800 to 83,500 people, whom he identifies as the rural population, while 160–225,000 people (the urban population) relied on imported grain.) Osborne (1987) 46 thinks that the whole population (put at 150,000) 'could' have been supported locally. Hansen (1988) 12, operating with higher population totals, argues that self-sufficiency was impossible even in good years. He therefore endorses G's view given here, assuming that one-half of the population could be supported locally in a normal year, fewer in a bad year (12–13). Oliver (1995) 30 agrees with G. that 120–150,000 people (or 130,000: cf. 37) could be fed but points out that warfare could interrupt this supply (38). Whitby (forthcoming) expresses doubts about the validity of existing calculations (including G's) and stresses the importance of the psychology of the market. He concludes that Attica and its dependencies could not have supported more than half the population of Attica.

'A serious disequilibrium between Athens' food needs and its capacity to meet them from Attica and nearby dependencies did not develop until well into the post-Persian war period' (pp. 194–5). Tausend (1989) argues that as early as the beginning of the sixth century BC, many Attic farmers switched from grain to olive cultivation and thereby created demand for grain imports, mainly from the Propontis region. Keen (1993) argues for the significance of early grain imports from the Black Sea region. Against an overrating of sixth-century imports, see Garnsey (1988) 107–19, esp. 112–13, and cf. 110–11 against a supposed takeover of olives in Athenian farming. Rhodes (1993) 769 considers the view by Garnsey (1988) 109–10 that Attica could subsist on locally grown corn well into the sixth century 'too optimistic' but offers no supporting argument.

G's recourse to a broad quantitative model has met with both support and criticism. Herz (1989) states that G's interpretation rests on many hypotheses but gives a defendable result. Morris (1994) 361 prefers G's treatment of Attica's grain supply to the analysis by Starr (1977) 156. A number of scholars follow G's lead whilst nuancing his picture, such as Osborne (1985) (1987); Hansen (1988); Sallares (1991). Whitby (forthcoming) opts for more divergent estimates. Stroud (forthcoming) and, implicitly, Ruschenbusch (1988, and personal communication), object to the use of IG II^2. 1672 in this context. At a more general level, Isager and Skydsgaard (1992) 108–14 express aprioristic scepticism in rejecting models *per se*: 'Not knowing the cultivated area and unable to verify the existence of one and only one system of cultivation, and furthermore not knowing the yield nor the amount of sowing per area-unit, we must conclude that such calculations should be relegated to scholar's desks as some kind of mental exercise' (113). This conclusion stems from a rather idiosyncratic view of the nature of historical research: 'As long as the alternative model is allowed to remain on the model stage, it is inoffensive, but when it is let loose on actual history, whatever this may be – as by Garnsey – caution is called for' (114). Is there is any historical reconstruction that does not involve some (deliberate or subconscious) modelling? In fact, it is not the use of models as such that is problematic. Rather they are more appropriately applied in some settings than in others. Thus, Morris (1994) 361 sensibly points out that since Athens was a much smaller system than other systems that have been subjected to modelling – such as the Roman empire – models are difficult to build because even small margins of error may seriously affect the results. (One might add that this can be shown to be the case with quantitative models of other individual cities, such as Pompeii: see Scheidel (1992b) 209–13, esp. n. 8, on Jongman (1988) 97–154.) This problem inevitably reduces the plausibility of any model of the grain supply of Attica: existing source references and probabilistic assumptions concerning the crucial variables of population size and grain yields create margins of error too wide to make possible anything other than very crude estimates of the average level of Athenian self-sufficiency in a given period.

12

THE YIELD OF THE LAND IN ANCIENT GREECE

I. INTRODUCTION

To inquire into the yield of the land in ancient Greece is to pursue a phantom. We need to know, essentially, production totals, area under cultivation, sowing rate for the major crops, in the various regions of Greece, over an extended period of time – in the course of which the natural and social environment did not stand still.

The data do not exist. This is not only because of the disappearance of private records and public documents and the non-survival of treatises of agronomy – we have several such treatises from Italy and are not much wiser for that on the issues in question. The ancients were uninterested in assembling the data we require. Worse still, they lacked key economic concepts like productivity, that is, the ratio of output over input. Or so it would seem.

What can be done, given this evidential blackout? A study of yield-related concepts would have value, in introducing us to the mentality of landowners from antiquity. There is scattered information for farming practices bearing on yield. We can also ask how far comparative evidence can fill the information gap. These matters are discussed in reverse order below.

But I begin by considering one direct piece of ancient evidence for yield, the First Fruits inscription from Eleusis dated to 329/8, *IG* II², 1672. I have previously discussed this inscription[1] without, however, facing possible objections to its use for the purposes in question. I want to deal with them now. The document has other points of interest, not least for religious history, but these are not my present concern.

II. AGRICULTURAL PRODUCTION IN ATTICA, 329/8 BC

The inscription in question purports to record the receipt by officials at the sanctuary of Eleusis of First Fruits (*aparchai*) of the wheat and barley

---

[1] Garnsey (1988) 98–106. I am grateful to Susan Alcock for criticism and suggestions.

crops for 329/8 BC from the ten tribes of Attica and a few dependent territories. Supposing that the payment was made at the rate of 1/1,200 of the wheat crop and 1/600 of the barley crop, as was the case in the late fifth century,[2] then by simple arithmetic we can obtain the yield figures for the areas in question, the only yield figures from ancient Greece.

There is no assurance that the exaction rates for First Fruits remained unchanged from the 420s to the 320s, but I see no reason for abandoning this assumption, at least until a determined sceptic emerges from the shadows.

The accuracy of the figures has been impugned by Ober, who writes:

> Although the amounts are listed by tribe, it is probable that each farmer would have had to make his own computation of the goddesses' percentage. Even allowing for the religious scruples of the rural population, it can hardly be doubted that the goddesses received less than their full share of the harvest. A relatively small amount of cheating becomes quite significant when multiplied by a factor of 600 or 1,200.[3]

The possibility of evasion in the form of deliberate under-reporting by large numbers of farmers must certainly be considered. But the exaction was tiny, 'chicken feed' one might say, in the case of the mass of small farmers who, according to the vision of Ober, inherited from Jones, peopled the territory of Attica in the classical period. Moreover, the payment was requested not by a foreign power as ‖ an exercise of imperialism, but by a sanctuary that was central to the life of the city.

The figures for First Fruits and total yield might be inaccurate for another reason, if small producers were systematically passed over because their contributions were felt to be inconvenient or even impossible to collect, and anyhow too insignificant to be worth collecting. How were 1/1,200 or 1/600 to be subtracted from a peasant's crop? And what would be the point of extracting such a piffling amount, supposing it were possible? So the Athenians might have thought, having in mind of course not the research interests of economic historians of later ages, but the material need of the personnel of the sanctuary (and the farmers of Attica).

I am not convinced by the argument from insignificance. Tiny amounts of grain become significant if there are enough of them. Let us suppose that Jones was roughly correct in his conjecture that there were around 6,000 thetic plots in classical Attica.[4] At, say, half a choinix per thete, that comes to 62.5 medimnoi, more than 10 per cent of the barley and approaching three times the wheat brought to Eleusis as First Fruits in 329/8.

There remains the logistical problem of collecting a large number of small contributions. Again, I am not persuaded that there is a genuine

[2] *IG* I³, 78 (c.425–415 BC).   [3] Ober (1985) 23–4.   [4] Jones (1957) 80.

dilemma here. Let us focus on the issue of how inconveniently small those contributions might have been.

Grower 1, a wheat farmer, had to produce 25 medimnoi of wheat (= 1,000 kg, at 1 med. = 40 kg), before his First Fruits came to 1 choinix (1 choinix = 1/48 medimnos, 1,200 choinikes = 25 medimnoi). The choinix is the smallest unit of dry measure named on the inscription.

Twenty-five medimnoi is about 40 per cent more than a household of four would have had to grow each year to sustain itself (if consumption was at the rate of 175 kg per person per year). One might therefore predict that a sizeable number of farmers might have been unable to contribute a basic First Fruits payment that was worth collecting.

But smaller measures existed, even if they are not mentioned in the inscription. There were two xestai in a choinix, and four kotulai. The wheat harvests of four small growers might together have made up First Fruits of one choinix, and got into the record that way.

In any case, how realistic is all of this? There was much less wheat grown in Attica than barley, and little of it would have been produced by small farmers. In semi-arid Attica, it was risky to grow wheat; barley was a much safer and more successful crop. I envisage only a small investment by smallholders in wheat. So, if wheat did go uncollected and unrecorded, this was because it really was insignificant in quantity.

Non-recording of barley is less likely. Grower 2, who specialized in barley, had to produce 12.5 medimnoi of barley (= 417.5 kg at 1 med. = 33.4 kg) before he could pay over one choinix as First Fruits at the rate of 1/600 of the crop. A household of four, consuming barley at the rate of 175 kg per person per year, had to grow for its own subsistence c.21 medimnoi, or 66 per cent over and above the 12.5 medimnoi, which divided by 600 equals one choinix. In a bad year First Fruits might have amounted to less than a choinix – but might still have been collectible in principle.

In sum, I see no reason for believing that large amounts of wheat or barley would necessarily have been excluded from the process of First Fruits collection. And I see no merit at all in the extreme position that the numbers recorded on the inscription were purely notional, and the harvest figures derived from them purely imaginary. How might such notional numbers have been arrived at? Would they have been adjustable according to the success or failure of the harvest, and if so, how were they adjusted? Would the Athenians have saved themselves any trouble by adopting such a ruse?

I am inclined therefore to accept the First Fruit figures as more or less accurate for the year in question, allowing for some margin of error due to evasion, non-collection or figure-rounding. Of course any modification made to the figures for any of these reasons would only increase their magnitude – and the size of the harvest.

All this said, the limitations of the inscription must be recognized. The figures are for one year's harvest – and one year is not enough on which to base a general assessment of the productivity of agriculture in Attica, or anywhere else in Greece. In any case, the inscription gives production figures, and does not allow us to infer productivity: for that we would need to know the sown area, and the sowing rate. Finally, the production figures are only for wheat and barley, and we do not know how much of Attica was given over to these crops, as distinct from other cereals, legumes, the vine, and, especially, the olive.

Thus no estimate of either total agricultural production, or the productivity of agriculture (and horticulture) in Attica can be drawn from the inscription.

This has not prevented scholars, myself included, from making their conjectures, and partly on the basis of their reading of the inscription. Barbagallo's pessimistic assessment of the productive capacity of Attica – 3 hl/ha (= 235 kg/ha) and 5 hl/ha (= 330 kg/ha) for wheat and barley respectively – is not unrelated to his assumption that the crop of 329/8 was a 'normal' one. There is, similarly, a correlation between my own more optimistic estimate and my conviction that 329/8 was a bad year and the harvest below the norm.[5]

I propose the following figures as appropriate for wheat and barley in a standard year:

Proportion of Attica under grain 17.5 per cent
Area under barley: area under wheat 4 : 1

yield per ha (wheat) 625 kg/ha (or 8 hl/ha at 1 hl = 78 kg wheat)
yield per ha (barley) 770 kg/ha (or 12 hl/ha at 1 hl = 64 kg barley)
total output wheat 5,250,000 kg (1/5 × 42,000 = 8,400 ha × 625)
total output barley 25,872,000 kg (4/5 × 42,000 = 33,600 ha × 770)
seed-yield : seed sown (wheat) 4.8 : 1 (at sowing rate 130 kg/ha)
seed-yield : seed sown (barley) 6 : 1 (at sowing rate 130 kg/ha) ||

The wheat harvest of 329/8 was 20 per cent as large as is envisaged in my model, and the barley harvest 44 per cent as large.

Assuming the same area sown,
yield per ha (wheat)   was 128 kg/ha = 1.65 hl/ha in 329/8
yield per ha (barley)   was 338 kg/ha = 5.25 hl/ha

Assuming the same sowing rate,
seed-yield : seed (wheat) was 1 : 1
seed-yield : seed (barley) was 2.6 : 1

[5] Barbagallo (1904); Garnsey (1988).

So much for yield figures from ancient Greece. Can comparative data plug the gap?

III. COMPARATIVE EVIDENCE

Comparative evidence will inevitably be turned to, and must be used with circumspection. In the first place, the incautious use of Italian data from antiquity does not help the cause. Columella, writing more than three centuries after Theophrastus, for an audience of gentlemen farmers operating essentially in the centre/west of Italy, once declared in an off-the-cuff aside that yields against seed for cereals (not specifically for wheat) in the greater part of Italy rarely rose as high as four to one. This statement, problematic enough for Italy, cannot simply be transferred over time or from one ecological zone and socio/political environment to another.[6]

Then again, yields recorded from Greece in other, pre-modern epochs are unusable unless broad comparability can be established on the ecological, economic and political levels.[7]

Such data must in any case be quantitatively significant to carry any impact. Barbagallo in his search for 'la produzione media relativa', cites for Greece the harvest of 1875 only (but for no obvious motive, since he completely discounts it). The harvest for 1921 in Greece provided Jardé with his only comparative material and with the basis of his general assessment of Greek (and Attic) production.[8]

Average yields of 629.1 kg/ha and 793.7 kg/ha in wheat and barley respectively for Attica between the years 1911–50 (with some gaps) provide a sounder basis for a comparative investigation of Attic productivity.[9] However, the production totals are to some extent problematic for comparative purposes, because the period in question saw the gradual and partial introduction into Greece of modern techniques and practices.

Even if we had as good a data sequence from a slightly earlier period, its transferrability would be far from automatic. As Paul Halstead has recently argued,[10] 'traditional agriculture' (not in any case a homogeneous entity) as practised in the Mediterranean in recent times before the

---

[6] Columella, *Rust.* 3.3.4; Garnsey and Saller (1987) 79–82. Columella's yield figure, if it did concern wheat (but the word used is not *triticum* but *frumenta*), would have been roughly equivalent to 540 kg/ha gross (400 kg/ha net).

[7] See e.g. Svoronos (1976) 57–8; Topping (1977) 284–7.   [8] Jardé (1925) 60, 203–8.

[9] Gallant (1991). The times-series data collected as part of a broader study by Gallant and myself of the Agroclimatology of the Mediterranean are more profitably employed in other ways, for example, to measure inter-annual variability. Cf. Gallant (1989) 397 (table 2).

[10] Halstead (1987); cf. Halstead and Jones (1989).

introduction of mechanization, artificial fertilizers and irrigation, cannot be assumed to be a replica of ancient agriculture.

IV. ANCIENT FARMING PRACTICES BEARING ON YIELD

Having witnessed an agricultural revolution (which is still in progress), the essential achievement of which has been a dramatic improvement in yields of sown crops, we should be less susceptible than earlier generations of scholars to exaggerating the potential of Mediterranean agriculture in a pre-industrial society. The problem is to decide whether Greek agriculture was advanced or primitive, whether yields were high or low, within the limits set by the state of scientific knowledge and technological development. We have sketchy knowledge of both the way the Greeks farmed and their natural environment. It may be that more information would actually make things more difficult; at least, it would complicate the task of generalization, since a 'pattern' of diversity and variability, already discernible in the ancient and comparative evidence, would become only more apparent. With these reservations in mind, we can try to assess the likely impact on production of particular ancient farming practices.

Among factors crucial to yield I single out weather, soil and seed. On seed I will have nothing to say except to give publicity to a recently published book by Robert Sallares. In it he presses the case, by means of an evolutionary argument, for the relatively low-yielding capacity of ancient seeds.[11]

Talk of the weather brings to mind the adage in Theophrastus: 'The harvest is the year's and not the field's.' A high level of variability is a defining characteristic of the Mediterranean climate, and its impact on yield is direct and powerful.[12] The fickle weather, however, is a given, something that Mediterranean farmers have had to adapt to and || learn to live with for millennia; it sets the limits to the development of agriculture in this region. The extent to which ancient farmers pressed against those limits is dictated less by their reaction to the weather than by their interaction with the soil. The soil too is a given; but, as Theophrastus frequently reminds his readers, it can be worked (*ergazein*) and husbanded (*therapeuein*).

What was the quality of the soils cultivated by the farmers of ancient Greece? One issue is how far they cultivated eroded soils, or, on the other hand, alluvium. It appears that there was little deterioration of the hillsides

---

[11] Sallares (1991).
[12] Theophr. *Caus. pl.* 3.23.4; *Hist. pl.* 8.7.6. The ongoing Agroclimatology Project of P. Garnsey and T. Gallant is studying *en gros* the effect of climatic fluctuations on yield in the Mediterranean. See Lamas and Shashoua (1973) (the Negev); Hadjichristodoulou (1982) (Cyprus). Both these studies showed that the *distribution* of precipitation was the main factor in grain yield.

or alluvial deposition in the plains (at least in the Argive and Thessalian plains, areas studied in exceptional depth) after the major erosion of the Bronze Age.[13] Between the Bronze Age and late Antiquity (another period of major erosion),[14] the soils of the plains would have suffered gradual loss of natural fertility if regularly worked and not renewed in some way. The question is how far this process of deterioration had gone by, say, the classical period in Greek history. One factor to be borne in mind is that the speed of decline can slow down to the point of insignificance, once fertility and yield have reached a low enough level. Arnon, who made this observation with the old soils of the Near East in mind, classed a yield of 500–700 kg/ha as 'very low'. A great deal evidently depends on one's point of comparison.[15]

Some effort was made to rejuvenate the soil in antiquity. The question is how great an effort, and how far it was successful in arresting the apparently otherwise inevitable decline. This is a negative formulation: it can be accepted that no significant improvement in soil and plant performance was possible through human action before the introduction of artificial fertilizers on a large scale. But within those limits there is plenty of room for argument between pessimists and optimists, or minimalists and progressives.

The key issues include manuring, the relation between the agricultural and pastoral economies, and the use of legumes as a field crop as an alternative to or in rotation with cereals or fallow. The issues are interconnected. Manuring (the application of animal and human dung and other organic substances) supplied phosphorus, nitrogen and other necessary nutrients. Whether grazing animals stayed on or near the farm or were moved to seasonal pastures in the uplands in the summer months made a difference to the amount of dung available from that source. The production of legumes for animal feed or fodder crops has obvious relevance in this connection; but in addition, legumes grown for food on any scale would have slowed down the process of nutrient depletion in the soil because of their notable nitrogen-fixing capacity.

I do not discuss any of these issues in any detail here; learned treatments have recently appeared or are imminent.[16] I limit myself to some general observations relating to manure and legumes, singling out the testimony of

[13] Van Andel, Runnels and Pope (1986); van Andel, Zangger and Demitrack (1996).
[14] Vita-Finzi (1969). But see Wagstaff (1981).
[15] Arnon (1972) 27, citing Littlejohn (1946).
[16] E.g. Hodkinson (1988); Skydsgaard (1988); cf. Thompson (1989). On manuring, see Alcock, Cherry and Davis (1994); cf. Spurr (1986) 126–32. Good introductions to ancient agriculture can be found in Spurr's book, and in Amouretti (1986). See also, somewhat more briefly, Osborne (1987) ch. 2; Skydsgaard (1987). See now Gallant (1991) and Sallares (1991).

Theophrastus. The absence of any treatment of livestock by this author, hardly to be anticipated in works entitled *Origins of Plants* and *Enquiry into Plants*, is the main reason for my passing over the issue of the integration of arable farming and livestock raising, though this and pastoralism in general have become fashionable subjects after long neglect.

I do not pretend that Theophrastus provides anything but partial coverage, or that the various other sources (however scattered) that exist can be dispensed with. If I privilege Theophrastus, this is because he is our main source for Greek farming in the classical period.[17] One might almost say that if Theophrastus does not treat a particular aspect of farming, then we are denied any detailed knowledge of it. I have just cited livestock-raising as an example.

Theophrastus appears in the two works on plants principally as a botanist. He did however read the missing agronomists and shows himself well-informed about at least some farming practices. To this extent he can be taken as proxy for a genuine agronomist, and as one who engaged in describing as well as prescribing. The difficulty in using Theophrastus is not so much in distinguishing prescription from description, but rather in deciding how widely and to what areas of Greece his descriptions apply. The problem is obvious in the case of descriptions which are non-localized, less obvious but still real in the case of those referring to a specific city or region in Greece. An example is green-manuring, a practice which Theophrastus associates with Thessaly and Macedonia (see below).[18] Then there is the question of || his audience and the scale of the farming enterprises that interested him. In general, Theophrastus betrays no interest in small-scale peasant farms. This was predictable but still worth bearing in mind if we are tempted to generalize about Greek farming on the basis of Theophrastus.

Manuring

For Theophrastus manuring is one of the standard operations of farming, in the case of trees, seed-crops of all kinds, garden shrubs and

---

[17] I support the positive remarks of Hodkinson (1988) 69–70 on this score. Xenophon, *Oikonomikos* provides some information on agricultural practice (and in particular on the attitudes of rich landowners), but is thin and eccentric.

[18] Theophr. *Hist. pl.* 8.9.1. In *Hist. pl.* 8.7.4, the practice of grazing and cutting down the young wheat in order to control its growth is associated with 'good soils', and illustrated from Thessaly. In *Caus. pl.* 4.16.1, the susceptibility of beans to consumption by worms is exemplified from Thessaly. The wording of *Hist. pl.* 8.9.1 is different: 'the people of Macedonia and Thessaly turn over the ground when it (sc. beans) is in flower'. On the surface this is purely a statement about the regions mentioned; but exclusivity is not necessarily implied.

vegetables[19] – though not in equal measure or without discrimination. Thus for example we are told that vines welcome manure every three years at most, cereals where the soil is poor;[20] and there is detail on types of manure and the matching of manures to plants and to soils.[21] Overall his treatment of the subject is of course far from comprehensive and must be filled out from other sources. Brief reference to tanner's manure and urine, and of course to human dung, is the only pointer he gives to the systematic waste collection and disposal from urban communities known from other evidence;[22] while the mention of litter manure as distinct from dung merely hints at the practice of the treatment of the fields with farmyard refuse (including broken pots, at once the joy and the bane of the survey archaeologist).[23] Again, one by-product of his silence on livestock raising is a total concentration on the human application of collected dung. Finally, his numerous references to manuring are not specific as to locality. This however matters less than it would in the case of a more sophisticated and recherché technique than the application of animal and human dung. Theophrastus' main message is that the practice was routine and, by inference, ubiquitous. Of course, all farmers were not equally zealous in applying manure. Equally obviously, all the manure produced was not put to agricultural use. Finally, all farming land was not treated evenhandedly. In this last matter, distance and the limited availability of animal and human power were differentiating factors. In any case, the type of landowner or land-user might make a difference, or the category of land, whether it was owner-occupied or rented out, private or public. The requirement appearing in the lease of public land from Arkesine on Amorgos that the lessee 'is to apply one hundred and fifty loads of dung a year with a basket holding a medimnos and four hemiekta, or pay a fine of half a drachma for each basket shortfall', was not apparently a standard clause.[24]

The prior question remains, whether sufficient manure was available to supply all the needs of agriculture, and it has always received a negative answer. Quite rightly. But more thorough investigation is required, with at least an attempt at quantification and a recognition of variation across space and time. An obvious starting point would be Attica in Theophrastus'

---

[19] E.g. Theophr. *Caus. pl.* 3.2.1; 3.9.5; 3.20.6; *Hist. pl.* 2.7.1; 8.7.7. Cf. Xen. *Oec.* 20.2.10. Note that sewage sludge proved more effective than commercial fertilizer in an experiment in south-west USA. See Day and Thompson (1988).

[20] Theophr. *Caus. pl.* 3.9.5; 3.20.2.

[21] E.g. Theophr. *Hist. pl.* 2.7.4; *Caus. pl.* 3.6.2; 3.9.3; 3.17.5.

[22] Theophr. *Caus. pl.* 3.9.3, cf. 3.17.5; Owens (1983); Vatin (1976).

[23] Theophr. *Hist. pl.* 2.7.4; 7.5.1; cf. Xen. *Oec.* 18.2. See Wilkinson (1982). For a comprehensive discussion see Alcock, Cherry and Davis (1994).

[24] *SIG*³, 963. Osborne (1987) 42–3, table 2, on the provisions of agricultural leases provides a useful check-list.

own time, the late fourth century, with the waste production of people and animals set against area under cultivation.

Legumes

One comes away from the works of Theophrastus with the firm conviction that seed legumes, or pulses, were a regular field crop in the Greece of his day, and not just garden vegetables (they were that as well). Cereals and legumes are often directly compared: in terms of yield, impact on the soil, vulnerability to damage, character of seed, speed of growth, sowing and harvesting patterns, suitability as food and as fodder. Legumes are said to bring higher yields than cereals.[25] It is also stated several times that legumes (with the exception of chickpeas) rejuvenate the soil, whereas wheat and barley exhaust it.[26]

This last claim is somewhat problematic. Legumes do not draw on soil nitrogen to the extent that cereals do, because of their capacity to fix atmospheric nitrogen. Yet in company with other crop plants, if harvested, they remove nutrients from the soil. In an experiment conducted on old soils in a semi-arid region of Cyprus, wheat yielded better following dry fallow than following a legume.[27] It seems to follow that the most satisfactory rotation system involving legumes in such environments would involve wheat/barley, legume and fallow, in that order. Theophrastus (unlike the elder Pliny, for Italy) does not disclose which cropping cycles were in operation in his time. Those leases from Attica which indicate that fallow was sometimes reduced to make room for legumes are no more informative in this respect.[28] Probably a variety of rotation systems were employed.

Theophrastus' comment about the soil-renewing capacity of legumes would not be at all problematic, if he had had in mind the practice of green manuring, where the plant is ploughed under rather than harvested. In the Cyprus experiment a wheat crop yielded half as much again after green manuring as after bare fallow (720 cf. 480 kg/ha). Theophrastus associates green manuring with Thessaly and Macedonia.[29] It does not follow that Greek farmers elsewhere did not know about or practise the technique. A related question is the extent to which such practices were employed throughout the farming community in Thessaly and Macedonia. It may have been standard practice, or, alternatively, confined to the more 'progressive' farmers among those with land to spare. But even they might

---

[25] Theophr. *Caus. pl.* 4.8.1f; *Hist. pl.* 8.3.4.
[26] Theophr. *Caus. pl.* 4.8. 1–3; *Hist. pl.* 8.7.2; 8.9. 1–3.
[27] Littlejohn (1946). For more recent experiments, but revolving around the use of fertilizers, see Krentos and Orphanos (1979), cf. Gregory, Shepherd and Cooper (1984).
[28] See e.g. *IG* I³, 252, lines 12–3; *IG* II², 1241, lines 22–4; *IG* II², 2493, lines 9–10.
[29] Theophr. *Hist. pl.* 8.9.1.

not have practised it invariably; it depended on their perception of their situation, in relation to such factors as the stage of a family's progress in the life-cycle, the amount of food in storage, and the scale of recent or anticipated expenditures. Decision-making was an infinitely flexible business.

In any case, it does seem legitimate to infer from Theophrastus that pulses were grown on a considerable scale for human food. This message is corroborated by other sources, for example, comic poets. Broad beans and lentils, in particular,[30] appear to have played an important role in the Greek diet. The apparent popularity of beans, particularly among the poorer classes, is not unparadoxical, considering their vulnerability to drought and their antinutritive qualities, which range from favism to flatulence.[31] These disadvantages apparently weighed less with the ancient Greek and other Mediterranean peoples, then as now, than their low cost, which is connected with their suitability for storage, and their nutritional value, which was intuited rather than understood. Pulses are protein-rich and contribute certain crucial amino acids in which wheat and barley are deficient. If Theophrastus in addition thought of them as good for the soil, the correct inference might well be that he or his sources knew of farmers who employed rotation systems which used legumes to advantage.

V. CONCEPTS OF YIELD

My title is 'The yield of the land in ancient Greece'. But is this a concept that the Greeks used or even recognized? At first sight, at any rate, it would seem that the ancients thought in terms of return on seed, not on land (though direct evidence for this comes from the Roman agronomists rather than the Greek sources). Return on seed is only one factor of production; and a high yield to seed ratio may be correlated with low return per unit area.[32] Here then we seem to have one more illustration of the 'failure' of ancient farmers to make rational calculations of the productivity, efficiency and profitability of their enterprises.

The ancient-modern comparison is sterile and uninformative.[33] Theophrastus or Aristotle could not have composed the article on Productivity in *The Encyclopedia of the Social Sciences*. But it does not follow that

---

[30] For modern accounts see e.g. Hebblethwaite, ed. (1983); Webb and Hawtin (1981).

[31] Antinutritive qualities: see Grmek (1983) 307–54. No doubt the rich consumed pulses much less than the poor. Theophrastus talks of legumes as a 'heavy' food, 'natural' to animals, in contrast with cereals, a lighter food, more suitable for human consumption, *Caus. pl.* 4.9. 1–3. Note that 'heavy' cereals were fed to slaves and considered appropriate for athletes, *Hist. pl.* 8.4.4f.

[32] See e.g. Topolski (1981). For antiquity, cf. Jongman (1988) 135 n. 5 (cf. on (mainly labour) productivity 26–7, 76–7, 87–90, 150–4). Theophrastus observes that when plants are sown thin they are more productive, *Caus. pl.* 2.12.4.

[33] Garnsey and Saller (1987), 77–8.

farmers, or proprietors, in antiquity did not think of relating the product of the farming operation to the various resources employed in its production.[34]

Production totals obviously mattered. Solon legislated the classification of Athenians in terms of the size of their (sc. average) harvests, with pentakosiomedimnoi, those who could produce 500 medimnoi, at the top of the hierarchy. Every year Greek farmers measured their harvests. Every year they decided how much of the harvest to set aside as seed – and so were in a position to calculate the yield of the seed. But just as regularly they decided how much land to put under cultivation, how much land to assign to each crop, and how much seed to sow for a given area. In other words, they had all the information they needed to work out the yield of the land.

Production totals and the yield of the land mattered to landowners at various social and economic levels, though for different reasons. Small farmers (tenants as much as owner-occupiers, if operating on a small scale) were growing food primarily for their own consumption; their very survival and that of their families depended on the performance of the crops they sowed. The rich, as Robin Osborne has reminded us in his conference paper, with reference to Athens, were obliged to raise cash in order to meet the expenses imposed on them by the polis and occasioned by their position in society. The burdens imposed on them under the Athenian democracy were as heavy as anywhere.[35] The rich, of course, also had more opportunity than those of lower economic station to raise their profit levels. They were in a position to invest in the necessary animals; they could buy in urban wastes, and were not short of labour for collecting and spreading it; they were also better placed to play the market.

The pull of the market was never powerful enough to engender a thoroughly entrepreneurial mentality. Profit was looked for, but not profit maximization, the 'productivity ratio' was understood partially, not in its totality.

However, there were doubtless rich gentleman farmers in all periods who were preoccupied or obsessed with the yield of the plant. Theophrastus and the Roman agronomists wrote at least in part, perhaps largely, for them. Theophrastus generally passes over the business of marketing produce, || while regularly giving advice as to how to grow crops that are both prolific and fine specimens.[36]

---

[34] Cf. Cipolla (1981).

[35] Xen. *Oec.* 2.5–8 is a mildly satirical summary of the burdens on wealthy Athenians.

[36] Theophr. *Caus. pl.* 1.13.9 (sale of early apples and pears on the market); 6.2.3–4 (export of herbs). As it happens, Theophrastus gives figures for yield on seed once only, for Babylon, *Hist. pl.* 8.7.4 (50-fold, 100-fold). But there is much talk about the quality of the produce, and on the production of heavy-bearing fruit trees and vines and 'many-eared' seed crops (cf. 8.8.2: Attic barleys make the most meal).

The quantity of land available to a landowner made a great deal of difference. So might labour and seed, but I single out land here as the most crucial factor.[37] The 'prize marrow (or blue-ribbon pumpkin?) syndrome', was more likely to be manifested by those with land to spare. Among subsistence peasants, or for that matter the small and middling farmers of overpopulated classical Attica, land was a finite and scarce commodity. In these circles we would expect attention to have been given, above all, to arriving at a crop-combination which would make the best use of the limited available resources, with the aim of producing what was needed for the family and a little more besides.

[37] Cf. Halstead (1990).

13

THE BEAN: SUBSTANCE AND SYMBOL

127. KUAMOS HELLENIKOS. Vicia Faba Bean

The Greeke beane is windy, flatulent, hard of digestion, causing troublesomme dreames; yet good for the Cough, & breeding flesh being in ye midst of hott and cold. Being sod with Oxymel, and eaten with the shucks, it stayes dysenteries and the fluxes of the Coeliaci, and being eaten it is good against vomiting. But it is made lesse flatulent, if the first water in which it was sod be cast away: but the green is worse for ye stomach and more windie. But the meale of the beane being applyed as a Cataplasme, either by itself or with Polenta, doth assuage the inflammations that comme of a stroake, & makes skarrs to be of one colour, & helps swelling and enflamed duggs, & doth extinguish milke. But with Hony and the meale of Foenigraec it doth dissolue ye Furunculi and the Parotidae, and ye bluenesse vnder ye eyes; with Roses, & franckincense, and the white of an egge, it doth represse the Procidentias Oculorum, & their Staphylomata, & ye Oedemata. Being kneaded with wine it helps the suffusions & stroakes of the eyes. And being chewed without the Huske it is layd on the forehead as an acollema for fluxes. Being sod in wine it cures ye inflammations of ye stones. And being applyed as a Cataplasme to ye place where the Pubes growes in children, it keeps them impuberes a long tyme; & it cleanseth ye vitiligines, but if the shucks of them be applyed as a Cataplasme, it makes ye haire that is extirpated to grow starveling and thinne. Being also applyed with Polenta, and Alumen Scissum, and old oyle, it dissolues ye Strumae, and ye decoction thereof dyes wool. It is applyed also to the fluxes of bloud occasioned by Leeches, being shuckt & divided in twoe partes, according as it grew, and the cutt half being closely prest on, it doth suppresse it.

Dioscorides 2.127, translated by John Goodyer in 1655
(*The Greek Herbal of Dioscorides,* edited by
Robert T. Gunther, New York, 1959).

INTRODUCTION

My subject is the fava bean, *vicia faba*, known as the broad bean, sometimes called the horse bean or field bean. The ancient bean was a diminutive version of the modern broad bean, *vicia faba minor* rather than *maior*.[1]

Introduced in the Neolithic Age, the bean has been a common item in the diet of Mediterranean peoples since it became established as a regular crop in the course of the Bronze Age.[2] The bean, along with other dry legumes, or pulses, is valued as a productive crop easy to store and nutritious to consume.[3]

In classical antiquity, this 'strong' (or 'heavy') food was also rich in its symbolic associations. The more adverse, even sinister, ideas or doctrines associated with the bean stem from various declared 'enemies' of the bean, in particular the Pythagoreans and Orphics.[4] Other superstitions have the flavour of folk-lore and seem likely to have circulated rather more widely. The question arises whether suspicion of the bean affected the dietary behaviour of ordinary people, or only a handful of 'sensitive spirits' in philosophical or religious circles.

The matter is more complicated than this, since much of the 'publicity' surrounding the bean was positive. Even philosophers – and gods – were not unanimously hostile. Pythagoras shunned beans, but Epicurus in a food shortage distributed them among his friends. Excluded from the festivals of Demeter, beans were nonetheless accepted by Apollo in the form of the sacred offering of bean soup at the feast of the Pyanepsia at Athens.[5]

---

[1] The fava bean is to be distinguished from the *phaseolus vulgaris* which arrived in the Mediterranean and Europe from South America in the sixteenth century. The historiography of the bean is strangely unbalanced. On the one hand, the role of beans (and of legumes in general) as acceptable or even staple food is rarely discussed (but see Olck (1899)), presumably because it is taken as read that they played a very minor role in comparison to cereals. On the other hand, beans as forbidden food are an object of endless fascination among students of anthropology, philosophy, religion and medicine. See, e.g., Grmek (1983) 307–54; Detienne (1970), (1977) ch. 3–4; Katz (1987). Also on cultural aspects, see Chirassi Colombo (1968) 39–54; Shepherd (1989). On the bean as food, see André (1981) 35–6. On the agronomy of the bean, see Arnon (1972) ch. 6; Hebblethwaite, ed. (1983); Hebblethwaite et al., eds. (1984).

[2] Origin of the bean: Renfrew (1973) 107ff.; Ladizinsky (1975), (1989); Zohary and Hopf (1988) 102–7. Legumes crop up everywhere in archaeological sites in Greece and the Eastern Mediterranean after the end of the Bronze Age (J. Hansen, personal communication). On archaic Rome, see Ampolo (1980).

[3] Aykroyd and Doughty (1982); and n. 16.

[4] On the mythology of the bean, see Grmek (1983) 307–54; Detienne (1970), (1977) ch. 3–4; Andrews (1949).

[5] Plut. *Demetr.* 34 (Epicurus); Paus. 8.15 (Demeter); *Schol. Aristoph. Ach.* 1076. Photios s.v. *Pyanepsion*, with Bruit (1990) 167–70 (Pyanepsia).

Later on we shall explore the possibility that the 'divisiveness' of beans cut deeper, separating people according to their means and position in society.

It will already be clear that my primary interest does not lie in the decipherment of 'bean-language', however fascinating this might be as an intellectual exercise. I am more intrigued by other matters, namely, the origins of the complex of meanings surrounding the bean, and the possible links between bean as symbol and bean as food.

I am aware that just by inquiring into the origins of bean metaphor and its impact on the consumer I might seem to be taking up a stance against theories of the autonomy and priority of symbol and ideology (food is 'good to think', wrote Lévi-Strauss), and leaning towards more materialistic explanations of food preferences and aversions, which stress environmental, biological, economic and political considerations.[6] I do not intend to justify my preference in any detail. The proof of the pudding is the eating.

BEAN AS SYMBOL

The fertile imagination of the Pythagoreans transformed a banal legume into a monstrous object of fear and repugnance. On this point Detienne's analysis is hard to improve on:[7]

> For strict vegetarians, every blood sacrifice is a murder, and ultimately an act of cannibalism, for which the horror is expressed by way of the broad bean. This legume, we hear, is the antithesis of spices, that wonderful food of the gods in the Golden Age. By virtue of its nodeless stalk and its affinities with the rotten, the broad bean establishes the same direct communication with the world of the dead as spices establish with the world of the gods. But in the Pythagorean system of thought, the broad bean is even more than this: it is a being of flesh and blood, the double of the man at whose side it grows and from whose rotten compost they both feed. In consequence, the Pythagoreans say, eating beans and gnawing at the head of one's parent are the same crime. For proof Pythagorean tradition furnishes a series of experiments. In a mysterious cooking process, a broad bean is placed in a pot or some closed vessel, hidden under a dunghill or buried in the ground. After quite a long period of gestation, the bean is transformed, either into female sex-organs to which is attached the barely formed head of a child, or into a human head with fully recognizable traits. In these experiments, the pot is a womb, charged with revealing the true nature of the bean. But that nature can be discovered also in the following way: a bean that has been gnawed or lightly crushed is exposed for a few moments to the sun. Immediately it releases, it is said, a smell which is

[6] Harris (1987). [7] Detienne (1977) 146–7.

either that of sperm or that of blood spilled in the course of a murder. The Pythagoreans are explicit: eating beans is feeding on human flesh; it is to eat the meat of all meats the most individual.

The analysis can be supported from texts of various kinds. But the historical Pythagoras, the mystical philosopher who established himself at Croton in S. Italy around 530 BC, is shrouded in mystery. It is possible that even when he was alive his reasons for banning bean consumption were unknown. They were perhaps, rather like the exclusion of beans from Demeter's ceremonies, 'a holy secret'.[8] The plethora of explanations and interpretations proposed by multiple commentators – from Aristotle in the fourth century BC to John the Lydian in the sixth century AD – and the contradictory traditions relating to his beliefs and dietary practices, prove beyond any doubt that the true reasons for which Pythagoras shunned beans remain inaccessible to us. Aristotle's list (sic) of possible motives, as recorded by Diogenes Laertius, can serve as an introduction to bean symbolism:

> Pythagoras counselled abstinence from beans either because they are like the genitals, or because they are like the gates of Hades, for they alone have no hinges; or again, because they spoil, or because they are injurious, or because they are like the form of the universe, or because of oligarchy, for they are used for drawing lots.[9]

These disparate elements, despite the brilliant attempt of Detienne to order them in a coherent whole, seem to me rather to have been put together at random.[10] The allusion at the end to democracy is particularly inappropriate, and cannot in any case be attributed to Pythagoras without anachronism.

This brings us to the positive side of bean symbolism. For the citizen of Athens at least, the bean became a metaphor for democracy, being used in the appointment by lot of numerous officials. Also at Athens, the council of 500 was designated the 'council of the bean'.[11]

Andrews, following an intuition of Delatte, captures the ambivalence and the mystique of beans in the following passage:

> The ancients felt toward beans a mingled respect and dread, a complex of emotions suggested by the Greek term *hieros*, which apparently was generally applied to an object believed to be charged with some supernatural force, contact with which might be either beneficial or harmful. Today we generally call this mysterious power *mana* in its helpful aspect and taboo in its harmful aspect.[12]

---

[8] Paus. 8.15.   [9] Diog. Laert. 8.34.   [10] Detienne (1970).
[11] Thuc. 8.66, cf. Ar. *Av.* 1022; Xen., *Mem.* 1.2.9; Plut. *Per.* 27; Lucian, *Vit. Auct.* 6.
[12] Andrews (1949) 277; cf. Delatte (1930) 33.

The ancient sources, when they expound the doctrine of Pythagoras, generally take account of these two aspects, the one sinister, the other more cheerful. Pliny the Elder wrote[13] that:

> (The bean) ... was thought to have a dulling effect on the senses, and also to cause sleeplessness, and it was under a ban with the Pythagorean system on that account – or as others have reported, because the souls of the dead are contained in a bean. At all events it is for that reason that beans are employed in memorial sacrifices to dead relatives. Moreover, according to Varro's account, it is partly for these reasons that a priest abstains from eating beans, though also because certain letters of gloomy omen are to be found inscribed on a bean-flower.... It is undoubtedly the case that the bean is the only grain that even when it has been grazed down by cattle fills out again when the moon is waxing.

But he also indicates that:

> In ancient ritual, bean pottage has a sanctity of its own in sacrifice to the gods ... There is a special religious sanctity attached to the bean; at all events it is the custom to bring home from the harvest a bean by way of an auspice, this being consequently called the harvest-home bean. Also it is supposed to bring luck at auctions if a bean is included in a lot for sale.

According to Mary Douglas,[14] food is a language which conveys messages. Bean-language is particularly involved and obscure. But beans are not only meaning, but also food, the ingestion of which affects bodily health in one way or another. Physiological responses may illuminate, or even hold the key to, the semantics of the bean. In this connection, it is very interesting that there is ambivalence and contradiction about the bean at the material as well as symbolic level. If as symbol beans have both positive and negative resonances, as food the bean is at once extremely nourishing and has conspicuous anti-nutritive qualities. Let us here leave structuralism and anthropology for medical history, the perspicacity of Detienne for the wisdom of Grmek.

BEAN AS FOOD

The nutritional value of beans was appreciated, if not understood, in Graeco-Roman antiquity.[15] Galen knew of the body-building qualities of beans, and fed them in bulk to the gladiators in his charge. Three

---

[13] Plin. *HN* 18. 117–19. [14] Douglas (1966), (1972).
[15] Galen 6.529; Macrob. *Sat.* 1.12.33; cf. Ov. *Fast.* 6.169–80; Diosc. 2.127.

centuries later (in the fifth century AD), Macrobius wrote that fat bacon and bean porridge were popular with the early inhabitants of Rome (and with their gods) 'because bodily strength is above all nourished by these things'. Beans, along with other members of the class of dry legumes, or pulses, are rich in protein. This means they are a possible substitute for meat (and have thus earned the sobriquet 'the poor man's meat'), and a useful complement to cereals, which have considerably less protein and are deficient in the key amino acid lysine. Legumes also supply other nutrients in which cereals are deficient, notably, calcium and Vitamin c.[16] (The complementarity of legumes and cereals is an important theme to which I will turn on another occasion.)

On the other hand, beans are associated with disorders ranging from flatulence to favism, which can be fatal.[17] The gases which give rise to flatulence, and also to severe intestinal cramps and diarrhoea, are caused by the concentration in fava beans of indigestible oligosaccharides (raffinose and stachiose). Beans are also high in L-dopa, which has been described as 'a potent psychoactive neurotransmitter'. Thirdly, beans contain b-glycosides (vicine and covicine), which are responsible for a nutritional disorder known as favism. This afflicts those deficient in the enzyme G6PD (glucose-6-phosphate dehydrogenase). The symptoms are weakness, pallor, jaundice and haemoglobinuria, and, in about 10 cent of cases, death can result.

Of these several disorders, the first is the most familiar. 'Why does bean soup blow out the belly but not the fire?' asks a character in an Attic comedy of the fourth century BC.[18] The second is recognizable in the frequent complaint that beans disturb sleep and give bad dreams.[19] But favism goes unnoticed in the primary sources. The scientific isolation and description of the disease is of course a relatively recent development. But one might have expected sufferers or observers in the pre-scientific world to have made connections between some of its symptoms and the ingestion of beans. Yet the literature is silent. The omission is the more remarkable if, as the experts claim, the disease was as common in the Mediterranean then as it is now, affecting about 30 per cent of the population.

The dilemma is acute: how could the bean have been retained as a significant crop through the centuries (supposing this be accepted, but see below) in an area where it is incompatible with the genetic constitutions of an important minority of the population?[20] Two promising approaches have been suggested. First, the very same properties that debilitate those

---

[16] Aykroyd and Doughty (1982); Pellett and Shadarevian (1970).
[17] Grmek (1983) 327–340; Buerg et al. (1984); Katz (1987) e.g., 138–9, 153.
[18] Ath. 9.408b.   [19] Cic. *Div.* 1.30.62; Plin. *HN* 18.118; *Geoponica* 2.35; etc.
[20] The analysis of Katz (1987) is to be recommended.

with G6PD deficiency reduced the susceptibility of normal people to malaria – which is also endemic to the Mediterranean region. Second, bean toxins can be removed or reduced in the food-preparation process, insofar as this involves soaking, boiling, shelling and the germination of the seed.

This is not the end of the matter. Two further questions are raised, and until they are resolved, favism must cast a shadow over the whole subject of bean consumption and avoidance. The first is, how far did the ancients practise the risk-reducing strategies just mentioned? And the second is, how far and by what processes, in a pre-scientific society, might knowledge have accumulated and circulated about the disease-inducing and disease-combating properties of beans? The silence of the sources is prima-facie evidence for the failure of the society as a whole to make the connection between beans and the disabilities associated with favism (and, by the same token, between beans and immunity from malaria). It remains possible that rejection of beans on a fairly large scale, though within individual families, lies behind the negative connotations of beans.

As for the veto on beans and the motivation of the known enemies of beans, is it possible that Pythagoras was aware that beans were bad for his health?[21] In a religious context, does the windiness of beans lie behind their rejection in the interests of ritual purity? Does the idea that the bean embodied spirit have the same background? Of course verification of any particular suggestion of this kind is not at hand. But one cannot dismiss speculation of this kind out of hand. The bean veto did not come out of nothing, and we are entitled to inquire into its origins. Meanwhile, the parallel ambiguity between beans as substance and beans as symbol with which I began this section is suggestive. Bean-language contains an uneasy combination of positive and negative images. Such confusion is just what one might expect to be associated with a food which can, on the one hand, induce good health, and on the other, seriously undermine it.

BEAN AS SOCIAL MARKER

To inquire further into the possible impact of bean symbolism we turn from the biological to the social context. Eating is an act of social as well as physiological significance. Food brings people together, but also erects boundaries between them. It marks off gods from humans, humans from animals. It reflects and creates divisions within humanity – between people of different cultures and religions, between countrymen and city dwellers,

[21] Arie (1959).

people of the plain and of the mountain, rich and poor, men and women, adults and children. Do patterns of bean consumption and ideology in the ancient world reflect the divisions of a stratified society?

There is a prior question concerning bean consumption which can no longer be postponed. Dry legumes are today a common ingredient, second to cereals, in the diet of the people of the less developed dry regions of the Mediterranean zone, especially in the Eastern Mediterranean, the Near East and North Africa. And in some parts, beans are the most successful legume. There is a presumption that beans, together with other key dry legumes (but not the field bean, phaseolus vulgaris, a sixteenth-century import from the New World), played a significant role in the diets of past Mediterranean societies.

But this may not be a safe assumption. The negative associations of beans may have made a direct impact on the dietary customs of a considerable number of consumers. As it happens, the assumption of those ancient historians who have interested themselves in food is that cereals provided the lion's share of nutritional needs for the mass of consumers. Foxhall and Forbes (1982) indeed have estimated average cereal consumption at 70–75 per cent of food energy requirements, and this figure has won wide acceptance. Moreover, a superficial reading of the nutritional literature might lead one to suppose that a diet that is heavily weighted towards cereals is fundamentally healthy, so that legumes are dispensable. Nutritionists appear to agree that those who eat enough cereal to satisfy the bulk of their caloric needs will at the same time ingest sufficient protein. This might seem to strengthen the case for treating legumes as a whole as marginal and might seem to justify their neglect by ancient historians.

Protein quality is relevant as well as quantity. If the balance of the protein is less than satisfactory because of the absence of legumes, and if other important nutrients supplied by legumes are lacking, consumers would be in an important sense 'malnourished'.

In any case, the 'hunch' of modern writers, who are not specialists in antiquity but assume that the consumption of beans (and dry legumes as a whole) has been widely prevalent in the Mediterranean ever since they were established in the region, can be supported from the ancient sources themselves (although a quantitative analysis of production or consumption rates of any legume, or any cereal for that matter, is of course impossible). I do not intend to argue the case in detail, and introduce only one or two of the more obvious sources, those which interest themselves in agriculture.

A close reading of Theophrastus or Columella leaves little room for doubt that beans, and some other legumes (including lentils, peas and chickpeas) were cultivated at an important level in the Graeco-Roman world.[22] For example, Theophrastus makes stray reference to the cultivation of beans in the open fields (as opposed to gardens, where also they were grown)[23] in Macedonia and Thessaly, in Apollonia in the Ionian Sea, at Cyzicus, in Lemnos and in Egypt.[24]

These same places, significantly, are better known for the cultivation of cereals. Sicily, too, was a country of cereals. Yet beans were grown there on a large scale.[25] Inscriptions from Taormina dated around the end of the Hellenistic Age present accounts of a Sitophylax over several years. One might have thought that this magistrate built up stocks of wheat (*sitos*) and saw to its distribution. But it was a question not of wheat, but of beans (*kuamoi*). These inscriptions confirm the coexistence of cereals and legumes in the Mediterranean, and raise the question, without furnishing the answer, about the social and economic status of the consumers of beans. The question remains unanswered, because the inscriptions give no information at all on context. We do not know if beans were distributed in this period when wheat supplies were deficient. Anyway, it appears certain that a lot of beans were grown in the region, and that ordinary people were in the habit of eating them.

And the rich? Clearly they would not have queued up for beans at Taormina. Did they in addition think of beans as a 'low-grade' food, as 'the poor man's meat'?

We are what we eat. Usually when the relation between food and society is mentioned, dry legumes are left out of the discussion. We read that meat is the classic sacrificial food, and that it is the monopoly of the rich. We read also that white bread is the preserve of the élite. And so forth. Some such distinctions are perfectly explicable. In a world dependent on sedentary agriculture, meat is rare, expensive to produce and to obtain; it is therefore out of the reach of the ordinary family and individual most of the time. Similarly, the cost of acquiring and processing the best breadwheat to make the lightest bread out of the most refined flour means that this product too was effectively monopolized by the rich.

Other foods were cheaper and more freely available, including barley. It does not follow however that barley was food only for animals, slaves and the poor. This view, long accepted by scholars in relation to consumers in Athens and Attica, has recently been shown by Gallo to be a considerable

---

[22] In fact, the question of the importance of the cultivation and consumption of beans (and of dry legumes in general) in antiquity is rarely posed. With the exception of Sarpaki (1992), modern commentators suppose either that most people ate beans since their arrival, or that beans (and dry legumes) were of little importance.

[23] Theophr. *Caus. pl.* 3.20.1, etc.

[24] Theophr. *Caus. pl.* 4.11.8, 12.3.8, 16.1; *Hist. pl.* 8.2.8, 11.3.

[25] *IG* XIV 423–9 (c. AD 100).

exaggeration.[26] Consumption of barley products, particularly the flat barley-cake, *maza*, was much too widespread among ordinary Athenians for that. It remains true that wheat had a certain cachet in Athens which barley lacked.

But not *any* wheat. Theophrastus knew that the wheat of Aenos in Thrace was fed to slaves because it was heavy.[27] What appealed to wealthy consumers was the light wheat from which good bread was made. The delights of leavened bread had only recently been discovered by Athenians of the classical period. The wheat that made the best bread had to be imported and paid for by the consumer. Its superior status was thereby guaranteed. Here was an additional item to separate off the rich from their social and economic inferiors.

The lightest wheat, as Theophrastus tells us, came from Pontus. This was *triticum vulgare* or *aestivum*, the soft winter wheat that was the ancestor of modern breadwheat. The wheat of Attica was apparently quite light (certainly lighter than Boeotian), but it was not *triticum vulgare*, and there was not much of it. Barley, not wheat, flourished in the dry conditions of Attica.[28]

The significant distinction in the minds of better-off Greeks, then, was not between wheat and barley; nor even was it between cereals and legumes. Theophrastus had discussed the two classes of seed-crops together, and his unified treatment is justified several centuries later in Galen's description of legumes as 'grains of Demeter'.[29] The distinction which represents the value-system of the élite is that which emerges in Theophrastus between:

(1) Wheat that is light and easily digestible by man.
(2) Heavier wheats, barleys and legumes – these are less easily digestible.
(3) Fodder crops, including some legumes.

The first category belongs to good bread wheat. The second includes barley and beans. Insofar as the capacity to make good bread was the principle of division, the two crops had much in common. With regard to beans, a sentence of Galen on legumes goes to the heart of the matter: 'Legumes is the name of those grains of Demeter out of which bread is not made.' In early Rome (for example), bean flour was added to the flour of cereal.[30] But beans were normally boiled and made into soup, or roasted, or eaten in a green and tender state as 'dessert' (as the botanist Phaenias of Eresos wrote[31]). Galen had earlier branded barley bread as inferior.[32] Athenians

[26] Gallo (1983).   [27] Theophr. *Hist. pl.* 8.4.4.
[28] Theophr. *Caus. pl.* 4.9.5; cf. *Hist. pl.* 8.4.5; 8.8.2. For *triticum vulgare* from Pontus, cf. van Zeist and Casparie (1984) 267–83.
[29] Galen 6.524.   [30] Plin. *HN* 18.117.   [31] Ath. 2.54.   [32] Galen 6.506.

ate their barley primarily in the form of flat cakes, *maza*, gruel, or roasted meal.

The mass of Athenian citizens patronized barley products, especially *maza*. The pauper ate these too, but his *maza* was full of chaff.[33] Beans also (and lentils) were food for the mass of ordinary citizens of the polis – not just slaves and paupers. The Athenian who in the comic fragment hurries off to the Pyanopsia with pot and beans is a respectable farmer from Acharnae.[34]

Food for ordinary citizens, or food for slaves and the poor? In the value system of the rich, it made little difference. Beans were a symbol of democracy. But *they* preferred oligarchy, almost without exception, and they characterized democracy as the rule of the lower classes over their betters.

Pythagoras is said by Aristotle to have imposed his ban on beans partly 'because of oligarchy, for they are used in drawing lots'. Whatever is to be made of this, there is no need to believe that the educated and wealthy élite of the Greek cities boycotted beans for ideological reasons. Their response, as might have been anticipated, was ambiguous. They did not avoid beans altogether; but they did not consume them in bulk. The 'beanfeast' was not set up for such as them. On the contrary, in traditional societies, it was organized by the rich for their workers and clients. As for them, they ate beans fresh whether as a dessert (*tragema*) or in the form of soup, ragout or exotic sauces, the kind to be found in the Cookery Book of Apicius. Two of these recipes, carrying the name of the Roman emperor and gourmet Vitellius, go like this:[35]

> Peas or beans à la Vitellius: I
> Boil the peas or beans, stir until smooth. Pound pepper, lovage, ginger; and over the spices put yolks of hard-boiled eggs, 3 oz. honey, liquamen, wine and vinegar. Put all this, including the spices which you have pounded, in the saucepan. Add oil, and bring to the boil. Season the beans with this. Stir until smooth if lumpy. Add honey and serve.
>
> Peas or beans à la Vitellius: II
> Boil the peas or beans. When the froth has been skimmed off, add leeks, coriander, and flowers of mallow. While this is cooking pound pepper, lovage, origan, fennel seed, moisten with liquamen and wine, put in the saucepan, add oil. When it boils again, stir. Pour over best oil and serve.

Tell me what you eat, with whom *and how* and I will tell you who you are.

CONCLUSION

The symbolism of the bean is very rich. The bean conjures up death, hell, blood, semen. But at the same time it is a good luck charm. In the Roman

[33] Ath. 2.60.   [34] Ath. 9.407e.   [35] Apicius 5.190.5.

Saturnalia or in the *fêtes des rois* of the Christian world, the person who draws the bean is crowned king.

As a food, the bean is at once nourishing and poisonous. It disturbs the mind. It provokes physical reactions that are either antisocial or dangerous. There is no evidence that anyone in antiquity saw a direct connection between beans and death or serious illnesses. Rather, it is a matter of prohibitions emanating from highly circumscribed philosophical or religious circles; and of the emergence of a justificatory mythology. Moreover, one can assume that the word passed down from fathers to sons in the context of individual families that beans were best avoided.

It doesn't look as if any of this had a profound effect on the consumption of beans in the Mediterranean. On the contrary, a great many countryfolk and consumers in general depended on the bean (in addition to other dry legumes) as a food capable of complementing, or, if need be, substituting for cereals.

Beans *were* the poor man's meat. As for the élite, they had no need of beans as a staple food, but at the same made use of it along with other plebeian foods, in such a way as to affirm their superiority over the lower orders in society.

14

MASS DIET AND NUTRITION IN THE CITY OF ROME

I. INTRODUCTION

In this paper I investigate the diet and health of the mass of Rome's inhabitants. This is not a subject that has roused much interest among historians.[1] The provenance of the foods that poured into the city of Rome, the 'decline' of Italian agriculture and the rise of provincial production, the growth of state intervention in the food supply of Rome, the public distribution system (*frumentatio*), its birth, development and periodic breakdown, its organization and politics – all these issues have been fully investigated and debated. But the discussion has more or less petered out at Rome's ports, warehouses, distribution points and rubbish dumps (notably, the mountain of broken oil-containers that is Monte Testaccio). The *plebs frumentaria*, once it has received its (unmilled) grain, has faded from view; while the group or groups of non-recipients have never come into focus. My object in this paper is to take the matter of the food supply of Rome into the area of food consumption, concentrating on ordinary Romans.

But who were the ordinary Romans of Rome? It is an integral part of my argument that the social structure of the population of Rome is essential background to any study of the nutritional status of its residents. Most Romans, most of the 750,000–1,000,000 residents of the city, were poor, but there were different levels of poverty. At the risk of being overschematic, I distinguish between the permanent poor and the temporary poor, and subdivide the former into the very poor and the ordinary poor, roughly corresponding || to the 'structural poor' and 'conjunctural poor' of recent analyses of late medieval and early modern European historians

---

[1] These themes are adumbrated in Garnsey, ed. (1989), but not with special reference to the city of Rome. I have greatly benefited from the criticisms and suggestions of Dominic Rathbone and Greg Woolf. Among those to whom I am indebted are the anthropologists and/or paleopathologists Sara Bisel, Gino Fornaciari, Roberto Machiarelli, Patricia Smith, the nutritionists Alison Paul and Roger Whitehead, and the historians Richard Duncan-Jones, Lin Foxhall and John Henderson.

(Pullan (1978); Woolf (1986); Henderson (1994); cf. Whittaker (1993b). The very poor were the truly destitute: they spent their lives in search of food, work and shelter. The ordinary poor lived at the edge of subsistence; they had some kind of lodgings, and provided unskilled, part-time or seasonal labour, when they could get it. By the temporary poor I mean small shopkeepers and artisans, who enjoyed a somewhat higher social and economic status, but were liable to slip into poverty in times of shortage or at difficult points in their life cycles. The distinction between recipients and non-recipients of state grain, which had significant consequences for economic status, diet and health, does not coincide with either of the distinctions just outlined. But it is hard to imagine that those at the lowest levels of Roman society had access to the *frumentatio*, even when the grain was available gratis, as it was from 58 BC, to those on the list. I will have occasion to refer also to those Romans of modest or middling wealth who were neither rich nor poor, and, in passing only, to slaves, for my main concern in the present instance is with the free. Among groups disadvantaged for reasons of gender and age, I give special attention to infants.

Studies of diet exist. André (1981) provides a list of the food resources available to and utilized by Romans and Italians. He is interested particularly in dietary changes over time, much less so in differences between the diets of rich and poor, and hardly at all in health. White (1976), Sippel (1988) and Evans (1980b) give some attention to health and nutrition. However, Evans (1980b) (like Frayn (1979)) is a study of peasant diets and has only marginal relevance to the condition of the poorer inhabitants of Rome, even if some residents of Rome would have furnished seasonal labour on nearby estates.

White's aims expressed at the beginning of his article include 'to examine the evidence for the diet of the working population of classical times; to evaluate it in terms of nutrition and general bodily health'. What he provides is more accurately described as a general discussion of food preparation and consumption with reference to cereals (though his treatment of the diet of soldiers is more comprehensive). He attempts no statement about the state of health of Romans of Rome, nor does his general assessment of 'Roman' diet relate specifically to them: 'The basic diet of both Greeks and Romans was strongly, though not exclusively, vegetarian, ǁ comprising a variety of cereals, vegetables (green and dried), and fruit (fresh and dried), with wine (diluted with varying proportions of water) as the only drink, apart from water. In Greece, the commonest meat was that of goats, in Italy, that of pigs, in the form of pork or bacon. Beef might be eaten occasionally after a sacrifice, but the cow, like the ox, was a working animal, and milk was normally obtained from sheep and goats, while olive oil took the place of butter and soap, as well as being the major source of domestic lighting. Fish (both fresh and salted) and poultry also featured in the diet of both peoples' (White (1976) 147).

White's research belongs to the tradition of scholarship represented by Jasny (1944) and Moritz (1958), lately joined by Amouretti (1986) for Greece, which has been concerned with cereals and the technology of their processing. A significant contribution in this area is Foxhall and Forbes (1982), which however breaks new ground in tackling the difficult problem of the quantity of cereals consumed, and in an innovative way, with attention to nutritional matters and with the aid of comparative evidence.

The message of Sippel's article is that 'serious malnutrition ... must ... have been present in Rome among the poorer classes'. This judgement would not surprise any student of urbanism in preindustrial societies of the past or developing societies of the present. Nevertheless it has not to my knowledge been voiced by any previous ancient historian.[2] In contrast, the poor living conditions of ordinary Romans is a well-worn theme, publicized three decades ago by Yavetz (1958) and recently powerfully revived by Scobie (1987); food consumption has no place in either study. Sippel explains the 'omission' in terms of the upper-class bias of the sources and their lack of interest in 'Romans at the bottom of the socioeconomic scale'. But the attitudes and assumptions of modern historians of Rome are also of interest. Some have perhaps assumed that the existence of the *frumentatio* renders the nutritional status of ordinary Romans unproblematic; while others may have thought that any dietary deficiencies were made up through the purchase of low-cost foods or through the medium of patronage.

Sippel's argument is the more arresting because he is commenting precisely on the position of recipients of state grain, not those excluded from the *frumentatio* (these he overlooks), many of whom || must have been worse off. In addition to passing over nonrecipients, Sippel has overestimated the numbers of recipients (he seems to be operating with a figure of 320,000), and has underestimated the nutritional value of the handout of five *modii* of grain per month (judged by him 'barely sufficient for an adult male'). In general, he is too pessimistic about the value of a diet dominated by cereals. He answers his own question 'But what exactly is the result of a diet composed predominantly of grain?' with 'An essentially vegetarian diet, as must have obtained (of necessity) among those on the lowest rung of the socioeconomic ladder in Rome, would inevitably lead to serious and widespread nutritional deficiency.' (I take it that he means by 'vegetarian diet' a diet restricted to cereals.) In any case, his article does not settle the

---

[2] Corvisier (1985), writing about health in Greece, considers the possibility of periodic shortage but not that of endemic malnutrition.

question how far the diet of ordinary Romans was cereal-dominated, and therefore how relevant his gloomy pronouncement is to their predicament, on his own terms. His statement on their diet is general, tentative and supported by a minimum of documentation: 'Most Romans, including the greater part of the upper class, must have been content with a much simpler diet composed mostly of wheat or barley in some prepared form, supplemented with a piece of pork or fish and some onions, garlic and beans. Below the middle economic level, the variety and availability of nutritive foods would have been considerably more restricted. The essential diet of the poor could have been little more than coarse bread washed down with water drawn fresh from one of the public fountains fed by the city's many aqueducts, and, perhaps, the rare addition of some pulses and wine of the roughest sort' (Sippel (1988) 47–8).

It may be that no more precise and informative statement on the subject of diet and health of ordinary, poor Romans can be made. My intention in this paper is to survey and evaluate the evidence, and to outline some approaches which may pay dividends in the future. I will be asking questions about wheat (how good a staple, how much consumed, by whom and at what cost?), the balance of the diet as a whole, and the prevalence of malnutrition and deficiency disease.

II. NUTRITIONAL VALUE OF WHEAT

I begin with the nutritional implications of the apparent fact that under the Principate 150,000 people (or 200,000) received gratis 5 *modii* (*c*.33 kg) of unmilled wheat every month by favour of the emperor and through the agency of his officials. ‖

The first thing that must be said, as a partial corrective of Sippel's argument, is that in wheat the Romans had a relatively good staple food, measured in terms of its contribution to human nutritional needs. These break down into food energy or calories, proteins or amino acids, and specific vitamins and minerals (table 14.1).

Wheat scores well as a source of food energy. Operating with the figure of 1,625–2,012 kcals per person per day as a minimum requirement (Clark and Haswell (1970) 58), and taking 3,330 kcals as the food energy value of 1 kg of soft wheat, we can estimate that basic needs, if met completely by wheat, would be satisfied by consumption of 490–600 gm of wheat, or, at a high extraction rate, 650–800 gm of wholemeal bread (or 2–2.4 Roman lbs.).[3] This represents minimum requirements, that is, sufficient to keep

---

[3] From flour to bread: Foxhall and Forbes (1982) 80, using Plin. *HN* 18.87 (weight of flour = 75 per cent weight of bread). Flour does not lose calories when made into bread, cf. Aykroyd and Doughty (1970) 34–5, 62. From grammes to pounds: Foxhall and Forbes

Table 14.1. *Calories and nutrient content of wheat/barley (per 100 gm)*

Cereal	Water	Cals	Prot.	Fat	Total carbohydrate incl. fibre	Ca mg	Fe mg	Thiamine mg	Riboflavin mg	Nicot. Acid mg
Wheat (hard)	12 gm	332	13.8	2.0 gm	70	37	4.1	0.45	0.13	5.4
Wheat (soft)	12	333	10.5	1.9	74	35	3.9	0.38	0.08	4.3
Barley	12	332	11.0	1.8	73	33	3.6	0.46	0.12	5.5

(Adapted from Aykroyd and Doughty (1970) 18, Table 2)

life going, not to attain good health. If 75 per cent of food energy requirements were taken in as cereals, a relatively high estimate (cf. Foxhall and Forbes (1982) 74; see table 14.2), then these figures reduce to 350–450 gm of wheat per day or, at a high extraction rate, 500–600 gm of wholemeal || bread. A side-glance at the *frumentatio* shows the recipient of 5 *modii* (about 3,700 kcals per day) was getting more than 1 kg of wheat per day or more than double his basic requirement.

A consumer eating enough wheat to fulfil his energy requirements would receive at the same time a more than adequate supply of protein (Clark and Haswell (1970) 7; cf. table 14.3). The same cannot be said of the polished rice, short in protein as well as other vital nutrients, that is consumed by many contemporary Asians, or of the sundry low-protein root crops to which many Africans are wedded – yams or sweet potatoes, or the 'false banana plant', ensete ventricosum, of the Ethiopian Gurage tribe, which supplies about one third of the protein of plain household white wheat flour (Shack (1978)). In other words, it can be said that PEM, protein-energy malnutrition (otherwise known as PCM, protein-calorie malnutrition) should not have been present to a significant degree || in the ancient Mediterranean, provided that the staple food was consumed in sufficient quantity.

This generalization has a rough and ready acceptability, but only that. It does not apply to children in periods of most rapid growth, or to pregnant

(1982) 84 (1 Roman pound = 327.45 gm). Barley also has high calorific value and in other respects too has a nutritional standing similar to that of wheat. Throughout this paper I refer only to wheat, as there is no good evidence known to me that barley was in regular use as food for humans in the city of Rome – in contrast with classical Athens. Barley consumption might serve as an indication of lower socio-economic status, as in Athens, but information is lacking.

Table 14.2. *Total calories from wheat in certain countries, 1960–5*

Country	Grammes of wheat per caput daily	% of total cals from wheat	wheat cals % of cals from all cereals and starchy foods	% total cals from all cereals and starchy foods
Turkey	516	58	82	71
Yugoslavia	416	48	75	64
Greece	404	48	89	54
Italy	331	43	83	51
Syria	313	47	77	61
Jordan	310	50	84	59
Lebanon	283	44	82	53
Iraq	259	42	75	56
Libya	229	44	71	63
Romania	340	38	58	65
Israel	301	37	88	42
Spain	286	37	74	50
France	261	30	80	37
United Arab Republic	239	31	43	73
Portugal	173	24	43	56
UK	204	22	74	30
USA	149	17	72	24

(Adapted from Aykroyd and Doughty (1970) 75–8, Tables 10–14)

Table 14.3. *Protein content of some staple foods*

Cereal or root crop	Protein (gms of protein per 100 gms)
Wheat (hard)	13.8
Wheat (soft)	10.5
Barley	11.0
Rye	11.0
Oats	11.2
Sorghum	9.7
Millet	10.3
Rice	7.5
Maize	9.5
Potato	1.7

(Adapted from Aykroyd and Doughty (1970) 19, Table 2; Wing and Brown (1979) 51, Table 4.3)

Table 14.4. *The essential amino acid composition of wheat gluten, yeast protein and a 50 : 50 mixture of these, compared with the FAO/WHO reference protein (mg amino acid/g Nitrogen)*

Amino acid	Wheat gluten	Yeast protein	Wheat + yeast	WHO/FAO reference protein
Isoleucine	267	310	288	250
Leucine	472	450	460	440
LYSINE	121	510	316	340
Methionine	95	110	102	
Cystine	130	60	95	
Met + Cys	225	170	197	220
Phenylalanine	364	270	317	
Tyrosine	248	230	239	
Phe + Tyr	612	500	556	380
THREONINE	167	300	234	250
Tryptophan	70	70	70	60
Valine	260	400	330	310

(Adapted from Simmonds (1981) 161, Table 10.3)

and lactating women. In addition, it glosses over the fact that wheat is notably deficient in the essential amino acid lysine, and to a lesser extent threonine (table 14.4) unless its flour is enriched with yeast, and it has to be supplemented by foods with a complementary amino acid pattern such as dry legumes.[4]

The discussion of the energy and protein value of cereals therefore raises important questions concerning both quantity and quality. Did ordinary Romans get enough of the staple to serve their basic food-energy and protein requirements? How far were the deficiencies of cereals made up for by the consumption of other foods? How far was the diet balanced?

The question of dietary balance recurs when we consider wheat as a source of vitamins and minerals. ||

Wheat is a good source of the B vitamins thiamin and (unlike maize) niacin, and of vitamin E, but, the germ of the grain apart, it is low in riboflavin (vitamin B_2) and deficient in vitamins A, C and D. These must be

---

[4] See Aykroyd and Doughty (1970) 26–32; Simmonds (1981) 161 (amino acids and wheat); Aykroyd and Doughty (1970) 28–9 (extraction rates make a difference); Simmonds (1981) 149; Aykroyd and Doughty (1970) 18–20 (variability of wheat proteins: 6–16 per cent, 7–24 per cent); Pal (1966) 163 (climate and soil as main determinants).

Table 14.5. *Summary of avitaminosis*

Fat-soluble vitamins	
Vitamin A	Night-blindness, xeropthalmia, keratomalacia, bone malformation, growth retardation
Vitamin D	Rickets, osteomalacia, osteoporosis
Vitamin E	Anaemia
Vitamin K	Haemorrhage
Water-soluble vitamins	
Ascorbic acid	Scurvy
Thiamin	Beri-beri
Riboflavin	Cheilosis, glossitis, angular stomatitis, eye changes
Niacin	Pellagra
Biotin	Dermatitis, muscle pain, anaemia
Pyridoxine	Anaemia, convulsions, dermatitis
Pantothenic acid	Cramps, depression, insomnia
Folic acid	Megaloblastic anaemia
Vitamin B_{12}	Pernicious anaemia

(Adapted from Wing and Brown (1979) Table 3.7)

supplied from other sources. Symptoms of the various forms of avitaminosis[5] are listed in summary form in table 14.5.

Those vitamin deficiencies bearing on wheat and barley consumers are the following:

Vitamin A deficiency: this results in afflictions of the eyes, very common in contemporary developing countries. They include night-blindness, xerophthalmia progressing to keratomalacia and blindness in the worst cases. They are associated with a diet short in animal products, and are prevalent in rice-eating areas, among children, notably in the third and fourth years of life.

Vitamin B_2 riboflavin deficiency: symptoms include swollen and cracked lips, inflammation of the tongue and the mucous lining of the mouth. ||

Vitamin C deficiency: this is scurvy, a disease of the connecting tissue preventing continued development of bones and teeth.

---

[5] On avitaminosis, see Scrimshaw, Taylor and Gordon (1968) 40ff., 87ff.; Jarrett (1979) 94–118; Ortner and Putschar (1981) 270ff.; Wing and Brown (1979) 36–40; Thylefors (1987).

Table 14.6. *Summary of hypomineralosis*

Calcium	Rickets, osteomalacia, osteoporosis, tetany
Phosphorus	Rickets, bone fragility
Magnesium	Vasodilation, soft tissue mineralization, atherosclerosis, tetany
Sodium	Nausea, anorexia, muscular weakness, cramps
Potassium	Weakness, anorexia, abdominal distension, tachycardia
Iron	Anaemia
Copper	Anaemia, demyelination of nerves, bone disorders
Manganese	Ataxia
Zinc	Hepatosplenomegaly, dwarfism, hypogonadism
Iodine	Goitre, cretinism
Fluorine	Dental caries
Cobalt	Anaemia
Chromium	Impaired glucose tolerance curve
Molybdenum	Poor growth
Selenium	Growth retardation

(Adapted from Wing and Brown (1979) 41, Table 3.8)

Vitamin D deficiency: rickets (in infants and children), osteomalacia (in adults, especially pregnant and lactating women), osteoporosis (in the elderly). There is a cessation of bone growth, a softening of existing bone, deformation. The cause may be genetic, dietary or environmental (lack of ultraviolet radiation), or a combination.

The main symptoms of deficiencies in key minerals[6] are set out in summary form in table 14.6.

Wheat (like barley) is an adequate source of calcium and iron. A moderately active man needs 40–50 mg of calcium per day, and 5–9 mg of iron. Wholemeal wheat will provide 36 mg of calcium per 100 gm edible portion (72–90 per cent of requirements) and 4 mg of iron ‖ (44–80 per cent of requirements). A moderately active woman requires about three times as much iron, and a pregnant or lactating woman more than twice as much calcium. A very serious question mark hovers over the nutritional status of pregnant and lactating women, or more generally, women of childbearing age.

There is a point of more general significance. The form in which key minerals are taken in makes a difference. A range of pathological conditions can be traced to deficiencies of minerals such as calcium, iron and zinc, and to vitamin D deficiency, where cereal consumption is not evidently

---

[6] On hypomineralosis, see Wing and Brown (1979) 40–4; Jarrett (1979) 118ff.; cf. Ortner and Putschar (1981) 257ff. (iron); and see next note.

insufficient in terms of quantity. These deficiencies have occurred in Asian immigrant communities in Britain (for example, rickets and the related condition osteomalacia in Glasgow, Birmingham and London), and in Middle Eastern countries such as Iran, and in Egypt. For example, investigators noticed in Iranian villagers the syndromes of iron deficiency anaemia. They originate in the high consumption of unleavened breads made from high extraction meals by primitive methods. The problem is caused by the action of phytate acid, which combines with calcium, iron and zinc in the diet to form compounds that are not readily absorbed in the alimentary canal. Thus wheat is a reasonable source of iron, but the absorption of the iron is impeded by the action of phytates. Phytates occur in the flour in greater proportion || as the extraction level is raised, for the reason that they are concentrated in the bran and germ.[7]

Thus in antiquity trouble might be anticipated wherever chappatis or the like, made from high extraction flour, were consumed as the staple food within a relatively undifferentiated dietary regime. In general, it is obvious enough that the poorer the consumers, the more primitive were their food-processing methods, the less efficiently their cereal was sieved, and the coarser the product turned out; and if their bread was baked without leaven, or if the indigenous yeast was not given the opportunity to permeate, then the absorption of vital minerals would have been impaired. Poets and philosophers (as distinct from agronomists or historians, who are silent) give the firm impression that the lower classes in Rome ate bad quality bread, laden with bran and impurities (Hor. *Epist.* 2.1.123; Sen. *Ep.* 18.7, 119.3; Mart. 11.56.8 etc.). The rich favoured the more refined, whiter breads.

III. HOW MUCH WHEAT CONSUMED?

'Ideally we should like to know the calorie and protein value of the food that families could command in England in the past, and how this varied over time and place. In practice, the evidence that we have on past diets is sparse and largely confined to aristocratic households and to institutions. We simply do not know in any detail the quantity and quality of the food of the people, how it varied over time, or what scope there was for substituting other foods in time of harvest deficiency' (Walter and Schofield (1989) 7).

There is nothing unusual about this pronouncement on the diet of ordinary Englishmen in the past. Few historians of medieval or early modern

---

[7] On phytates, see Ford et al. (1972); Goel and Arneil (1982); Reinhold (1971); Sarrain et al. (1969).

European societies would be justified in displaying greater optimism.[8] Historians of antiquity are by no means isolated in their ignorance.

The grain dole at Rome offered perhaps 150,000 people free grain to the quantity of 5 *modii* per month. This monthly figure, || equal to more than 1 kg daily, is not however to be taken as a figure for an individual's wheat consumption, for several reasons.

Five *modii* represent more than double the minimum food-energy requirement in wheat (assuming for the moment that 25 per cent of calorific needs came from other kinds of food); they are likely therefore to have been consumed by more than one individual. No doubt people in possession of 5 *modii* of grain ate more than the bare minimum needed for survival, at any rate if they were without dependents. How much they ate in fact must have depended on their family circumstances. A man and woman could have survived on the wheat from the dole, even if the woman was fed less than the man, on whatever grounds.

Again, the 5 *modii* of wheat is unlikely to have been usable in its entirety. The grain had travelled far; if of Egyptian origin, it was at best the grain of the year before. More likely it was older than this by the time it reached the consumer, having been stored in warehouses for some time. Not all of it would have been fit for human consumption. It would have deteriorated further after distribution, while stored in some dark corner, waiting to be processed and eaten. Wheat easily deteriorates if not stored in optimum conditions (such as were not available in the crowded tenements of Rome), and it is prone to attack by sundry pests and diseases.

There is another sense in which the monthly grain handout may not have been available to the consumer in toto: if some of it was handed over in lieu of a cash payment to millers and bakers, or for storage. There is no information on the subject.

The central point is that the 5 *modii* handout represents a maximum, and in practice was not normally available in its entirety to the individual recipient and consumer. In other words, the figure cannot serve as the basis of an estimate of the average rate of consumption of wheat or bread among the recipients of state grain.

It would be appropriate to add a footnote on the rations of slaves, for the reasons that they were a significant (if unknown) proportion of the population of Rome, and that we happen to know the diet prescribed by the elder Cato for rustic slaves (*De Agricultura* 56ff.; Etienne (1981)). There was a heavy cereal component, amounting to 3 *modii* per month (*c.*2,220 kcals) for the administrative and domestic staff and shepherds,

---

[8] See e.g. the articles collected in Hermardinquer (1970); *Annales ESC* 1975; *Archeologia Medievale* 1981.

4 *modii* (c.2,960 kcals) for the slave workers in the winter, and 4.5 *modii* (c.3,330 kcals) for the same group in the summer. In addition, Cato gave his slaves a *pulmentarium* which was at base oil, salt and vinegar, but might include in appropriate seasons olives, allec (a sauce of partially decomposed fish) and figs. It is not clear what inferences if any can be drawn from this for food consumption of slaves (and ex-slaves) in Roman households. Urban *familiae* were doubtless given cereals in quantity, but they may also have had authorized or unauthorized access to a wide range of foodstuffs not usually available to rural slaves, or, for that matter, to ordinary freeborn Romans.

IV. THE STAPLE FOOD: COST TO THE CONSUMER

The *frumentatio* as introduced by Gaius Gracchus in 123 BC involved the payment of 6⅓ asses (about 1½ sesterces) per *modius*, and five times that amount for the actual handout. The charge was abolished by the law of Clodius of 58 BC. Thus for most of the last century of the Republic even those of the lowest socioeconomic groups who were eligible for the *frumentatio* had to find cash to obtain it. This is an important consideration to bear in mind in any evaluation of the benefits of the *frumentatio* to poor Romans. However, in order to simplify matters I will treat the late Republican period as transitional, and anchor the discussion in the period of the Principate when the *frumentatio* was fully developed, and the grain was handed out gratis.

The grain cost nothing, but it was unmilled and as such inedible. Did the ordinary members of the *plebs frumentaria* have their own grinding or baking facilities? To the extent that they did not (and the existence of some home or communal milling, at any rate, cannot be ruled out), they would have had to pay in some way for the processing of their grain. Pliny (*HN* 18.90) gives a price of twelve sesterces per *modius* for ordinary wheat flour, perhaps double the normal market price for unmilled wheat, estimated at six to eight sesterces per *modius* (Duncan-Jones (1982) 345–7). The finest quality flour cost twenty sesterces. Baking costs had still to be met – unless the customer was content with *puls*, porridge, rather than bread. Bread and wine were the preferred combination in late Republican Rome and subsequently, among those who could afford them. Most poor Romans would probably have made do with porridge or flat loaves.

The larger baking establishments were equipped to perform the milling as well as baking operations. A flashy baker of freedman status called Eurysaces set up at the Porta Maggiore an extravagant monument to himself and his wife in the reign of Augustus; on the friezes of the monument are depicted the grinding of the grain (by means of two donkey-driven grain mills) as well as the kneading of the dough and the baking itself.[9]

Bakers could become rich. I suspect they made their money mainly at the expense of the 'middle classes' of Rome (see below), who could avoid the 'grind' of home preparation.

Food processing, then, cost money. So did storage, for those who looked for more space and security than their own lodgings could offer.

More significantly, not everyone received free grain. Fronto, writing in the reign of Marcus Aurelius, makes a distinction between *plebs frumentaria* and *plebs urbana* which indicates that they were not coextensive (Fronto, *Ep.* 200.4–5, ed. van den Hout). The former was in fact a privileged group within the latter.

The grain recipients did not include non-citizens, foreigners and slaves: citizenship and domicile in Rome were necessary qualifications.

Women and girls were not ordinarily on the list.[10] Widows in particular must have been in a precarious position. Poor relief records from fourteenth century Florence show that females, presumably mainly widows, received much more aid than males: they made up 88 per cent of those receiving charity (Henderson (1988) 264).

Some people were in theory qualified to receive but were in practice excluded from the list because of the enforcement of a *numerus clausus*. Even if the list when revised and fixed by Augustus had included all those eligible at the time, which is unlikely, this would not have been the situation for long. A category would have inevitably grown up of citizens resident in Rome and not on the list.

In short, the grain dole was a guarantee against starvation for each recipient and, potentially, one other adult. But some residents of Rome were more vulnerable because they did not receive the dole: many of them had to purchase most or all their food in the market.

Even in the case of the *plebs frumentaria*, the state did not provide all the grain that was needed (cf. Le Gall (1971) 267). The grain given to each recipient in the *frumentatio* was sufficient to keep two adults alive. Any family with more than two adult members and only one recipient of state grain would have had to buy more grain or flour in the market, at commercial rates, or bread, perhaps at subsidized rates if made by bakers under contract to the state (Herz (1988) 40, 78, 110ff.).

There is one qualification: a sub-adult male could apparently receive state grain in his own right if he was ten years old (or perhaps fourteen). If he came from a family already involved in the *frumentatio*, his family would be doing well. Trajan may have added 5,000 new infant grain

---

[9] Zimmer (1982) nos. 18–33.
[10] Exceptions are discussed by van Berchem (1939) 34–45; Rickman (1980) 182–5.

recipients; the source is the panegyric of the emperor by Pliny the Younger, and it is unclear whether the author is talking about grain dole or cash handouts (*congiaria*) (Plin. *Pan.* 51; cf. 26–8).

To sum up, the claims of conservative politicians such as Cicero and Augustus (Cic. *Sest.* 103; Suet. *Aug.* 40), that the grain dole turned the *plebs* into fainéants, might have been good propaganda, but did not reflect the realities of life in Rome – as Le Gall observed in a useful article almost two decades ago (Le Gall (1971)). The state grain was only a beginning; in order to capitalize on this bonanza, the recipient had to have money, which meant that he had to have a job, and a job that paid enough to cover the rent and other basic expenses as well as the food bill.

Did patronage render employment unnecessary or less important? The city of Rome did not offer anything approaching optimal conditions for the development of patron-client relations between rich and poor, and there is very little evidence for their operation below the sub-élite level.[11] None is provided in the poetry of Martial and Juvenal, two representatives of the sub-élite, who nevertheless say a lot about patronage (Mohler (1931); Gérard (1976)). The operation of charity cannot be ruled out, but in pagan society this would have been ad hoc and irregular, largely in the hands of the slave cooks and kitchenhands at the back doors, or just possibly slave and freedman footmen at the front doors, of the elegant houses of the rich. I suspect that the closest approximation to patrons known to Romans of low socioeconomic standing were the bosses who ruled on the building sites and on the wharves. It was they who handed out the wage labour that stood between the poor and starvation (or a life of begging, scavenging and petty theft). ||

Employment was crucial. Tacitus says that the flood of AD 69 deprived the common people of food and the jobs with which they might have earned the money to buy it (*Hist.* 1.73). The emperor Vespasian is alleged to have rejected out of hand a labour-saving device for moving heavy building materials, with the words: 'How then could I feed my poor *plebs* (*plebicula*)?' (Suet. *Vesp.* 18).

That many Romans had to buy grain is clear from other texts, most obviously those describing the popular reaction when wheat prices rose. The protesters would have been drawn from both receivers of state grain and non-receivers, because both were drawn into the grain and bread market.

V. A BALANCED DIET?

Perhaps 25 per cent of the food energy requirement was derived from sources other than cereals (cf. table 14.7). This is merely a guess. We

---

[11] Le Gall (1971) 270–2 is ambivalent on the presence of small men among receivers of patronal *sportulae*, but holds that the mass of citizens could not live off *sportulae*.

Table 14.7. *The calorific value of selected plant foods in kcal per 100 g edible portion*

Olive oil	900
Dried pulses	350–375
Dried fruits (fig, apple, plum, grape)	280–300
Nuts: walnut	700
acorn	270
pistachio	640
chestnut	200
Bulbs	40–50
Roots	30–50
Greens (leaves, stalks, shoots)	20–50
Mushrooms	25
Cereals	350–360
Green pulses	50–100
Fresh fruit (fig, apple, cherry, berry)	65–90

(*Source*: Halstead (1981) 315, Table 11.1)

cannot know the true figure, or how it was made up. As with the question of the quantity of cereals consumed, the problem of the quality of the diet of ordinary people is one shared by historians of most other pre-modern periods.

As working hypotheses, I propose the following:

(1) Within the *plebs urbana* diets were various.

(2) The key variables that determined the nature of the diet in each individual case were jobs (their existence and nature) and connections.

(3) The poor of Rome, except the truly destitute, could usually count on consuming in addition to cereals a modest amount of dry legumes, wine and olive oil (all of the cheaper variety), as long as they were in employment. The base rate for an unskilled labourer was about three sesterces per day (Duncan-Jones (1982) 54).

(4) Low-quality fish, fish-sauce and cheap vegetables were sometimes available to poor Romans, but most of the products of horticulture, cheese (and other dairy products), meat, and eggs were largely inaccessible.

I am under no illusion as to the limitations of the sources and the extent of the support that they can lend to this or any summary statement about diet. But I do not accept that nothing at all can be said on the subject, or that the Roman poor as a whole were ordinarily restricted to bread and water. ‖

The first two points listed above are closely connected and need only brief further discussion. The quality of the diet hinged on the spending power of the consumer, and this in turn depended on the character of his employment (regularity, rate of pay or profit), the state of the food market (for the variety and amount of foodstuffs, and therefore their cost, will have fluctuated) and the cost of non-food necessities, in particular, housing, clothing and fuel for heating. The importance of employment and therefore income, given the dependence of Romans on the market, has already been stressed in connection with cereals. Caligula's 'market tax' (*macelli vectigal*, Plin. *HN* 19.56), was apparently imposed on all foodstuffs (*edulibus*, Suet. *Calig.* 40) and provoked a furore among the common people, presumably because of the inflationary effect it had on prices. The operation of patronage (or charity for the very poor) is not to be completely ruled out, but is more or less invisible. Further under the heading of connections, one can admit the existence of family links between inhabitants of city and countryside, which might have been characterized by a regular or sporadic inflow of food into ordinary Roman households, especially those of recent immigrants from rural communities not far from Rome. Again this remains conjectural.

Points three and four concern the consumption of foods other than cereals in Rome. Wine, oil and dry legumes are commonly regarded as staples throughout the Mediterranean region, and special reasons have to be found for denying their presence to some ‖ degree in the diet of the ordinary people of Rome (as opposed to countryfolk with more direct access to the products of the countryside). Extreme poverty and unemployment (and underemployment) count as special reasons. Until free oil and wine were added to grain in the distributions, under Septimius Severus (at the turn of the second century) and Aurelian (in the early 270s) respectively, these commodities had to be purchased even by those on the *frumentatio* list, and they cost more in Rome than elsewhere. Aurelian's other innovation, the distribution of bread rather than wheat, also reduced costs for participants in the *frumentatio* (SHA, *Sev.* 18.3; *Aurel.* 35.2, 48.1).

Consumption of wine (of some kind or other) must have been more or less ubiquitous in Rome, as the literary and archaeological sources indicate (Tchernia (1980), (1986); Panella (1981)). Wine could apparently be purchased in Rome for around 1–2 sesterces per litre (1.27–1.84 per *sextarius* = 0.539 litres) (Duncan-Jones (1982) app. 15), about half the daily wage for unskilled work. Yet even low quality wine would not always have been freely and cheaply available. On one occasion in the reign of Augustus, the 'populus' complained that wine was dear and in short supply, and were sharply reminded by the emperor that Agrippa had provided water free of charge (Suet. *Aug.* 42).

Prices for olive oil are lacking, but the impression given by the agricultural writers is that olive production was less profitable than viticulture, and, if so, low-quality oil, in the amounts required for food consumption, probably cost very little. It has been suggested that in the Mediterranean world on average around 20 litres of oil per person per year were consumed as food (Amouretti (1986) 181–3; Mattingly (1988a) 33–4; (1988b) 159, 161); this works out at around 490 kcals per day (100 g gives 900 kcals, 1 kg is a little more than 1 litre). Cato's agricultural slaves were allowed about 6.5 litres per year (c.160 kcals per day) plus quite a lot of pickled olives (Cato, *Agr.* 58). But no inference is possible about oil consumption rates among ordinary, poor Romans of Rome from these figures, or for that matter from the volume of amphoras on Monte Testaccio (Rodriguez-Almeida (1984) 116–19).

Apart from cereals, dry legumes, in particular lentils, chickpeas and broad beans, were the main source of protein as of calories in the Mediterranean basin as a whole (except where olive oil was consumed in great quantities, as it was in modern Crete: Allbaugh (1953); Foxhall and Forbes (1982) 65ff.). Dry legumes also supplied || the amino acids in which wheat and barley were low, and the missing vitamin A. The flour of legumes was commonly blended with wheat flour to make bread (e.g. Plin. *HN* 18.117; Ath. 158e). Beans are associated by Martial with artisans (*faba fabrorum*, 10.48.16), chickpeas are the food of the humbler section of the theatre audience, according to Horace (*Ars P.* 249), and a would-be politician is depicted by the same poet as having impoverished himself by showering the Circus crowd with chickpeas, beans and lentils (*Sat.* 2.3.184). Horace presumably had in mind the distribution of presents to the public on the last day of the spring festival, the Floralia; in a parallel passage, Persius has an aspiring politician dispense chickpeas at the Floralia (5.177ff.). Martial indicates that a kind of pease pudding made of chickpeas was sold in the streets hot (1.41.6), and at low cost (1.103.10, 1 as, or ¼ sesterce). A hint of mass consumption of dry legumes in Rome is provided in the recently discovered tablets of Murecine in the Bay of Naples. These tablets speak of quantities of Egyptian lentils and chickpeas alongside Egyptian grain in storage at Puteoli, presumably on their way to Rome (*AE* 1972, 86–7 and 1973, 143: AD 37).

In addition, cheap vegetables such as cabbage, leeks, beet, garlic and onions are associated in imaginative literature with the poor (cf. Juv. 1.134; 3.293; 5.87; Pers. 3.114; Mart. 13.13.1; Plaut. *Poen.* 1314; etc.). Pliny the Elder refers to garden produce that could be purchased cheaply (*cibo etiam uno asse venali*), but then complains (not without rhetorical exaggeration, no doubt) that the high-spending rich have forced up the price even of vegetables, so that most of them are out of the reach of the average Roman (*tribus*) (Plin. *HN* 19.52ff.). Some Romans may have had direct access as tenants or labourers to the produce of the *horti* in the suburbs and immediate hinterland of Rome, where vegetables, fruit (and flowers) were produced for sale in the market. It is hard to imagine ordinary Romans as proprietors of these plots, however small. Pliny the Elder's *'hortus ager pauperis erat'* refers to an idealized past, not the harsh present. It was better off Romans who exploited the *horti*, including it seems, some enterprising freedmen.[12] ||

It is difficult to find other items with which to expand the regular diet of ordinary Romans. It is important not to be led astray by the 'humble' or 'modest' meals paraded by the poets and Cicero: they were well beyond the reach of the poor (Hor. *Sat.* 2.2; Juv. 11.56ff.; Mart. 5.78; Cic. *Sen.* 56).

As with olive oil, so with fish and fish-products, it is tempting but unwarranted to draw inferences about consumption patterns among the poor of Rome from the evidence for the size of the 'industry' (Ponsich and Tarradell (1965); Panella (1973) 512–22, (1981) 68–9; Peacock and Williams (1986) 33–9, 113–14, 117–31; McCann (1987) 141–55). Fish, it seems, was generally expensive, but those breeding in polluted sections of the Tiber, old and smelly fish, small fry and low-quality fish sauce may sometimes have been consumed by the poor. But on this point we are at the mercy of passages like the following from Juvenal, on a miser's rations, showing (if anything) how out of touch he was with the poor:

> In the middle of September he will save up the mincemeat of yesterday; in summer-time he will preserve under seal for tomorrow's dinner a dish of beans, with a bit of mackerel, or half a stinking sprat, counting the blades of the cut leeks before he puts them away. No beggar from a bridge would accept an invitation to such a meal. (14.128ff.)

As for meat, it may be true that the Romans of Rome consumed more meat then the Athenians, pork in particular, but this does not mean that meat was regularly available to Romans of the lower socioeconomic levels, until, that is, the introduction of free pork by Aurelian in the 270s AD. In late antique Rome, 120,000 people could expect to receive 20–25 kg of meat per annum (cf. Chastagnol (1953), (1960) 58–9, 330; Jones (1964) 702–3, 1289–91; Barker (1982); Corbier (1989)). In the early Empire, however, ordinary Romans could probably aspire to little better than the sausages or blood puddings of dubious content that could be purchased in the sundry cookshops of the city (Juv. 11.143–4; Hor. *Epist.* 1.15.34; Corbier (1989) 244–5; cf. pp. 224–35).

---

[12] Carandini (1989) 339–58 is more optimistic than Champlin (1982) 107–8 about access of poor Romans to the *horti*. Purcell (1987) stresses the significance for market sales and consumption of non-cereal foodstuffs of smallscale production in the extra mural 'suburban' areas of Rome. But he shows that even tiny allotments were expensive (p. 38), and theorizes that 'small people' had access to them through dependency relationships (pp. 40–1).

Choicer food was sometimes to be had at public festivals or following imperial cash handouts (*congiaria*) or through private benefactions (cf. Per. 6.50). Such events were not common enough to have made much difference nutritionally.

Archaeology furnishes a new kind of evidence for ancient diet, still to be considered. I have in mind not so much animal and plant remains in and around human sites, or faecal evidence, as human || skeletal remains – the bones and teeth that are regularly unearthed, and often thrown away, on archaeological sites all over the old world. Anthropologists, paleonutritionists and paleopathologists are asking new questions of these materials, questions about diet and nutrition, and they are using newly developed scientific techniques to obtain answers.[13]

Two techniques are especially relevant to matters of diet. The first is trace element analysis.[14] This is a biochemical analysis of bone samples, animal and human, plus soil samples, for a variety of minerals, especially calcium, phosphorus, magnesium, zinc and strontium. Trace element analysis shows the absolute levels of food of plant and animal origin, as indicated by the strontium and zinc values, respectively. Zinc is taken into the body through the consumption of animal foods, and strontium through plant products (strontium also occurs in significant quantities, though still only in trace, in sea-food.) The obvious next step is to make a deduction about the comparative significance of foods derived from plants (and/or sea-food), on the one hand, and from animals on the other. On this basis scholars have felt able to make a general classification of an economy as agricultural, pastoral or mixed. The second technique is stable carbon isotype analysis, still in the process of being perfected by scientists, which is designed to separate out the various foodstuffs which contribute to the trace element deposit: for example, it will enable us to distinguish the strontium deriving from terrestrial and marine sources.[15]

The city of Rome (as opposed to some sites in Tuscany, Campagna and the Abruzzi) is not a fertile field for human skeletal analysis, or not yet.

---

[13] In some cases, for example, the measuring of stature from large bones as an index of nutritional status, older techniques (for the method, Trotter and Glaser (1958)) are being put to more profitable use.

[14] Toots and Voorhies (1965) (animal bones); Brown (1973); Wing and Brown (1979); Bisel (1980); Sillen and Kavanagh (1982); Rathbun (1984); Martin, Goodman and Armelagos (1985); Klepinger (1984); Beck (1985); Bumsted (1985); Gilbert and Mielke (1985); Lambert et al. (1985); Pate and Brown (1985); Waldron (1987); Machiarelli, Salvadei and Catalano (1988) 262ff.

[15] Lewin (1983); Schoeniger, Tauber and de Niro (1983); Zurer (1983). The other main diseases await detailed investigation. Diarrhoea etc. and relevant eye-diseases, like bladder stone, were evidently common. Kwashiorkor can certainly occur in a Mediterranean setting (Gerbasi (1956)), as can rickets (Lapatsanis, Deliyanni and Doxiadis (1968); Doxiadis et al. (1976)).

The main reason is that Romans largely cremated their ‖ dead in the late Republic and early Principate (before the second century AD); and that buried bones are the more informative. Thus far the skeletal samples are of only vestigial interest: they are few, and they come form the 'suburbs' of Rome rather than the city itself: Grottaferrata near the Alban mount (first century AD), the so called 'Villa dei Gordiani' on the via Prenestina (two samples, fourth century AD) (Machiarelli (1987); Fornaciari, Menacagli Trevisani and Ceccanti (1984)). Of these, the latter produces a most interesting contrast: the individuals buried in one location (the Mausoleum) have a significantly higher level of zinc (and also of lead) in their bones than those buried elsewhere (in the Basilica). The implications are that the diet of the former was richer in meat and perhaps dairy products (and also that greater use was made of eating and drinking utensils with a high lead content).

In summing up this section, I return to my first proposition, that within the *plebs urbana* dietary regimes will have varied considerably. There were important differences between recipients of state grain and non-recipients: these differences sprang from the fact that the former had perhaps 30-40 sesterces more to spend per month than the latter (5 *modii* × 6–8 sesterces); but they may also have enjoyed privileged access to cash handouts. Other differences reflected socioeconomic position: Romans might be regularly employed, or underemployed or unemployed. Moreover, among the employed, some worked as unskilled labourers on basic rates, while others had more marketable skills. Finally, a sizeable 'middle class' existed in Rome whose members ate well in terms both of quantity and quality. They were a 'middle class' in the sense that they were neither particularly rich nor particularly poor. They benefited from whatever bounty the state provided, but in addition gained a reasonable living working either on their own behalf or in the service of the rich. They were often or typically freedmen. Freedmen formed the commercial infrastructure of Roman society; but it is men of this status and economic position too, not the poor (freeborn or freed), who are associated in the sources with the *horti* of the suburbs.

VI. MALNUTRITION IN ROME

The earlier discussion highlighted the weak position of the poor or very poor in the city of Rome: those who could hope for only irregular, typically unskilled employment, and within this class, ‖ those excluded from the *frumentatio*. The emphasis has been on adult males, inevitably, because they dominated the *frumentatio*, and also (if to a lesser extent), the labour market. Women, particularly widows, and young children, more especially girls, were mentioned above only in passing as non-recipients and as potentially vulnerable groups.

A comparative approach, starting from the much better known contemporary developing societies, would redress the balance by focusing on women of child-bearing age and, in particular, infants. These are the two groups most liable to nutritional stress (cf. Garnsey, ed. (1989) 25ff., 50ff.). The discussion that follows centres on infants, whose position was especially precarious.

In contemporary developing countries malnutrition is above all an affliction of very young, though it carries implications for the growth pattern, health and survival of older children and adults. Malnutrition is closely allied to the equally familiar phenomenon of high infant mortality. The lesson to be learned by social historians of antiquity is that an assessment of the health of an ancient population should begin with, and be constructed around, an evaluation of the rate of foetal and infant mortality and of the nutritional experience of neonates and infants.

My present intention is limited to sketching out a programme of research. The first stage is to derive a profile of diseases of infancy from third world data (with special attention to the Mediterranean basin), concentrating on ailments carrying dietary implications as opposed to infectious diseases. Kwashiorkor and marasmus are the most familiar and conspicuous forms of clinical malnutrition, bearing witness to an intake of calories and protein which is seriously deficient. In fact, however, gastro-intestinal disorders, diarrhoea and dysentery, are responsible for most infant deaths in the developing nations. They are particularly active at the period of weaning, hence the term 'weanling diarrhoea' (Scrimshaw, Taylor and Gordon (1968) 216–61; Rowland (1986)); they strike when the 'weanling' is making the precarious transition from human milk to more or less adult food that is frequently short in nutrients and prone to contamination. In addition infants are particularly prone to specific deficiency diseases including anaemia, eye diseases, bladder stone, and (less commonly) rickets.

Iron-deficiency anaemia is a typical disease of infants and women of reproductive age (Dallmann (1986); De Maeyer and Adiels-Tegman (1985)). Nightblindness and xerophthalmia leading in the worst cases to total loss of sight are associated with diets poor in Vitamin A, derived predominantly from foods of animal origin (Thylefors (1987)). The cause of bladder stone is dietary, a mainly farinaceous diet low in milk and other animal products. It is particularly a boy's disease, and it strikes the poor, mostly city dwellers living in overcrowded unhygienic conditions (Ellis (1969); van Reen, ed. (1977); Makler (1980)). Rickets has a complex aetiology. Genetic background may be a factor, but also diet (shortage of Vitamin D) and lack of exposure to sunlight (Belton (1986)).

The next step involves searching the literature of antiquity for the deficiency diseases that are a feature of modern developing countries.

My preliminary impression is that there is a significant amount of pertinent evidence waiting to be assembled. The main dilemma, not yet resolved to my satisfaction, is how to weigh it. The first difficulty lies in the way the evidence is presented. The ancient writers, including the medical writers who inevitably take centre stage, had only the most primitive notions of nutrition and of disease. Our approach must therefore be indirect. We have to ask questions of the ancient sources which they do not themselves ask. The best and most useful sources will be those which describe in detail, and in terms which do not allow confusion, diet and diet-related diseases, even if they do not appreciate their import. A second difficulty is the social bias of the medical (and other) writers, whose observations cannot be assumed to have any direct relevance to the mass of the population. A third difficulty lies in the prescriptive nature of much of the medical writing, which creates special problems of evaluation.

In the following, abbreviated discussion of diet-related diseases I take bladder stone and rickets as examples.

Bladder stone receives a lot of attention in the sources, and may be assumed to have been common – though I suppose it is still open to a determined sceptic to explain that it was frequently mentioned simply because conspicuous and painful. As Pliny the Elder wrote:

> The experience of time has concluded that the disease causing the sharpest agony is strangury from stones in the bladder; next comes disease of the stomach, and after that pains produced by diseases of the head; these being the only diseases that are responsible for suicides. (*HN* 25.7.23)

Pliny in fact refers over forty times to the affliction, but only once associates it with boys, and never ascribes a cause – being concerned only with (uniformly mad) remedies. No ancient author improves on the diagnosis of the Hippocratic writer that it was caused by bad milk and bad water (*Airs, Water, Places* 9). Finally, the sources do not indicate the social (or geographical) spread of the affliction. It is left to us to deduce, as we reasonably can, that it affected all classes (and Romans of Rome as well as others).

Unlike bladder stone, rickets is not identified as a specific ailment, and receives scant notice from the sources, being referred to once by Soranus and once by Galen (Soran. *Gyn.* 2.43ff.; Galen, *de san. tuend.* 7). The passage of Soranus is the more revealing of the two (of the author's prejudices, among other things):

When the infant attempts to sit and to stand, one should help it in its movements. For if it is eager to sit up too early and for too long a period, it usually becomes hunchbacked (the spine bending because the little body has as yet no strength). If moreover it is too prone to stand up, and desirous of walking, the legs may become distorted in the region of the thighs.

This is observed to happen particularly in Rome; as some people assume, because cold waters flow beneath the city and the bodies are easily chilled all over; as others say, because of the frequent sexual intercourse the women have or because they have intercourse after getting drunk – but in truth it is because they do not make themselves fully acquainted with child rearing. For the women in this city do not possess sufficient devotion to look after everything as the purely Grecian women do. Now if nobody looks after the movements of the infant, the limbs of the majority become distorted, as the whole weight of the body rests on the legs, while the ground is solid and hard, being paved in most cases with stones. And whenever the ground upon which the child walks is rigid, the imposed weight heavy, and that which carries it tender – then of necessity the limbs give in a little, since the bones have not yet become strong. (*Gyn*. 2.43ff.)

This is Rome (predominantly), the children come from families of some standing, and the condition is common (in the time of Soranus, the mid-second century AD). The 'aetiology' provided by Soranus is of course worthless. In fact Soranus sheds more light on the origins of the disease in the passage where he prescribes the swaddling of infants for the first three months of life. This treatment, if coupled with confinement indoors, might well have deprived the newborn of a readily available source of vitamin D. A younger contemporary, Galen, supplies the missing link in one of his treatises on venesection (always supposing that he is conveying genuine information) in a gratuitous tilt at the female sex, 'who stay indoors, neither engaging in strenuous labour nor exposing themselves to direct sunlight' (*De venae sectione adversus Erasistratum liber*, Kühn, 164).

Was rickets confined to the élite? Hardly. As already indicated, the aetiology of rickets is complex; it belongs to a group of disorders (including iron deficiency anaemia, hepatosplenomegaly, hypogonadism, dwarfism and geophagia or pica) which can be traced to deficiencies of key minerals due to their malabsorption. In our world they occur among people whose overwhelmingly farinaceous diet revolves around the consumption of bread which is low in yeast and made from high extraction flour carrying high values of phytate. The poor of ancient Rome were prime candidates for rickets (and the adult equivalent, osteomalacia).

There remain to be considered human skeletal remains as a source of information on deficiency diseases – as opposed to infectious diseases, the traditional concern of paleopathologists.

We cannot as yet turn to skeletal data to fill out our knowledge of the incidence of rickets in Rome. Rickets rarely appears in the much more numerous non-Roman skeletal samples. But then, one might expect rickets in antiquity to have occurred above all in large, densely populated urban agglomerations such as Rome was.

The two skeletal samples that we do have from Rome (or its environs) highlight two other indices of malnutrition which are familiar to paleonutritionists and new-breed paleopathologists. In the study of the skeletons from the Villa Gordiani, the authors find a correlation between low zinc and high strontium counts and cribra orbitalia (Fornaciari, Menacagli-Trevisani and Ceccanti (1984) 172–3). Cribra orbitalia is a pathological lesion on the superior border of the orbits (parallel to lesions of the frontal, parietal and occipital cranium bones, often called porotic hyperostosis); the bone surface develops a porous appearance, or in severe cases, it is overrun by a trabecular lattice pattern. The cause is often dietary, specifically, iron deficiency anaemia, and it is particularly prevalent among children and women (Goodman et al. (1984) 29; Nathan and Haas (1966); Hengen (1971)).

Secondly, the Grottaferrata data (which await full publication) show a bone condition known as osteopenia, a low bone mass, as estimated from humeral cortical thickness (Machiarelli, Salvadei and Catalano (1988) 258). This is a symptom of malnutrition not unlike porotic hyperostosis and cribra orbitalia, which are also characterized by a thinning of the outer dense cortical bone. The condition is common among women of child-bearing age; a study of some Near Eastern samples concludes that osteopenia observed in skeletons of females is to be ascribed to a predominantly cereal diet rich in phytates, aggravated by the calcium drain associated with pregnancy and lactation (Smith, Bloom and Berkowitz (1984) 609). The condition can also of course occur in adult males, as at Grottaferrata.

There are other indices of malnutrition and nutritional stress.[16] I single out at this juncture only the developmental lesions known as dental hypoplasia, a defect in the enamel of the tooth which takes the form of an indented horizontal line, pointing to a shortage of calcium or certain vitamins in the body at a particular time. The condition is very common in children in developing countries (Smith and Peretz (1986)), and is a familiar occurrence in skeletal populations in Italy and elsewhere in the Mediterranean.

VII. CONCLUSION

Political and economic factors, in a word, the joint operation of a command economy and market demand, guaranteed that an enormous quantity and variety of foodstuffs poured daily into Rome. Romans were in principle well placed to enjoy a rich and balanced diet.

[16] For Harris (stress) lines, see Martin, Goodman and Armelagos (1985) 253–65.

As in all other societies, the political and social hierarchy, and the nature of the economy, ensured an unequal distribution and consumption of available food.

To arrive at the specifically Roman forms of inequality, it is not enough to think in terms of a two-tier structure of propertied and non-propertied, rich and poor, or to imagine that the *plebs urbana* was one monolithic block. For example, intermediate groups, a sizeable 'middle class', existed. These were people of middling resources, who were more favourably placed as consumers of food than those with little or no property.

In any case we must go beyond a simple analysis of the social structure in economic terms, and examine socio-political factors which worked in combination with the economy to produce a distinctive || and heterogeneous society. Among such factors I would single out, on the one hand, state intervention, that is, free grain distribution, extended towards the end of our period to take in selected non-cereal foods, and, on the other hand, private relief systems operating through networks of dependency.

The labour market can in a sense be subsumed under the headings of public and private relief; that is to say, most jobs were created by the requirements of, on the one hand, the government, and on the other, rich private individuals.

These relief systems created and perpetuated inequalities within the *plebs urbana* because not all were beneficiaries; they created divisions between those on and those off the register of grain recipients, and between those who were or who were not patronized by wealthy families.

The generosity of the state and of rich or moderately well off private citizens had its limits. These limits are most visible in the case of the public distribution system, which for the bulk of the period of the Principate concerned only grain, grain that was insufficient for a family, and that still had to be milled, baked, and stored.

On the basis of the social and economic hierarchies thus exposed, one can make conjectures about the diets of the *plebs urbana*. One must say diets, because they were various, depending on the purchasing power and dependency relationships of the individual; one must say 'conjectures about diets', because our evidence will only take us so far, and leads to rival interpretations. More, and less, optimistic judgements of what and how much ordinary Romans ate have been reached, on the basis of the same evidence. However, the 'data base' is not static. I have pointed to new kinds of evidence, specifically, the scientific analysis of skeletons, which should in the course of time become highly significant.

Also on the basis of these same social and economic hierarchies, one can identify groups vulnerable to malnutrition within the wider *plebs urbana*.

In the investigation of nutritional status, a bold approach is fruitful. In the first place, comparison with the contemporary third world pays dividends. Thanks to the attention of nutritionists, medical scientists, social anthropologists, developmental economists, and so on, we can extend the range of questions we might be inclined to ask of the ancient evidence, and in the process bring into play texts that otherwise might have been peripheral to the analysis || or simply overlooked. More particularly, we might have completely passed over the matter of infant malnutrition, under the influence of the mainstream medical writers of antiquity, who do not notice, or fail to comment on, the phenomenon. Yet in contemporary developing countries infants are easily identifiable as a group especially at risk, notably during the early periods of fast growth. Armed with this information, we can search the ancient evidence for relevant deficiency diseases. Such an investigation is only partially successful if we stay with the conventional medical sources, which are not interested in presenting a systematic discussion of infant diseases. Paleopathology plays a key supplementary role, that is, the new paleopathology, which is concerned to trace the impact on the human skeleton of deficiency diseases rather than merely infectious diseases. It does this by identifying, on the one hand, deficiency disease, and on the other, periodic stress at the foetal, neonatal and older infant stages – and for that matter, among other vulnerable groups, in particular, women of child-bearing age.

This paper, as predicted, has arrived at no firm conclusions. It has achieved its aim if it has produced a list of questions which might profitably be asked of the ancient evidence, and a survey of the approaches, new and old, which might be used fruitfully in pursuing these questions. It is offered in respect and admiration to an eminent scholar whose own work first led me to confront the food supply of the city of Rome. ||

Addendum

Adumbrating more extensive future research, this paper explores the character and quality of the diet of the ordinary people of Rome. G. argues against the prevailing tendency to reduce diet to an undifferentiated list of foods consumed, and introduces the scientific analysis of human skeletal remains as a means of establishing patterns of endemic malnutrition.

The grain dole in the city of Rome (pp. 228, 236) has been the subject of several recent studies which focus on the technical and administrative dimension of this system of food supply: see Herz (1988); Sirks (1991); Virlouvet (1995). Concerning the question of a balanced diet (pp. 239–45), see Whittaker (1993b) 285–6, on nutrition and its health implications among the urban poor, and Nutton (1995) 364–5, on Galen's references to low-quality food in large cities. With reference to G's comments on malnutrition in the capital (pp. 245–9),

Cherry (1993) discusses chronic hunger in late Republican Rome and argues that although this condition is not safely attested in the sources, it is possible to deduce from various parameters such as the incidence of documented food crises, the cost of living and levels of income that it must have been widespread among the poor. On the impact of infectious diseases which would interact with and aggravate the effects of malnutrition (cf. p. 246), see Scheidel (1994b), (1996a) 141–53; Shaw (1996). Sperduti (1995) is an example of ongoing work and progress in the field of palaeodemography (pp. 248–9). This approach will be expanded by G. in future publications.

15

CHILD REARING IN ANCIENT ITALY

The history of childhood in European history takes off in the early modern period, around the sixteenth century. Historians of classical antiquity and the Middle Ages have until recently shown little interest in the topic, largely because their preoccupations have traditionally been different.[1] Shortage of evidence is not an adequate reason or excuse for this neglect. The reconstruction of infant life in early modern Europe is admittedly also a hazardous business. Indeed, Peter Laslett opted to study household size and composition because of the lack of data on infancy. His forthright criticism includes both primary sources (such as personal diaries) and secondary sources (such as advice literature): 'It is well known how intractable the analysis of any body of documents of this kind can be; so untidy is it, so variable, so contradictory in its dogmas and doctrines, so capricious in what it preserves and what it must leave out' (Laslett (1977) 66). Linda Pollock is perhaps more representative of early modern social historians in her willingness to work with the sources, while admitting their deficiencies: 'We still know little about how parents actually reared their children' (Pollock (1983) 203, 212, 234).

For antiquity, scattered literary discussions and references, though different from the early modern diaries, serve a similarly limited purpose. Between the literary texts, and such diverse sources as papyri recording wet-nurse contracts in Egypt, stone epitaphs for dead infants, and skeletal remains, we do not lack ‖ information (of variable quality and quantity, to be sure) on parent-child attitudes, birth rituals, the treatment of babies, feeding patterns, and the nutritional status of infants. Again, the secondary

---

[1] In addition to the monographs by Néraudau (1984); Boswell (1988); and Wiedemann (1989), useful contributions on a smaller scale include Bradley (1980), (1986); Brind'Amour and Brind'Amour (1971), (1975); Dixon (1988) ch. 5; Golden (1988); Rousselle (1983) ch. 3; and Wiesehöfer (1988). I am grateful to Josef Wiesehöfer for sending me a prepublication copy of his article and for permission to cite it. Among those who helped me improve this chapter, I have special reason to thank Keith Bradley, Robert Sallares, and Greg Woolf. Robert Hinde and Keith Wrightson provided invaluable bibliographical assistance.

253

literature from antiquity includes works whose influence on adult behaviour and attitudes toward children in later periods of European history has been profound: they range from Soranus' *Gynaecology* to the various treatises wherein Augustine expounds the doctrine of original sin.[2]

Antiquity has not been a closed book to social historians who are not by training ancient historians. One thinks on the one hand of the work of Michel Foucault on sexuality and, on the other, of histories of paediatrics, breast feeding, and wet nursing, which have serviceable opening chapters on antiquity (Foucault (1984); Still (1931); Abt and Garrison (1965); Fildes (1986), (1988)). The judgements of ancient attitudes and practices that are found in such works, however, are often superficial and inappropriate. Philippe Ariès, the founder of modern childhood history, for example, writes: 'This feeling of indifference towards a too fragile childhood is not really very far removed from the callousness of the Roman or Chinese societies which practised the exposure of new-born children. We can now understand the gulf which separates our concept of childhood from that which existed before the demographic revolution or its preceding stages. There is nothing about this callousness which should surprise us: it was only natural in the community conditions of the time' (Ariès (1962) 37).

The approach of Ariès and those influenced by him (Hunt (1972); DeMause (1974); Shorter (1976); Stone (1977)) is coloured by an assumed ancient (or medieval) 'before', with which is juxtaposed a modern 'after' and an early modern transition. Such schematization carries obvious dangers; it gives the impression, for example, that attitudes and behaviour toward children in ancient and early modern societies were sharply contrasting. But the issues are similar: crucially, a high rate of infant mortality was a shared feature of all premodern societies, and it should not simply be assumed that classical, medieval, and early modern societies coped with this in different ways. As it is, the behaviours that are usually taken as barometers of parental attitudes, in particular, the abandonment of unwanted babies, wet nursing, and swaddling, occurred in all the societies in question (though not necessarily to the same degree or for the same reasons from one society to another or, within any individual society, from one social class to another).[3] Thus it is quite wrong to suppose that

---

[2] The influence of Christianity on attitudes toward childhood is too large a subject to be treated here. Continuities with and divergences from the Jewish and pagan traditions merit exploration. (Keith Thomas has some suggestive comments on baptism as a *rite de passage*: (1971) 36.) The main theme is the comprehensive reorientation of attitudes about childhood that was achieved by the church fathers, in particular, Augustine.

[3] With regard to antiquity, I have in mind mainstream Graeco-Roman society. I am aware, for example, that exposure was not practised by the Jews (cf. Tac. *Hist.* 5.5) or the Egyptians (Diod. 1.80.3; Strab. 17.2.5; Masciadri and Montevecchi (1982)).

the abandonment of infants was practised to a significant extent only in ancient communities, or in ancient pagan communities.[4]

In fact, the whole procedure of inferring attitudes from behaviour is problematic. The sources pose a number of problems, of which the first and most obvious is that the behaviour in question is often flimsily recorded and (in any case) cannot be quantified. We do not and cannot know how common the exposure of children was in Graeco-Roman antiquity (Patterson (1985); Boswell (1988) 46-9), or what proportion of abandoned children survived. In addition, parental behaviour must be placed in a cultural and socioeconomic context if it is to receive anything but a superficial interpretation. Advocates of the 'indifference thesis' are vulnerable to the criticism that their analyses are one-dimensional. Nor are their critics themselves entirely immune, for example, in their response to Lawrence Stone's judgement of a culture that practised wet nursing as bleak and non-caring (Stone (1977) 65). These critics maintain that personal diaries reveal a quite different society, in which the high mortality rate 'led not to indifference but to a persistent anxiety for their children in the face of the hazards of illness and accident' (Wrightson (1982a) 109), a society in which 'affection and deep concern' for children was conspicuous (Macfarlane (1986) 52; compare Pollock (1983) 58). The effectiveness of such responses depends on the size and representativeness of the sample, both in this case strictly limited. The part of Stone's argument that pertains to the miserable and brutal life of the poor, who swaddled, smothered, and abandoned their children, remains untouched.[5]

Likewise, one cannot achieve any major breakthrough by summoning up from antiquity touching epitaphs and stray anecdotes to show that sometimes dead babies were mourned and surviving infants valued (among the élite and || the upwardly mobile). Such evidence can do little more than justify the assertion that 'there was no general absence of tender feeling for children as special beings' (Boswell (1988) 37). A more significant

---

[4] It might even be argued that the standard classification of abandonment as a form of infanticide (cf. Scrimshaw (1983)) is inappropriate in the case of pagan antiquity, because values and institutions (e.g., slavery) ensured a significant degree of 'circulation' of the abandoned, and therefore a reasonable survival rate. For abandonment in the (Christian) late Roman Empire, see Boswell (1988) 69-75, 138-79. Wrightson (1982b) suggests for the Christian Era, with special reference to the early modern period, that a Christian social morality, especially its condemnation of illegitimacy, increased the rate of abandonment. For Italy, from the late Middle Ages onward, see, e.g., Trexler (1973a), (1973b) (Florence); Tittarelli (1985) (Perugia); and Hunecke (1989) (Milan). Daly and Wilson (1984) argue, in a comprehensive comparative survey, that two-thirds of the societies of the contemporary world are infanticidal.

[5] The division of society into rich and poor with which Stone operates is, of course, an oversimplification.

riposte to the indifference thesis is to show, as Fildes does for the early modern period, that wet nurses did not invariably neglect the infants in their care, and that wet nursing might have been resorted to as a means of spacing children close together or of reducing absence from full-time employment (Fildes (1988)).

With respect to Graeco-Roman antiquity as well, the recourse to a wet nurse, and other aspects of the regimen imposed on infants, must be explained with reference not just to parental emotions, but also to the socioeconomic circumstances of individual families and to cultural practices and social values. The cultural context in particular tends to get short shrift in the history of childhood. In the matter of the abandonment of children, the *rites de passage* of birth and (infant) death thus provide an essential part of the background against which to assess the decisions of parents.[6]

To summarize, a better understanding of childhood in antiquity is of importance not only in itself, but also as a contribution to a better founded 'history of childhood' – better founded in the sense that it would not privilege the quest for 'conscious human emotions' at the expense of the analysis of the norms and practices and the socioeconomic conditions of the society in question.

NEONATES: THE DEAD AND THE UNWANTED

The newborn were survivors of that most dangerous operation, birth. Or they were temporary survivors. Many neonates, most according to Aristotle, died in the first days: 'Most are carried off before the seventh day, and that is why they give the child its name then from the belief that it has now a better chance of survival' (*Hist. an.* 588a5). On the basis of comparative evidence, and assuming an average expectation of life at birth of twenty-five years, one can calculate that in ancient Rome 28 per cent of those born alive, or 280 out of || 1,000 children, died in the course of the first year, and around 50 per cent died before the age of ten (compare Hopkins (1983) 225).

[6] *Rites de passage* have been studied (see especially, for Rome, Brind'Amour and Brind'Amour (1971), (1975)), but as far as I know, they have not previously been brought centrally into the debate about parental attitudes. But see Golden (1988) 156, referring to the role of 'customary and well-accepted child-rearing practices' and 'more or less elaborate ritual practices and eschatological beliefs', which reduce anxiety and 'help parents come to terms with their grief'. Wiesehöfer (1988) 23 comes close to my argument when he infers from the legal texts and the underrepresentation of infants in funerary inscriptions 'dass jene Kinder eben noch nicht also vollwertige soziale Persönlichkeiten angesehen wurden und als Träger familiärer Traditionen ausfielen' (that such children were not yet acknowledged to be full members of society and were judged deficient as bearers of family traditions).

The concept of infant mortality rate as customarily used by demographers refers to numbers of deaths in the first year of life proportionate to live births. Some historians of childhood use the term rather more loosely to cover the first five or six years of life (Pollock (1983) 25). This does not matter much, as long as the five-year period is not treated as monochrome, as if parents can be assumed to have responded to the death of an infant in the same way, whatever its age. The reconstructions of Ariès and of his adherents envisage parental indifference and neglect persisting in a kind of steady state throughout the period of infancy.

One would expect parents to be more deeply affected by the deaths of older children than those of the very young. This is confirmed by the early modern English and American diaries, at least for the diary-compiling classes (Pollock (1983) 141). The Roman evidence appears to be corroborative. But we need to ask not just how individual parents reacted to the premature deaths of their children (a question that brings us face to face with the exiguity and problematic nature of the evidence), but also what kind of behaviour was normative and culturally sanctioned.

Funerary monuments and epitaphs suggest in the first place that a lower evaluation was placed on neonates and young infants than on older children and adults. Of more than sixteen thousand tombstones from the city of Rome and elsewhere in Italy that recorded ages at death, only 1.3 per cent were those of babies under twelve months. The proportion rises significantly for children between the ages of one and four (expected: 21 per cent of all deaths; observed 13 per cent). That is to say, all children under five were underrepresented in commemorations, but by far the most pronounced underrepresentation was that of infants in the first year of life (Hopkins (1983) 225). Of course, a child who did not receive commemoration in an epitaph was not necessarily denied a formal burial. In some Roman North African samples, there is an interesting discrepancy between tombstone commemorations and actual burials. At the town of Sitifis, 39 per cent of all burials ($N = 228$) were of children under one ($N = 88$), and 62 per cent those of children under ten ($N = 141$) (compare Saller and Shaw (1984) 130 n. 27).

Funerals of babies were simple and accomplished with dispatch (Néraudau (1984) 373–92). Plutarch, talking of his own Greek society, says that infants who died young, presumably before the naming ceremony (see below), did not receive the normal burial rites (*Mor.* 612). Sources for Rome suggest that the dead were escorted at night with torches outside the city walls, to diminish their terror (according to Seneca, *Hercules Furens* 849ff.) or to dispel pollution (Serv. ‖ *Ad. Aen.* 11.143). Fear of pollution did not prevent parents in certain societies (for example, early Rome) from burying their babies in or under the house. This practice, and the custom of not cremating babies who had yet to cut teeth (Pliny, *HN* 7.72; cf. Juv. 11.139–40), suggest that the very young were considered not yet to have made the transition from nature into the human community.

Displays of grief at an infant's funeral were considered inappropriate. It was enshrined in law that children under twelve months should not be mourned at all, whereas those between one and three years might receive some measure of mourning (*Fr. Vat.* 321). The inference is not that babies were never mourned, or that parents were indifferent. Instead of parental indifference or worse (the scope for moralizing at the expense of past societies is endless), we might prefer to talk of stern realism in the face of high levels of foetal, perinatal, and infant mortality.

The *rites de passage* associated with birth should throw light on social attitudes, not merely those of individual parents. Another dimension is added to the argument if parents experiencing one of the great crises of human existence are seen as members of a wider community, carrying out ritual customs and practices imposed by tradition (compare van Gennep (1960) ch. 5).

A Roman child was named on the *dies lustricus*, on the eighth day after birth for girls and the ninth for boys, in what was at once a ceremony of purification (as its name indicates) and a ceremony of admission into the household (Paulus 107–8L; Macrob. *Sat.* 1.16.36; Brind'Amour and Brind'Amour (1971), (1975)). Until that day, the child was, as it were, in limbo, 'more like a plant than an animal' (Plut. *Quaest. Rom.* 102.288c). During the ceremony the child was subject or subjected to a succession of 'ritual dangers,' corresponding to the physical peril it had faced in the first week of life. As has been seen, Aristotle made a straightforward connection between the postponement of the naming ceremony (held on the seventh day, in his account) and heavy neonate mortality.[7]

The birth rituals were designed, at different levels, to clear pollution from the newborn and its mother, protect them against the evil powers, assess the baby's capacity to survive, and test the willingness of its parents, particularly the father, to bring up the infant. The child (in its foetal as well as newborn state) was ringed around by a host of supporting deities, for which Varro, filtered through Augustine, is our main source. The Carmentes were the Fates, Postverta and Prorsa presided over regular and breech births, Diespater and Lucina had responsibilities for the birth, Vaticanus presided over the first cry, Opis placed the newborn on the

---

[7] It cannot be assumed that rituals were invariably carried out as ordained by law or custom. See Scheper-Hughes (1985) 311, on the postponement of naming (and christening) at Alto do Cruzeiro; cf. Berry and Schofield (1971) on the variety of ages at baptism in early modern England, in spite of official regulations that countenanced a delay of up to seven days before c.1650 and up to fourteen days thereafter.

ground, and Levana raised it again. Intercidona, Pilumnus, and Deversa were represented by three men who guarded the house of the newborn with axe, pestle, and broom. Inside, Cunina watched over the child's cradle, Rumina the feeding at the breast, and Potina and Educa the baby's drinking and eating, while Paventia protected it from terror (August. *De civ. D.*4.11; compare 6.9). Augustine was eager to lay bare the farcical fragmentation of the pagan pantheon. But *we* can see a community engaged in a desperate battle against hostile powers to reproduce itself.

Seen in this light, birth was a time of acute danger and a source of pollution and disruption, met by a complex of rituals designed to define and limit both the dangers to child and mother and the anxieties of the family. Thus thinking in terms of parental indifference to, or distancing from, the newborn child becomes difficult, and judging the attitude and behaviour of parents by our own values more obviously improper.

The problem of the unwanted child is also clarified if set against this background. *Infanticide*, which is often used as an umbrella term embracing exposure, abandonment, and actual killing of babies (inaccurately, according to Boswell (1988) 41-5), is a stumbling block for some who are otherwise unconvinced by the indifference thesis. Hopkins rejects the inference from the tombstones that Roman parents 'passively tolerated, or pretended not to care about the death of babies and young children'. But he goes on to admit that 'infanticide' gives rise to 'nagging doubts' (Hopkins (1983) 225).

The counterpart to the official recognition of the newborn child by its father, symbolized by his lifting the child from the ground (*tollere, suscipere*), was its rejection, which led to ritual exposure. This is clearly illustrated for the world of classical Athens by a playful passage in Plato's *Theaetetus*.[8] Socrates, acting as midwife to Theaetetus, who is labouring to give birth to a truth, asserts that the || product must be inspected and put to the test as if it were a newborn baby undergoing the *amphidromia* rite (compare Vernant (1983) 152-6; Parker (1983) 48-66; Hamilton (1984)): 'Well, we have at last managed to bring this forth, whatever it turns out

---

[8] Because of the need to focus on Italy I have made only limited use of the Greek evidence. This is an embarrassment, as there are interesting comparisons to be made (cf. Brind'Amour and Brind'Amour (1975)). Moreover, the Greek and Roman worlds grew closer together under the political domination of Rome, and there were cultural consequences, for example, in the realm of medicine. What cultural classification should be assigned to the prescriptions of Soranus and Galen, both Greek doctors who practised in Rome? A full study of Greek initiation rites for children should consider not only the Amphidromion, but also the Anthesteria and Apaturia festivals (see, e.g., Deubner (1959)). In addition, the complex classificatory vocabulary applied to children from birth to the end of infancy has implications for conceptions of childhood. See Aristophanes of Byzantium frag. 1, ed. Nauck, p. 88. I owe this reference to Eva Cantarella.

to be; and now that it is born, we must in very truth perform the rite of running around with it in a circle – the circle of our argument – and see whether it may not turn out to be after all not worth rearing, but only a wind-egg, an impostor. But perhaps you think that any offspring of yours ought to be cared for and not put away? Or will you bear to see it examined and not get angry if it is taken away from you, though it is your first-born?' (Pl. *Tht.* 160c–161a).

The implication is that the physical condition of the baby and its prospects for survival and good health primarily determined whether it was 'worth rearing'. This is also the only motive offered, five centuries later, by Soranus, for not bringing up the child:

> Now the midwife, having received the newborn, should first put it upon the earth, having examined beforehand whether the infant is male or female, and should make an announcement by signs as is the custom of women. She should also consider whether it is worth rearing or not. And the infant which is suited by nature for rearing will be distinguished by the fact that its mother has spent the period of pregnancy in good health, for conditions which require medical care, especially those of the body, also harm the foetus and enfeeble the foundations of its life. Second, by the fact that it has been born at the due time, best at the end of nine months, and if it so happens, later: but also after only seven months. Furthermore by the fact that when put on the earth it immediately cries with proper vigour; for one that lives for some length of time without crying, or cries but weakly, is suspected of behaving so on account of some unfavourable condition. Also by the fact that it is perfect in all its parts ... And by conditions contrary to those mentioned, the infant not worth rearing is recognized. (Soranus, *Gyn.* 2.10)

Was this 'merciless selection' (Etienne (1976) 131), stern realism, or something else? A physically imperfect child had little chance of surviving to adulthood, and the sooner it died, the more easily its loss could be borne – if, that is, we allow Roman parents some human emotions, as Plato apparently allowed their Greek counterparts.

Physically weak babies were born to and rejected by rich and poor alike. Only the poor systematically abandoned babies because they could not feed them. Feeble by nature or doomed to malnourishment – these categories merged together. An anthropologist studying destitute women in a north Brazilian shantytown noted their habitual 'equanimity and resignation' as they sent their superfluous babies into 'circulation' through informal adoption or abandonment – or just let them fade away. But maternal passivity could give ‖ way to intense grief at the loss of a particular child in whom hopes had been invested. If there was neglect, it was 'selective,' and a product of grim necessity (Scheper-Hughes (1985)).

To return to classical antiquity, for children who could not be supported from available resources, the rate of abandonment probably fluctuated seasonally (so that an autumn baby, conceived in the winter month of Gamelion, self-evidently a popular month for marriage in Athens, had a better chance of being reared than one born in the spring before the harvest). The prevailing economic climate (the size of harvests and the incidence of drought and shortage) was also a determining factor.

The fateful decision might be made on other grounds, for example, the illegitimacy of the child (who thus infringed political, religious, or moral rules). Among those with wealth and high status, the desire to keep property intact in a society where partible inheritance was practised might also provide sufficient motive.[9] Finally, the sex of the child was sometimes of consequence.[10]

Only those suffering from physical weakness or deformity are likely to have met with direct infanticide more or less invariably. Other unwanted babies were often preserved (compare Powell (1988) 354–7; Boswell (1988) 129) or given some chance of survival. The important points are these: the rejection of a child normally occurred before he or she was (culturally) considered to have achieved the status of full humanity (compare Harris and Ross (1987) 7); and that rejection was integrated into a sequence of rituals designed to protect the newborn (and its mother) in its most vulnerable period. Far from holding them cheap, Romans placed a high value on their babies (compare Schama (1987) ch. 7).

THE SURVIVING INFANT: SWADDLING AND FEEDING

Indifference and neglect become even less appropriate descriptions of parental attitudes toward children once the newborn had survived the perinatal crisis and secured formal admission to the family. In the words of the Hippocratic Corpus: 'Curriers stretch, rub, brush, wash; that is the treatment given to children' (Hipp. Corp., *On Regimen* 1.19). It was important that the child be beautiful, well proportioned, and healthy.[11] ||

Much of the attention given to the survivors was misguided and not conducive to their good health and future prospects. Greeks and Romans, including their leading scientists – Hippocrates, Aristotle, Soranus, and

---

[9] The three reasons for infanticide outlined thus far are considered by Daly and Wilson (1984) in their full comparative survey to have been the most significant. For a critique of their methodology and assumptions, see Hinde (1987) 99–100.

[10] For references to female infanticide in antiquity, see Eyben (1980–1) 16–17; for general discussion, see Dickemann (1975).

[11] The themes of this and the following sections are given preliminary treatment in Garnsey, ed. (1989).

Galen, and the rest – were groping in a thick fog of ignorance, which incidentally did not lift until about a century ago. Soranus' *Gynaecology* was authoritative as late as the nineteenth century. One's reaction to such works is to wonder whether children were not safer in the hands of humble midwives than those of fashionable doctors. There is some overlap, however, between ancient and modern wisdom in the matter of the feeding and care of children.

The twisted wisdom of the medical profession began to have an impact on the newborn baby soon after birth – at least among those families who patronized such doctors. Soranus, it is true, disapproved both of dousing the baby in cold water (a custom among Germans, Scythians, and some Greeks) and of washing it with wine (pure or mixed with brine) or with 'the urine of an innocent child'. He favoured cleansing the child with salt, possibly combined with honey, olive oil, or the juice of barley or fenugreek or mallow, and then bathing it twice in lukewarm water (Soranus, *Gyn.* 2.12–13). But the swaddling that immediately followed and continued for around three months was potentially dangerous, if coupled with confinement indoors and, as the child became more mobile and independent, an inadequate weaning diet. An off-the-cuff remark of Galen's about the habits of Roman women, that they 'stay indoors, neither engaging in strenuous labour nor exposing themselves to direct sunlight' has implications for early infancy (Galen, *De venae sectione adversus Erasistratum liber*, Kühn 164, translated in Brain (1986) 25).

The main disability to which such infants were liable was rickets. The aetiology of rickets is complex. Genetic background, diet, and lack of exposure to sunlight are all possible factors. People have contracted rickets in a Mediterranean climate in modern times (Belton (1986); compare Lapatsanis, Deliyanni, and Doxiadis (1968); Doxiadis et al. (1976)), as well as in antiquity.[12] Soranus, who quite obviously did not understand the condition, writes:

> When the infant attempts to sit and to stand, one should help it in its movements. For if it is eager to sit up too early and for too long a period, it usually becomes hunchbacked (the spine bending because the little body has as yet no strength). If, moreover, it is too prone to stand up and desirous of walking, the legs may become distorted in the region of the thighs.
>
> This is observed to happen particularly in Rome; as some people assume, || because cold waters flow beneath the city and the bodies are easily chilled all over; as others say, because of the frequent sexual intercourse

---

[12] Grmek (1983) 118–20 finds rickets rare in antiquity before the Roman period brought the growth of huge cities and with it, pauperization and dietary change in an urban context. Cf. Garnsey (1991) [= chapter 14].

the women have or because they have intercourse after getting drunk – but in truth it is because they do not make themselves fully acquainted with child rearing. For the women in this city do not have sufficient devotion to look after everything as the purely Greek women do. Now if nobody looks after the movements of the infant the limbs of the majority become distorted, as the whole weight of the body rests on the legs, while the ground is solid and hard, being paved in most cases with stone. And whenever the ground upon which the child walks is rigid, the imposed weight heavy, and that which carries it tender – then of necessity the limbs give in a little, since the bones have not yet become strong. (Soranus, *Gyn.* 2.43ff.)

After describing the techniques of swaddling and putting the baby to bed, Soranus turns to food:

Now, after putting the newborn to bed subsequent to the swaddling, one must let it rest and, in most cases, abstain from all food up to as long as two days... After the interval one must give food to lick... honey moderately boiled... one must gently anoint the mouth of the newborn with the finger, and must then drop lukewarm hydromel into it...

From the second day on after the treatment, one should feed with milk from somebody well able to serve as a wet nurse, as for twenty days the maternal milk is in most cases unwholesome, being thick, too caseous, and therefore hard to digest, raw, and not prepared to perfection. Furthermore, it is produced by bodies which are in a bad state, agitated and changed to the extent that we see the body altered after delivery when, from having suffered a great discharge of blood, it is dried up, toneless, discoloured, and in the majority of cases feverish as well. For all these reasons, it is absurd to prescribe the maternal milk until the body enjoys stable health.

Therefore we ought to censure Damastes, who orders the mother to give the newborn the breast immediately, contending that it is to this end that nature too has provided for the production of milk beforehand so that the newborn may have food straightaway. And one must also blame those who follow his opinion in these things, like Apollonius called Biblas... If, however, a woman well able to provide milk is not at hand, during the first three days one must use the honey alone, or mix goat's milk with it. Then one must supply the mother's milk, the first portion having been sucked out beforehand by some stripling (for it is heavy) or squeezed out gently with the hand, since the thick part is hard to suck out and also apt to clog up in newborn children on account of the softness of their gums. (*Gyn.* 2.17–18)

Distrust of colostrum has a long history in Europe and persists in present-day Third World societies (Jelliffe and Jelliffe (1978)). Yet colostrum is about three times as rich in protein as mature human milk (Stini (1985) 203ff.) and has || important protective functions in the first six weeks of life: its antibodies and proteins guard the newborn against infections, particularly in the gastrointestinal tract (Fildes (1986) 81, compare 199-204).

Aristotle assumed that the child would be given the breast from the first day and had nothing to say against colostrum (*Gen. an.* 776a). Evidently the medical profession in Soranus' day was divided on the subject, though Galen makes no comment. Like other medical controversies, this would have had limited impact outside an upper-class clientele. Ordinary people may have regarded colostrum as acceptable or rejected it as bad milk. There is no way of telling. What is clear is that the denial of colostrum would have significantly reduced the life chances of the children concerned.

MOTHER OR WET NURSE?

Nutritionists are agreed that maternal milk is the best food for the newborn baby; that in developing countries supplementary or substitute foods, whether traditional (and often of low nutrient content) or commercial, jeopardize the health of the infant; and that even in advanced societies the early introduction of supplementary foods increases the infant's vulnerability to infection and food allergy. The contemporary debate is over requirements and how best to test dietary adequacy. By recent WHO and FAO estimates, the average baby needs to take in 120 kilocalories of milk per kilogram of body weight in the first three months, falling to 110 kcals at six to eight months and 106 kcals at one year. Such levels of milk production, however, are beyond the capacity of average mothers, whether in advanced or poorer societies. Department of Health and Social Security figures are lower by more than ten per cent, but are still too high, judging from many contemporary societies, where babies apparently in reasonable health take in a 'less than adequate' volume of milk. An alternative approach, which seeks to measure milk requirement with reference to growth patterns, confirms that official estimates are unrealistically high, especially for the three- to nine-month-period, sandwiched between periods of high growth velocity (Whitehead and Paul (1981), (1988); Whitehead, Paul and Cole (1982), (1989); Paul et al. (1988)). The discussion continues.

The medical writers of antiquity were agreed that mother's milk was best for babies, other things being equal. Galen writes: 'They require a completely moist regime, since their constitution is more moist than that of other ages . . . Thus nature herself planned for children and provided them with mother's milk as a moist sustenance. And mother's milk is equally best for all children, provided it be not by chance diseased, and not least for the child of the best constitution, whom we are now discussing, for it is likely that his mother's || whole body and her milk are free from disease. So that those children who are nourished by their mother's milk enjoy the most appropriate and natural food' (Galen, *Hyg.* 7.22).

For psychological as well as nutritional reasons, however, the milk of a woman who had given birth two to three months previously was believed to be of better quality than that of the more recently delivered mother. Soranus makes this point with the aid of a quaint simile from gardening:

> But if circumstances allow a choice of women able to suckle, one must select the best, and not necessarily the mother, unless she also shows the attributes characteristic of the best nurses. To be sure, other things being equal, it is better to feed the child with maternal milk; for this is more suited to it, and the mothers become more sympathetic toward the offspring, and it is more natural to be fed from the mother after parturition just as before parturition. But if anything prevents it one must choose the best wet nurse, lest the mother grow prematurely old, having spent herself through daily suckling. For just as the earth is exhausted by producing crops after sowing and therefore becomes barren of more, the same happens with the woman who nurses the infant; she either grows prematurely old having fed one child, or the expenditure for the nourishment of the offspring necessarily makes her own body quite emaciated. Consequently, the mother will fare better with a view to her own recovery and to further childbearing if she is relieved of having her breasts distended too. For as vegetables are sown by gardeners into one soil to sprout and are transplanted into different soil for quick development, lest one soil suffer by both, in the same way the newborn, too, is apt to become more vigorous if borne by one woman but fed by another, in case the mother, by some affliction, is hindered from supplying the food. (Soranus, *Gyn.* 2.18)

The attention given to wet nursing by the medical writers, and the controversy it aroused among the educated classes, indicate that wet nursing was common at least among the wealthy in Rome and in the empire at large (see Gell. *NA* 12.1; Tac. *Dial.* 2.39; Ps.-Plut. *De lib. educ.* 5). Moreover, the rich employed wet nurses (usually slaves or humble free women) not only for their legitimate children, but also for infant slaves, including no doubt some they had themselves fathered (for example, Bradley (1986) 211).

Why wet nurses? According to Lawrence Stone, many infant and child deaths resulted from the indifference and neglect of their parents. In the case of the rich, they 'sent their children away to wetnurses for the first year, despite the known negligence of nurses which resulted in a death rate double that of maternally fed babies' (Stone (1977) 65). Doubtless some parents in all ages have deserved Stone's strictures, or have fitted Bradley's more sensitive characterization: 'It is within this area of class mentality that perhaps the best explanation for the prevalence of wetnursing is to be found, therefore, because the custom provided parents with a mechanism which operated against the over-investment of emotion in their children, or a cushion against the foreseeable loss of children and the accompanying emotional trauma. By driving a wedge between parent and child, wetnursing fulfilled for the parent a self-protective function, diminishing the degree and impact of injury in the event of loss in a society where such loss was commonly experienced' (Bradley (1986) 220).

Parental feelings were complex, and any generalization about motives is suspect. Behind Soranus' discussion lies the assumption that wet nursing was an efficient means of rearing children, and this no doubt influenced rich parents and slave owners alike. Other considerations varied from a mother's vanity to the desire for more children, or for more closely spaced children. It was appreciated in antiquity that lactation inhibited pregnancy (Arist. *Hist. an.* 587b; *Gen. an.* 777a). That nurturing the newborn imposed a heavy burden on the mother was also recognized.

Maternal death and incapacity would have increased the demand for wet nurses significantly in rich and poor households alike. Poor families, however, could hardly compete with the rich for wet nurses. If no nurse was available in the family, or among friends and neighbours, the poor would have had recourse to such grimmer remedies as early weaning (see below), abandonment, or sale.

Nor should we forget the displaced babies of the wet nurses themselves: Soranus (*Gyn.* 2.20) pronounced that women who had given birth two to three months previously made the best nurses. As Richard Trexler wrote regarding late medieval Florence, 'Infants put out to nurse were given to mothers whose own infants had either died, been abandoned, or themselves been given to wetnurses. The lives of the innocents, like those of any child put to nurse, depended on the death or dislocation of cohorts' (Trexler (1973b) 260).

Only a minority of families had the luxury of choice whether to employ a wet nurse. Insofar as wet nursing was standard practice among the propertied classes and not among the poor, then the latter scored over the rich – for a baby who is fed by his or her own mother is endowed with greater resistance to disease. This advantage must be weighed against the possibility that many humble mothers were chronically malnourished and unable adequately to feed their babies, who were in any case likely to have been small at birth and fragile || afterward. 'Undernourished mothers have undersized babies and undersized babies have high mortality rates' (Stini (1985) 218).

WEANING

Modern nutritionists and health experts familiar with contemporary developing countries are very aware that infants being weaned (those who have survived the crises of pregnancy, birth, and the neonatal stage) are particularly vulnerable to disease. There are two periods of particular danger (Whitehead (1980); Whitehead and Paul (1981); Whitehead, Paul and Cole (1982); Wharton, ed. (1986)). The first, beginning around three months, coincides with the initial introduction of supplementary foods that are nutritionally suspect and unhygienically prepared and administered. The characteristic features of this critical period are increased morbidity and, in particular, the prevalence of 'weanling diarrhoea'. This stage begins earlier for children prematurely weaned or fed artificially more or less from birth, and their chances of survival are much slimmer. The current wisdom is that supplementary foods are rarely needed and should not be introduced before the end of the third month. This can be accepted as a rule of thumb, even if vigorous debate continues about the length of time breast feeding can completely satisfy the infant's requirements, and whether indeed those requirements can be generalized, given differences in sex, size, pattern of baby activity, growth velocity, and metabolic needs. A complication is the capacity of infants (and indeed humans of all ages) to adapt to lower than 'desirable' nutrient intakes.

The second period of high vulnerability to disease occurs when the supply of breast milk is lagging well behind need and the child is increasingly dependent on inadequate weaning foods. This period begins, typically, at about nine months, when there is a significant upturn in the velocity of growth, and may be prolonged for more than a year. It is often characterized by nutritional deficiency, a high susceptibility to infection, and malnutrition.

For information on weaning foods in classical antiquity, we turn to the prescriptive works of the medical writers. Soranus talks of 'crumbs of bread softened with hydromel or milk, sweet wine, or honey wine,' and later also of 'soup made from spelt, a very moist porridge, and an egg that can be sippled' (*Gyn.* 2.46). Galen prescribes 'first bread, and then vegetables and meat and other such things' (*Hyg.* 10.31). Ordinary people would have depended on cereal as the basic weaning food. The well-off family had a distinct advantage at the weaning stage because of its access to a wider range of foodstuffs, including some that were rich protein sources. But the phasing out of milk in favour of solid food would undermine the child's health if it happened too early. The || ordinary family had the choice of transferring the infant to cheap solid food that was low in protein, or delaying the weaning process (always supposing that breast milk was still available).

In all this, the weaning timetable was of crucial importance. Galen prescribes milk alone until the baby has cut its first teeth (in about the seventh month), and thereafter a gradual introduction of solid food until the end of the second year (*Hyg.* 9.29, 10.31). Soranus' treatment is more detailed:

> Those women are too hasty who, after only forty days, try to give cereal food (as do those for the most part who find nursing a burden). Yet, on the other hand, it is also bad not to change to other food when the body has already become solid – not only because the body becomes moist and therefore delicate if fed on milk for too long a time, but also because in case of sickness the milk easily turns sour.
> For this reason, when the body has already become firm and ready to receive more solid food, which it will scarcely do successfully before the age of six months, it is proper to feed the child also with cereal food...
> As soon as the infant takes cereal food readily, and when the growth of the teeth assures the division and trituration of more solid things (which in the majority of cases takes place around the third or fourth half-year), one must stealthily and gradually take it off the breast and wean it by adding constantly to the amount of other food but diminishing the quantity of milk...
> One should not, however, pay attention to Mnesitheus and Aristanax, who maintain that one should wean a female six months later because it is weaker; for they do not realize that some female infants are both stronger and fleshier than many males... (*Gyn.* 2.46–48)

In sum, Soranus knew of babies denied the breast in the second month, but like Galen, favoured the introduction of solid food in the seventh month. He envisaged final weaning in the course of the second year; he disapproved of advice to delay the weaning of girls, presumably into the third year.

Both authorities, as already indicated, wrote for a social milieu in which the hiring of wet nurses was common. So did later medical writers (notably Aetius, Oribasius, Paulus of Aegina), who made similar recommendations (compare Fildes (1986)). Wet-nursing contracts in Egypt ran from six months to three years, with two years the most typical (Bradley (1980)). People who could afford wet nurses in principle could also provide a supporting diet of solid food of reasonable quality; the extent to which they did so cannot be determined. The risks involved in late weaning did not apply so much to this class as to those ordinary and poor families who could offer only a decreasing quantity of mother's milk and inadequate supplementary foods.

Early weaning, however, posed the greatest danger. In other premodern || societies, and in the contemporary Third World, it is associated with poverty, working mothers, and urbanization. The combination of the mother's poor diet and her need or obligation to work in the fields or in the cities leads to reduced milk output, at a time when the child needs to build up and preserve passive immunity (Schofield (1979) 103). As a mid-sixteenth-century French doctor, Simon de Vallambert, wrote, 'Long before the first teeth appear, even before the age of three months, the women of the countryside, and the poor women of the towns, give bouilli to their children, because if the latter took no other nourishment beside milk, they would not be able to go so long without sucking as they do, during the time when mothers are absent and held down by their work... Because of their continual labour and poor life, these mothers do not have a lot of milk, so that they would not be capable of feeding the child if he did not take other nourishment in addition to milk from the breast' (cited in Fildes (1986) 247).

The emotional lives of families in past societies is a most elusive subject. Yet bold assertions are made about affective relationships within the Roman family to the effect that parents, in the face of high mortality at birth and early infancy, showed indifference to or distanced themselves from their infants, and displayed sheer cruelty and callousness toward those babies they did not want to bring up. Infants who survived the perinatal period were turned over to wet nurses even if the mother was both available and capable of feeding her own child. Why? Apparently to prevent mother-child bonding, preserve the figure, follow the fashion that high society dictated, or maximize the mother's child-bearing potential. The lack of systematic treatment of infant diseases in the medical sources is interpreted as betraying a casual attitude on the part of both doctors and parents to the suffering of children.

Parental indifference, neglect, and cruelty did exist, but not as general or distinctive features of Roman society. One can begin constructing an alternative theory by citing individual cases of anxious or grief-stricken parents (from literature and gravestones). In spite of the problematic nature of some of the sources, they suggest that in certain social circles some parents cared deeply about their children from birth. A more effective strategy would take cognizance of socioeconomic factors, including the poverty of the mass of the population and the lack of adequate methods of birth control, and yet would see infant-rearing practices as culturally defined and sanctioned. In the first days of life, the baby hovered in a kind of no man's land, the object of purifying, protective, and testing ritual. If it survived the ordeals imposed by nature and by man until the *dies lustricus*, the eighth or ninth day after birth, it was named and formally accepted by the father and other family representatives – always || supposing the family had the will and the resources to prolong its existence. The three most prevalent reasons for rejection of a baby were its poor fitness potential, inadequate parental resources, and illegitimacy.

Rejection of one child did not necessarily carry adverse implications for the treatment of those admitted into the family and receiving the formal commitment of the parents to its care. From this time onward, the chief point of interest becomes how much the child-rearing methods of Roman parents undermined the health and survival prospects of their children. In the Roman world of the high Empire, at least in the circles in which Soranus and company moved, babies were frequently denied colostrum, the hiring of a wet nurse was expected, swaddling was standard practice, weaning foods were nutritionally inadequate (though wealthier families may have provided more varied and nutritious fare), early weaning was common enough to be singled out for criticism, and late weaning recommended; other sources, especially papyri, suggest that late weaning was often practised. Given the close connection between infant feeding practices and infant malnutrition, disease, and mortality – obvious to anyone familiar with contemporary developing countries – we may confidently hypothesize a high incidence of undernourishment and disease among the under-five population of Rome and the Roman world.

It is not my present purpose to test this particular hypothesis. That would require an analysis not only of the conventional medical literature, but also of paleopathological evidence, both cumulative deficiency disease in children (porotic hyperostosis and cribra orbitalia, bone damage traceable frequently to iron deficiency anaemia) and periodic stress at the foetal, neonatal, and older infant stages (as revealed in a dental condition known as enamel hypoplasia). For the present, I confine myself to the observation that the regimen prescribed for infants by fashionable doctors, and the unsatisfactory nutritional status achieved by many infants so treated, are to be accounted for with reference not to theories of affective relationships, but to the social norms and cultural practices of a prescientific society. ‖

Addendum

This paper addresses a problem that has long been fashionable among historians of more recent periods, namely, attitudes to small children. Rather than falling back on the evidence of epitaphs and isolated anecdotes in literature for what they supposedly reveal about parental emotions, G. argues that one must address this question with reference to cultural practices and social values as revealed in literary texts, especially medical treatises, which concern themselves with early rites of passage such as feeding, swaddling and weaning.

Rawson (1991) 10–17 covers some of the same ground. Bradley (1993) 245–6 briefly discusses this paper. On infant death (pp. 256–61), see also Néraudau (1987); on exposure and infanticide (p. 261), cf., e.g., Brulé (1992) (on Greece). On breastfeeding (pp. 263–6), Huffman and Lamphere (1984) is still useful.

For comparative purposes, see Golden (1990), a sophisticated study of childhood in Athens, and cf. also Golden (1997) on the valuing of children in the Greek world. Golden (1992) provides a thoughtful overview of the study of childhood in antiquity. Krause (1992) contains a wealth of references to earlier research. The most comprehensive study on attitudes to infants and infant death in the context of very high mortality is now Scheper-Hughes (1992), on a Brazilian slum, who argues that a massive incidence of infant and child mortality reduces parental attachment to the child; for different views, cf. Folta and Deck (1988); Nations and Rebhun (1988).

16

FAMINE IN HISTORY[1]

> 'Nothing is more shamelessly demanding
> than an empty belly,
> which commands attention,
> even if the body is heavy with weariness,
> the heart laden with grief.'
>
> HOMER (Odysseus)

> 'And waking early before the dawn was red
> I heard my sons, who were with me, in their sleep
> Weeping aloud and crying out for bread.'
>
> DANTE (Count Ugolino)

Hunger has always been part and parcel of the human experience – in archaic Greece, late medieval Italy, Tudor England, Stalinist Russia, and present-day Asia, Africa and Latin America.

Indeed, hunger, undernourishment, malnutrition rather than famine, is the scourge of the developing nations today. In the Third World, hunger is endemic and universal. In the words of the famine theorist Amartya Sen:

> Most often hunger does not take its toll in a dramatic way at all, with millions dying in a visible way (as happens with famines). Instead, endemic hunger kills in a more concealed manner. || People suffer from nutritional deficiency and from greater susceptibility to illness and disease. The insufficiency of food, along with the inadequacy of related commodities (such as health services, medical attention, clean water, etc.), enhances both morbidity and mortality. It all happens rather quietly without any clearly visible deaths from hunger. Indeed so quiet can this process be that it is easy to overlook that such a terrible sequence of deprivation, debilitation and decimation is taking place, covering – in different degrees – much of the population of the poorer countries in the world.

---

[1] Important studies include Sen (1981); Arnold (1988); Devine (1988); Harrison (1988); O'Grada (1988); De Waal (1989); Walter and Schofield, eds. (1989); Newman, ed. (1990).

FAMINE AND HUNGER

Endemic hunger – the subject offers multiple opportunities for the historian. Did malnutrition exist on a large scale in the past? Were pre-industrial European, or traditional Mediterranean societies, in this respect 'third worlds'? These are questions historians have hardly begun to ask themselves. This is partly because the primary sources on which we depend have not conceptualized the *state* of endemic hunger, as opposed to the *event*, going hungry. Famine, in contrast, is no novelty to the historian. On the other hand, general treatments of the phenomenon by historians are rare. David Arnold's book is an honourable exception. Historians of famine tend to be well-versed only in their own famines. Thus the subject of famine poses a challenge too.

FAMINE AS CATASTROPHE

Is famine a catastrophe? The question may seem otiose. First, is not hunger-induced death the most pitiful way to die? Count Ugolino in the Ninth Circle of Hell, again:

> I gnawed at both my hands for misery:
> and they, who thought it was for hunger plain
> and simple, rose at once and said to me:
>
> O Father, it will give us much less pain
> If you will feed on us; your gift at birth
> was this sad flesh, strip it off again. ||

Multiply the Ugolino family by hundreds of thousands, and there is a disaster too painful to contemplate: the Ukraine in 1933; Bengal in 1943; China in 1959–61.

In famine, then, the burden of human responsibility is heavy. There is commonly a human input in the form of negligence, selfishness, maladministration, ideological blindness or dogmatism, without which there would be no famine. In this respect, famine is more comparable to war than to other human catastrophes.

But there is a problem: the 'frequency' of famine is a standard theme of historical writing. If famine has been a frequent occurrence in history, can it be, by definition, catastrophic? What is the likelihood that catastrophe in the form of famine struck China between 206 BC and AD 1911 on no fewer than 1828 occasions (to cite an often repeated statistic)? Or that catastrophic famine, to quote Fernand Braudel, the eminent historian of early modern Europe and the Mediterranean world, 'recurred so consistently for centuries on end that it became incorporated into man's biological regime and built into his daily life'? Braudel reports, for example, that the city of Florence in around 400 years between 1371–1791 experienced sixteen 'very good' harvests and 111 years of 'disette'. This word, which should mean 'shortage', is more or less interchangeable with 'famine' in Braudel's discussion. This may point the way to a resolution of the problem. Perhaps famine has been confused with associated or similar phenomena.

There is need, in my view, of a ground-clearing operation, which sets out to clarify the nature of famine, to lay down guidelines as to how to identify it in the records of the past, and to point to trends in the historical development of famine. Such is the purpose of this paper. I do not present detailed case-studies of particular famines, but rather use those already in existence as a basis for generalization. I gladly acknowledge my debt at this juncture to all 'faminists', past and present, without whose work this chapter could not have been written, not forgetting the father of them all, the one time Fellow of Jesus College, Cambridge, Thomas Malthus.

FAMINE AND SHORTAGE

Famine is not endemic hunger, as I have already implied. Endemic hunger, or chronic malnutrition, is a condition of long-term food deprivation, whereas famine is a particularly acute food emergency. The two phenomena may be closely related. In some settings, for example in pre-industrial Europe and in the modern developing world, the state of endemic hunger is periodically punctuated by episodic famine; while a famine emergency characteristically sinks a society deeper into the mire of chronic undernourishment and poverty. Thus Garcia and Escuderos can talk daringly of famine and hunger together with drought as bringing 'constant catastrophe' upon the contemporary Third World.

Famine is not shortage. Both are hunger-related crises, but of different degrees of seriousness. Historians tend to collapse famine into shortage, or variants such as dearth, scarcity or hunger; the same writers, significantly, write of famine as a frequent occurrence. A consequence is that a qualitative account of famine is hard to derive from their discussions. We cannot say on the basis of Braudel's account how many of the 111 Florentine food crises were catastrophic: how many, in my terms, were famines.

An Egyptian landowner called Hekanakht, who lived around 4,000 years ago, points the way forward. In a frosty letter to some discontented dependents, he wrote:

> I have managed to keep you alive until this day. Take heed that you do not fall into anger ... Being half alive is better than dying altogether. One

should use the word hunger only in regard to real hunger. They have begun to eat people here.

Following Hekanakht, we should build into our concept of famine a recognition that there are different levels of human suffering and social dislocation; and we should be prepared to give famine a strong definition. My provisional summary definition of famine is as follows:

> *Famine* is a critical shortage of essential foodstuffs, leading through hunger to a substantially increased mortality rate in a community or region, and involving a collapse of the social, political and moral order. ‖

A subsistence crisis that is less than a famine I call a food shortage, defined thus:

> *Food shortage* is a short-term reduction in the amount of available foodstuffs, as indicated by rising prices, popular discontent and hunger, in the worst cases leading to death by disease or starvation.

I use *food crisis*, or subsistence crisis, not as a synonym of food shortage, but as an umbrella term, encompassing any kind of food emergency.

I submit that famines, thus defined, are, and always have been, rare; they are genuine catastrophes. When historians and commentators say that famines were frequent, they are actually talking about food shortages, or lesser food crises.

To illustrate: let us glance at a food crisis in Florence in 1329, which I would characterize as a shortage rather than a famine. We are given a privileged view of this crisis through the eyes of Giovanni Villani, a contemporary chronicler and government official, and Domenico Lenzi, grain dealer and market official of Orsanmichele, the grain market in the centre of Florence. Lenzi kept a ledger (*Il Libro del Biadaiolo*) recording the prices of grains and legumes in 1320–35, filled out and enlivened with his own observations and reflections. From data he presents it can be seen that in June 1329 the price of wheat was roughly four times higher than in the previous June, and that other seed crops (rye, beans, barley and spelt) rose with wheat.

Lenzi's book is ornamented with full-page miniatures. One shows a harvest scene in times of plenty. An angel is trumpeting the good news of joy (*allegrezza*) and abundance (*abbondanzia*). But there are ominous rumblings coming from the third trumpet. God issues the warning: 'I can take it all away; you had better be grateful'.

The companion miniature depicts a harvest scene in less happy times. The devil is in the ascendant, having routed the angel and broken his trumpet. God summons the defeated angel: 'Come back to heaven; it is cleaner and purer here'. ‖

In a second pair of miniatures, we see the grain market in happy and in unhappy times. In the first, the scene is orderly. The grain bins are full, there is *allegrezza*, singing and dancing below. In the second, there is confusion in both heaven and earth. The angel is in retreat and the trumpets are broken. The dialogue reads:

> ANGEL: I am happy and content in my refuge.
> GOD: Nourish the soul, let the body be punished.
> DEVIL *(to God)*: I will do as you have permitted me.
> *(to the crowd)*: Weep, you have reason to. The good is past.
> In hunger and want I shall make you suffer.
> CROWD: Grief upon grief. God is abandoning us to the worst of fates.

So the miniaturist; Lenzi has the crowd shouting something like this (I paraphrase):

> Those merchants are behind the shortage. We should do away with the lot of them and make off with their goods ... A curse on those corrupt politicians for leaving us without food. Let's go to the houses of the robbers who are hoarding the grain and burn them down, with their owners too, for starving us. ‖

According to Villani, the officials met the risk of disorder by calling in the commune militia. They also had an execution block and axe brought into the piazza, and threatened to amputate the foot or hand of anyone caught stealing. ‖

In the miniature, we see the people battling for such grain as is available, while the commune militia stands close by to protect grain and merchants.

But in the side panel charity is shown in operation. Food is being distributed to the established categories of 'respectable' poor through ‖ the agency of the Confraternity of the Miraculous Madonna of Orsanmichele.

This is a shortage, not a famine. Prices have rocketed, the people are discontented. Food is short, and there is a scramble for residual ‖ grain. For there is some grain, the barrels are low but not empty, charities are active, and the little people (*popolo minuto*), according to Villani, are receiving rations from the commune. There is even something left for the strangers and rustics, who, having been (according to the fiercely patriotic Lenzi) thrown out of 'perverse tormenter and lunatic' Siena, were received and fed at Florence ‖ (outside the walls, however). Finally, Villani says nothing about deaths.

In contrast, Ireland in the Great Potato Famine of 1846–50 experienced at least one million deaths and an overall rise in the crude death rate (the numbers dying per thousand of the population) of 100 per cent. Or, take the Soviet Union in 1933. The crude death rate for the European provinces of the USSR in 1933 was about double that of the previous year; in one of those provinces, the Ukraine, it tripled; and within the Ukraine in the city of Kharkov it almost quadrupled. ‖

THE FOOD CRISIS CONTINUUM

The famine/shortage dichotomy is not a precision tool by which historians can readily differentiate between catastrophic and lesser food crises. The idea of a dichotomy holds out less promise than that of a spectrum or continuum of food crises. Any particular food crisis occupies a place on a continuum leading from mild shortage to disastrous famine.

The food crisis continuum has two main advantages. Firstly, it does not imply the existence of a distinct boundary between famine and ‖ shortage. It is not at all obvious how such a boundary could be demarcated.

Secondly, the food crisis spectrum is more compatible with the idea of famine as a dynamic process, in the course of which a population ‖ moves in stages from dearth through destitution to considerably increased mortality and social disintegration. Advocates of this view are reacting against what they see as a tendency to focus exclusively on the last stage of famine. My position is not necessarily incompatible with theirs; it is that only those subsistence crises that have evolved as far as that terminal phase are properly termed famines.

A strong definition of famine, one that reserves the word for the most severe food crises – for catastrophes – does create problems in approaching historical societies. It exposes one to the accusation of imposing an academic definition that is at variance with actual historical usage. Documents that survive from the ancient, medieval and early modern worlds use the word famine or an equivalent to describe events that might not qualify under my definition.

This is to broach a problem familiar to historians, namely, the interpretation of primary source materials. Here it is appropriate to refer to a critique of the use of literary sources by modern historians, presented with characteristic forthrightness by Cambridge historian and former Master of Darwin, Moses Finley. His criticisms apply, not just to historians of antiquity, but also to medievalists and early modernists. The gist of his complaint is that we tend to approach historians of past societies as if they possessed the conceptual framework and technical skills with which the historian of today is equipped. The historian in approaching his sources should be fully aware of the differences between his and their intellectual horizons and traditions.

Finley had in mind authors such as Herodotus, Thucydides and Livy. But we often have to deal with annals and chronicles that are much more rudimentary, much less high-genre, than the works of mainline historians such as these – works such as those that furnished the raw material for Sir William Wilde's *Table of Cosmical Phenomena, Epizootics, Famines and Pestilences in Ireland, 900–1850*.

There are considerable obstacles in the way of composing a qualitative account of famine in medieval Ireland on the basis of entries such as these.

1099 'Great dearth of provision in all Ireland.' (*Annals of Ulster*)
'Plunderings, and the evil deeds of war and famine . . . ' (*Annals of Innisfallen*)

1137 'A great scarcity [*tacha*], in the province of Connaught, of which multitudes died.' (*Annals of Kilronan*)

1153 'A great famine raged in Munster, and it spread all over Ireland, being occasioned by the vehemence of the war.' (*Annals of Innisfallen*)

The entries lengthen as we approach Wilde's composition date of 1851, as elaborate eyewitness accounts become available. But they have a rhetoric of their own that is hard to penetrate. I illustrate this time from Scotland. Robert Somers composed his *Letters from the Highlands: After the Great Potato Famine of 1846* for the North British Daily Mail after touring the Scottish Highlands in the autumn of 1847:

> Anyone who witnessed the groups of wretched creatures who crowded into our large towns during last summer and autumn – who knows the want and privation which there awaited them – who saw hundreds of families lying night after night on the cold damp grass of Glasgow Green, or amid the still more pestilential vapours of the wynds and lanes, and who listened to the barking coughs of the infants, as if their little bosoms were about to rend, can require no statistics to satisfy their minds of the fearful destruction of human life occasioned by the ejectment of the peasantry from the parishes in which they were born and had lived, and the property of which should have been made responsible for their sustenance in the day of famine. This country was last year the scene of a Massacre of the Innocents, which has had no equal since the days of Herod the Infanticide.

One can admit the value of Somers' work while recognizing its limitations as a historical document. 'A Massacre of the Innocents' 'no equal since the days of Herod the Infanticide' 'anyone who witnessed [it] . . . can require no statistics'. It was precisely the mortality figures, much less impressive in Scotland than in contemporary Ireland, which led Devine to raise the question whether the title famine was merited in this case.

In sum: the literary sources will make most sense to the historian of famine if they are approached with a firm set of criteria for famine, drawn from a wider survey of food crises than any primary sources can control, and arrived at with the aid of a conceptual framework lacking to earlier historians and chroniclers.

In practice, the debate about the meaning and nature of famine is conducted almost exclusively among social scientists and Third World experts. It goes without saying that historians of famine in past societies can ill afford to be ignorant of the course of their lively and ongoing discussions. Does the preceding argument need modification in the light of the debate?

My strong definition of famine appears to be consistent with the usage of Amartya Sen and some other modern famine experts. In a recent paper, Frances d'Souza shows an interesting reluctance to classify as famines the 'food emergencies' in Lesotho in 1983–5 and Mozambique in 1982–5. The title of famine is reserved for the Ethiopian experience (1983–5), for the reason that of the three countries in question, only Ethiopia suffered mass starvation and long-term disruption.

This position must meet the challenge of Alex de Waal. His argument is that famine must be given a broad and flexible meaning, one which (in particular) embraces not only 'famines that kill', but also emergencies that are not markedly destructive of human life, if, that || is, one is to produce analyses that are consistent with the perceptions of famine sufferers themselves. And this is an imperative, not a mere option, because, to judge from de Waal's experiences in the Sudan, the judgements of famine sufferers are more accurate, their understanding of their predicament and how to deal with it deeper, than that of visitors from outside, however expert.

De Waal's polemic against the 'disaster visitors', typically the representatives of international agencies and relief organizations, is sustained and effective, and appears to undercut my advice to the historian as to how best to approach famine in societies of the past. The contradiction is only superficial. De Waal regards dependence on documents as suspect, preferring to base his account of famine in the Sudan on oral information culled from the people on the ground, and on his own observation. This approach recalls Finley's scepticism in the face of the primary sources. The crucial difference lies less in attitude to the sources than in the range of sources available to the historian of past societies, on the one hand, and the social scientist observing contemporary societies, on the other.

As to how broad one's definition of famine should be: de Waal's approach is comparable to that of the 'famine as process' theorists referred to earlier, who would apply the term famine to the whole course of a food emergency rather than merely to the last stage; he would, furthermore, call those food emergencies that stop short of a catastrophic last stage, famines, not merely those 'that kill'. Whether or not we as historians choose to follow his lead in this is perhaps unimportant. We are not 'disaster visitors' who, for better or for worse, will decide the fate of Sudanese or Ethiopians. De Waal's most useful contribution for our purposes is his subtle analysis of the evolving strategies of a population in the grip of a food-crisis. Along the way, he makes the kind of distinctions between one food-crisis and another that we are interested in making, without being able to draw on the perceptions of the suffering populations themselves.

For ultimately it is more worthwhile to ask whether one food-crisis was less serious or more serious than another, and what kind of structural differences are revealed by the comparison, than to decide whether to confer or withhold the title famine from either or both. In asking the former questions, we are exploiting the advantages of the food-crisis continuum: we are in effect engaged in placing a particular food-crisis on the continuum both in relation to other crises, and in relation to the two poles. Is it to be placed towards the famine end of the continuum, or alternatively towards the mild-shortage end? In the section that follows I ask by what criteria we can make such judgements. In the meantime I stand by my strong definition of famine, which in any case seems implied by the concept of a food-crisis spectrum, which opposes a 'famine end' and a 'shortage end'. My response to those who prefer a broad definition is to point to the advantages for a comparative analysis of making firm unambiguous distinctions. And every historian of famine must be a comparativist in some degree.

CRITERIA OF FAMINE: MORTALITY INCREASE

My provisional definition of famine involves a sharp rise in the mortality rate and social, political and moral collapse.

Collapse of the social, political and moral order is the central, also the controversial, element of my definition. I come to it in the final section. Dramatic increase in mortality, by contrast, is a standard defining characteristic of famine, heading most people's lists. In the 'revised version' of my definition, I make it a leading symptom of social collapse, but only one of several symptoms. There are two main problems in applying this criterion. The first is how to decide what might count, in the context of food deprivation, as a dramatic rise in mortality, a mortality crisis; the second is, how to distinguish between mortality increase that is caused by food deprivation and mortality increase with other origins.

HOW MANY MUST DIE?

The question has little practical relevance for || historians of pre-statistical societies, for example England before the second half of the sixteenth century when burial records in parish registers become available. But how are mortality figures to be used when they are available?

There is of course the familiar problem of imprecise, discrepant and manipulated statistics, which I do no more than mention here.

One possible index is absolute numbers of deaths; so, Ireland, the Great Potato Famine: at least 1 million dead; Bangladesh, 1974–5: around 1.5 million; Bengal in 1943: around 2 million; the Soviet Union, that is, Ukraine and other European provinces, 1933: 4–5 million; China in 1959–61: officially 15 million, in reality probably many more.

Another index is an increase in the crude death rate (CDR), the numbers dying per thousand of the population. One can plot the increase in crude death rate above a moving average of deaths over a designated period of time.

The most useful indices will be those allowing us to take account of differences in population levels as between societies.

But again, where is the famine line to be drawn? Must mortality rise by 100 per cent, as Andrew Appleby suggested in his study of famine in Tudor and Stuart England? The consequence of applying that estimate would be almost to banish famine from English and European history. The Europe-wide food crisis of 1816–19, called by John Post 'the last great subsistence crisis of the western world' would be revealed as of less than famine proportions. The crisis of 1846–7 in the western Highlands of Scotland, dubbed by T. M. Devine 'the great highland famine', would lose its title. In English history, the so-called Great Famine of 1315–16, in which some towns are thought to have suffered mortality increases in the range of 8–20 per cent might have to be renamed. In early modern England we find mortality rates of 21 per cent above the norm in 1596–7, 26 per cent in the following year and 18 per cent in 1623–4. These are of course national figures, disguising regional differences, roughly between the north, which suffered greatly, and the south, which suffered less. In the Great Irish Famine the impact || of the famine was again uneven, but the death rate really did double over the nation as a whole.

How to escape the *reductio ad absurdum*: no famine unless the death rate has doubled? We could tinker with the figures; we could say that mortality must rise not by 100 per cent, perhaps, but by 50 per cent, or 25 per cent for there to be a famine. Any new figure would be just as much open to the charge of arbitrariness as the old one. It would be better to stop thinking in terms of a numerical cut-off point, for behind that approach lies the unrealistic assumption that there is a sharp dichotomy between famine and lesser food crises.

Wrigley and Schofield, the historical demographers of early modern England, arrive at a workable compromise; they employ a one-star, two-star and three – star classification, corresponding to a mortality rise of, respectively, 10–20 per cent, 20–30 per cent, and over 30 per cent, above a moving 25-year average.

Their concern is with ranking mortality crises in general (for the years between 1541 and 1871), not hunger-related crises in particular; and in fact the graver crises in their list were not famines at all. This leads me to the second problem to do with the mortality criterion of famine: how to distinguish between mortality crises induced by famine, those induced by epidemic disease, and mixed crises.

Famine and disease

The two often strike together and are hard to disentangle in the evidence. In ancient Greek, the words themselves are easily confused: *limos* is severe hunger or starvation, *loimos* epidemic disease. In Greek literature, the two work in harness. Starvation and disease are the punishment of Zeus for the violent and evil city in Hesiod's poem *Works and Days*; in Herodotus' *History*, they together pursue the Cretans returning from Troy.

Of course, the ancient Greeks could tell apart food crises and epidemics, if for example people were stricken with disease in the absence of food crisis – as in fact happened in Athens in the second year of the great war of 431–403 BC between Athens and Sparta, described by Thucydides. Further, the copious medical writings that || survive from antiquity provide the basis for a distinction between death from starvation, death from hunger-related diseases (especially dysentery and 'famine diarrhoea') and death from infectious diseases acting independently (measles, smallpox, plague, etc.), even if the distinctions were not yet fully conceptualized. For example, Galen, the doctor/philosopher from Pergamum in Asia Minor in the second century AD, knew that starvation was a rare form of death ('people do not die primarily because of want of food'), and found the main cause of death in famine conditions to be what we might call secondary infections. He has a colourful description of a peasantry succumbing to such diseases (the identities of which are not uniformly easy to determine) following the consumption of unwholesome substitute foods:

> The food crises (*limoi*) occurring in unbroken succession over a number of years among many of the peoples subject to the Romans have demonstrated clearly, to anyone not completely devoid of intelligence, the important part played in the genesis of diseases by the consumption of unhealthy

foods... The country people finished the pulses during the winter, and so had to fall back on unhealthy foods during the spring; they ate twigs and shoots of trees and bushes, and bulbs and roots of indigestible plants; they filled themselves with wild herbs and cooked fresh grass... And so one could see some of them at the end of spring and virtually all of them at the beginning of summer catching numerous skin diseases, though these diseases did not have the same form in each case; some were erysipelatous, some inflamed, some with a lichen-like growth, some psoriatic, and some of leprous character... But with several of them anthrax or cancerous tumours occurred along with fevers, and killed many people over a long period of time, with scarcely any surviving. Numerous fevers occurred without skin diseases; defecation was evil-smelling and painful, and there followed constipation or dysentery; the urine was pungent or indeed foul-smelling, as some had ulcerous bladders. Some broke out in a sweat, evil-smelling at that, or in decaying abscesses. Those to whom none of these things happened all died either from what was clearly inflammation of one of the intestines or because of the acuteness and malignity of the fevers. ‖

Galen did not appreciate the finer points of the synergistic relationship between malnutrition and disease. He was, however, dimly aware that malnourishment can actually be a protection against certain epidemic diseases, such as malaria. This is now common knowledge.

Among modern historians, the complex interactions between nutrition and disease have been explored mainly by historians of early modern England. The Tudor and Stuart historian Andrew Appleby did pioneering work in disentangling the causal roles of epidemic disease and food deprivation (he called the latter famine), and in exploring the connection between the two. Recent research has taken considerably further the investigation of the relationships between nutrition and disease, and between, on the one hand, high grain prices and, on the other, food availability, famine, deaths from epidemic disease and mortality crises in general. This research is tending towards three main conclusions. I summarize the discussion of Walter and Schofield and, to avoid confusion retain their terminology of famine, famine-related mortality, and so on, rather than substituting my own. These conclusions are:

(1) Mortality fluctuations in early modern England and France were overwhelmingly determined by the prevalence of epidemic diseases, not by famine.
(2) Even in mixed crises, in which grain prices and the incidence of diseases appear to fluctuate independently, the role of famine is ambiguous.
(3) The effect of famine is largely indirect. Famine causes dislocation; it stimulates migration from one country centre to another, or from the

country to already crowded and unhygienic cities; and it is in this way that infection, the real killer, is spread.

This last observation applies more pertinently to shortage than to famine. Indeed, the discussion of Walter and Schofield as a whole contains an implicit contrast between, on the one hand, 'standard' harvest fluctuations, which provoked, *inter alia*, disease-spreading || migration, and, on the other, exceptional shortage, which as in Galen's vignette of the peasants of Asia Minor induces life-threatening action, including the consumption of bad food or non-foods. This is my own shortage/famine distinction in embryonic form.

The net result of this exploration of the causes of mortality crises is that the role of famine is reduced and its historical presence in general diminished. This supports my earlier suggestion that famine is a comparatively rare event. More narrowly, it suggests that too much weight has been put on the requirement of a dramatic rise in mortality. Other criteria of famine, including other demographic variables, should be introduced to share the burden of defining famine. A full discussion would include the impact of food crisis on fertility. I confine my remarks here to migration.

Migration

This is commonly seen as a safety-valve, reducing the death toll at home. But there are three qualifications to be made: first, migration does not always hold much hope for the migrant; second, it is not always possible; third, it may have adverse effects on the home community.

The first point needs no extended discussion: migration may not improve the prospects of a migrant, where for example he is destined to die in a refugee camp or migrant ship.

Opportunities for migration may be limited, especially in the case of the poorer members of an afflicted community, those most at risk in a food crisis. Or consider the ancient Egyptians. In a food crisis the best they could do was to move up or down the Nile into another administrative district. But that district might be expected to be in difficulties also, if the source of the problem was the absence of a Nile flood and therefore the lack of opportunity to plant a crop. The desert offered no escape to the fellahin. Moreover, in some historical periods at least, for example, the period of Roman domination, the route into the Mediterranean was closed to those without a special government-issued permit. Egyptians had nowhere to go – as a race. High levels of mortality in famine conditions are predictable, and stories of cannibalism become intelligible against this background. ||

Finally, mass migration can have negative consequences. Consider the emergency in the Scottish Highlands from 1846. The death toll was so modest that the historian of this famine felt obliged to pose the question whether it was a famine at all. But what happens if large-scale emigration is introduced as an index of famine? Outmigration from the Highlands was already under way before the first of the failures of the potato harvest in 1846, but it accelerated in the decade that followed. (Similarly, in Ireland, migration was considerable in the three decades preceding the potato famine and was then stepped up.) It was migration that enabled the Scottish Highland communities to avoid a mortality crisis of Irish proportions. But from the point of view of the home community, the results in Scotland and Ireland may not have been so dissimilar. Emigration reduced the population of the West Highland parishes by one quarter to one half in the 1840s and 1850s. In short, emigration might operate not only as a safety valve but also as a destroyer of communities. In this latter, destructive, role, migration deserves to be joined with mortality as a defining characteristic of famine. One can still agree that the Scottish famine was much less serious than the Irish famine, in which at least a million died and over 400,000 emigrated. But in making this judgement I am not relying solely on mortality statistics.

There are other criteria for identifying famine (and assessing the relative gravity of food crises) in addition to mortality and migration. But rather than fragment the definition I prefer to subsume all such criteria under what I regard as the central defining characteristic of famine – that it entails the social, political and moral collapse of the community.

CRITERIA OF FAMINE: FAMINE AS BREAKDOWN OF A SOCIETY

Any reasonably stable community has evolved a system of political authority, social relationships and economic mechanisms for distributing available food throughout the population. It is human decision and action which shore up this system or alternatively || undermine it, causing crisis, and in the worst cases, famine. Famine is a catastrophe that no society or polity can survive, at least in the short term.

Symptoms of a disintegrating society include: political corruption, instability or anarchy, economic dislocation, descent into lawlessness and disorder, and the breakdown of the moral economy – all this resulting in severe food deprivation as indicated by the recourse to last-resort substitute foods, heavy loss of life, and large-scale emigration. In what follows I focus on the political dimension of famine and on the moral economy, and I play off these factors against two others that bulk large in most accounts of the aetiology of famine, namely, natural disasters, and, more briefly, prevailing economic and environmental conditions.

Famine and politics

Famine has occurred periodically in times of political disruption. In particular, there has always been a close causal link between war, foreign or civil, and famine. One thinks of contemporary events in the horn of Africa or of the sufferings in the Second World War of Russians, Dutch, Greeks, and of Polish Jews in the Warsaw Ghetto. Historians of classical antiquity are aware that many famine narratives are set in times of war and culminate in the starvation of a population under siege – Athens in 403 BC at the end of the war with Sparta, Athens again under siege from the Romans under Sulla in 83 BC, Rome in the midst of civil war in 42–36 BC, and so on.

Political ideology has fathered famines. Stalin starved the peasantry of the Ukraine in 1932–3 by requisitioning their grain to feed the industrial workforce in the cities and to pay for imports of machinery and ferrous metals. Mao Zedong's Great Leap Forward killed more than 15 million Chinese in 1959–61 by inducing a sharp fall in supply, milking the countryside to the advantage of urban consumers, and smashing the bureaucracy. The Chinese bureaucracy had played a vital role in earlier times in preventing famine, notably in the eighteenth century, which has been called 'the golden age of famine relief' in China. ||

The relation between political stability and the welfare of the population was unusually intimate in Egypt. The Egyptian economy, until quite recently, depended on the ability of the central authority to monitor and control the flooding waters of the Nile through a complex network of irrigation channels, and to store the surplus of good years against the inevitable but unpredictable bad years, when sowing was restricted or prevented by a too low or too high flood. Famine in Egypt is often associated with rulers who were corrupt, inefficient or preoccupied with domestic or foreign enemies.

In the history of Europe, governments have created or aggravated food emergencies through a policy of minimal intervention, while requisitioning grain or permitting it to be exported. Peripheries of empire are vulnerable to such treatment. One could illustrate from the Roman empire, with reference to the peasants of Asia Minor whose sufferings were witnessed by the doctor (and social historian) Galen, or from a strange happening of AD 99 when grain was shipped from Rome to Egypt, that is to say, *sent back* from the parasitical imperial capital to its place of origin. Or one could illustrate the point from Finland, decimated by famine in 1696–7, while its Swedish overlords permitted traders to sell abroad the wheat surplus from Scania; or again, from Ireland between 1846–8 under the direct rule of Westminster. The British government, guided by its famine administrator Charles Trevelyan, high priest of the new orthodoxy of 'sound political economy', distributed food to the 'incorrigibly indolent' Irish belatedly and reluctantly, and only after the failure of its preferred policy of creating jobs. In addition, the export of grain out of famine-stricken areas was tolerated. Imperialist attitudes and economic dogmas combined to undermine the old ideology of the moral economy.

The moral economy

The term was coined by E. P. Thompson to refer to a consistent, traditional assumption on the part of the mass of consumers that their rulers were morally obliged to protect them from starvation. Some governments advertised their commitment to the moral economy by issuing official regulations – examples are the Famine Codes of India of the 1880s, and the Books of Orders of Elizabethan England. In other societies, government involvement might be minimal. In the cities of the ancient Mediterranean world, the alleviation of food crises was characteristically undertaken by private benefactors, not by governments. In rural England of the early modern period, the wealthy were expected as a matter of course to provide grain to the poor in times of dearth. In addition, charitable institutions funded by state, church or private foundations play an increasingly active part in European society from the late Middle Ages, as we witnessed earlier in the case of fourteenth-century Florence.

To round off this sketch of the moral or social economy, it may be noted that in addition to the vertical links between rich individuals or institutions and the poor, there operated in traditional societies a horizontal support system between kin, neighbours, friends within the community and further afield. These links were fundamental; they are less often discussed because they are less well documented.

The same phenomena can be analysed, following Amartya Sen, in terms of entitlements, where entitlement refers to the basic ability of individuals to command the food resources they need for survival. Sen's theory is primarily an economic theory. What he called the exchange entitlement of an individual was measured primarily in terms of occupation and place in the network of economic relationships. Access by agricultural labourers to food hinges on their capacity to sell their labour power, which is much less in demand in a food emergency. Craftsmen and traders must buy food at high prices at a time when the demand for their own products and services has sharply declined. And so on.

In traditional societies, people do not depend entirely on the market for their food. As has been mentioned, a complex relief system operates at several levels. Translating into the language of entitlement, we can talk in terms of 'dependency entitlements' (vertical links) complementing 'reciprocal exchange entitlements' (horizontal links).

In a famine, this structure breaks down. The horizontal support system loses its utility: destitute peasants have nothing to exchange. Vertical links between large landowners and their tenants, labourers and other dependents prove fragile. A major theme of Scottish and Irish famine history is the mass eviction of peasants as a cost-saving exercise. As for public relief, governments of regions that are chronically vulnerable to food emergencies are commonly unable or unwilling to cope effectively with famine. There is little the poor can do in a famine to stimulate public authorities into relief action. Grain riots are a hallmark of shortages, not famines. It has been provocatively asked || whether hunger rioters in early modern England were actually hungry. The point being made is that such riots were in part political, designed to remind the authorities of their obligations under the moral economy. In a famine, unrest is ineffectual and shortlived; it soon gives way to the desperate search for substitute foods, and then to apathy:

> Great destitution at Oranmore, county Galway: Whole families are living on chicken-weed, turnip-tops, and sea-weed; they did not ask for anything, no one spoke, a kind of insanity, a stupid despairing look, was all that was manifested. (*Dublin Evening Mail,* September 1847)

> They sit on wooden benches, crowded close together and all looking in the same direction, as if in the pit of a theatre. They do not talk at all; they do not stir; they look at nothing; they do not appear to be thinking. They neither expect, fear nor hope for anything from life. (A poorhouse in Dublin through the eyes of De Tocqueville)

FAMINE: THE ROLES OF NATURE AND OF MAN

My account of famine places a heavy burden of responsibility for famine on people. For this reason, famine is, among catastrophes, unlike earthquakes or volcanic eruptions, which are natural disasters. However, Nature, and in addition, underlying economic structures, have traditionally been assigned leading roles in famine-genesis.

Now, humanity is heavily implicated in the deterioration of the natural environment. It is unnecessary to dwell on this obvious, and in the contemporary world, frightening, truth. In addition, the causal links between natural disaster, economic backwardness and famine are complex, and human action or inaction almost invariably has to be built into the sequence. This point does need some exegesis.

Rhys Carpenter argued that drought killed off the civilization of Mycenae around 1200 BC. Barbara Bell offered a similar explanation for the disappearance of other ancient societies. ||

The onus is on the drought theorists to establish the existence of cycles of drought, and to show that these cycles had the enormous impact on history that is postulated. Instead, Bell attempted to prove the existence of the supposed droughts from the historical record. The attempt was not successful, and in any case it is a difficult and dangerous game to play.

Climatologists have suggested that the Mycenaean region might have suffered a run of unusually dry winters comparable to that of the winter of 1954–5, when the rain-bearing cyclonic depressions passed over Greece about 100 miles further north than usual. At most they have provided a model of what might have been. This is far from a demonstration that things happened in that way, and it is hard to see what pertinent evidence could be adduced. Phenomena such as droughts leave little trace in the geological record. Techniques such as tree-ring analysis might in time have something to offer; bad years show up as sequences of less than average growth. However, even if cycles of drought at the appropriate times could be pinpointed, it would still have to be shown that such conditions, through their impact on human society, changed the course of history.

The difficulties may be briefly illustrated from Turkish West-Central Anatolia between 1560–1620. An enterprising investigator has found suggestive sequences of years of restricted tree-growth in this region at this time. Putting this evidence together with scattered literary references, he presents a bleak picture of 'shortages' and 'famines'. However, the dimensions of the tree-rings cannot be shown to correlate closely with the position of consumers in Turkish Anatolia. For example, prohibitions on grain export, a sure sign of shortage, operated in 1565–7, but in those years above-average or near-average tree-growth is reported. This is an invitation to introduce non-climatic factors into the causal sequence. The period in question is acknowledged to have been one of 'peasant unrest, even revolt (the so-called Celali Rebellions), large-scale changes in land use, and unexpectedly large fluctuations in urban populations'.

It can be agreed that short-term climatic changes *may* fatally undermine humanity's capacity to manage the environment, especially in || areas where the ecological balance is inherently precarious. The case is not yet proven for Mycenaean Greece or early modern Turkish Anatolia. But Cambridge historian John Iliffe, in his study of poverty in Africa, has drawn attention to the half century or so of natural disasters in precolonial and colonial Africa from the 1880s. The prolonged droughts and severe environmental degradation of Africa in the 1970s and 1980s, not to mention flooding in Bangladesh, are too familiar to need extended comment.

The question is, how exceptional such circumstances have been in human history. I suggest that Nature, whether in the form of climatic irregularities, environmental stress or crop disease (as in Ireland and Scotland in the 1840s) is more commonly the proximate cause of famine than the final determinant.

Nature may trigger off famine. But there is no straightforward causal chain leading from climatic irregularity through harvest failure and food shortage to famine.

Harvest failure, however caused, is not a necessary cause of famine. Sen noted that the Great Bengal Famine of 1943 followed a harvest only 5 per cent down on a five-year average for the region. Famine can occur, and usually does occur, when there is no absolute food shortage. Nor is harvest failure a sufficient condition of famine. There was no famine in Bengal in 1941, although the harvest was 13 per cent lower than that of two years later, the year of the Great Famine. Even in ancient Egypt, the combination of efficient storage and distribution systems could counter one bad year or several; this appears to be the message of the Joseph story in Genesis. The example should not be pressed. Pharaoh had a Joseph to interpret his dreams. Would he have stored so much grain otherwise, and over so long a period (though a drought of precisely seven years is not an authentic detail)? And would it have been reasonable to expect him to do so?

I turn finally and very briefly to the role of underlying economic structures. In famine, the link is broken between a community and the resources that ordinarily sustain and reproduce it. This has been a fragile link, easily jeopardized, in numerous societies, for example, in the traditional underdeveloped societies of the pre-industrial West, || or in modern developing countries. Such societies are characterized by low productivity in agriculture, primitive transport facilities, poverty and low entitlement among the mass of consumers. I prefer to put it in these terms, rather than say, following Malthus, that famine follows from the conjunction of too little food and too many mouths to feed. However, people have not been passive in the face of recurring, though not precisely predictable, environmental disasters and economic setbacks. They have evolved flexible long-term strategies for the survival of their societies. History has shown how easily communities slip into shortage, hunger and destitution, and how determinedly they resist the plunge into famine.

CONCLUSION

Thus, if we are to ask why famine occurs, or occurs more commonly in one society rather than another, we can begin with the environmental background; we can pass to the economic system and consider the level of agricultural productivity, the transport system, and the degree of market integration. But it is necessary to go beyond these factors to investigate the social or moral economy, the effectiveness of private relief systems in insulating the more vulnerable sections of the community against starvation, and the supplementary role of institutions and governments. This is an essential part of the explanation of how, for example, England slipped the shadow of famine by the end of the eighteenth century, leaving Scotland and Ireland behind; or how China in the eighteenth century was relatively famine-free.

If today the poorer countries of the world could in principle be protected from famine, this is not only because there is enough food to go around, but also because a supra-national relief system, a world moral economy, has come into existence, capable of staving off famine – if only local governments will co-operate, and if only relief organizations will diagnose correctly the needs of the communities at risk.

This is a notable advance. There remain, however, those food emergencies that are terrible enough from the point of view of the || victims, but fail to engage the conscience or even attract the notice of the nations of the world, because they are not 'famines that kill'. Finally, one can ask whether the main opponent has been identified. Is it famine, or not rather malnutrition? It may be in our power to abolish episodic famine. Endemic hunger, the constant or continuing catastrophe, remains.

Addendum

This is a more general paper which in its original format was presented as a Darwin College Lecture to a wider audience of non-specialists. It is theoretical and comparative in nature and elaborates on the distinction between famine and shortage introduced in Garnsey (1988). G. criticizes previous scholarship for the loose use of the terminology of food crisis which causes confusion and impedes accurate and sensible comparative analysis.

The distinction between famine and food crisis is the starting point of Garnsey (1988) who contrasts the 'frequency of food crisis' with the 'infrequency of famine' (8–39). At the same time, this differentiation was independently brought up by Kohns (1988) who distinguishes between catastrophes and 'specific hunger', i.e., general want (103). He prefers the term 'Versorgungskrise' (supply crisis, shortage) to 'Hungersnot' (famine), and refers to the interchangeability of such terms in previous research (104–5, cf. 112). Migeotte (1991) 19 n. 1 (on the

Hellenistic world) accepts G's distinguishing of 'famine' from 'disette', as does Henderson (1994) 278 and n. 123; cf. 283 n. 148 (on Florence), with reference to Garnsey (1988) and the present paper. Devereux (1993) 9–20 discusses various definitions of famine. Watkins and Menken (1985) point out that severe famines were generally rare in world history (653) and therefore lacked serious demographic impact (665). Recent work on famine includes Seavoy (1986) and Devereux (1993).

Garnsey (1988) is the first comprehensive treatment of famine and food shortage in classical antiquity (cf. Herz (1989)); for briefer surveys, see Garnsey (1986a), (1990), (forthcoming a, b). See also Gallant (1991) 113–96. Conditions in the Hellenistic world, largely passed over in G's studies, are addressed by Migeotte (1991); see also Gallant (1989); Quaß (1993) 230–4, 253–5. On hunger in late Republican Rome, see Cherry (1993) (above, addendum to chapter 14).

BIBLIOGRAPHY

Abramenko, A. (1992) 'Liberti als Dekurionen: einige Überlegungen zur lex Malacitana', *Laverna* 3: 94-103
Abramenko, A. (1993) *Die munizipale Mittelschicht im kaiserzeitlichen Italien: zu einem neuen Verständnis von Sevirat und Augustalität*. Frankfurt a. M.
Abt, A. F. and Garrison, F. H. (1965) *History of pediatrics*. Philadelphia and London
Alcock, S. E. (1993) *Graecia Capta: the landscapes of Roman Greece*. Cambridge
Alcock, S. E., Cherry, J. F. and Davis, J. L. (1994) 'Intensive survey, agricultural practice and the classical landscape of Greece', in I. Morris, ed., *Classical Greece: ancient histories and modern archaeologies*. Cambridge, 137-70
Alföldy, G. (1961) 'Die Sklaverei in Dalmatien zur Zeit des Prinzipats', *AAntHung* 9: 121-51
Alföldy, G. (1972) 'Die Freilassung von Sklaven und die Struktur der Sklaverei in der römischen Kaiserzeit', *RSA* 2: 97-129
Alföldy, G. (1984) 'Drei städtische Eliten im römischen Hispanien', *Gerión* 2: 193-238
Alföldy, G. (1985) *The social history of Rome*. London and Sydney
Allbaugh, L. G. (1953) *Crete: a case study of an underdeveloped area*. Princeton
Amelotti, M. (1966) *Il testamento romano*. Florence
Amouretti, M.-C. (1986) *Le pain et l'huile dans la Grèce antique*. Besançon
Ampolo, C. (1980) 'Le condizioni materiali della produzione: agricoltura e paesaggio agrario', *DArch* 2: 15-46
Anderson, P. (1974) *Passages from antiquity to feudalism*. London
André, J. (1981) *L'alimentation et la cuisine à Rome*. Paris
Andreau, J. (1973) 'Remarques sur la société pompéienne (à propos des tablettes de L. Caecilius Iucundus)', *DArch* 7: 213-54
Andreau, J. (1974) *Les affaires de monsieur Jucundus*. Rome
Andreau, J. (1993) 'The freedman', in Giardina, ed. (1993), 175-98
Andrews, A. C. (1949) 'The bean and Indo-european totemism', *American Anthropologist* 51: 274-92
Andreyev, V. N. (1974) 'Some aspects of agrarian conditions in Attica in the fifth to third centuries BC', *Eirene* 12: 5-46
Arangio-Ruiz, V. (1936) 'Epigrafia giuridica greca e romana (1933-1935)', *SDHI* 2: 429-520
Arbos, P. (1922) *La vie pastorale dans les Alpes françaises*. Paris
Archi, G. G. et al., eds. (1956) *Pauli sententiarum fragmentum Leidense*. Leiden
Arias Bonnet, J. A. (1982) 'Capitalismo y suelo urbano su reflejo en las fuentes jurídicas romanas', in *Plinio il vecchio sotto il profilo storico letterario*. Como, 285-94

Arie, T. H. D. (1959) 'Pythagoras and beans', *Oxford Medical School Gazette* 2: 75-81
Ariès, P. (1962) *Centuries of childhood*. London
Arnold, D. (1988) *Famine: social crisis and historical change*. Oxford
Arnon, I. (1972) *Crop production in dry regions*, vol. 2. London
Attolini, I. et al. (1991) 'Political geography and productive geography between the valleys of the Albegna and the Fiora in the northern Etruria', in Barker and Lloyd, eds. (1991), 142-52
Aubert, J.-J. (1994) *Business managers in ancient Rome: a social and economic study of institores, 200 BC-AD 250*. Leiden
Avi-Yonah, M. (1958) 'The economy of Byzantine Palestine', *IEJ* 8: 39-51
Avram, A. (1985) 'Zur Rentabilität der Kolonenarbeit in der römischen Landwirtschaft', *StudClas* 23, 85-99
Aykroyd, W. R. and Doughty, J. (1970) *Wheat in human nutrition*. Rome
Aykroyd, W. R. and Doughty, J. (1982) *Legumes in human nutrition*. Rome
Backhaus, W. (1981) 'Bemerkungen zur Bedeutung von Lohnarbeit und Sklavenarbeit in der römischen Landwirtschaft', in Mommsen, H. and Schulze, W., eds., *Vom Elend der Handarbeit: Probleme historischer Unterschichtenforschung*. Stuttgart, 93-107
Baldacci, P. (1967-8) 'Alcuni aspetti dei commerci nei territori cisalpini', *AttiCSDIR* 1: 5-20
Baldacci, P. (1977) 'Comum et Mediolanum: rapporti tra le due città nel periodo della Romanizzazione', in *Colloques internationaux du centre de la recherche scientifique, 542: thèmes de recherches sur les villes antiques d'occident*. Paris, 99-120
Bandelli, G. (1983) 'Per una storia della classe dirigente di Aquileia repubblicana', in *Les 'bourgeoisies'* (1983), 175-203
Barbagallo, C. (1904) 'La produzione media relativa dei cereali e della vite nella Grecia, nella Sicilia e nell'Italia antica', *Rivista di storia antica* 8: 477-504
Barbieri, G. (1952) *L'albo senatorio da Settimo Severo a Carino*. Rome
Barja de Quiroga, P. (1991) 'La dependencia económica de los libertos en el alto imperio Romano', *Gerión* 9: 163-74
Barja de Quiroga, P. L. (1992) *La dependencia política y económica de los libertos en el Alto Impero romano: el ejemplo de Ostia*. Madrid
Barja de Quiroga, P. L. (1995) 'Freedmen social mobility in Roman Italy', *Historia* 44: 326-48
Barker, G. (1973) 'Cultural and economic change in the prehistory of central Italy', in C. Renfrew, ed., *The explanation of cultural change: models in prehistory*. London, 359-70
Barker, G. (1975) 'Prehistoric territories and economics in central Italy', in E. S. Higgs, ed., *Palaeoeconomy*. Cambridge, 111-75
Barker, G. (1977) 'The archaeology of Samnite settlement in Molise', *Antiquity* 51: 20-4
Barker, G. (1982) 'The animal bones', in D. Whitehouse et al., 'The schola praeconum I: the coins, pottery, lamps and fauna', *PBSR* 50: 53-101, at 81-91

Barker, G. (1985) 'Landscape archaeology in Italy', in Malone and Stoddart, eds. (1985), 1–19
Barker, G. (1989) 'The archaeology of the Italian shepherd', *PCPhS* 215: 1–19
Barker, G. (1991) 'Approaches to archaeological survey', in Barker and Lloyd, eds. (1991), 1–9
Barker, G. (1995a) *A Mediterranean valley: landscape archaeology and Annales history in the Biferno valley*. London and New York
Barker, G. (1995b) 'Landscape archaeology in Italy – goals for the 1990s', in Christie, ed. (1995), 1–11
Barker, G. and Lloyd, J., eds. (1991) *Roman landscapes: archaeological survey in the Mediterranean region*. London
Barker, G., Lloyd, J. and Webley, D. (1978) 'A classical landscape in Molise', *PBSR* 46, 35–51
Barnes, T. D. (1970) 'A senator from Hadrumetum, and three others', in *Bonner Historia-Augusta-Colloquium 1968/69*. Bonn, 45–58
Baticle, Y. (1974) *L'élevage ovin dans les pays européens de la Méditerranée occidentale*. Paris
Beck, L. A. (1985) 'Bivariate analysis of trace elements in bone', *Journal of Human Evolution* 14: 493–502
Beloch, J. (1886) *Die Bevölkerung der griechisch-römischen Welt*. Leipzig
Belton, N. R. (1986) 'Rickets – not only the "English Disease"', in Wharton, ed. (1986), 68–75
Belvedere, O. (1995) 'Land tenure and settlement in Roman Sicily', in T. Fischer-Hansen, ed., *Ancient Sicily*. Copenhagen, 195–208
Bernardi, A. (1976) 'I Celti nel Veneto', in *L'Italia settentrionale nell'età antica: convegno in memoria di Plinio Fraccaro*. Como, 71–82
Bertolone, M. (1939) *Repertorio dei ritrovamenti e scavi di antichità romane avvenuti in Lombardia*, vol. 1. Milan
Berry, B. M. and Schofield, R. S. (1971) 'Age at baptism in pre-industrial England', *Population Studies* 25: 453–63
Bintliff, J. and Snodgrass, A. M. (1988) 'The end of the Roman countryside: a view from the East', in R. F. J. Jones et al., eds., *First millennium papers: western Europe in the first millennium AD*. Oxford, 175–217
Bisel, S. (1980) 'A pilot study in aspects of human nutrition in the ancient eastern Mediterranean, with particular attention to trace minerals in several populations from different time periods', unpublished PhD thesis, University of Michigan
Bjerg, B. et al. (1983) 'Antinutritional and favism inducing factors in *Vicia Faba* L.', in Hebblethwaite, ed. (1983), 287–96
Blache, J. (1933) *L'homme et la montagne*. Paris
Blake, M. E. (1959) *Roman construction in Italy from Tiberius through the Flavians*. Washington DC
Blanks, D. R. (1995) 'Transhumance in the Middle Ages: the eastern Pyrenees', *Journal of Peasant Studies* 23, 64–87
Bloedow, E. F. (1975) 'Corn supply and Athenian imperialism', *AC* 44: 20–9

Blok, A. (1968) 'South Italian agro-towns', *CSSH* 10: 121-35
Boeswillwald, E., Cagnat, R. and Ballu, A. (1905) *Timgad, une cité africaine sous l'empire romain*. Paris
Boethius, A. (1960) *The Golden House of Nero: aspects of Roman architecture*. Ann Arbor
Boffo, L. (1977) 'Per la storia della antica navigazione fluviale padana: un *collegium nautarum* o *naviculariorum* a Ticinum in età imperiale', *RAL* ser. 8, 32: 623-32
Boswell, J. (1988) *The kindness of strangers: the abandonment of children in western Europe from late antiquity to the Renaissance*. London
Bottema, S. (1974) *Late quaternary vegetation history of north-western Greece*. Groningen
Bowersock, G. W. (1965) *Augustus and the Greek world*. Oxford
Bowersock, G. W. (1969) *Greek sophists in the Roman empire*. Oxford
Bradford, J. (1949) '"Buried landscapes" in southern Italy', *Antiquity* 23: 58-72
Bradford, J. (1950) 'The Apulia expedition: an interim report', *Antiquity* 24: 84-95
Bradford, J. (1957a) *Ancient landscapes: studies in field archaeology*. London
Bradford, J. (1957b) 'The ancient city of Arpi in Apulia', *Antiquity* 31: 167-9
Bradley, K. R. (1980) 'Sexual regulations in wet-nursing contracts from Roman Egypt', *Klio* 62: 321-5
Bradley, K. R. (1986) 'Wet-nursing at Rome: a study in social relations', in B. R. Rawson, ed., *The family in ancient Rome: new perspectives*. London and Sydney, 201-29
Bradley, K. R. (1987a) 'Dislocation in the Roman family', *Historical Reflections* 14: 33-62
Bradley, K. R. (1987b) 'On the Roman slave supply and slave breeding', in M. I. Finley, ed., *Classical slavery*. London, 42-64
Bradley, K. (1993) 'Writing the history of the Roman family', *CPh* 88: 237-50
Brain, P. (1986) *Galen on bloodletting*. Cambridge
Bravo, B. (1983) 'Le commerce des céréales chez les Grecs de l'époque archaïque', in Garnsey, P. and Whittaker, C. R., eds., (1983), 17-29
Brenner, R. (1976) 'Agrarian class structure and economic development in pre-industrial Europe', *P&P* 70: 30-75
Breuer, S. (forthcoming) *Stand und Status: munizipale Oberschichten in Brixia und Verona*. Bonn
Brind'Amour, L. and P. (1971) 'La deuxième satire de Perse et le *dies lustricus*', *Latomus* 30: 999-1024
Brind'Amour, L. and P. (1975) 'Le *dies lustricus*, les oiseaux de l'aurore et l'amphidromie', *Latomus* 34: 17-58
Bringmann, K. (1985) *Die Agrarreform des Tiberius Gracchus: Legende und Wirklichkeit*. Stuttgart
Brockmeyer, N. (1968) *Arbeitsorganisation und ökonomisches Denken in der Gutswirtschaft des römischen Reiches*. Bochum

Brockmeyer, N. (1971) 'Der Kolonat bei römischen Juristen der republikanischen und augusteischen Zeit', *Historia* 20, 732-42
Brown, A. B. (1973) 'Bone strontium as a dietary indicator in human skeletal populations', unpublished PhD thesis, University of Michigan
Brown, P. (1978) *The making of late antiquity*. Cambridge, Mass. and London
Bruit, L. (1990) 'The meal at the Hyakinthia: ritual consumption and offering', in O. Murray, ed., *Sympotica: a symposium on the symposion*. Oxford, 162-74
Brulé, P. (1992) 'Infanticide and abandon d'enfant: pratiques grecques et comparaisons anthropologiques', *DHA* 18: 53-90
Brunt, P. A. (1962) 'The army and the land in the Roman revolution', *JRS* 52: 68-86
Brunt, P. A. (1971) *Italian manpower 225 BC-AD 14*, Oxford (repr. 1987)
Brunt, P. A. (1975) 'Two great Roman landowners', *Latomus* 34: 619-35
Brunt, P. A. (1980) 'Free labour and public works at Rome', *JRS* 70: 81-100
Buckland, W. W. (1908) *The Roman law of slavery*. Cambridge
Buckler, W. K. (1923) 'Labour disputes in the province of Asia', in *Anatolian studies presented to W. M. Ramsay*. Manchester, 27-50
Buckler, W. K. (1953) 'A trade union pact of the 5th century', in G. E. Mylonas and D. Raymond, eds., *Studies presented to David Moore Robinson on his seventieth birthday*, vol. 2. St. Louis, 980-4
Bumsted, M. P. (1985) 'Past human behavior from bone chemical analysis – respects and prospects', *Journal of Human Evolution* 14: 539-51
Buonocore, M. (1986) 'Insediamenti e forme economiche nell'Abruzzo romano dei primi due secoli dell'impero', *Studi classici e orientali* 36: 279-92
Burford, A. (1972) *Craftsmen in Greek and Roman society*. London
Burford, A. (1993) *Land and labor in the Greek world*. Baltimore and London
Burford-Cooper, A. (1977-8) 'The family farm in Greece', *CJ* 73: 162-75
Bürge, A. (1988) 'Cum in familia nubas: zur wirtschaftlichen und sozialen Bedeutung der familia libertorum', *ZRG* 105: 312-33
Bürge, A. (1990) 'Der mercennarius und die Lohnarbeit', *ZRG* 107: 80-135
Burian, J. (1964) 'Die einheimische Bevölkerung Nordafrikas von den Punischen Kriegen bis zum Ausgang des Prinzipats', in F. Altheim and R. Stiehl, eds., *Die Araber in der Alten Welt*, vol. 1. Berlin, 420-549
Byrne, A. H. (1920) *T. Pomponius Atticus*. Bryn Mawr
Calderini, A. (1940) *Aquileia romana*. Milan
Calderini, A. (1953) *Storia di Milano*. Milan
Camodeca, G. (1980) 'Ricerche sui *curatores rei publicae*', *ANRW* II.13: 453-534
Campbell, J. K. (1964) *Honour, family and patronage: a study of institutions and moral values in a Greek mountain community*. Oxford
Capogrossi Colognesi, L. (1986) 'Grandi proprietari, contadini e coloni nell' Italia romana (I-III D.C.)', in A. Giardina, ed., *Società romana e impero tardoantico, I: istituzioni, ceti, economie*. Bari, 325-65
Carandini, A. (1989) *Schiavi in Italia: gli strumenti pensanti dei Romani fra tarda Repubblica e medio Impero*. Rome
Carcopino, J. (1951) *Cicero: the secrets of his correspondence*. London

Carlyle, M. M. (1962) *The awakening of southern Italy*. London
Carrié, J.-M. (1993) 'L'economia e le finanze', in A. Schiavone, ed., *Storia di Roma, 3: l'età tardoantica*. Rome, 751–82
Carter, L. B. (1986) *The quiet Athenian*. Oxford
Cartledge, P. (1995) 'Classical Greek agriculture II: two more alternative views', *Journal of Peasant Studies* 23: 131–9
Cary, M. (1949) *The geographic background of Greek and Roman history*. Oxford
Castrén, P. (1975) *'Ordo populusque pompeianus': polity and society in Roman Pompeii*. Rome
Castrén, P. (1981) 'Le aristocrazie municipali ed i liberti dalla guerra sociale all'epoca Flavia', *Opuscula Instituti Romani Finlandiae* 1: 15–24
Cebeillac-Gervasoni, M., ed. (1996) *Les élites municipales de l'Italie péninsulaire des Gracques à Néron: Actes de la table ronde de Clermont-Ferrand (28–30 novembre 1991)*. Paris
Celuzza, M. G. and Regoli, E. (1982) 'La Valle d'Oro nel territorio di Cosa: Ager Cosanus e ager Veientanus a confronto', *DArch* 4: 31–62
Ceresa Mori, A. (1995) *'Mediolanum* dall'*oppidum* celtico alla città romana', in Christie, ed. (1995), 465–76
Champlin, E. (1982) 'The *suburbium* of Rome', *AJAH* 7: 97–117
Chaniotis, A. (1995) 'Problems of "pastoralism" and "transhumance" in classical and hellenistic Crete', *Orbis Terrarum* 1: 39–89
Charlesworth, M. P. (1934) 'Caius and Claudius', in *CAH* 10: 653–701
Chastagnol, A. (1953) 'Le ravitaillement de Rome en viande au Ve siècle', *Revue Historique* 210: 13–22
Chastagnol, A. (1960) *La préfecture urbaine à Rome sous le Bas Empire*. Paris
Chastagnol, A. (1976) *La fin du monde antique*. Paris
Chastagnol, A. (1978) *L'album municipal de Timgad*. Bonn
Chelotti, M. (1990) 'Mobilità sociale e legami familiari alla luce dell'albo dei decurioni di Canosa (*CIL* IX, 338)', *MEFRA* 102: 603–9
Chelotti, M., Gaeta, R., Morizio, V. and Silvestrini, V., eds. (1990) *Le epigrafi romane di Canosa*, vol. 1. Bari
Cherry, D. (1993) 'Hunger at Rome in the late Republic', *EMC* 37 (n.s. 12): 433–50
Chilver, G. E. F. (1941) *Cisalpine Gaul: social and economic history from 49 BC to the death of Trajan*. Oxford
Chirassi Colombo, I. (1968) *Elementi di culture precereali nei miti e riti greci*. Rome
Christie, N., ed. (1995) *Settlement and economy in Italy 1500 BC–AD 1500: papers of the fifth conference of Italian archaeology*. Oxford.
Christol, M. (1992) 'Les ambitions d'un affranchi à Nîmes sous le Haut-Empire: l'argent et la famille', *Cahiers du Centre G. Glotz* 3: 241–58
Cipolla, C. M. (1981) 'Per una storia della produttività nei secoli del medioevo e del rinascimento', in S. Mariotti, ed., *Produttività e tecnologie nei secoli XII–XVII: Istituto internazionale di storia economica 'F. Datini' Prato, Atti della 'terza settimana di studio' (23 aprile–29 aprile 1971)*. Florence, 3–7

Clark, C. and Haswell, M. (1970) *The economics of subsistence agriculture*. 4th edn. London
Claude, D. (1969) *Die byzantinische Stadt im 6. Jahrhundert*. Munich
Connaert, E. (1948) 'Les guildes médiévales (Ve–XIVe siècles)', *Revue historique* 199: 22–55, 208–43
Corbier, M. (1981) 'Proprietà e gestione della terra: grande proprietaria ed economia contadina', in Giardina and Schiavone, eds. (1981), vol. 1: 427–44
Corbier, M. (1983) 'Fiscus and patrimonium: the Saepinum inscription and transhumance in the Abruzzi', *JRS* 73: 126–31
Corbier, M. (1989) 'The ambiguous status of meat in ancient Rome', *Food and Foodways* 3: 223–64
Corvisier, J.-N. (1985) *Santé et société en Grèce ancienne*. Paris
Cracco Ruggini, L. (1971) *Le associazioni professionali nel mondo romano-bizantino*. Turin
Curchin, L. A. (1986) 'Non-slave labour in Roman Spain', *Gerión* 4: 177–87
Curchin, L. A. (1987) 'Social relations in central Spain: patrons, freedmen and slaves in the life of a Roman provincial hinterland', *Anc. Soc.* 18: 75–89
Curti, E., Dench, E. and Patterson, J. (1996) 'The archaeology of central and southern Roman Italy: recent trends and approaches', *JRS* 86: 170–89
Dahl, G. and Hjort, A. (1976) *Having herds: pastoral herd growth and household economy*. Stockholm
Dalby, A. (1996) *Siren feasts: a history of food and gastronomy in Greece*. London and New York
Dal Cason Patriarca, F. (1995) 'Considerazioni demografiche sulla lista decurionale della Tabula di Canusium', *Athenaeum* 83: 245–64
Dallmann, P. R. (1986) 'Iron deficiency in the weanling: a nutritional problem on the way to resolution', in Wharton, ed. (1986), 59–67
D'Altroy, T. N. and Earle, T. K. (1985) 'Staple finance, wealth finance, and storage in the Inka political economy', *Current Anthropology* 26: 187–206
Daly, M. and Wilson, M. (1984) 'A sociobiological analysis of human infanticide', in G. Hausfater and S. B. Hrdy, eds., *Infanticide: comparative and evolutionary perspectives*. New York, 487–502
D'Arms, J. H. (1974) 'Puteoli in the second century of the Roman empire: a social and economic study', *JRS* 64: 104–24
D'Arms, J. H. (1976) 'Notes on municipal notables of imperial Ostia', *AJPh* 97: 387–411
D'Arms, J. H. (1979) 'Rapporti socio-economici fra città e territorio nella prima età imperiale', *AAAd* 15: 549–73
D'Arms, J. H. (1981) *Commerce and social standing in ancient Rome*. Cambridge, Mass. and London
D'Arms, J. H. (1990) 'Italien', in Vittinghoff, ed. (1990), 375–426
Daube, D. (1957) 'Three notes on Digest 18.1, conclusion of sale', *Law Quarterly Review* 73: 379–98
Davis, J. (1973) *Land and family in Pisticci*. London

Davis, J. (1977) *People of the Mediterranean: an essay in comparative social anthropology*. London

Davis, J. L. (1996) 'A page turns in the history of Greek regional studies', *JRA* 9: 458–65

Day, A. D. and Thompson, R. K. (1988) 'Effects of dried sewage sludge on wheat cultivars in the southwestern U.S.', *Journal of Arid Environments* 14: 93–9

Day, J. (1942) *An economic history of Athens under Roman domination*. New York

Degrassi, A. (1967) 'Il supposto municipio di Classe e l'amministrazione di Ravenna', in id., *Scritti vari di antichità*, vol. 3. Trieste, 285–93

De Laet, S. J. (1949) *Portorium: étude sur l'organisation douanière chez les Romains, surtout à l'époque du haut-empire*. Bruges

Delano Smith, C. (1966) 'Ancient landscapes of the Tavoliere, Apulia', *Transactions of the Institute of British Geographers* 41: 203–8

Delano Smith, C. (1979) *Western Mediterranean Europe: a historical geography of Italy, Spain and southern France since the Neolithic*. London

Delatte, A. (1930) 'Faba Pythagorae cognata', in *Serta Leodiensia*. Liège, 33–57

De Ligt, L. (1990) 'Demand, supply, distribution: the Roman peasantry between town and countryside: rural monetization and peasant demand', *MBAH* 9, 2: 24–56

De Ligt, L. (1991) 'Demand, supply, distribution: the Roman peasantry between town and countryside: supply, distribution and a comparative perspective', *MBAH* 10, 1: 33–77

De Ligt, L. (1993) *Fairs and markets in the Roman empire: economic and social aspects of periodic markets in a pre-industrial society*, Amsterdam

De Ligt, L. (1994) 'The imprint of imperialism: Greece under the empire', *Archaeological Dialogues* 1: 170–3

Della Corte, M. (1926) 'Publius Paquius Proculus', *JRS* 16: 145–54

Della Corte, M. (1954) *Casi ed abitanti de Pompei*. 2nd edn. Rome

De Maeyer, E. and Adiels-Tegman, M. (1985) 'The prevalence of anaemia in the world', *World Health Statistics Quarterly* 38: 302–8

De Martino, F. (1986) 'Schiavi e coloni tra antichità e medioevo', *StTardoant* 2: 7–44

De Martino, F. (1991) 'L'economia', in B. Andreae et al., eds., *Princeps urbium: cultura e vita sociale dell'Italia romana*. Milan, 225–336

De Mause, L., ed. (1974) *The history of childhood*. London

Demougin, S. (1994) 'A propos des élites locales en Italie', in *L'Italie d'Auguste à Dioclétien*. Rome, 353–76

De Neeve, P. W. (1984a) *Colonus: private farm-tenancy during the Republic and the early empire*. Amsterdam

De Neeve, P. W. (1984b) *Peasants in peril: location and economy in Italy in the second century BC*. Amsterdam

De Neeve, P. W. (1990) 'A Roman landowner and his estates: Pliny the Younger', *Athenaeum* 78, 363–402

De Pachtere, F. G. (1912) 'Les Campi Macri et le sénatus-consulte hosidien', in *Mélanges Cagnat*. Paris, 169–86

Desplanques, H. (1969) *Campagnes ombriennes: contribution à l'étude des paysages ruraux en Italie centrale*. Paris
Despois, J. (1940) *La Tunisie orientale: Sahel et basse steppe. Etude géographique*. Paris
Detienne, M. (1970) 'La cuisine de Pythagore', *Archives de sociologie* 29: 141–62
Detienne, M. (1977) *Dionysos mis à mort*. Paris
Deubner, L. (1959) *Attische Feste*. Hildesheim
Devereux, S. (1993) *Theories of famine*. New York
Devine, T. M. (1988) *The Great Highland Famine: hunger, emigration and the Scottish Highlands*. Edinburgh
De Waal, A. (1989) *Famine that kills: Darfur, Sudan 1984–1985*. Oxford
Dickemann, M. (1975) 'Demographic consequences of infanticide in man', *Annual Review of Ecology and Systematics* 6: 107–37
Di Niro, A. (1977) *Il culto di Ercole tra i Sanniti Pentri e Frentani: nuove testimonianze*. Salerno
Dixon, S. (1988) *The Roman mother*. London and Sydney
Douglas, M. (1966) *Purity and danger: an analysis of concepts of pollution and taboo*. New York
Douglas, M. (1972) 'Deciphering a meal', *Daedalus* 101: 61–82
Dovring, F. (1960) *Land and labor in Europe 1900–1950: a comparative survey of recent agrarian history*. 2nd edn. The Hague
Downey, G. (1961) *A history of Antioch in Syria from Seleucus to the Arab conquest*. Princeton
Doxiadis, S. et al. (1976) 'Genetic aspects of nutritional rickets', *Archives of Disease in Childhood* 51: 83–90
Dumont, J. C. (1986) 'Les *operarii* de Varron (*res rusticae*, 1, 17, 2–3)', *RPh* 60: 81–8
Duncan, G. (1958) 'Sutri (Sutrium)', *PBSR* 13: 63–134
Duncan-Jones, R. P. (1962) 'Costs, outlays and summae honoriae from Roman Africa', *PBSR* 17: 47–115
Duncan-Jones, R. P. (1963) 'Wealth and munificence in Roman Africa', *PBSR* 18: 159–77
Duncan-Jones, R. (1982) *The economy of the Roman empire*. 2nd edn. Cambridge
Duncan-Jones, R. (1990) *Structure and scale in the Roman economy*. Cambridge
Dupont, F. (1977) *Le plaisir et la loi*. Paris
Duthoy, R. (1970) 'Notes onomastiques sur les Augustales: cognomina et indication de statut', *AC* 39: 88–105
Duthoy, R. (1974) 'La fonction de l'augustalité', *Epigraphica* 36: 134–54
Dyson, S. L. (1978) 'Settlement patterns in the Ager Cosanus', *JFA* 5: 251–68
Eck, W. (1978) 'Abhängigkeit als ambivalenter Begriff: zum Verhältnis von Patron und Libertus', *Memorias de historia antigua* 2: 41–50
Egger, R. (1961) *Die Stadt auf dem Magdalensberg: ein Grosshandelsplatz*. Vienna
Ellis, H. (1969) *A history of bladder stone*. Oxford
Elvin, M. (1973) *The pattern of the Chinese past*. London
Escurac-Doisy, H. d' (1967) 'Notes sur le phénomène associatif dans le monde paysan à l'époque du haut-empire', *Antiquités Africaines* 1: 59–71

Etienne, R. (1960) *Le quartier nord-est de Volubilis*. Paris
Etienne, R. (1976) 'Ancient medical conscience and children', *Journal of Psychohistory* 4: 131–62
Etienne, R. (1981) 'Les rations alimentaires des esclaves de la "familia rustica" d'après Caton', *Index* 10: 66–77
Evans, J. K. (1980a) '*Plebs rustica*: the peasantry of classical Italy I. The peasantry in modern scholarship: a methodological critique', *AJAH* 5: 19–47
Evans, J. K. (1980b) '*Plebs rustica*: the peasantry of classical Italy II. The peasant economy', *AJAH* 5: 134–73
Evans, J. K. (1991) *War, women and children in ancient Rome*. London and New York
Eyben, E. (1980–1) 'Family planning in Graeco-Roman antiquity', *AncSoc* 11–12: 5–82
Fabre, G. (1981) *Libertus: recherches sur les rapports patron – affranchi à la fin de la république romaine*. Rome
Faraguna, M. (1992) *Atene nell'età di Alessandro: problemi politici, economici, finanziari*. Rome
Feger, R. (1956) 'T. Pomponius Atticus', *RE Suppl.* 8: 503–26
Fildes, V. A. (1986) *Breasts, bottles and babies: a history of infant feeding*. Edinburgh
Fildes, V. A. (1988) *Wet nursing: a history from antiquity to the present*. Oxford
Finley, M. I. (1952) *Studies in land and credit in ancient Athens, 500–200 BC: the horos-inscriptions*. New Brunswick
Finley, M. I. (1959) 'Was Greek civilization based on slave labour?', *Historia* 8: 145–64 (repr. in Finley (1981) ch. 6)
Finley, M. I. (1960) 'The servile statuses of ancient Greece', *RIDA* 7, 165–89 (repr. in Finley (1981) ch. 8)
Finley, M. I. (1965) 'Technical innovation and economic progress in the ancient world', *Economic History Review* 18: 29–45 (repr. in Finley (1981) ch. 11)
Finley, M. I., ed. (1968) *Slavery in classical antiquity*, Cambridge
Finley, M. I. (1973a) *The ancient economy*. London
Finley, M. I. (1973b) *Democracy ancient and modern*. London
Finley, M. I. (1976) 'Private farm tenancy in Italy before Diocletian', in Finley, ed. (1976), 103–21
Finley, M. I., ed. (1976) *Studies in Roman property*. Cambridge
Finley, M. I. (1981) *Economy and society in ancient Greece* (B. D. Shaw and R. P. Saller, eds.). London
Finley, M. I. (1985) *The ancient economy*. 2nd edn. London
Folta, J. R. and Deck, E. S. (1988) 'The impact of children's death on Shona mothers and families', *Journal of Comparative Family Studies* 19: 433–51
Forbes, H. A. (1982) 'Strategies and soils: technology, production and environment in the peninsula of Methana, Greece', unpublished PhD thesis, University of Pennsylvania
Ford, J. A. et al. (1972) 'Rickets and osteomalacia in the Glasgow Pakistani community, 1961–71', *British Medical Journal* 17 June: 677–80

Fornaciari, G., Menacagli Trevisani, E. and Ceccanti, B. (1984) 'Indagini paleonutrizionali e determinazione del piombo osseo mediante spettroscopia ad assorbimento atomico sui resti scheletrici di epoca tardo-romana (IV secolo d.c.) della "Villa dei Gordiani" (Roma)', *Archivio per l'antropologia e l'etnologia* 114: 149-76
Foss, C. (1976) *Byzantine and Turkish Sardis*. Cambridge, Mass.
Foucault, M. (1984) *L'usage des plaisirs*. Paris
Foxhall, L. (1990) 'The dependent tenant: land leasing and labour in Italy and Greece', *JRS* 80: 97-114
Foxhall, L. (1993) 'Farming and fighting in ancient Greece', in J. Rich and G. Shipley, eds., *War and society in the Greek world*. London and New York, 134-45
Foxhall, L. and Forbes, H. A. (1982) '*Sitometreia*: the role of grain as a staple food in classical antiquity', *Chiron* 12: 41-90
Franciosa, L. (1951) 'La trasumanza nell'Appennino centro-meridionale', *Memorie di geografia economica* 4: 7-97
Frank, T. (1933) *An economic survey of ancient Rome* vol. 1. Baltimore
Frayn, J. M. (1979) *Subsistence farming in Roman Italy*. London
Frayn, J. M. (1984) *Sheep-rearing and the wool trade in Italy during the Roman period*. Liverpool
Frayn, J. M. (1993) *Markets and fairs in Roman Italy*. Oxford
Frederiksen, M. W. (1959) 'Republican Capua: a social and economic study', *PBSR* 27: 80-130
Frederiksen, M. W. (1970-71) 'The contribution of archaeology to the agrarian problem in the Gracchan period', *DArch* 4-5, 330-57
Frederiksen, M. W. (1976) 'Changes in the patterns of settlement', in P. Zanker, ed., *Hellenismus in Mittelitalien*. Göttingen, 341-55
Frederiksen, M. W. and Ward-Perkins, J. B. (1957) 'The ancient road systems of the central and northern Ager Faliscus', *PBSR* 25: 67-208
Frier, B. W. (1977) 'The rental market in early imperial Rome', *JRS* 67: 27-37
Frier, B. W. (1978) 'Cicero's management of his urban properties', *CJ* 74: 1-6
Frier, B. W. (1980) *Landlords and tenants in imperial Rome*. Princeton
Frier, B. W. (1992) 'Statistics and Roman society', *JRA* 5: 286-90
Fulford, M. (1989) 'The economy of Roman Britain', in M. Todd, ed., *Research on Roman Britain: 1960-1989*. London
Gabba, E. (1972) 'Urbanizzazione e rinnovamenti urbanistici nell'Italia centro-meridionale del I sec. a.C.', *SCO* 21: 73-112
Gabba, E. (1976) *Republican Rome: the army and the allies*. Oxford
Gabba, E. (1977) 'Considerazioni sulla decadenza della piccola proprietà contadina nell'Italia centro-meridionale del II sec. a. C.', *Ktèma* 2: 269-284
Gabba, E. and Pasquinucci, M. (1979) *Strutture agrarie e allevamento transumante nell'Italia romana (III– I sec. a. C.)*. Pisa
Gallant, T. W. (1983) 'An examination of two island polities in antiquity: the Lefkas-Pronnoi survey', unpublished PhD thesis, University of Cambridge

Gallant, T. W. (1989) 'Crisis and response: risk-buffering behavior in Hellenistic Greek communities', *Journal of Interdisciplinary History* 19: 393-413
Gallant, T. W. (1991) *Risk and survival in ancient Greece: reconstructing the rural domestic economy*. Cambridge
Gallo, L. (1983) 'Alimentazione e classi sociali: una nota su orzo e frumento in Grecia', *Opus* 2: 449-72
Gallo, L. (1984) *Alimentazione e demografia della Grecia antica: ricerche*: Salerno
Gardner, J. F. (1989) 'The adoption of Roman freedmen', *Phoenix* 43: 236-57
Garnsey, P. (1970) *Social status and legal privilege in the Roman empire*. Oxford
Garnsey, P. (1971a) 'Honorarium decurionatus', *Historia* 20: 309-25
Garnsey, P. (1971b) '*Taxatio* and *pollicitatio* in Roman Africa', *JRS* 61: 116-29
Garnsey, P. (1975) 'Descendants of freedmen in local politics: some criteria', in B. Levick, ed., *The ancient historian and his materials: essays in honour of C. E. Stevens*. Farnborough, 167-80
Garnsey, P. (1976) 'Peasants in Roman society', *Journal of Peasant Studies* 3, 221-35
Garnsey, P. (1978) 'Rome's African empire under the Principate', in Garnsey, P. and Whittaker, C. R., eds., *Imperialism in the ancient world*. Cambridge, 223-54
Garnsey, P. (1979) 'Where did Italian peasants live?', *PCPhS* 225, 1-25
Garnsey, P. (1980) 'Non-slave labour in the Roman world', in Garnsey, ed. (1980), 34-47
Garnsey, P., ed. (1980) *Non-slave labour in the Greco-Roman world*. Cambridge
Garnsey, P. (1981) 'Independent freedmen and the economy of Roman Italy under the Principate', *Klio* 63: 359-71
Garnsey, P. (1982a) 'Probleme der römischen Landwirtschaft zur Zeit der Republik und des frühen Prinzipats', in Herrmann, J. and Sellnow, I., eds., *Produktivkräfte und Gesellschaftsformationen in vorkapitalistischer Zeit*. Berlin, 343-9
Garnsey, P. (1982b) 'Slaves in "business"', *Opus* 1,1: 105-8
Garnsey, P. (1983) 'Introduction', in Garnsey and Whittaker, eds. (1983) 1-5
Garnsey, P. (1985) 'Les travailleurs du bâtiment de Sardes et l'économie urbaine du bas-empire', in P. Leveau, ed., *L'origine des richesses dépensées dans la ville antique*. Aix-en-Provence, 147-60
Garnsey, P. (1986a) 'Famine in the ancient Mediterranean', *History Today* 36, May: 24-30
Garnsey, P. (1986b) 'Mountain economies in southern Europe: thoughts on the early history, continuity and individuality of Mediterranean upland pastoralism', in M. Mattmüller, ed., *Wirtschaft und Gesellschaft in Berggebieten*. Basle, 1-25
Garnsey, P. (1988) *Famine and food supply in the Graeco-Roman world: responses to risk and crisis*. Cambridge
Garnsey, P., ed. (1989) *Food, health and culture in classical antiquity: Cambridge Department of Classics Working Papers No.1*. Cambridge

Garnsey, P. (1990) 'Responses to food crisis in the ancient Mediterranean world', in L. Newman, ed., *Hunger in history: food shortage, poverty, and deprivation*. Oxford, 126-46

Garnsey, P. (1991) 'Mass consumption and diet in the city of Rome', in A. Giovannini, ed., *Nourrir la plèbe: actes du colloque tenu à Genèvre les 28 et 29. IX. 1989 en hommage à Denis van Berchem*. Basle and Kassel, 67-101

Garnsey, P. (1992) 'Yield of the land', in B. Wells, ed., *Agriculture in Greece*. Stockholm, 147-53

Garnsey, P. (forthcoming, a) 'Famine', in P. Brown, G. Bowersock and A. Grabar, eds., *Guide to late antiquity*. Cambridge, Mass.

Garnsey, P. (forthcoming, b) 'Les raisons de la politique', in J. Flandrin and M. Montanari, eds., *Histoire de l'alimentation*

Garnsey, P., Gallant, T. and Rathbone, D. (1984) 'Thessaly and the grain supply of Rome in the second century BC', *JRS* 74: 30-44

Garnsey, P. and Saller, R. (1982) *The early Principate, Augustus to Trajan*. Oxford

Garnsey, P. and Saller, R. (1987) *The Roman empire: economy, society and culture*. London

Garnsey, P. and Whittaker, C. R., eds. (1983) *Trade and famine in classical antiquity*. Cambridge

Garnsey, P. and Woolf, G. (1989) 'Patronage of the rural poor in the Roman world', in A. Wallace-Hadrill, ed., *Patronage in ancient society*. London and New York, 153-70

Garzetti, A. (1968) *Le valli dell'Adda e della Mera in epoca romana*. Chiavenna

Gauthier, P. (1981) 'De Lysias à Aristote (Ath. Pol. 51.4): le commerce du grain à Athènes et les fonctions des sitophylaques', *RD* 59: 5-28

Georgoudi, S. (1976) 'Quelques problèmes de la transhumance dans la Grèce ancienne', *REG* 87: 155-81

Gérard, J. (1976) *Juvénal et la réalité contemporaine*. Paris

Gerbasi, M. (1956) 'Kwashiorkor in Sicilia', *Pediatria* 64: 941-1003

Gernet, L. (1909) *L'approvisionnement d'Athènes en blé au Ve et au IVe siècle*. Paris

Giardina, A. (1982) 'Lavoro e storia sociale: antagonismi e alleanze dall'ellenismo al tardoantico', *Opus* 1: 115-46

Giardina, A., ed. (1993) *The Romans*. Chicago and London

Giardina, A. and Schiavone, A., eds. (1981) *Società romana e produzione schiavistica*, vols. 1-3. Bari

Gilbert, R. I. and Mielke, J. H., eds. (1985) *The analysis of prehistoric diets*. Orlando

Goel, K. M. and Arneil, G. C. (1982) 'Rickets, old and new', *Pediatric Nutrition* 9: 219-44

Golden, M. (1988) 'Did the ancients care when their children died?', *G&R* 35: 152-63

Golden, M. (1990) *Children and childhood in classical Athens*. Baltimore and London

Golden, M. (1992) 'Continuity, change and the study of ancient childhood', *EMC* 11: 7–18
Golden, M. (1997) 'Change or continuity? Children and childhood in Hellenistic historiography', in M. Golden and P. Toohey, eds., *Inventing ancient culture: historicism, periodization, and the ancient world*. London and New York, 176–91
Gomme, A. W. (1933) *The population of Athens in the fifth and fourth centuries BC*. Oxford
Goodman, A. H. et al. (1984) 'Indications of stress from bone and teeth', in M. N. Cohen and G. J. Armelagos, eds., *Paleopathology at the origins of agriculture*. Orlando, 13–49
Goold, G. P. (1964) Review of R. A. B. Mynors, ed., *C. Plini Caecili Secundi epistularum libri decem*. Toronto 1963, *Phoenix* 18: 320–8
Gordon, M. L. (1931) 'The freedman's son in municipal life', *JRS* 21: 65–77
Graindor, P. (1922) *Chronologie des archontes athéniens sous l'empire*. Brussels
Gregory, P. J., Shepherd, K. D. and Cooper, P. J. (1984) 'Effects of fertilizer on root growth and water use of barley in northern Syria', *Journal of Agricultural Science* 103: 429–38
Griffith, G. T. (1935) *Greek mercenaries of the Hellenistic world*. Cambridge
Grmek, M. D. (1983) *Les maladies à l'aube de la civilisation occidentale*. Paris
Gruaz, J. (1910) 'Sur une médaille en or romaine trouvée à Sainte-Croix en 1876', *Revue suisse de numismatique* 16: 297–301
Grundy, G. B. (1948) *Thucydides and the history of his age*. Oxford
Gualtieri, M. and de Polignac, F. (1991) 'A Rural Landscape in western Lucania', in Barker and Lloyd, eds. (1991), 194–203
Gubler-Gross, R. (1962) *Moderne Transhumanz in der Schweiz*. Winterthur
Guillet, D. (1981) 'Land tenure, ecological zone and agricultural regime in the central Andes', *American Ethnologist* 8: 139–56
Gummerus, H. (1906) *Der römische Gutsbetrieb als wirtschaftlicher Organismus nach den Werken des Cato, Varro und Columella*. Leipzig
Gummerus, H. (1916) "Industrie und Handel, B. Bei den Römern", *RE* 9, 1439–535
Hadjichristodoulou, A. (1982) 'The effects of annual precipitation and its distribution on grain yield of dryland cereals', *Journal of Agricultural Science* 99: 261–70
Halstead, P. (1981) 'Counting sheep in Neolithic and Bronze Age Greece', in I. Hodder, G. Isaac and N. Hammond, eds., *Pattern of the past: studies in honour of David Clarke*. Cambridge, 307–39
Halstead, P. (1984) 'Strategies for survival: an ecological approach to social and economic change in the early farming communities of Thessaly, N. Greece', unpublished PhD thesis, University of Cambridge
Halstead, P. (1987) 'Traditional and ancient rural economy in Mediterranean Europe: plus ça change?', *JHS* 107: 77–87
Halstead, P. (1990) 'Quantifying Sumerian agriculture – some seeds of doubt and hope', *Bulletin on Sumerian Agriculture* 5: 187–95

Halstead, P. and Jones, G. (1989) 'Agrarian ecology in the Greek islands: time stress, scale and risk', *JHS* 109: 41–55
Hamilton, R. (1984) 'Sources for the Athenian amphidromia', *GRBS* 25: 243–51
Hammond, N. G. L. (1976) *Migrations and invasions in Greece and adjacent areas.* Park Ridge, NJ
Hanfmann, G. M. A. and Waldbaum, J.-C. (1975) *A survey of Sardis and the major monuments outside the city walls.* Cambridge, Mass.
Hannestad, K. (1962) *L'évolution des ressources agricoles de l'Italie du 4ème au 6ème siècle de notre ère.* Copenhagen
Hansen, M. H. (1981) 'The number of Athenian hoplites in 431 BC', *SO* 56: 19–32
Hansen, M. H. (1985) *Demography and democracy: the number of Athenian citizens in the fourth century BC.* Herning
Hansen, M. H. (1988) *Three studies in Athenian demography.* Copenhagen
Hansen, M. H. (1989) 'Demography and democracy – a reply to Eberhard Ruschenbusch', *AHB* 3: 40–4
Hansen, M. H. (1994) 'The number of Athenian citizens *secundum* Sekunda', *EMC* 38: 299–310
Hanson, V. D. (1995) *The other Greeks: the family farm and the agrarian roots of western civilization.* New York
Harmand, L. (1955) *Libanius, Discours sur les patronages.* Paris
Harris, M. (1987) 'Foodways: historical overview and theoretical prolegomenon', in M. Harris and E. B. Ross, eds., *Food and evolution: towards a theory of human food habits.* Philadelphia, 57–90
Harris, M. and Ross, E. B. (1987) *Death, sex and fertility: population regulation in preindustrial and developing societies.* New York
Harris, W. V. (1980) 'Towards a study of the Roman slave trade', in J. H. D'Arms and E. C. Kopff, eds., *The seaborne commerce of ancient Rome: studies in archaeology and history.* Rome, 117–40
Harrison, G. A. (1988) *Famine.* Oxford
Hayashi, N. (1989) 'Die *pecunia* in der *pollicitatio ob honorem*', *Klio* 71: 383–98
Hayes, J. W. and Martini, I. P., eds. (1994) *Archaeological survey in the lower Liri valley, central Italy.* Oxford.
Haywood, R. M. (1938) 'Roman Africa', in *ESAR* 4: 1–119
Hebblethwaite, P. D., ed. (1983) *The Faba Bean (Vicia Faba L.).* London
Hebblethwaite, P. D. et al. (1984) *Vicia Faba: agronomy, physiology and breeding.* The Hague
Heitland, W. E. (1921) *Agricola: a study of agriculture and rustic life in the Greco-Roman world from the point of view of labour.* Cambridge
Helen, T. (1975) *Organization of Roman brick production in the first and second centuries AD: an interpretation of Roman brick stamps.* Helsinki
Henderson, J. (1988) 'The parish and the poor in Florence at the time of the Black Death: the case of S. Frediano', *Continuity and Change* 3: 247–72
Henderson, J. (1994) *Piety and charity in late medieval Florence.* Oxford
Hengen, O. P. (1971) 'Cribra orbitalia: pathogenesis and probable etiology', *Homo* 22,2: 57–76

Herlihy, D. (1985) *Medieval households*. Cambridge, Mass.
Hermardinquer, J.-J. (1970) *Pour une histoire de l'alimentation*. Paris
Herz, P. (1988) *Studien zur römischen Wirtschaftsgesetzgebung: die Lebensmittelversorgung*, Stuttgart
Herz, P. (1989) Review of Garnsey (1988a), *Gnomon* 61: 135–42
Heurgon, J. (1971) *Recherches sur l'histoire, la religion et la civilisation de Capoue préromaine des origines à la deuxième guerre punique*. (repr.) Paris
Hinde, R. A. (1987) *Individuals, relationships and culture*. Cambridge
Hinrichs, F. T. (1974) *Die Geschichte der gromatischen Institutionen*. Wiesbaden
Hitchner, B. (1994) 'Image and reality: the changing face of pastoralism in the Tunisian high steppe', in J. Carlsen, P. Oersted and J. E. Skydsgaard, eds., *Landuse in the Roman empire*. Rome, 27–43
Hodkinson, S. (1988) 'Animal husbandry in the Greek polis', Whittaker, ed. (1988), 35–74
Hoeg, C. (1925) *Les Saracatsanes: un tribu nomade grecque*. Copenhagen
Hölkeskamp, K.-J. (1987) *Die Entstehung der Nobilität: Studien zur sozialen und politischen Geschichte der Römischen Republik im 4. Jhdt. v. Chr.* Stuttgart
Holmes, T. R. (1923) *The Roman Republic and the founder of the empire*, vol. 1. Oxford
Hopkins, K. (1978a) *Conquerors and slaves: sociological studies in Roman history 1*. Cambridge
Hopkins, K. (1978b) 'Economic growth and towns in classical antiquity', in P. Abrams and E. A. Wrigley, eds., *Towns in societies: essays in economic history and historical sociology*. Cambridge, 35–77
Hopkins, K. (1980) 'Taxes and trade in the Roman empire (200 BC–AD 400)', *JRS* 70: 101–25
Hopkins, K. (1983) *Death and renewal: sociological studies in Roman history 2*. Cambridge
Hopper, R. J. (1979) *Trade and industry in classical Greece*. London
Hornblower, S. (1983) *The Greek world 479–323 BC*. London
Horstkotte, H. (1984) 'Magistratur und Dekurionat im Lichte des Albums von Canusium', *ZPE* 57: 211–24
Houston, J. M. (1964) *The western Mediterranean world: an introduction to its regional landscapes*. London
Huffman, S. L. and Lamphere, B. B. (1984) 'Breastfeeding performance and child survival', in W. H. Mosley and L. C. Chen, eds., *Child survival: strategies for research*. Cambridge, 93–116
Hunecke, V. (1989) *I trovatelli di Milano*. Bologna
Hunt, D. (1972) *Parents and children in history: the psychology of family life in early modern France*. New York
Huttunen, P. (1974) *The social strata in the imperial city of Rome*. Oulu
Isager, S. and Hansen, M. H. (1975) *Aspects of Athenian society in the fourth century BC*. Odense
Isager, S. and Skydsgaard, J. E. (1992) *Ancient Greek agriculture: an introduction*. London and New York

Jacobone, N. (1925) *Un antica e grande città dell'Apulia, Canusium: ricerche di storia e di topografia.* Canosa
Jacques, F. (1984) *Le privilège de liberté: politique impériale et autonomie municipale dans les cités de l'Occident romain (161–244).* Rome
Jameson, M. H. (1977–8) 'Agriculture and slavery in classical Athens', *CJ* 73: 122–45
Jardé, A. (1925) *Les céréales dans l'antiquité grecque: la production.* Paris
Jarrett, R. J., ed. (1979) *Nutrition and disease.* London
Jashemski, W. F. (1973) 'The discovery of a large vineyard at Pompeii: University of Maryland excavations, 1970', *AJA* 77: 27–41
Jasny, N. (1944) *The wheats of classical antiquity.* Baltimore
Jelliffe, D. M. and E. F. P. (1978) *Human milk.* Oxford
Johannowsky, W. (1970–71) 'La situazione in Campania', *DArch* 4–5: 267–89
Johne, K.-P., Köhn, J. and Weber, V. (1983) *Die Kolonen in Italien und den westlichen Provinzen des römischen Reiches: eine Untersuchung der literarischen, juristischen und epigraphischen Quellen vom 2. Jahrhundert v.u.Z. bis zu den Severern.* Berlin
Jones, A. H. M. (1937) *The cities of the eastern Roman provinces.* Oxford
Jones, A. H. M. (1940) *The Greek city from Alexander to Justinian.* Oxford
Jones, A. H. M. (1956) 'Slavery in the ancient world', *Economic History Review* ser. 2, 9: 185–99
Jones, A. H. M. (1957) *Athenian democracy.* Oxford
Jones, A. H. M. (1960) 'The cloth industry under the Roman empire', *Economic History Review* 13: 183–92
Jones, A. H. M. (1964) *The later Roman empire, 284–602: a social, economic and administrative survey.* Oxford
Jones, A. H. M. (1970) 'The caste system of the later Roman empire', *Eirene* 8: 79–96
Jones, A. H. M. (1974) *The Roman economy: studies in ancient economic and administrative history* (P. A. Brunt, ed.). Oxford
Jones, C. P. (1968) 'A new commentary on the letters of Pliny', *Phoenix* 22: 111–42
Jones, G. D. B. (1962) 'Capena and Ager Capenas: part I', *PBSR* 30: 116–207
Jones, G. D. B. (1963) 'Capena and Ager Capenas: part II', *PBSR* 31: 100–58
Jones, G. B. D. (1973) 'Civil war and society in southern Etruria', in M. R. D. Foot, ed., *War and society.* London, 277–87
Jones, M. (1981) 'The development of crop husbandry', in M. Jones and G. Dimbleby, eds., *The environment of man: the Iron Age to the Anglo-Saxon period.* Oxford, 95–127
Jongman, W. (1988) *The economy and society of Pompeii.* Amsterdam
Joshel, S. R. (1992) *Work, identity, and legal status at Rome: a study of the occupational inscriptions.* Norman OK and London
Kahane, A., Threipland, L. M. and Ward-Perkins, J. (1968) 'The Ager Veientanus, north and east of Rome', *PBSR* 36: 1–213
Kahrstedt, U. (1960) *Die wirtschaftliche Lage Grossgriechenlands in der Kaiserzeit.* Wiesbaden

Kaser, M. (1971) *Das römische Privatrecht*. 2nd edn. Munich
Katz, S. H. (1987) 'Fava bean consumption: a case for the co-evolution of genes and culture', in M. Harris and E. B. Ross, eds., *Food and evolution: towards a theory of human food habits*. Philadelphia, 133–59
Kayser, B. and Thompson, F. (1964) *Economic and social atlas of Greece*. Athens
Kedar, Y. (1957) 'Ancient agriculture at Shivtah in the Negev', *IEJ* 7: 178–89
Keen, A. (1993) '"Grain for Athens": notes on the importance of the Hellespontine route in Athenian foreign policy before the Peloponnesian War', *Electronic Antiquity* 1.6
Kehoe, D. P. (1988a) *The economics of agriculture on Roman imperial estates in North Africa*. Göttingen
Kehoe, D. P. (1988b) 'Allocation of risk and investment on the estates of Pliny the Younger', *Chiron* 18, 15–40
Kehoe, D. P. (1989) 'Approaches to economic problems in the 'Letters' of Pliny the Younger: the question of risk in agriculture', *ANRW* II 33.1, 555–90
Kehoe, D. P. (1993) 'Investment in estates by upper-class landowners in early imperial Italy: the case of Pliny the Younger', in H. Sancisi-Weerdenburg et al., eds. (1993), 214–37
Kennedy, H. (1985) 'The last century of Byzantine Syria: a reinterpretation', *Byzantinische Forschungen* 10: 141–83
Khazanov, A. M. (1983) *Nomads and the outside world*. Cambridge
Kirschenbaum, A. (1987) *Sons, slaves, and freedmen in Roman commerce*. Jerusalem
Kirsten, E. (1983) 'Gebirghirtentum und Sesshaftigkeit – die Bedeutung der Dark Ages für die griechische Staatenwelt', in S. Deger-Jalkotzy, ed., *Doris und Sparta: Akten des Symposions von Stift Zwettl 1.–4. Okt. 1980*. Vienna, 355–443
Kleijwegt, M. (1991) *Ancient youth: the ambiguity of youth and the absence of adolescence in Greco-Roman society*. Amsterdam
Klein, J. (1920) *The Mesta: a study in Spanish economic history 1273–1836*. Cambridge, Mass.
Klepinger, L. L. (1984) 'Nutritional assessment from bone', *Annual Review of Anthropology* 13: 75–96
Knoop, D. and Jones, G. P. (1967) *The medieval mason: an economic history of English stone building in the later Middle Ages and early modern times*. 3rd edn. Manchester
Kohns, H. P. (1988) 'Hungersnot und Hungerbewältigung in der Antike', in H. Kloft, ed. (1988) *Sozialmaßnahmen und Fürsorge: zur Eigenart antiker Sozialpolitik*. Graz and Horn, 103–21
Kolendo, J. (1985) 'Le attività agricole degli abitanti di Pompei e gli attrezzi agricoli ritrovati all'interno della città', *Opus* 4: 111–24
Kolendo, J. (1991) *Le colonat en Afrique sous le haut–empire*. 2nd edn. Paris
Kolendo, J. (1993) 'The peasant', in Giardina, ed. (1993), 199–213
Kornemann, E. (1905) 'Polis und Urbs', *Klio* 5: 72–92

Kosminsky, E. A. (1956) *Studies in the agrarian history of England in the thirteenth century*. Oxford

Koster, H. (1977) 'The ecology of pastoralism in relation to changing patterns of land use in the North East Peloponnese', unpublished PhD thesis, University of Pennsylvania

Krause, J.-U. (1987) *Spätantike Patronatsformen im Westen des Römischen Reiches*. Munich

Krause, J.-U. (1992) *Bibliographie zur römischen Sozialgeschichte 1: Die Familie und weitere anthropologische Grundlagen*. Stuttgart

Krentos, V. D. and Orphanos, P. I. (1979) 'Nitrogen and phosphorus fertilizers for wheat and barley in a semi-arid region', *Journal of Agricultural Science* 93: 711–17

Kudlien, F. (1984) 'Anniversarii vicini: zur freien Arbeit im römischen Dorf', *Hermes* 112: 66–84

Kühn, G. (1910) *De opificum romanorum condicione privata quaestiones*, Halle-Wittenberg

Kuniholm, P. I. and Striker, C. L. (1983) 'Dendrochronological investigations in the Aegean and neighbouring regions 1977–1982', *JFA* 10: 411–20

Kupiszewski, H. (1979) 'Des remarques sur les *statuliberi* en droit romain classique', in I. Bienzunska-Malowist and J. Kolendo, eds., *Actes sur le colloque sur l'esclavage, Nieborow 2–6 XII 1975*. Warsaw, 227–38

Kurz, K. (1963) 'Gnoseologische Betrachtungen über die statistisch-epigraphische Methode', *LF* 86: 207–22

Ladizinsky, G. (1975) 'On the origin of the broad bean', *Israel Journal of Botany* 24: 80–8

Ladizinsky, G. (1989) 'Origin and domestication of the south west Asian grain legumes', in D. R. Harris and G. C. Hillmann, eds., *Foraging and farming: the evolution of plant exploitation*. London, 375–89

Laffi, U. (1974) 'Problemi dell'organizzazione paganico-vicana nelle aree abruzzesi e molisane', *Athenaeum* 52: 336–9

Lamas, J. and Shashoua, Y. (1973) 'The effect of rainfall on wheat yields in an arid region', in *Plant response to climatic factors: proceedings of the Uppsala symposium, 1970*. Uppsala, 531–8

Lambert, J. (1934) *Les operae liberti: contribution à l'histoire des droits de patronat*. Paris

Lambert, J. B. et al. (1985) 'Bone diagenesis and dietary analysis', *Journal of Human Evolution* 14: 477–82

Lamboglia, C. (1921) 'La trasumanza nelli Alpi Ligure', in *Atti dell' VIII congresso geografico italiano*, vol. 2, Florence, 421–7

Langdon, M. K. (1991) 'On the farm in classical Attica', *CJ* 86: 209–13

Langhammer, W. (1973) *Die rechtliche und soziale Stellung der 'Magistratus municipales 'und der' 'Decuriones' in der Übergangsphase der Städte von sich selbstverwaltenden Gemeinden zu Vollzugsorganen des spätantiken Zwangsstaates (2.–4. Jahrhundert der römischen Kaiserzeit)*. Wiesbaden

Lapatsanis, P., Deliyanni, V. and Doxiadis, S. (1968) 'Vitamin D deficiency rickets in Greece', *Journal of Pediatrics* 73: 195-202

La Regina, A. (1970) 'Note sulla formazione dei centri urbani in area sabellica', in *Studi sulla città italica preromana: Atti del convegno di studi sulla città etrusca e italica preromana*. Bologna, 197-207

La Regina, A. (1970-71) 'Contributo dell'archaeologia alla storia sociale: territori sabellici e sannitici', *DArch* 4-5: 443-59

La Regina, A. (1975) 'Centri fortificati preromani nei territori sabellici dell'Italia centrale adriatica', *Posebna Izdania* 24: 271-84

Laslett, P. (1977) *Family life and illicit love in earlier generations: essays in historical sociology*. Cambridge

Last, H. (1934) 'The social policy of Augustus', in *CAH* 10, 1st edn: 425-64

Latron, A. (1936) *La vie rurale en Syrie et en Liban*. Beirut

Lauffer, S. (1971) *Diokletians Preisedikt*. Berlin

Le Gall, J. (1971) 'Rome, ville de fainéants?', *REL* 49: 266-77

LeGlay, M. (1990) 'La place des affranchis dans la vie municipale et dans la vie religieuse', *MEFRA* 102: 621-38

Lehmann, D. (1982) *Ecology and exchange in the Andes*. Cambridge

Le Lannou, M. (1941) *Pâtres et paysans de la Sardaigne*. Tours

Lepelley, C. (1967) 'Déclin ou stabilité de l'agriculture africaine au bas-empire? A propos d'une loi de l'empereur Honorius', *AntAfr* 1: 135-44

Lepelley, C. (1979-81) *Les cités de l'Afrique romaine au bas-empire*, 2 vols. Paris

Lepore, E. (1950) 'Orientamenti per la storia sociale di Pompei', in *Pompeiana: raccolta di studi per il secondo centenario degli scavi di Pompei*. Naples, 144-66

Les 'bourgeoisies' municipales italiennes aux IIe et Ier siècles av. J.-C. Centre Jean Bérard, Institut Français de Naples, 7-10 décembre 1981. Paris and Naples, 1983

Leschi, L. (1948) 'L'album municipal de Timgad et l'ordo salutationis du consulaire Ulpius Mariscianus', *REA* 50: 71-100

Leschi, L., et al. (1952) *Tablettes Albertini: actes privés de l'époque vandale (fin de Ve siècle)*. Paris

Leveau, P. (1983) 'La ville antique et l'organisation de l'espace rurale: *villa*, ville, village', *Annales ESC* 38: 920-42

Lewin, R. (1983) 'Isotopes give clues to past diets', *Science* 220: 1369

Lewis, D. M. (1973) 'The Athenian rationes centesimarum', in M. I. Finley, ed., *Problèmes de la terre en Grèce ancienne*. Paris, 187-212

Lewit, T. (1991) *Agricultural production in the Roman economy, AD 200-400*. Oxford

Lewthwaite, J. (1981) 'Plain tails from the hills: transhumance in Mediterranean archaeology', in A. Sheridan and G. Bailey, eds., *Economic archaeology*. Oxford, 57-66

Lewthwaite, J. (1982) 'Acorns for the ancestors: the prehistoric exploitation of woodland in the West Mediterranean', in: M. Bell and S. Limbrey, eds., *Archaeological aspects of woodland ecology*. Oxford, 217-30

Lewthwaite, J. (1984) 'Pastore, padrone: the social dimensions of pastoralism in prenuragic Sardinia', in W. H. Waldren et al., eds., *The Deya conference of prehistory: early settlement in the western Mediterranean islands and their peripheral areas*. Oxford, 251-68
Lézine, A. (1969) 'Sur la population des villes africaines', *AntAfr* 3: 69-82
Liebeschuetz, J. H. W. (1972) *Antioch: city and imperial administration in the later Roman empire*. Oxford
Littlejohn, L. (1946) 'Some aspects of soil fertility in Cyprus', *Empire Journal of Experimental Agriculture* 14: 123-34
Lloyd, J. (1991) 'Forms of rural settlement in the early Roman empire', in Barker and Lloyd, eds. (1991), 233-40
Lloyd, J. and Barker, G. (1981) 'Rural settlement in Roman Molise: problems of archaeological survey', in Barker, G. and Hodges, R., eds., *Archaeology and Roman society: prehistoric, Roman and medieval studies*. Oxford, 289-304
Loane, H. J. (1938) *Industry and commerce of the city of Rome (50 BC–AD 200)*. Baltimore
Lo Cascio, E. (1982) ' "Obaerarii" ("obaerati"): la nozione della dipendenza in Varrone', *Index* 11: 265-84
Lo Cascio, E. (1985/90) 'I *greges oviarici* dell'iscrizione di Sepino (*CIL* IX 2438) e la transumanza in età imperiale', *Abruzzo* 23-8: 557-69
Lo Cascio, E. (1993) 'Considerazioni sulla struttura e sulla dinamica dell'affitto agrario in età imperiale', in Sancisi-Weerdenburg et al., eds. (1993), 296-316
Lohmann, H. (1993) *Atene: Forschungen zur Siedlungs- und Wirtschaftsgeschichte des klassischen Attika*. Cologne
Los, A. (1987) 'Les affranchis dans la vie politique à Pompéi', *MEFRA* 99: 847-73
Los, A. (1992a) 'Les intérêts des affranchis dans l'agriculture italienne', *MEFRA* 104: 709-53
Los, A. (1992b) '*Quibus patet curia municipalis*: remarques sur la structure de la classe dirigeante de Pompéi', *Cahiers de Centre G. Glotz* 3: 259-97
Los, A. (1995) 'La condition sociale des affranchis privés au Ier siècle après J.-C.', *Annales: Histoire, Sciences Sociales* 50: 1011-43
McCann, A. M. (1987) *The Roman port and fishery at Cosa*. Princeton
Macfarlane, A. (1986) *Marriage and love in England: modes of reproduction 1300–1840*. Oxford
Machiarelli, R. (1987) *La necropoli di età romana di Grottaperfetta (Roma, 1 sec. AD): analisi bio-antropologica preliminare del materiale scheletrico*. Rome
Machiarelli, R., Salvadei, L. and Catalano, P. (1988) 'Biocultural changes and continuity throughout the 1st millennium BC in central Italy: anthropological evidence and perspectives', *Rivista di antropologia*, suppl. to vol. 66: 249-72
MacMullen, R. (1959) 'Roman imperial building in the provinces', *HSCPh* 64: 207-36
MacMullen, R. (1963) *Soldier and civilian in the later Roman empire*. Cambridge, Mass.

MacMullen, R. (1970) 'Market-days in the Roman empire', *Phoenix* 24: 333-41
MacMullen, R. (1974a) *Roman social relations, 50 BC to AD 284*. New Haven
MacMullen, R. (1974b) 'Peasants, during the Principate', *ANRW* II.1, 253-61
MacMullen, R. (1988) *Corruption and the decline of Rome*. New Haven and London
Macqueron, J. (1958) *Le travail des hommes libres dans l'antiquité romaine*, Aix-en-Provence
Maiuri, A. (1942) *L'ultima fase edilizia di Pompei*. Rome
Makler, P. T. (1980) 'New information on nutrition in ancient Greece', *Klio* 62: 317-9
Mansuelli, G. A. (1961a) 'La civilisation en Italie septentrionale après la conquête romaine (IIe-Ie siècle av. J.-C. - Ier siècle ap. J.-C.)', *RA* 2: 35-61
Mansuelli, G. A. (1961b) 'L'urbanistica della regio VIII: problemi, scoperte recenti e programma di lavoro', in *Atti del settimo congresso internazionale di archaeologia classica*, vol. 2. Rome, 325-45
Marasco, G. (1984) 'Sui problemi dell'approvvigionamento di cereali in Atene nell'età dei Diadochi', *Athenaeum* 62: 286-94
Marcone, A. (1988) *Il colonato tardoantico nella storiografia moderna (da Fustel de Coulanges ai nostri giorni)*. Como.
Maróti, E. (1989) 'Die Rolle der freien Arbeitskraft in der *Villa*-Wirtschaft im Zeitalter der Republik', *AAntHung* 32: 95-110
Marquardt, J. (1881) *Römische Staatsverwaltung*, vol. 1. Leipzig
Martin, D. L., Goodman, A. H. and Armelagos, G. J. (1985) 'Skeletal pathologies as indicators of quality and quantity of diet', in Gilbert and Mielke, eds. (1985), 227-79
Martin, R. (1971) *Recherches sur les agronomes latins et leurs conceptions économiques et sociales*. Paris
Martin, S. (1989) *The Roman jurists and the organization of private building in the late Republic and early empire*. Brussels
Masciadri, M. A. M. and Montevecchi, O. (1982) 'Contratti di baliatico e vendite fiduciarie', *Aegyptus* 62: 148-61
Mattingly, D. J. (1988a) 'Oil for export? A comparison of Libyan, Spanish and Tunisian olive oil production in the Roman empire', *JRA* 1: 33-56
Mattingly, D. J. (1988b) 'Olea mediterranea?' *JRA* 1: 153-61
Mattingly, D. J. (1993) 'Understanding Roman landscapes', *JRA* 6: 359-66
Meiggs, R. (1960) *Roman Ostia*. Oxford
Merrill, E. T. (1903) 'Notes on Pliny's letters', *CR* 17: 52-5
Michel, J. H. (1962) *La gratuité en droit romain*. Brussels
Mickwitz, G. (1936) *Die Kartellfunktion der Zünfte und ihre Bedeutung bei der Entstehung des Zunftwesens: eine Studie in spätantiker und mittelalterlicher Wirtschaftsgeschichte*. Helsinki
Migeotte, L. (1991) 'Le pain quotidien dans les cités hellénistiques: à propos des fonds permanents pour l'approvisionnement en grain', *Cahiers du Centre G. Glotz* 2: 19-41
Mitteis, L. and Wilcken, U. (1912) *Grundzüge und Chrestomathie der Papyruskunde*, vol. 1, 2. Leipzig and Berlin

Mócsy, A. (1974) *Pannonia and Upper Moesia: a history of the middle Danube provinces of the Roman empire*. London
Moeller, W. O. (1976) *The wool trade of ancient Pompeii*, Leiden
Mohler, S. L. (1931) 'The cliens in the time of Martial', in G. D. Hadzsits, ed., *Classical studies in honor of J. C. Rolfe*. Philadelphia, 239–64
Möller, C. (1993) 'Die mercennarii in der römischen Arbeitswelt', *ZRG* 110: 296–330
Mommsen, T. (1888) *Römisches Staatsrecht*, vol. 2. Leipzig
Moritz, L. (1958) *Grain mills and flour in classical antiquity*. Oxford
Morley, N. (1996) *Metropolis and hinterland: the city of Rome and the Italian economy 200 BC–AD 200*. Cambridge
Morris, I. (1992) *Death-ritual and social structure in classical antiquity*. Cambridge
Morris, I. (1994) 'The Athenian economy twenty years after *The ancient economy*', *CPh* 89: 351–66
Morris, J. (1964) 'Leges annales under the Principate', *LF* 12: 316–37
Mossé, C. (1966) *Le travail en Grèce et à Rome*. Paris
Mouritsen, H. (1988) *Elections, magistrates and municipal élite: studies in Pompeian epigraphy*. Rome.
Mouritsen, H. (1990) 'A note on Pompeian epigraphy and social structure', *C&M* 41: 131–49
Mrocewicz, L. (1989) *Arystokracja municypalna w rzymskich prowincjach nad Renem i Dunajem w okresie wczesnego cesarstwa*. Posen
Mrozek, S. (1977) 'Die Goldbergwerke in römischen Dazien', in *ANRW* II.6, 95–109
Mrozek, S. (1989) *Lohnarbeit im klassischen Altertum: ein Beitrag zur Sozial- und Wirtschaftsgeschichte*. Bonn
Murga, J. L. (1975) 'Sobre una nueva calificación del "aedificium" por obra la legislación urbanística imperial', *Iura* 26: 41–78
Murga, J. L. (1976a) *Protección a la estética en la legislación urbanística del Alto Impero*. Seville
Murga, J. L. (1976b) 'El senado consulto aciliano: *ea quae iuncto sunt aedibus legari non possunt*', *BIDR* 18: 155–92
Murra, J. V. (1972) 'El "control vertical" de un maximo de pisos ecologicos en la economia de las sociedades andinas', in *Visita de la provincia de Leon de Huanuco en 1562*, vol. 2. Huanuco, 429–76
Murra, J. V. (1975) *Formaciones economicas y politicas andinas*. Lima
Nathan, H. and Haas, N. (1966) 'Cribra orbitalia: a bone condition of the orbit of unknown nature: anatomical study with etiological considerations', *Israel Journal of Medical Sciences* 2,2: 171–91
Nations, M. and Rebhun, L.-A. (1988) 'Angels with wet wings can't fly: maternal sentiment in Brazil and the image of neglect', *Culture, Medicine, and Psychiatry* 1: 141–200
Neesen, L. (1981) 'Die Entwicklung der Leistungen und Ämter (munera et honores) im römischen Kaiserreich des zweiten bis vierten Jahrhunderts', *Historia* 30: 203–35

Néraudau, J.-P. (1984) *Etre enfant à Rome*. Paris
Néraudau, J.-P. (1987) 'La loi, la coutume et le chagrin – réflexions sur la mort des enfants', in F. Hinard, ed., *La mort, les morts et l'au-delà dans le monde romain*. Caen, 195–208
Netting, R. McC. (1972) 'Of men and meadows: strategies in Alpine land use', *Anthropological Quarterly* 45: 132–44
Netting, R. McC. (1982) *Balancing on an alp: ecological change and continuity in a Swiss mountain community*. Cambridge
Newman, L., ed. (1990) *Hunger in history: food shortage, poverty and deprivation*. Oxford
Nicolet, C. (1977) *Rome et la conquête du monde méditerranéen 264–77 av. J.C., I: les structures de l'Italie romaine*. Paris
Nicols, J. (1988), 'On the standard size of the ordo decurionum', *ZRG* 105: 712–9
Noè, E. (1974) 'La produzione tessile nella Gallia cisalpina in età romana', *RIL* 108: 918–32
Noonan, T. S. (1973) 'The grain trade of the northern Black Sea in antiquity', *AJPh* 94: 231–42
Nörr, D. (1965) 'Origo', *RE Suppl.* 10: 433–73
Nörr, D. (1965) 'Zur sozialen und rechtlichen Bewertung der freien Arbeit in Rom', *ZRG* 82, 67–105
Nutton, V. (1971) 'Two notes on immunities: *Digest* 27,1,6,10 and 11', *JRS* 61: 52–63
Nutton, V. (1995) 'Galen and the traveller's fare', in Wilkins, Harvey and Dobson, eds. (1995), 359–70
Ober, J. (1985) *Fortress Attica: defense of the Athenian land frontier 404–322 BC*. Leiden
O'Grada, C. (1988) *Ireland before and after the famine: explorations in economic history, 1800–1925*. Manchester
Olck, F. (1899) 'Bohne', *RE* 3: 609–27
Oliver, G. J. (1995) 'The Athenian state under threat: politics and food supply, 307 to 229 BC', unpublished D.Phil. thesis, University of Oxford
Orlove, B. S. (1980) 'Ecological anthropology', *Annual Review of Anthropology* 9: 235–73
Ortner, D. J. and Putschar, W. G. J. (1981) *Identification of pathological conditions in human skeletal remains*. Washington DC
Osborne, R. G. (1982) 'Rural structure and the classical polis: town-country relations in Athenian society', unpublished PhD thesis, University of Cambridge
Osborne, R. (1985) *Demos: the discovery of classical Attika*. Oxford
Osborne, R. (1987) *Classical landscape with figures: the ancient Greek city and its countryside*. London
Osborne, R. (1995) 'The economics and politics of slavery at Athens', in A. Powell, ed., *The Greek world*. London and New York, 27–43
Ostrogorsky, G. (1966) 'Agrarian conditions in the Byzantine empire in the Middle Ages', in *The Cambridge economic history of Europe*, vol. 1, 2nd edn. Cambridge, 205–34

Overbeck, J. (1875) *Pompeji in seinen Gebäuden, Alterthümern und Kunstwerken*. 3rd edn. Leipzig
Owens, E. J. (1983) 'The koprologoi at Athens in the fifth and fourth centuries BC', *CQ* 33: 44–50
Packer, J. E. (1971) *The insulae of imperial Ostia*. Rome
Pal, B. P. (1966) *Wheat*. New Delhi
Pallottino, M. (1970–71) 'La città etrusco-italica come premessa alla città romana: varietà di sostrati formativi e tendenze di sviluppo unitario', *AttiCSDIR* 3: 11–22
Panella, C. (1973) 'Appunti su un gruppo di anfore della prima, media e tarda età imperiale', in *Ostia III. Studi miscellanei*, vol. 21. Rome, 463–633
Panella, C. (1981) 'La distribuzione e i mercati', in Giardina and Schiavone, eds. (1981), vol. 2: 55–80
Pani, M. (1977) 'Su un nuovo cippo graccana dauno', *RIL* 111: 389–400
Panitschek, P. (1990) 'Der spätantike Kolonat: ein Substitut für die "Halbfreiheit" peregriner Rechtssetzungen?', *ZRG* 107: 137–54
Parker, R. (1983) *Miasma: pollution and purification in early Greek religion*. Oxford
Parkin, T. G. (1992) *Demography and Roman society*. Baltimore and London
Parsons, J. J. (1962) 'The acorn-hog economy of the oak woodlands of southwestern Spain', *Geographical Review* 52: 211–35
Pasquinucci, M. (1979) 'La transumanza nell'Italia romana', in E. Gabba and M. Pasquinucci, (1979) 79–182
Pasquinucci, M. (1984) 'Aspetti dell'allevamento transumante nell'Italia centro-meridionale adriatica', in *Sannio: Pentri e Frentani dal VI al I sec. a.C. Atti del convegno Campobasso, 10–11 novembre 1980*. Matrice, 99–102
Pate, D. and Brown, K. A. (1985) 'The stability of bone strontium in the geochemical environment', *Journal of Human Evolution* 14: 483–91
Patlagean, E. (1977) *Pauvreté économique et pauvreté sociale à Byzance, 4e–7e siècles*. Paris
Patterson, C. (1981) *Pericles' citizenship law of 451–50*. New York
Patterson, C. (1985) '"Not worth the rearing": the causes of infant exposure in ancient Greece', *TAPhA* 115: 103–23
Patterson, J. R. (1985) 'The Upper Volturno valley in Roman times', in R. Hodges and J. Mitchell, eds., *San Vicenzo al Volturno: the Archaeology, art and territory of an early medieval monastery*. Oxford, 213–26
Patterson, J. R. (1987) 'Crisis: what crisis? Rural change and urban development in imperial Apennine Italy', *PBSR* 55: 115–46
Paul, A. A. et al. (1988) 'Breastmilk intake and growth in infants from two to ten months', *Journal of Human Nutrition and Dietetics* 1: 437–50
Payne, S. (1985) 'Zoo-archaeology in Greece: a reader's guide', in N. C. Wilkie and W. D. E. Coulson, eds., *Contributions to Aegean archaeology: studies in honor of W. A. McDonald*. Minneapolis, 211–44
Peacock, D. P. S. and Williams, D. F. (1986) *Amphorae and the Roman economy*. Edinburgh

Pearse, L. (1974) 'The organization of Roman building during the late Republic and early empire', unpub. PhD thesis, University of Cambridge
Pellett, P. L. and Shadarevian, S. (1970) *Food composition tables for use in the Middle East*. Beirut
Persson, A. W. (1923) *Staat und Manufaktur im römischen Reich*. Lund
Philippson, A. (1892) *Der Peloponnes*. Berlin
Philippson, A. (1952) *Die griechischen Landschaften*, vols. 1,3. Frankfurt
Phillips, E. J. (1973) 'The Roman law on the demolition of buildings', *Latomus* 32: 86–95
Piganiol, A. (1965) 'La politique agraire d'Hadrien', in *Les empereurs romains d'Espagne*. Paris, 135–46
Pleket, H. W. (1971) 'Sociale stratificatie en sociale mobiliteit in de Romeinse keizertijd', *Tijdschrift voor Geschiedenis* 84: 215–51
Pleket, H. W. (1983) 'Urban elites and business in the Greek part of the Roman empire', in P. Garnsey, K. Hopkins and C. R. Whittaker, eds., *Trade in the ancient economy*. Cambridge. 131–44
Pleket, H. W. (1990) 'Wirtschaft', in Vittinghoff, ed. (1990), 25–160
Pleket, H. W. (1993) 'Agriculture in the Roman empire in comparative perspective', in Sancisi-Weerdenburg et al., eds. (1993), 317–42
Pollock, L. A. (1983) *Forgotten children: parent-child relations from 1500 to 1900*. Cambridge
Pollock, L. A. (1987) *A lasting relationship: parents and children over three centuries*. London
Ponsich, M. and Tarradell, M. (1965) *Garum et industries antiques de salaison dans la Méditerranée occidentale*. Paris
Postan, M. M. (1954) *The famulus: the estate labourer in the XIIth and XIIIth centuries*. Cambridge
Potter, T. W. (1979) *The changing landscape of south Etruria*. London
Potter, T. W. (1987) *Roman Italy*. London
Powell, A. (1988) *Athens and Sparta: constructing Greek political and social history from 478 BC*. London
Pucci, G. (1973) 'La produzione della ceramica aretina: note sull' "industria" nella prima età imperiale romana', *DArch* 7: 255–93
Pucci, G. (1976–7) 'Considerazioni sull'articolo di J. Andreau, "Remarques sur la société pompéienne (à propos des tablettes de L. Caecilius Iucundus)"', *DArch* 9–10: 631–47
Pugliese, G. (1957) 'In tema di "actio exercitoria"', *Labeo* 3: 308–43
Pullan, B. (1978) 'Poveri, mendicanti e vagabondi, secoli XIV–XVII', in *Storia d'Italia: Annali I: dal feudalismo al capitalismo*. Turin, 981–1047
Purcell, N. (1987) 'Tomb and suburb', in H. von Hesberg and P. Zanker, eds., *Römische Gräberstrassen: Selbstdarstellung-Status-Standard. Kolloquium in München 28.–30. Okt. 1985*. Munich, 25–41
Quaß, F. (1993) *Die Honoratiorenschicht in den Städten des griechischen Ostens: Untersuchungen zur politischen und sozialen Entwicklung in hellenistischer und römischer Zeit*. Stuttgart

BIBLIOGRAPHY

Quézel, P. (1967) 'La végétation des hauts sommets du Pinde et de l'Olympe de Thessalie', *Vegetatio* 14: 127-227
Rachet, M. (1970) *Rome et les Berbères: un problème militaire d'Auguste à Dioclétien*. Brussels
Rainer, W. (1987) *Bau- und nachbarrechtliche Bestimmungen im klassischen römischen Recht*. Graz
Rasmussen, T. (1991) 'Tuscania and its territory', in Barker and Lloyd, eds. (1991), 106-14
Rathbone, D. W. (1981) 'The development of agriculture in the 'Ager Cosanus' during the Roman Republic: problems of evidence and interpretation', *JRS* 71: 10-23
Rathbone, D. (1991) *Economic rationalism and rural society in third-century AD Egypt: the Heroninos archive and the Appianus estate*. Cambridge
Rathbun, T. A. (1984) 'Skeletal pathology from the paleolithic through the metal ages in Iran and Iraq', in M. N. Cohen and G. J. Armelagos, eds., *Paleopathology at the origins of agriculture*. Orlando, 137-67
Ravis-Giordani, G. (1983) *Bergers corses: les communautés villageoises du Niolu*. Aix-en-Provence
Rawson, B. (1991) 'Adult-child relationships in Roman society', in B. Rawson, ed., *Marriage, divorce, and children in ancient Rome*. Oxford, 7-30
Reinhold, J. G. (1971) 'High phytate content of rural Iranian bread: a possible cause of human zinc deficiency', *American Journal of Clinical Nutrition* 24: 1204-6
Renfrew, C. and Wagstaff, M., eds. (1982) *An island polity: the archaeology of exploitation in Melos*. Cambridge
Renfrew, J. (1973) *Palaeoethnobotany*. New York
Reynolds, J. M. (1969) 'Q. Otacilius Pollinus of Aventicum', *Bulletin de l'association pro Aventico* 20: 53-7
Reynolds, S. (1977) *An introduction to the history of English medieval towns*. Oxford
Rhoades, R. E. and Thompson, S. I. (1975) 'Adaptive strategies in alpine environments: beyond ecological particularism', *American Ethnologist* 2: 535-51
Rhodes, P. J. (1981) *A commentary on the Aristotelian* Athenaion Politeia. Oxford
Rhodes, P. J. (1993) *A commentary on the Aristotelian* Athenaion Politeia. 2nd edn. Oxford
Rickman, G. R. (1980) *The corn supply of ancient Rome*. Oxford
Rink, B. (1993) 'Sklavenfreilassungen in der späten römischen Republik als Beispiel für soziale Mobilität', *Laverna* 4 (1993) 45-54
Robertis, F. M. de (1955) *Il fenomeno associativo nel mondo romano: dai collegi della repubblica alle corporazioni del basso impero*. Naples
Robertis, F. M. de (1963) *Lavoro e lavoratori nel mondo romano*. Bavi
Rodriguez-Almeida, E. (1984) *Il Monte Testaccio*. Rome
Romanelli, P. (1929) 'Brevi note sulla distribuzione della piccola e grande proprietà agricola nell'Africa romana', in *Atti del I° congresso nazionale di studi romani*, vol. 1. Rome: 341-8

Rosafio, P. (1991) 'Studies in the Roman colonate', unpublished PhD thesis, Cambridge
Rostovtzeff, M. (1957) *The social and economic history of the Roman empire.* 2nd edn. Oxford
Rousselle, A. (1983) *Porneia: de la maîtrise du corps à la privation sensorielle, IIe-IVe siècles de l'ère chrétienne.* Paris
Rowland, M. G. M. (1986) 'The weanling's dilemma: are we making progress?', in Wharton, ed. (1986), 33-42
Rowland, R. J. (1982) 'The Sardinian Condaghi: neglected evidence for medieval sex ratios', *Florilegium* 4: 117-22
Roy, J. (1988) 'Demosthenes 55 as evidence for isolated farmsteads in classical Athens', *LCM* 13, 57-60
Ruggini, L. (1961) *Economia e società nell'Italia annonaria: rapporti fra agricoltura e commercio del IV e VI secolo d.C.* Milan
Rupprecht, G. (1975) *Untersuchungen zum Dekurionenstand in den nordwestlichen Provinzen des römischen Reiches.* Kallmünz
Ruschenbusch, E. (1988) 'Getreideerträge in Griechenland in der Zeit von 1921 bis 1938 n. Chr. als Maßstab für die Antike', *ZPE* 72: 141-53
Russi, A. (1986) 'I pastori e l'esposizione degli infanti nella tarda legislazione imperiale e nei documenti epigrafici', *MEFRA* 98: 855-72
Ste. Croix, G. E. M. de (1966) 'The estate of Phaenippus (Ps.-Dem. XLII)', in E. Badian, ed., *Ancient society and institutions: studies presented to Victor Ehrenberg.* Oxford, 109-14
Ste. Croix, G. E. M. de (1972) *The origins of the Peloponnesian War.* London
Ste. Croix, G. E. M. de (1981) *The class struggle in the ancient Greek world from the archaic age to the Arab conquests.* London
Sallares, R. (1991) *The ecology of the ancient Greek world.* London
Saller, R. P. (1994) *Patriarchy, property and death in the Roman family.* Cambridge
Saller, R. P. and Shaw, B. D. (1984) 'Tombstones and Roman family relations in the Principate: civilians, soldiers and slaves', *JRS* 74: 124-56
Salmon, E. T. (1967) *Samnium and the Samnites.* Cambridge
Salmon, E. T. (1969) *Roman colonization under the Republic.* London
Salomon, N. (1995) 'Atene e Lemno: ricerche sulle cleruchie ateniensi', unpublished dissertation, Pisa
Salvioli, G. (1906) *Le capitalisme dans le monde antique.* Paris
Salzman, L. F. (1952) *Building in England down to 1540: a documentary history.* Oxford
Sancisi-Weerdenburg, H. et al., eds. (1993) *De agricultura: in memoriam Pieter Willem de Neeve (1945-1990).* Amsterdam
Sander, E. (1958) 'Das Recht des römischen Soldaten', *RhM* 101: 152-234
Sargenti, M. (1982) 'La disciplina urbanistica a Roma nella normativa di età tardo-repubblicana e imperiale', in *Plinio il vecchio sotto il profilo storico letterario.* Como, 265-84
Sarpaki, A. (1992) 'The palaeoethnobotanical approach: the Mediterranean triad or is it a quartet?', in B. Wells, ed., *Agriculture in ancient Greece:*

proceedings of the seventh international symposium at the Swedish Institute at Athens, 16-17 May, 1990. Goteborg, 61-76
Sartori, F. (1967-8) 'I confini del territorio di *Comum* in età romana', *AttiCSDIR* 1: 273-290
Sartori, F. (1970-1) 'Città e amministrazione locale in Italia meridionale: Magna Graecia', *AttiCSDIR* 3: 43-60
Sarrain, M. et al. (1969) 'Zinc nutrition in human pregnancy in Fars province, Iran', *American Journal of Clinical Nutrition* 22: 726-32
Schama, S. (1987) *The embarrassment of riches: an interpretation of Dutch culture in the Golden Age*. London
Scheidel, W. (1989) 'Zur Lohnarbeit bei Columella', *Tyche* 4: 139-46
Scheidel, W. (1990) 'Quasikolonen bei Vergil?', *Klio* 72, 166-72
Scheidel, W. (1992a) '*Coloni* und Pächter in den römischen literarischen Quellen vom 2. Jh. v. Chr. bis zur Severerzeit: eine kritische Betrachtung (*Colonus*-Studien I)', *Athenaeum* 80: 331-70
Scheidel, W. (1992b) 'Neuen Wein in leere Schläuche: Jongman's Pompeii, Modelle und die kampanische Landwirtschaft', *Athenaeum* 80: 207-13
Scheidel, W. (1993a) 'Pächter und Grundpacht bei Columella (*Colonus*-Studien II)', *Athenaeum* 81: 391-439
Scheidel, W. (1993b) 'Sklaven und Freigelassene als Pächter und ihre ökonomische Funktion in der römischen Landwirtschaft (*Colonus*-Studien III)', in Sancisi-Weerdenburg et al., eds. (1993), 182-96
Scheidel, W. (1994a) *Grundpacht und Lohnarbeit in der Landwirtschaft des römischen Italien*. Frankfurt a. M.
Scheidel, W. (1994b) 'Libitina's bitter gains: seasonal mortality and endemic disease in the ancient city of Rome', *AncSoc* 25: 151-75
Scheidel, W. (1996a) *Measuring sex, age and death in the Roman empire: explorations in ancient demography*. Ann Arbor
Scheidel, W. (1996b) 'Instrumentum vocale: Bauern und Sklaven in der römischen Landwirtschaft', *Historicum* 47: 23-9
Scheidel, W. (1997) 'Quantifying the sources of slaves in the early Roman empire', *JRS* 87 (in press)
Scheidel, W. (forthcoming) 'Death and renewal in a Roman municipal élite: the *album* of Canusium reconsidered'
Scheper-Hughes, N. (1985) 'Culture, scarcity and maternal thinking: maternal detachment and infant survival in a Brazilian shantytown', *Ethos* 13: 291-317
Scheper-Hughes, N. (1992) *Death without weeping: the violence of everyday life in Brazil*. Berkeley, Los Angeles and London
Schiller, A. A. (1971) 'The business relations of patron and freedman in Roman law' (1935), in id., *An American experience in Roman law*. Göttingen, 24-40
Schoeniger, M. J. (1985) 'Tropic level effects on 15 N/14 N and 13 C/12 C ratios in bone collagen and strontium levels in bone material', *Journal of Human Evolution* 14: 515-25
Schoeniger, M. J., Tauber, H., and de Niro, M. J. (1983) 'Stable nitrogen isotope ratios of bone collagen reflect marine and terrestrial components of prehistoric human diet', *Science* 220: 1381-3

Schofield, S. (1979) *Development and the problem of village nutrition*. London
Schtajerman, E. M. (1964) *Die Krise der Sklavenhalterordnung im Westen des römischen Reiches*. Berlin
Schulze-Oben, H. (1989) *Freigelassene in den Städten des römischen Hispanien: juristische, wirtschaftliche und soziale Stellung nach dem Zeugnis der Inschriften*. Bonn
Scobie, A. (1987) 'Slums, sanitation and mortality in the Roman world', *Klio* 68: 399–433
Scramuzza, V. A. (1940) *The emperor Claudius*. Cambridge
Scrimshaw, N., Taylor, C. E. and Gordon, J. E. (1968) *Interactions of nutrition and infection*. Geneva
Scrimshaw, S. C. M. (1983) 'Infanticide as deliberate fertility control', in R. Bulatao and R. Lee, eds., *Determinants of fertility in developing countries, 2: fertility regulation and institutional influences*. New York, 245–66
Scullard, H. H. (1967) *The Etruscan cities and Rome*. London
Seavoy, R. E. (1986) *Famine in peasant societies*. New York, Westport and London
Sekunda, N. V. (1992) 'Athenian demography and military strength 338–322 BC', *BSA* 87: 311–55
Sen, A. (1981) *Poverty and famines: an essay on entitlement and deprivation*. Oxford
Serrano Delgado, J. M. (1988) *Status y promoción social de los libertos en Hispania Romana*. Seville
Shack, W. A. (1978) 'Anthropology and the diet of man', in J. Yudkin, ed., *Diet of man: needs and wants*. London, 261–80
Shaw, B. D. (1983) 'Soldiers and society: the Army in Numidia', *Opus* 2,1: 133–60
Shaw, B. D. (1996) 'Seasons of death: aspects of mortality in imperial Rome', *JRS* 86: 100–38
Shepherd, G. (1989) 'Food as symbol: beans', in Garnsey, ed. (1989), 148–59
Sherwin-White, A. N. (1966) *The letters of Pliny: a historical and social commentary*. Oxford
Shorter, E. (1976) *The making of the modern family*. London
Sillen, A. and Kavanagh, M. (1982) 'Strontium and paleodietary research', *Yearbook of Physical Anthropology* 25: 67–90
Silverman, S. F. (1968) 'Agricultural organisation, social structure, and values in Italy: amoral familism reconsidered', *American Anthropologist* 70: 1–20
Silverman, S. F. (1975) *Three bells of civilization: the life of an Italian hill town*. New York
Silvestrini, M. (1990) 'Aspetti della municipalità di Canusium: l'albo dei decurioni', *MEFRA* 102: 595–602
Simmonds, D. H. (1981) 'Wheat proteins, their chemistry and nutritional potential', in L. T. Evans and W. J. Peacock, eds., *Wheat science: today and tomorrow*. Cambridge, 149–66
Sippel, D. V. (1988) 'Dietary deficiency among the lower classes of the late Republican and early imperial Rome', *AncW* 16: 47–54

Sirks, B. (1991) *Food for Rome: the legal structure of the transportation and processing of supplies for the imperial distributions in Rome and Constantinople.* Amsterdam

Sirks, B. (1993) 'Reconsidering the Roman colonate', *ZRG* 110: 331-69

Skydsgaard, J. E. (1974) 'Transhumance in ancient Italy', *ARID* 7: 7-36

Skydsgaard, J. E. (1976) 'The disintegration of the Roman labour market and the clientela theory', in *Studia romana in honorem Petri Krarup septuagenarii.* Odense, 44-8

Skydsgaard, J. E. (1987) 'L'agricoltura greca e romana: tradizioni e confronto', *ARID* 16: 7-24

Skydsgaard, J. E. (1988) 'Transhumance in ancient Greece', in Whittaker, ed. (1988), 75-86

Small, A. M., ed. (1977) *Monte Irsi, southern Italy.* Oxford

Small, A. (1991) 'Late Roman rural settlement in Basilicata and western Apulia', in Barker and Lloyd, eds. (1991), 204-22

Smith, P., Bloom, R. A. and Berkowitz, J. (1984) 'Diachronic trends in humerical cortical thickness of near eastern populations', *Journal of Human Evolution* 13: 603-11

Smith, P. and Peretz, B. (1986) 'Hypoplasia and health status: a comparison of two lifestyles', *Human Evolution* 1: 1-10

Smutny, R. J. (1951) 'The sources of Cicero's income', *CW* 45: 49-56

Solin, H. (1971) *Beiträge zur Kenntnis der griechischen Personennamen in Rom.* Helsinki

Sperduti, A. (1995) 'I resti scheletrici umani della necropoli di età romano–imperiale di Isola Sacra (I–III sec. d. C.): analisi paleodemografica'. Unpublished dissertation, Rome

Spitzl, T. (1984) *Lex municipii Malacitani.* Munich

Sprengel, U. (1971) *Die Wanderherdenwirtschaft im mittel-und südostitalienischen Raum.* Marburg

Spurr, M. S. (1986) *Arable cultivation in Roman Italy c.200 BC–AD 100.* London

Staerman, E. M. (1969) *Die Blütezeit der Sklavenwirtschaft in der römischen Republik.* Wiesbaden

Staerman, E. M. and Trofimova, M. K. (1975) *La schiavitù nell'Italia imperiale I–III secolo.* Rome

Stahl, M. (1978) *Imperiale Herrschaft und provinziale Stadt: Strukturprobleme der römischen Reichsorganisation im 1.-3. Jh. der Kaiserzeit.* Göttingen

Starr, C. G. (1941) *The Roman imperial navy.* Ithaca, NY

Starr, C. G. (1977) *The economic and social growth of early Greece, 800–500 BC.* New York

Stazio, A. (1968) 'La documentazione archaeologica in Puglia', in *La città e il suo territorio: Atti del settimo convegno di studi sulla Magna Graecia, Taranto, Ottobre 1967.* Naples, 265-86

Stein, P. (1959) 'The mutual agency of partners in the civil law', *Tulane Law Review* 33: 595-606

Still, G. F. (1931) *The history of pediatrics.* London

Stini, W. A. (1985) 'Growth rates and sexual dimorphism in evolutionary perspective', in Gilbert and Mielke, eds. (1985), 191–226
Stone, L. (1977) *The family, sex and marriage in England 1500–1800*. London
Strack, M. L. (1914) 'Die Freigelassenen in ihrer Bedeutung für die Gesellschaft der Alten', *HZ* 112, 1–28
Stroud, R. S. (forthcoming) *An Athenian law on the grain-tax in the islands*
Svoronos, N. (1976) 'Remarques sur les structures économiques de l'empire byzantin au XIe siècle', *Travaux et mémoires* 6: 49–67
Syme, R. (1951) 'Tacfarinas, the Musulamii and Thubursicu', in P. R. Coleman-Norton, ed., *Studies in Roman economic and social history in honor of A. C. Johnson*. Princeton, 113–30
Tate, G. (1989) 'Les campagnes de la Syrie du Nord à l'époque protobyzantine', in C. Morrison and J. Lefort, eds., *Hommes et richesses dans l'antiquité byzantine*. Paris, 63–77
Tausend, K. (1989) 'Die Reformen Solons und der attische Handel', *MBAH* 8, 2: 1–9
Taylor, L. R. (1924) '*Seviri Equitum Romanorum* and municipal *Seviri*: a study in pre-military training among the Romans', *JRS* 14: 158–71
Taylor, L. R. (1960) *The voting districts of the Roman republic*. Rome
Tchalenko, G. (1953) *Villages antiques de la Syrie du nord*, vols. 1–3. Paris
Tchernia, A. (1980) 'Quelques remarques sur le commerce du vin et les amphores', in J. H. D'Arms and E. C. Kopff, eds., *The seaborne commerce of ancient Rome: studies in archaeology and history*. Rome, 305–12
Tchernia, A. (1986) *Le vin de l'Italie romaine: essai d'histoire économique d'après les amphores*. Paris
Thomas, K. (1971) *Religion and the decline of magic: studies in popular belief in sixteenth- and seventeenth-century England*. London
Thompson, J. S. (1989) 'Transhumant and sedentary sheep-raising in Roman Italy, 200 BC–AD 200', unpublished PhD thesis, University of Cambridge
Thylander, H. (1952) *Etude sur l'épigraphie latine*. Lund
Thylefors, B. (1987) 'A simplified methodology for the assessment of blindness and its main causes', *World Health Statistics Quarterly* 40,2: 129–41
Tibiletti, G. (1955) 'Il sviluppo del latifondo in Italia dall'epoca graccana al principio del impero', *Relazioni del X congresso internazionale di scienze storiche*, vol. 2. Rome, 237–92
Tibiletti, G. (1967) 'Mediolanum e le città vicine', *Notizie chiostro del Monasterio Maggiore* 1
Tittarelli, L. (1985) 'Gli esposti all'Ospedale di S. Maria della Misericordia in Perugia nei secoli XVIII e XIX', *Bollettino della deputazione di storia patria per l'Umbria* 82: 23–130
Toots, J. and Voorhies, M. R. (1965) 'Strontium in fossile bones and the reconstruction of food chains', *Science* 149: 854–5
Topolski, J. (1981) 'Les études sur les rendements du grain en tant que facteur de l'analyse de la croissance économique (remarques méthodologiques)', in S. Mariotti, ed., *Produttività e tecnologie nei secoli XII–XVII: Istituto inter-*

nazionale di storia economica 'F. Datini' Prato, Atti della 'terza settimana di studio' (23 aprile – 29 aprile 1971). Florence, 77–88
Topping, P. (1977) *Studies in Latin Greece AD1205–1715*. London.
Torelli, M. (1970–71) 'Contributo dell'archeologia alla storia sociale: 1 – L'Etruria e l'Apulia', *DArch* 4–5: 431–42
Torelli, M. (1976) 'La situazione in Etruria', in P. Zanker, ed., *Hellenismus in Mittelitalien*. Göttingen, 97–110
Toynbee, A. J. (1965) *Hannibal's legacy: the Hannibalic war's effect on Roman life*, vols. 1–2. Oxford
Toynbee, A. (1973) *Constantine Porphyrogenitus and his world*. London
Tozzi, P. (1972) *Storia padana antica: il territorio fra Adda e Mincio*. Milan
Treggiari, S. M. (1969) *Roman freedmen during the late Republic*. Oxford
Treggiari, S. M. (1980) 'Urban labour in Rome: *mercennarii* and *tabernarii*', in Garnsey, ed. (1980), 48–64
Trexler, R. (1973a) 'Infanticide in Florence: new sources and first results', *History of Childhood Quarterly* 1: 98–116
Trexler, R. (1973b) 'The foundlings of Florence, 1395–1455', *History of Childhood Quarterly* 1: 259–84
Trotter, M. and Glaser, G. C. (1958) 'A reevaluation of estimation of stature based on measurements of stature taken during life and of long bones after death', *American Journal of Physical Anthropology* 16: 79–124
Trousset, P. (1977) 'Nouvelles observations sur la centuriation romaine à l'est d'El Jem', *AntAfr* 11: 175–207
Ucelli, P. G. (1967–8) 'Iscrizioni sepolcrali di Milano dal I. al IV. secolo d.C. ed il problema della loro datazione', *AttiCSDIR* 1: 107–28
Ulbert, G. (1959) *Die römischen Donau-Kastelle Aislingen und Burghöfe*. Berlin
Vallat, J.-P. (1987) 'Les structures agraires de l'Italie républicaine', *AESC* 42: 181–218
Van Andel, T. H., Runnels, C. N. and Pope, K. O. (1986) 'Five thousand years of land use and abuse in the southern Argolid, Greece', *Hesperia* 55: 103–28
Van Andel, T. H., Zangger, E. and Demitrack, A. (1996) 'Land use and soil erosion in prehistoric and historic Greece', *JFA* 17: 379–96
Van Berchem, D. (1939) *Les distributions de blé et d'argent à la plèbe romaine sous l'empire*. Geneva
Van Dommelen, P. (1993) 'Roman peasants and rural organization in central Italy: an archaeological perspective', in E. Scott, ed., *Theoretical Roman archaeology: first conference proceedings*. Aldershot and Brookfield, Vt, 167–86
Van Gennep, A. (1960) *The rites of passage*. London
Van Ossel, P. (1992) *Etablissements ruraux de l'antiquité tardive dans le nord de la Gaule*. Paris
Van Reen, R., ed. (1977) *Idiopathic urinary bladder stone disease*. Washington DC
Van Zeist, M. and Casparie, W. (1984) *Plants and ancient man*. Rotterdam
Vatin, C. (1976) 'Jardins et services de voirie', *BCH* 100: 555–64

Velkov, V. (1962) 'Les campagnes et la population rurale en Thrace au IVe-VIe siècle', *Byzantino-Bulgarico* 1: 31–66
Vera, D. (1986) 'Forme e funzioni della rendita fondiaria nella tarda antichità', in A. Giardina, ed. (1981), vol. 1, 367–447, 723–60
Vera, D. (1988) 'Aristocrazia romana ed economie provinciali nell'Italia tardoantica: il caso siciliano', *Quaderni Catanesi di Studi Classici e Medievali* 10: 115–72
Vera, D. (1992) 'Conductores domus nostrae, conductores privatorum: concentrazione fondiaria e redistribuzione della ricchezza nell'Africa tardoantica', in: M. Christol et al., eds., *Institutions, société et vie politique dans l'empire romain au IVe siècle ap. J.-C: Actes André Chastagnol (Paris, 20–21 janvier 1989)*. Rome, 465–90
Vera, D. (1992–3) 'Schiavitù rurale e colonato nell'Italia imperiale', *Scienze dell'antichità* 6–7: 291–339
Vera, D. (1994) 'L'Italia agraria nell'età imperiale: fra crisi e trasformazione', in *L'Italie d'Auguste à Dioclétien*. Rome, 239–48
Vernant, J.-P. (1983) *Myth and thought among the Greeks*. London
Veyne, P. (1961) 'Vie de Trimalchion', *AESC* 2: 213–47
Veyne, P. (1991) *La société romaine*. Paris
Virlouvet, C. (1995) *Tessera frumentaria: les procédures de distribution du blé public à Rome à la fin de la République et au début de l'Empire*. Rome
Vita-Finzi, C. (1969) *The Mediterranean valleys: geological changes in historical times*. Cambridge
Vittinghoff, F. (1982) 'Zur Entwicklung der städtischen Selbstverwaltung – einige kritische Anmerkungen', in: id., ed., *Stadt und Herrschaft: Römische Kaiserzeit und Hohes Mittelalter*. Munich, 107–46
Vittinghoff, F., ed. (1990) *Europäische Wirtschafts- und Sozialgeschichte in der römischen Kaiserzeit*. Stuttgart
Wace, A. J. B. and Thompson, M. S. (1914) *The nomads of the Balkans: an account of life and customs among the Vlachs of Northern Pindus*. London
Wagstaff, J. M. (1981) 'Buried assumptions: some problems in the interpretation of the "Younger Fill" raised by recent data from Greece', *JArchSc* 8: 247–64
Walbank, M. B. (1983a) 'Leases of sacred properties in Attica, Part I', *Hesperia* 52: 100–35
Walbank, M. B. (1983b) 'Leases of sacred properties in Attica, Part II', *Hesperia* 52: 177–99
Waldron, T. (1987) 'The potential of analysis of chemical constituents of bone', in A. Boddington, A. N. Garland and R. C. Janaway, eds., *Death, decay and reconstruction: approaches to archaeology and forensic science*. Manchester, 149–59
Waldstein, W. (1986) *Operae libertorum: Untersuchungen zur Dienstpflicht freigelassener Sklaven*. Stuttgart
Walter, J. H. and Schofield, R. (1989) 'Famine, disease and crisis mortality in early modern society', in Walter and Schofield, eds. (1989), 1–74

Walter, J. H. and Schofield, R., eds. (1989) *Famine, disease and the social order in early modern society.* Cambridge
Waltzing, J.-P. (1896) *Etude historique sur les corporations professionelles chez les Romains depuis les origines jusqu'à la chute de l'empire d'occident*, vol. 2. Brussels
Ward-Perkins, J. B. (1970) 'Città e pagus: considerazioni sull'organizzazione primitiva della città nell'Italia centrale', in *Studi sulla città italica preromana: Atti del convegno di studi sulla città etrusca e italica preromana.* Bologna, 293–7
Wasowicz, A. (1968) 'Le problème du rapport et l'aménagement du territoire et du plan de cité', in *La città e il suo territorio: Atti del settimo convegno di studi sulla Magna Graecia, Taranto, Ottobre 1967.* Naples, 195–202
Wasowicz, A. (1969) 'La campagne et les villes du littoral septentrionale du Pont Euxin', *Dacia* 13: 73–100
Watkins, S. C. and Menken, J. (1985) 'Famines in historical perspective', *Population and Development Review* 11: 647–75
Watson, A. (1967) *The law of persons in the later Roman Republic.* Oxford
Webb, C. and Hawtin, G. (1981) *Lentils.* Slough
Weber, V. (1993) 'Die Munizipalaristokratie', in K.-P. Johne, ed., *Gesellschaft und Wirtschaft des Römischen Reiches im 3. Jahrhundert.* Berlin, 245–317
Wells, C. M. (1973) *The German policy of Augustus.* Oxford
Westermann, W. L. (1925) 'Hadrian's decree on renting state domains in Egypt', *JEA*: 165–78
Wharton, B., ed. (1986) *Food for the weanling: proceedings of a Farley Health Products symposium on feeding the older infant and toddler, held 10 December, 1985 at the Royal College of Physicians, London.* Oslo
Whitby, M. (forthcoming) 'The grain trade of Athens in the fourth century BC', in H. Parkins and C. Smith, eds., *Trade, traders and the ancient city.* London and New York
White, K. D. (1970) *Roman farming.* London
White, K. D. (1976) 'Food requirements and food supplies in classical times in relation to the diet of the various classes', *Progress in Food and Nutrition Science* 2: 143–91
White, L. (1962) *Medieval technology and social change.* Oxford
Whitehead, R. G. (1980) 'The better use of food resources for infants and mothers', *Proceedings of the Royal Society in London*, ser. B 209: 59–69
Whitehead, R. and Paul, A. A. (1981) 'Infant growth and human milk requirements: a fresh approach', *Lancet*: 161–3
Whitehead, R. and Paul, A. A. (1988) 'Comparative infant nutrition in man and other animals', in K. Blaxter and I. MacDonald, eds., *Comparative nutrition.* London, 199–213
Whitehead, R., Paul, A. A. and Cole, T. J. (1982) 'How much breast milk do babies need?', *Acta Paediatrica Scandinavica*, suppl. 299: 43–50
Whitehead, R., Paul, A. A. and Cole, T. J. (1989) 'Diet and the growth of healthy infants', *Journal of Human Nutrition and Dietetics* 2: 73–84

Whittaker, C. R. (1976) 'Agri deserti', in Finley, ed. (1976), 137–65, 193–200 (repr. in Whittaker (1993a) ch. 3)
Whittaker, C. R. (1978) 'Land and labour in North Africa', *Klio* 60: 331–62 (repr. in Whittaker (1993a) ch. 1)
Whittaker, C. R. (1980) 'Inflation and the economy in the fourth century AD', in C. E. King, ed., *Imperial revenue, expenditure and monetary policy in the fourth century AD*. Oxford, 1–22 (repr. in Whittaker (1993a) ch. 10)
Whittaker, C. R., ed. (1988) *Pastoral economies in classical antiquity*. Cambridge
Whittaker, C. R. (1990) 'The consumer city revisited: the *vicus* and the city', *JRA* 3: 110–18 (repr. in Whittaker (1993a) ch. 8)
Whittaker, C. R. (1993a) *Land, city and trade in the Roman empire*. Aldershot and Brookfield, Vt.
Whittaker, C. R. (1993b) 'The poor', in Giardina, ed. (1993), 272–99 (repr. in Whittaker (1993a) ch. 7)
Whittaker, C. R. (1994) *Frontiers of the Roman empire: a social and economic study*. Baltimore and London
Wickham, C. (1982) *Studi sulla società degli Appennini nell'alto medioevo: contadini, signori e insediamenti nel territorio di Valva (Sulmona)*. Bologna
Wickham, C. (1983) 'Pastoralism and underdevelopment in the early Middle Ages', *Settimane di Studio* 31: 3–53
Wiedemann, T. (1981) *Greek and Roman slavery*. London and Canberra
Wiedemann, T. (1985) 'The regularity of manumission at Rome', *CQ* 35: 162–75
Wiedemann, T. (1989) *Adults and children in the Roman empire*. London
Weigand, G. (1894) *Die Aromunen: ethnographisch-philologisch-historische Untersuchungen über das Volk der sogenannten Makedo-Romanen oder Zinzaren*. Leipzig
Wiesehöfer, J. (1988) 'Zur Ernährung von Säuglingen in der Antike'. Unpublished typescript
Wightman, E. M. (1970) *Roman Trier and the Treveri*. London
Wightman, E. M. (1985) *Gallia Belgica*. London
Wightman, E. M. and Hayes, J. W. (1994a) 'Settlement patterns and society', in Hayes and Martini, eds. (1994), 34–40
Wightman, E. M. and Hayes, J. W. (1994b) 'Society, economy and the environment', in Hayes and Martini, eds. (1994), 41–7
Wilkins, J., Harvey, D. and Dobson, M., eds. (1995) *Food in antiquity*. Exeter
Wilkinson, T. J. (1982) 'The definition of ancient manuring zones by means of extensive sherd sampling techniques', *JFA* 9: 323–33
Wilson, F. H. (1935) 'Studies in the social and economic history of Ostia, Part 1', *PBSR* 13: 41–68
Wilson, R. J. A. (1990) *Sicily under the Roman empire: the archaeology of a Roman province, 36 BC–AD 535*. Warminster
Wing, E. S. and Brown, A. B. (1979) *Paleonutrition: method and theory in prehistoric foodways*. New York
Winnifrith, T. (1983) 'Greeks and Romans', in T. Winnifrith and P. Murray, eds., *Greece old and new*. London, 65–94
Wolff, H. (1982) Review of Rupprecht (1975), *BJ* 182: 665–78

Wood, E. M. (1988) *Peasant-citizen and slave: the foundations of Athenian democracy*. London and New York
Woolf, S. (1986) *The poor in western Europe in the eighteenth and nineteenth centuries*. London
Wrightson, K. (1982a) *English society, 1580–1680*. London
Wrightson, K. (1982b) 'Infanticide in English history', *Criminal Justice History* 1: 1–20
Yavetz, Z. (1958) 'The living conditions of the urban plebs in Republican Rome', *Latomus* 17: 500–17
Yntema, D. (1993) *In search of an ancient countryside: the Amsterdam Free University field survey at Oria province of Brindisi, South Italy (1981–1983)*. Amsterdam
Zimmer, G. (1982) *Römische Berufsdarstellungen*. Berlin
Zoepffel, R. (1988) 'Il contadino nell'antichità', *Annali della Facoltà di Lettere e Filosofia dell'Università di Siena* 9: 1–17
Zohary, D. and Hopf, M. (1988) *Domestication of plants in the Old World*. Oxford
Zurer, P. S. (1983) 'Archaeological chemistry: physical science helps to unravel human history', *Chemical and Engineering News* 61: 26–44

INDEX

(Romans authors and emperors are listed under their most familiar name)

Abruzzi, 170–1, 175
Acraephia, 5
Aecae, 120
aediles, *see* city councillors
P. Aelius Aristides, 11
Aesernia, 123, 130, 170
Africa, North, 13, 86, 94, 97–8, 101–4, 136, 139–40, 144–5, 155–7, 257
ager publicus, 100–1
agrarian laws, 100–1, 118
agriculture, 56–7, 67, 70, 73, 114, 117, 129, 132–3, 135, 138–9, 151–65, 169, 185–93, 196–8, 204–11; *see also* land, tenancy
agri deserti, *see* land (abandoned)
Agrippa, *see* Vipsanius
agronomists, Roman, *see* Cato, Columella, Varro
Alba Fucens, 123
Alexander the Great, 98–9
Alföldy, G., 30–3
Alps, 47–8, 53, 172–3
Altinum, 47
anaemia, 246, 249, 270
Andes, 167, 174–5
Andreau, J., 37–8
Anicius Maximus, 13
L. Annius Secundus, 17
Antioch, 96, 157
Antoninus Pius (emperor), 7, 10
M. Antonius Priscus, 17
Apulia, 47–8, 111, 114, 119–20, 171–2
Aquileia, 47, 51, 62, 99–100
aristocracy, *see* city councillors, landowners, senate
Arretium, 39, 41, 48, 146–7
Aristotle, 92, 217, 256
army, 55, 93–4, 102, 105

Arpi, 119
artisans, 28, 35–6, 51–2, 77–87, 145–8, 150, 227, 287
Asculum, 120
Asia/Asia Minor, 14, 86, 96, 99, 282–3, 289
Ateii (gens), 41
Athens/Attica, 5, 91–4, 106, 133, 183–205, 212–13, 215, 217, 222–4, 259, 282; *see also* barley, cereals, climate, consumption, food supply, imports, land, population, wheat, yields
M. Atilius Regulus, 138
Aurelianus (emperor), 241, 243
M. Aurelius (emperor), 7–9, 33, 238
Augustus (emperor), 16, 29, 43, 52–3, 102, 108, 116–17, 167, 239, 241
Aventicum, 53

bakers, 54, 69, 236–8
Balkans, 160, 169, 171, 177
Bangladesh, 281
barley, 168, 184–9, 192–3, 201–5, 222–4, 229–30, 233–4
bean, 211, 214–25, 242
Bengal, 273, 281, 290
Beneventum, 170
Biferno valley, 109–10, 129, 171
Bithynia, 4–6, 13, 16–17
Black Sea region, 184, 195, 199
bladder stone, 246–7
Bologna, *see* Bononia
Bononia, 99, 127
Bosporan kings/kingdom, 184, 193–4
Bradford, J., 114
Brazil, 271
bread, 229–30, 237–8, 241

INDEX

breast milk, 263–6
Brescia, 128
bricks, 39
Britain, 160, 162–3
Buckler, W. K., 78–9, 81
builders, 39, 64, 77–87, 146
burials, 245

Cadiz, *see* Gades
C. Caecilius Isidorus, 29
Caecilius Iucundus, 37
Caesar, *see* Iulius
Caligula (emperor), 241
Callistratus (jurist), 6, 12, 83
Campania, 41, 112, 117–19, 122
Canusium, 17–27
Capena, 116
capital, *see* investment
Capua, 117–18, 127
Caracalla (emperor), 11
Carcopino, J., 66–7
cash crops, *see* olive, wine
Catiline, *see* Sergius
Cato, 138, 143–5, 236–7, 242
cattle, 47, 173
Celts, 57–8, 60, 127–8
centonarii, 50–2, 55, 58, 60–1
centuriation, 101–2, 111, 114, 120, 128
cereals, 51, 138, 168, 184, 221–2, 227–8, 239, 267, 275–6; *see also* barley, grain, wheat
cheese, 175
chickpea, 242
children, 233, 238–9, 246, 248, 253–71; attitude toward, 254–5, 257, 260, 269, 271; birth of, 258–9; commemoration of, 257; death/mortality of, 246, 254–5, 256–8, 265, 270–1; examination of, 259–60; exposure of, 255, 259, 261; feeding of, 263–9; killing of, 259; naming of, 258; newborn, 256–61; swaddling of, 262–3; weaning of, 246, 266–9
China, 105, 273, 281, 286
Cicero, 64–8, 118, 135, 145, 239
T. Quinctius Cincinnatus, 138

Cisalpina, Gallia, 45–6, 51, 128
cities, 3–87 *passim*, 116–19, 123, 145; 'agro towns', 112–14, 131–2; liturgies, 6–12, 25; territory of, 55, 123, 125, 128, 157, 186; rents, 63, 65–6, 68, 71; size of, 123; urban property, 63–76; *see also* city councillors, colonies, urbanization
city councillors, 3–27; in Athens, 5; in Bithynia, 4–6; in Canusium, 17–27; in Clazomenai, 6; decline of, 3–4; aediles, 12; duovirs, 12; fees, 12, 25; in Malaca, 5; in Mediolanum, 56, 58, 60–1; *novitas* of, 20–2, 26; *ordo decurionum*, 19, 25; *pedani*, 23, 26; plebeians as, 23–4, 27; *praetextati*, 20, 22–3, 26; *quinquennalicii*, 19; recruitment of, 4, 7–8, 15–27, 62; stratification among, 6–8, 15, 25, 27; *see also* freedmen
Claudius (emperor), 5, 72–5
Clazomenai, 6
clients, *see* patronage
climate, 168, 173–4, 176, 206, 289–90; of Attica, 189, 193
P. Clodius Pulcher, 237
Cnaeus Pompeius, 16, 22
collegia, 77–87
colonate, 105, 163
colonus, 105, 139–40, 163; *urbanus*, 130; *see also* tenancy
colonies/colonization, 98–102, 111, 118, 120–1, 123–7, 131
Columella, 120, 130, 137, 141, 171, 205
Comum, 53–5
Constantine (emperor), 158
Constantinople, 158–60
consumption/consumers, in Athens, 184, 187, 193; in Rome, 227–8, 236; *see also* food supply
L. Cornelius Sulla, 101
Corsica, 175
Cosa, 131
Crassus, *see* Licinius
Cremona, 123–6, 128
Crete, 14, 242
cribra orbitalia, 249, 270

Cyprus, 210
Cyrrhus, 157

Dalmatia, 30
Damasippus, 64
Danube, 47, 160–1
debt, 7; -bondage, 137, 143
decurions, see city councillors
deforestation, 176–7
demand, see consumption, trade
Demeter, 215, 217, 223
Demosthenes, 184–5, 193–5
Dertona, 49–50
de Waal, A., 279–80
diet, 168, 222–4, 226–52; see also children (feeding)
Dio of Prusa, 13
Diocletian (emperor), 11, 47, 85, 140
Dioscorides, 214
disease, 233–5, 246–9, 251–2, 267, 270, 272, 282–3
Domitian (emperor), 5
Drymos, 192
duovirs, see city councillors
Dupont, F., 42

Edessa, 152–3
Egypt, 94, 96, 102, 104, 136, 140, 145, 153, 163, 222, 236, 242, 268, 274–5, 286, 290
England, 281, 287
Epicurus, 215
Epirus, 64
epitaphs, 257
equestrians, 45
Ethiopia, 279
Etruria, 109, 111, 115–17; Etruscans, 113, 116
Eurysaces, 237–8
exchange, see trade
exploitation, of peasants, 96–7, 105, 164–5
exports, 47, 287, 289; see also imports, trade

fabri, 50–2, 58, 60–1, 80
Falerii, 116–17

fallow, 186, 191, 196
famine, 272–92 *passim*; definition of, 274–5, 277, 279–80, 291–2; and disease, 282–3; and migration, 284–5; and mortality, 276–7, 280–2, 283–6; rarity of, 284; and social relations, 285–8
farm/farm size, see peasants
favism, 219–20
Finland, 287
Finley, M. I., 34, 277–8
First Fruits, from Eleusis, 184, 201–3
fish, 243
flatulence, 214, 219–20
Florence, 238, 266, 274–6
flour, 237, 248
food crisis, 277–80; see also famine, food shortage
food distribution, 241, 243, 250; see also grain distribution
food, famine-, 275, 282–3, 288
food shortage, 274–6, 291; definition of, 275
food supply, of Athens, 183–200; of Constantinople, 158–9; of Rome, 159, 226, 236
food taboo, 215–17, 220
Frank, T., 65–6
freedmen, 28–44, 54, 58–9, 147–8, 150, 237, 245; as agents, 34, 40; as business managers, 34–5; dependence of, 30–4, 43; descendants of, as city councillors, 20, 26, 62; independence of, 29, 34, 37–9, 43–4, 148; *operae* of, 33, 35–6; as *socii*, 35–6; wealth of, 29, 38
Fronto, 238
funerals, 257–8

Gades, 45
Gaius (jurist), 11, 31, 134
Galatia, 14
Galen, 218, 223, 248, 262, 267, 282–3
Gallienus (emperor), 55
Gaul, 97, 160, 162
Gellius, 68
Genova, 49–50

goats, 172, 174
Gomme, A. W., 183-4, 191
Goths, 158, 161
government, local, *see* city councillors
Gracchus, *see* Sempronius
grain, distribution of, 226, 229-30, 236-9, 250-1, 276; rations of, 236-7; *see also* barley, cereals, wheat
Greece, 133, 136, 159, 163, 165, 176-7, 201-13, 222, 289
guilds, 80

Hadrian (emperor), 6, 10-11, 104, 156
Hannibal, 170
harvest, deficiency of, 185, 187, 189, 196, 235; failure of, 193, 290; variability of, 193, 198, 203, 206, 275
Heitland, W. E., 110
Herdonia, 120
Herodes Atticus, 93
Histria, 47-8
Honorius (emperor), 155-6
Hopkins, K., 32-4, 164
Horace, 242
horticulture, 243
housing, 68-9, 71-6
hunger, *see* famine, food crisis
hypoplasia, dental, 249, 270

Imbros, 192
immunity, from liturgies, 10-11
imperialism, 95, 98, 183
imports, 47, 183-5, 193-5, 199, 236, 249; *see also* exports, trade, traders
infants, *see* children
infanticide, *see* children (killing)
Interamna, 132
investment, 41; in livestock, 170; in manufacture, 41; in trade, 41; in urban property, 63-71, 76
Iran, 235
Ireland, 276, 278-9, 281, 285, 287-8
Italy, 93, 95, 100-1, 103, 106-33, 135, 140, 169-70, 173, 179, 205; central compared to southern, 112
C. Iulius Caesar, 53, 100-1, 117-18

Jardé, A., 183, 185-8, 191
Jones, A. H. M., 152-5, 164-5
Julian (jurist), 35
Julian (emperor), 157

Kühn, G., 146-7

Labeo (jurist), 9, 35
labourers, agricultural wage, 107, 112, 118-19, 135, 137, 139, 143-5, 150, 163, 287; urban wage, 79, 81-2, 239-40
Lambaesis, 102
land, abandoned, 104, 154-8, 160-1; assignment of, 99-100, 103, 111, 119-20, 122-5, 127, 138; carrying capacity, 183-200; extent of arable in Athens, 185-6, 189, 191-3, 195-6, 204; imperial, 97-8, 155-6; -owners, 54-9, 63, 65-6, 95-6, 104, 112, 127, 135, 138, 145, 153-4, 191, 212; productivity of, 162-5, 189-90, 201, 290-1; soil quality, 206-7; system of tenure, 112; *see also* yields, public, *ager publicus*
language, 17, 21
Larinum, 126
lead, 245
legumes, 210-11, 221, 240, 242; *see also* bean
Lemnos, 188-9, 192, 196, 222
lentils, 242
Lenzi, D., 275-6
Leo (emperor), 84
lex, Aelia Sentia, 31; *Fufia Caninia*, 31; *Hadriana*, 104
Libanius, 96-7, 164
M. Licinius Crassus, 65
Liguria, 49-50, 121, 167-8
liturgies, *see* cities
livestock, 121, 157, 168, 169, 170-5, 177, 179, 187, 207-8
locatio conductio, 79; *see also* tenancy
Luceria, 120-2, 126
Lugudunum, 41, 53
Lyon, *see* Lugudunum

Macedonia, 14, 208, 210, 222
Macrobius, 219
Mactar, 136, 144
Malaca, 4–5, 25, 72
malnutrition, 228, 230, 233–5, 246–9, 266, 270, 272, 274
manufacture, 39, 47, 51–2
manumission, 31–3; *see also* freedmen
manure, 207–10
Marcianus (jurist), 6–7
markets, 130, 276
Martial, 64, 242
meat, 51, 167, 169, 175, 227–9, 240, 243, 245
medicine, ancient, 260, 262–5, 267–8
Mediolanum, 45–6, 51–62
Melania the Younger, 142
mercennarii, see labourers
metalware, 47, 48, 52
Mickwitz, G., 78, 82
'middle class', in Rome, 238, 245, 250
midwives, 260, 262
Milan, *see* Mediolanum
millers/milling, 236–8
Momigliano, A., 153
Mommsen, T., 52
money lending, 63
mortality, *see* children (death), famine (mortality), starvation
mountains, 167–8, 172–4, 176–7
Mutina, 47–8, 72, 99
Mycenae, 289

N. Naevius Hilarus, 39
Narbo, 121
Nepos, 64
Neratius (jurist), 11
Nero (emperor), 72, 74
nexum, see debt-bondage
Nemausus, 43
Nile, 284, 286
Nîmes, *see* Nemausus
Noricum, 47–8, 55
nutrition, *see* diet, food, malnutrition

obaerarii, see debt-bondage
olive/olive oil, 47–51, 69, 97, 120, 138, 157, 162, 168, 190, 237, 240–2

onomastics, 19–22, 26
ordo decurionum, see city councillors
Oropos, 192
osteopenia, 249
Ostia, 39, 43, 68–9, 146

Padua, *see* Patavium
Palestine, 158
Papinian (jurist), 34
Parma, 47, 99
pastoralism, 101, 166–79
Patavium, 45, 47–9, 51
patronage, and freedmen, 30–7; and peasants, 105, 112; and the poor, 239, 241
Paulus (jurist), 23–4, 27, 36–7
pea, 224
peasants, 91–179 *passim*, 227, 283; in Athens, 91–4, 106, 191, 202–3; definition of, 91; displacement of, 93–4, 129, 147; farm size, 98–100, 103, 110–11, 115, 120, 125, 138, 191; fragmentation of holdings, 112; in politics, 92–3, 106; in Rome, 91, 93–106; as soldiers, 93–4, 102, 108; as tenants, 93, 96–7, 107, 109, 140; as wage labourers, 93, 107, 144–5; *see also coloni*, colonies, labourers, tenancy
peculium, of slaves, 34
pedani, see city councillors
Pericles, 92
Petronius, 42
Phainippos, 186
Philiskus, 11
Philostratus, 11
Philostratus of Lemnos, 11
pigs, 177–8
Pisa, 41
Placentia, 123
Plato, 190, 259–60
plebs frumentaria, see grain (distribution)
Pliny the Elder, 29, 50, 218, 242–3, 247
Pliny the Younger, 4, 13, 16, 140–1
Po, 46, 49, 50, 62
Pola, 111, 114

INDEX 335

Pompeii, 25, 37–9, 69–71, 118–19, 145–6, 200
Pompey, *see* Cnaeus
Pomponius (jurist), 12
T. Pomponius Atticus, 63–5
population, 45, 121, 123, 125, 136, 159–61; of Athens/Attica, 183–4, 187, 191–2, 197–9; of Rome, 226–7, 229, 236
porotic hyperostosis, *see* cribra orbitalia
ports, 49–51
pottery, 39, 41, 47–8, 53, 146
poverty/the poor, 226–7, 238, 241, 245, 251, 276
praetextati, *see* city councillors
prices, 142, 237, 241–2, 275, 283
priests, 54–5, 58–61
production, *see* manufacture, peasants
property, *see* cities, land
protein, 230–1
Puglia, 169
Puteoli, 39
Pythagoras, 215–18, 220, 224

quinquennalicii, *see* city councillors

rainfall, *see* climate
Ravenna, 50–2
Reate, 169, 172
rents, rural, 140; urban, 63, 65–6, 68, 71; *see also* cities, land
Rhine/Rhineland, 47, 103, 160
rickets, 246–7, 248–9, 262
Rome, city of, 39, 41, 68, 74, 76, 146–7, 226–52; *see also* colonies, freedmen, food distribution, food supply, grain (distribution), imports, malnutrition, population, senate, slaves, taxation, trade, traders, wheat
Romulus, 99
Rudiae, 119

Sabine country, 144
Salamis, 192
Samnium, 109, 121, 123, 169–70
Sardinia, 175–6

Sardis, 77–87
Scaevola (jurist), 10, 35
Scotland, 281, 285, 288
securities, 7
C. Sempronius Gracchus, 237
T. Sempronius Gracchus, 94, 100, 121
senate/senators, 15–16
Senatus Consultum, Hosidianum, 72–3, 76; *Volusianum*, 72
Septimius Severus (emperor), 4, 241
L. Sergius Catilina, 137
P. Servilius Rullus, 118
servus quasi colonus, 142, 149
settlement patterns, 112–33, 159
sheep, 169, 172, 174, 177–8
Sicily, 132, 135, 159, 163, 222
Silverman, S. F., 112
Sippel, D. V., 228–9
skeletons, analysis of, 244–5, 248–9, 251–2
Skyros, 192
slaves, 30–4, 47, 53, 94–6, 108–9, 130, 134–7, 142–4, 147–50, 163–4, 223, 236–7, 239
Soranus, 247–8, 260, 262–3, 265–8
Spain, 25, 43, 48–9, 167, 169, 174–6, 178
Sparta, 92
speculation, 64–5, 74–6
Starr, C. G., 185–7
starvation, 282
Strabo, 45–7, 49–51, 167–8
Sulla, *see* Cornelius
Ser. Sulpicius Rufus, 35
Sybaris, 119
Syria, 96–7, 99, 157–8, 161, 164

Tarentum, 71, 119, 126
Tauromenium, 222
taxation, 93, 96–7, 105, 152–4, 156–7, 164, 241; *see also* First Fruits
tenancy/tenants, 94, 104–5, 107, 109, 129–30, 137, 139–43, 148–9, 156, 158–9, 163; *see also coloni*, peasants, *servus quasi colonus*
textiles, 39, 47–9, 146, 175
Thamugadi, 17, 25, 27, 69
Theodoret, 157

Theophrastus, 190, 206, 208, 210, 222
Thessaly, 208, 210
Thrace, 160-1
Thugga, 27
Tiber, 64, 243
trade, 46-51, 53-4, 62, 67, 152-3, 167-8, 184, 193-5, 199
traders, 10, 28, 35, 50, 53-4, 87, 153, 287
Trajan (emperor), 4-6, 12-14, 16-17, 56
transhumance, 168-79
Transpadana, Gallia, 46, 50-1, 55
transport, 46, 49, 50, 51, 290-1; *see also* trade
Trimalchio, 29, 40, 42-4

Ukraine, 273, 277, 281, 286
Ulpian (jurist), 7, 36, 83
Umbria, 144, 178
urbanization, 113, 115-17, 129
Urso, 72

Varro, 136-7, 143, 169, 172
vegetables, 242
Veii, 115-16, 129, 131-2
Veleia, 95
Vercellae, 54-5
L. Verus (emperor), 7, 9, 33
Vespasian (emperor), 144, 239
veterans, 11, 98-103, 117
Veyne, P., 29-30, 37-40, 44

villages, 57, 96-7, 112, 116, 119, 150, 157-8, 160, 164
Villani, G., 275-6
villas, 56-7, 64, 95, 97, 109, 114, 119, 143, 149; *see also* slaves
M. Vipsanius Agrippa, 241
vitamins, 232-5, 246
Vitellius (emperor), 224
viticulture, *see* wine
Vitruvius, 68
Volubilis, 69, 71

wage labour, *see* labourers
Waltzing, J.-P., 78, 82
war, 52-3, 160-1, 170
wealth, 63, 70
weaning, 246, 266-9
wet-nursing, 255-6, 263-6
wheat, 121, 184, 186-9, 192-3, 201-5, 210, 223, 229-34, 236, 241
wine, 47, 48, 50-1, 119-20, 168
women, 230-1, 238, 246, 248-9, 261, 268-9
wool, *see* textiles

yeast, 232
yields, 168, 187-90, 193, 198, 201, 204-6, 210-11; *see also* land (productivity)

Zeno (emperor), 84-5

Printed in the United States
By Bookmasters